Decolonized Approaches to Human Rights and Social Work

Melinda Madew • Marcin Boryczko • Mark Lusk
Editors

Decolonized Approaches to Human Rights and Social Work

Springer

Editors
Melinda Madew
Department of Social Work
Protestant University of Applied Sciences
Ludwigsburg
Ludwigsburg, Germany

Department of Social Work
University of Johannesburg
Johannesburg, South Africa

Marcin Boryczko
Department of Social Work
Faculty of Social Sciences
University of Gdańsk
Gdańsk, Poland

Mark Lusk
School of Social Work
New Mexico State University
Las Cruces, NM, USA

ISBN 978-3-031-33029-2 ISBN 978-3-031-33030-8 (eBook)
https://doi.org/10.1007/978-3-031-33030-8

This Springer imprint is published by the registered company Springer Nature Switzerland AG
The registered company address is: Gewerbestrasse 11, 6330 Cham, Switzerland

Foreword by Rory Truell

I congratulate the editors and authors who have brought this book into the world. It provides a clear contribution on the need to recognize the different traditions in social work, and it acutely addresses the requirement to rebalancing the Western bias that dominates so much of the professional literature. The book also contributes to debates beyond social work and speaks directly to the world's global norms and methodologies now largely based on Western traditions – norms that are failing to address climate change, exacerbated inequality and dwindling democracy.

Indigenous social work is alive and thriving in many parts of the world. It has always been there offering distinctly different worldviews in the application of social work. These approaches are marked by the principles of 'reciprocal relationships,' so that people benefit together, 'interconnection' realizing that our wellbeing is fully intertwined with others, 'belonging' and 'responsibility' highlighting that people's real experience of rights lie in each other's day-to-day actions. Yet has the profession dominated by more than 100 years of Western values, based on individual merit, been willing to listen, to understand and to embrace wisdoms that are likely to provide answers to the global challenges that affect us all?

The tide is turning, and this book is another wave drawing us closer to a profession that can articulate global contributions and action for a new sustainable world philosophy. If there was a specific date that pinpointed this tidal change, it would in July 2014. In Melbourne at the IFSW General Assembly, the decades of indigenous social work voices were finally heard. There was different consequential action, one was the formal founding of an IFSW Indigenous Committee (now a Commission) that provided recognition of indigenous social work's specific voice and identity. The Indigenous Commission is now a formal structure within IFSW which has the ability to shape the global policies and standards that glue the profession together.

In July 2014, the IFSW General Assembly also agreed on a new International Definition of Social Work, along with the International Association of Schools of Social Work. There were four major changes to the earlier definition and three of these had been advocated for by indigenous social workers. This included a reference to 'collective responsibilities' to sit alongside of the promotion of human rights. Rights, they advocated, need to be embedded in systems and cultures, along with everyone's sense of cultural duty to act towards fulfilling the rights of others. The new Definition also highlighted 'respect for diversities,' paving the way to develop shared understandings of how differing cultural views can contribute to our sustainable shared futures. And further, the Definition named 'indigenous knowledges' equally along with other forms of knowing.

Since then, the global profession has developed a global theme on Ubuntu, which spurred writings, webinars and gatherings across the world. In Africa, the continent home of Ubuntu, we heard social work practitioners say, 'We had to say goodbye to indigenous practice when we undertook our social work studies at the university, but after graduating we had to reincorporate the traditional wisdom as we worked in the communities. Now for the first time we feel we can talk about this in the profession's international forums.' In other countries and cultures, social workers held discussion groups reflecting, 'What is the Ubuntu in our traditional cultures and how can we integrate this knowledge into our practice.'

Through these processes, the international social work profession has altered its global positioning, messaging and actions. Following on from the worldwide theme Ubuntu, the profession highlighted 'Co-building a New Eco-Social World: Leaving No One Behind.' Implicit in this message are the aforementioned principles advanced by our indigenous colleagues: reciprocity/interconnection (co-building together), belonging and responsibility (leaving no one behind) in joint action. The 'new eco-social world' aspect of the message also derives from indigenous wisdom recognizing the human place within nature, eco-systems and the climate. It is a realization that people also need to respect nature and the environments in which we live for our own and their sustainability.

From that global theme another was launched: Respecting diversity through joint social action. This again speaks to the need for a fundamental shift from the West Knows Best to the incorporation of differing philosophies that are needed right now to develop and secure nature and people's place within it.

Yet the world and the profession of social work still have a long way to go. There are still many countries, particularly in the industrialized Western countries, where social work practice is driven by individualism and degrading benefit policies and systems. These approaches falsely put all the responsibility of wellbeing on the shoulders of each sole person, neglecting the reality that our cultures, communities and social relationships are a massive determining factor in our lives. When that fails, the system (sometimes) offers the person a minimal amount of support, but never enough to transform their lives and often contributing to a diminished self-image.

Books such as this are an important part in the profession's continuous change process. The writings hold us to account for social work's past and sometime current involvement in colonial oppressive frameworks and Western dominance. It introduces non-Western approaches that promote individuality in the communal context, but not individualism. IFSW expresses its sincere thanks to all who have contributed.

IFSW Secretary-General
Rheinfelden, Switzerland
February 2023

Rory Truell

Foreword by Susan Mapp

As Audre Lorde stated, "The master's tools will never dismantle the master's house" (Lorde, 1979/1984). Nations in the Global South were actively impoverished – first through plunder of their natural and human resources and then through global trade structures that sought to disadvantage them through trade barriers and predatory loans. Decolonization must occur not only in those nations subjected to colonization but in the colonizer countries as well. In the United States, its Indigenous peoples were colonized and people from Africa were forcibly brought to its lands for enslavement. To decolonize social work, we must look to address harmful structures rather than focusing on those people the structures produce, and we must seek within cultures for appropriate tools. By drawing together authors and knowledge from around the globe in both colonized and colonizer nations, these editors have amassed a font of knowledge that helps to move us from the theoretical to the practical in achieving this goal.

As noted by these editors, political decolonization does not equate cultural decolonization, and impacts on belief systems – what is the "right" way to do things – can linger long past forms of government. Social workers are too often in positions of power where they judge those they are tasked to help and determine if they meet pre-established standards. This book is a critical step in moving social work from a charity-based or need-based approach to the rights-based approach. With its formal origins in lying in helping people adjust to larger structures – be that people in poverty or those newly arrived in a city/nation– it is not surprising that early social work operated from a charity model. While there certainly was some focus on changing those structures – introducing child labor laws, for example – there was still a top-down approach that was reliant on the benevolence of the giver, rather than that to which people had a right.

In contrast, the rights-based approach, rather than focusing on what we believe people need or deserve, helps us to actualize what they are entitled to by dint of being human (Gatenio Gabel, 2016). Implementing human rights into social work practice – utilizing a rights-based approach – necessitates honoring process along with outcome (Gatenio Gabel et al., 2022). It matters not just what we achieve, but how we achieve it, with participation of the service user being essential. The rights-based approach also focuses accountability on those in power, not on those whom they serve (Androff, 2016).

In seeking to decolonize social work practice, we should include methods of restorative justice, but we must also recognize that in some cases there has always been a lack of justice and thus we must evoke transformative justice. We cannot restore justice where it never was, but we can seek to transform a system to one that is equitable and just. Transformative justice focuses on "collective, community-based responses" rather than governmental systems thus shifting to support from networks rather than formal power (Kim, 2021, p. 168). Thus, the realization of justice becomes an "everyday democratic act," that is open to anyone as a member of society rather than reserved for those acting on behalf of the state (Kim, 2021, p. 170).

Social work educators play a critical role in realizing this shift to decolonization and a rights-based approach. It matters how we educate students – future social workers. It matters what methods we use, what theories we teach, the language we employ, and whose processes are valued. It matters what and how we train the providers of the future, regardless of where they will practice and with whom. As one example, as social work evolves to face new challenges and recognize additional sources of knowledge, we are abandoning the idea of "international social work" with its demarcation between "our" problems and "their" problems, as though issues end at national borders. We are moving towards "global social work" where we acknowledge the commonality of human issues, while also recognizing the impact of local culture in affecting their occurrence and resolution (Mapp & Gatenio Gabel, 2022).

It is only when we recognize these shared issues and seek to learn from each other, rather than replicating the top-down methods from our origins that we will truly be able to make progress. To truly realize the rights-based approach and decolonize their practice, social workers must aim to revitalize previously suppressed indigenous knowledge. This necessitates a constructivist view – an attempt to understand the world through the perspective of their reality rather than from the hegemonic view of the Global North. Rather than seeing another's culture as "other" or "exotic," and its people in need of our aid, we must be seeking to raise it up and honor their wisdom.

When social work educators take or send students to other nations, which approximately 75% of US social work programs do (Mapp & Gatenio Gabel, 2019), it matters how it is done. Such trips, if done from a traditional framework, reinforce the idea of a recipient/donor framework for both parties – a charity-based approach with the donor (student) as generous and the recipient, the citizens of that nation as needy (Lough & Carter-Black, 2015). If educators laud themselves for such trips and emphasize the learning students gain, rather than partnering with a local community and centering their concerns, they reinforce colonization of the mind for all involved (Mapp & Rice, 2019). This happens within colonizer nations as well, where some send students out for service learning to a community, where rather than establishing a partnership, students arrive and do what they believe to be helpful, and then depart without looking back over their shoulder to see what the community thought about it or if there was any lasting impact, replicating colonial methods.

Therefore, social workers must critically examine, and update where needed, educational methods and materials. Our profession must honor the knowledge that everyone brings to addressing social issues and recognize that answers will often lie outside of the formal systems we have established. Bringing service users into positions of power in the academy and recognizing them as "experts by experience," lifting up their voices and perspectives in developing curricula, such as is done in Britain, is one method (Adamson et al., 2022, p. 1). We need to shift away from the focus on clinical social work to ensure just systems, since doing so will likely reduce the need for micro level interventions. It is through knowledge such as is contained in this volume that we can actualize a just world.

Associate Provost for Institutional
Effectiveness and Innovation
Elizabethtown College
Elizabethtown, PA, USA

Susan Mapp

References

Adamson, K., Goulden, A., Logan, J., & Hammond, J. (2022). Service user involvement in social work education: A scoping review. *Social Work Education*. Advance online publication. https://doi.org/10.1080/02615479.2022.2097213

Androff, D. (2016). *Practicing rights: Human rights-based approaches to social work practice*. Routledge.

Gatenio Gabel, S. (2016). *A rights-based approach to social policy analysis*. Springer.

Gatenio Gabel, S., Mapp, S., Androff, D., & McPherson, J. (2022). Looking back to move us forward: Social workers as human rights professionals delivering justice. *Advances in Social Work, 22*(2), 416–435. https://doi.org/10.18060/24971

Kim, M. E. (2021). Transformative justice and restorative justice: Gender-based violence and alternative visions of justice in the United States. *International Review of Victimology, 27*(2), 162–172. https://doi.org/10.1177/0269758020970414

Lorde, A. (1984). The master's tools will never dismantle the master's house (Comments at the "The personal and the political panel," Second Sex Conference, New York, September 29, 1979). In Sister outsider (pp. 110–113). Sister Visions Press. (Original work published 1979).

Lough, B., & Carter-Black, J. (2015). Confronting the white elephant: International volunteering and racial (dis)advantage. *Progress in Development Studies, 15*(3), 207–220. https://doi.org/10.1177/1464993415578983

Mapp, S. C., & Gatenio Gabel, S. (2019). Educating students on international social work issues in U.S. social work programs: How is it done*? Journal of Social Work Education, 55*(2), 238–250. https://doi.org/10.1080/10437797.2018.1513881

Mapp, S., & Gatenio Gabel, S. (2022). Moving social work from international social work to global social work through aligning SDG principles and social work education standards. *Social Work Education: The International Journal, 41*(7), 1412–1426. https://doi.org/10.1080/02615479.2022.2089647

Mapp, S. C., & Rice, K. (2019). Conducting rights-based short-term study abroad experiences. *Social Work Education: The International Journal, 38*(4), 427–438. https://doi.org/10.1080/02615479.2018.1560403

About the Book

This book is an edited collection that is useful both as a textbook for students and teachers and as a practitioner's reference. As a textbook, it is useful in courses such as Postcolonial Social Work, History of Human Rights and Social Work, Critical Social Work Theory and Practice, Decolonizing Approaches in Social Work, and Indigenous Eco-Social Work. The editors introduce the book in sections and chapters that cover decolonization theory and the history of human rights through philosophy and legal theory. Chapters review the history and theory behind United Nations principles, international and regional conventions and declarations. The book identifies how social work can draw insights from history in order to identify paths forward in building an ecologically just world.

Contents

About the Editors

Melinda Madew is Professor in International Social Work at the Protestant University of Applied Sciences Ludwigsburg, Germany, and a Research Associate at the University of Johannesburg, South Africa. She serves as Board Member of the European Social Work Research Association. Her teaching and research are in the areas of gender politics, postcolonial social work and indigenous knowledge, and practice in community organizing. She has served as education and research consultant for international development organizations. She conceptualized and implemented international projects under the auspices of European Union educational programs for North-South university collaboration.

Marcin Boryczko is an Associate Professor at the University of Gdańsk, Poland, where he teaches Social Work on bachelors and masters levels. He serves in the board of several international and national associations such as the Polish Federation of Social Workers and Social Service Employees Unions (Polska Federacja Związków Zawodowych Pracowników Socjalnych i Pomocy Społecznej), the European Social Work Research Association, the International Advisory Board of the *European Social Work Research Journal*, and Polish representative in the International Federation of Social Workers (IFSW). His main research interests include social work education, critical social work theory, human rights, decolonization, neoliberal governmentality, and populism in Central Europe.

Mark Lusk is a faculty member in the School of Social Work at New Mexico State University. Professor Lusk was Senior Fulbright Scholar at the Catholic University of Peru in Lima and also a Fulbright Research Scholar at the Catholic University of Rio de Janeiro in Brazil. He currently works with forced migrants and refugees from Central America and Mexico and related human rights issues. Dr. Lusk was Founding Director of the School of Social Work at Boise State University (Idaho) and has served as Associate Provost at the University of Georgia.

Contributors

Erica Balderrama Department of Social Work, College of Health Sciences, University of Texas at El Paso, El Paso, TX, USA

Marcin Boryczko Department of Social Work, Faculty of Social Sciences, University of Gdańsk, Gdańsk, Poland

Kris Clarke Department of Social Work, Faculty of Social Sciences, University of Helsinki, Helsinki, Finland

Araceli Garcia Department of Social Work, College of Health Sciences, University of Texas at El Paso, El Paso, TX, USA

Emilio Jose Gómez Ciriano Faculty of Social Work, University of Castilla-La Mancha, Cuenca Campus, Cuenca, Spain

Tanja Kleibl Social Work Department, Technical University of Würzburg-Schweinfurt, Wurzburg, Germany

Department of Social Work, University of Johannesburg, Johannesburg, South Africa

Jason M. Leung Department of Environmental Studies, Benguet State University, La Trinidad, Benguet, Philippines

Philippine Department of Science and Technology Research – Extractive Mining and Indigenous Communities, Baguio City, Philippines

Mark Lusk School of Social Work, New Mexico State University, Las Cruces, NM, USA

Melinda Madew Department of Social Work, Protestant University of Applied Sciences Ludwigsburg, Ludwigsburg, Germany

Department of Social Work, University of Johannesburg, Johannesburg, South Africa

María Inés Martínez Herrero International University of La Rioja, Logroño, La Rioja, Spain

Eva M. Moya Department of Social Work, College of Health Sciences, University of Texas at El Paso, El Paso, TX, USA

Border Biomedical Research Center, El Paso, TX, USA

Nicholas D. Natividad Department of Criminal Justice, Department of Borderlands and Ethnic Studies, New Mexico State University, Las Cruces, NM, USA

Tomasz Nowicki Department of Social Work, Faculty of Social Sciences, University of Gdańsk, Gdańsk, Poland

Ndangwa Noyoo Department of Social Work, University of Cape Town, Cape Town, South Africa

Prospera Tedam Department of Social Wellbeing, United Arab Emirates University, Abu Dhabi, United Arab Emirates

Samuel Terrazas Department of Social Work, University of Texas Permian Basin, Odessa, TX, USA

Kiran Thampi Department of Social Work, Rajagiri College of Social Sciences, Kochi, Kerala, India

Nycil Romis Thomas Department of Social Work, Rajagiri College of Social Sciences, Kochi, Kerala, India

Part I
Social Work and the Decolonization Project

Chapter 1
Human Rights and the Decolonization of Social Work

Marcin Boryczko, Mark Lusk, and Melinda Madew

Introduction

Social work has a long history of advocating for and promoting human rights. This tradition began before the term "human rights" was widely used as it has been since the end of the global conflicts of the mid-twentieth century. It was at that time that global society had to confront and become reconciled with the catastrophes of World War II and the Holocaust by creating international institutions, covenants, and legal documents that require nations to abide by universal set of obligations that recognize and protect the inherent human dignity and worth of all people – a core tenet of social work since its founding.

The profession of social work originated in large part as a result of a recognition that the industrial era, with its attendant urbanization, mechanization, and exploitation of workers, brought with it a perverse set of outcomes that violated basic human dignity, such as child labor, poor and dangerous working conditions, low wages, deficient living conditions, environmental degradation, malnutrition, discrimination against women, poor sanitation, and inadequate health care (Stearns, 2019). Early

M. Boryczko (✉)
Department of Social Work, Faculty of Social Sciences, University of Gdańsk, Gdańsk, Poland
e-mail: marcin.boryczko@ug.edu.pl

M. Lusk
School of Social Work, New Mexico State University, Las Cruces, NM, USA
e-mail: marklusk@nmsu.edu

M. Madew
Department of Social Work, Protestant University of Applied Sciences Ludwigsburg, Ludwigsburg, Germany

Department of Social Work, University of Johannesburg, Johannesburg, South Africa
e-mail: m.madew@eh-ludwigsburg.de

M. Madew et al. (eds.), *Decolonized Approaches to Human Rights and Social Work*, https://doi.org/10.1007/978-3-031-33030-8_1

social workers largely addressed these issues from the framework of charity and did not assertively engage the status quo by advocating for significant changes in the social and economic structures that engendered such adverse outcomes for workers, children, and the poor – a framework that still holds sway in contemporary social work despite the enormous changes in society since the outset of industrialization.

It could be argued that not much has changed at the fundamental level in social work since its inception. Social work education and practice have been built on working primarily with individuals and groups at the expense of advocating for and instigating significant changes in the social and economic structures that are at the root of individual problems. Although many social work professionals worldwide have been active on questions of racism, economic inequality, social injustice, and human rights, too little has been done to update the social work paradigm to address long-standing and profound problems created by industrial monopolies and power elites that are sustained by governments that enact policies and laws from neoliberal and conservative ideologies.

In this book, the author/contributors make the case for considering the centrality of human rights and decolonization to a progressive vision for the future of social work. These two intellectual traditions can inform a renaissance of social work as it grappled with the challenges of addressing social problems in a postcolonial, postindustrial, and increasingly fragmented global society.

Human Rights

Although the term human rights is of fairly recent historical origin, its antecedents can be found in early philosophical and theological traditions. Most religions hold human dignity and the inherent worth of all persons as part of the core of their doctrines. While many religions emphasize moral duties and obligations over individual rights, the world's great religious traditions also include humanistic ideals that stress the importance of seeing all people as equal at the most fundamental level. Ancient philosophy also anticipates and provides part of the foundation for contemporary human rights. Confucius, for example, contended that all people, including the so-called commoners, each have human qualities and sensibilities of reason and awareness and the role of the state is to cultivate these traits by caring for the moral welfare of its members (Ishay, 2008). In classical Western philosophy, notable attention was given to ideals that provided a further foundation for human rights and ethics. The stoics, for example, contended that humans are rational creatures who are subject to natural law and by extension are equals under the law and entitled to just and fair treatment (Horowitz, 1974). The classical concept of natural law emphasizes moral responsibilities over entitlements but also referred to equity and justice (Lloyd, 2005).

Further advances toward a theory of human rights exploded during the Enlightenment (see Chap. 6). Western philosophers such as Rousseau, Locke, Condorcet, and others developed the concept of a "social contract" wherein democratic governments, which exist at the will of the people, provide for the protection of citizens and guarantee freedoms of expression and self-governance. The foundational Enlightenment thinkers provide the basis for dissolving unnatural hierarches, such as monarchic rule, and served as part of the rationale for the American and French Revolutions. The Enlightenment thinkers also promulgated ideas that were core elements of key legal documents, such as the American Constitution and French *Declaration des Droits de l'Homme et du Citoyen.*

But catastrophic events of the mid-twentieth century were responsible for the emergence of a doctrine of human rights and the institutional structure to advance them. Both world wars in the last century were massive industrial killing machines in which the rights of civilians, combatants, and targeted minorities were utterly ignored. The Holocaust in particular with its unprecedented genocide was so shocking and soul-wrenching that countries around the world agreed to found the United Nations (1945) for the purpose of "…maintaining international peace and security, developing friendly relations among nations and promoting social progress, better living standards and human rights" (United Nations, 2022a). The UN undertook a major step to advance human rights and after careful international deliberation enacted the Universal Declaration of Human Rights (UDHR) in 1948. Since then, the UN has adopted nine core human rights conventions and covenants covering the rights of women, racial minorities, indigenous peoples, and children as well as documents on civil and political rights and conventions against torture and enforced disappearance (United Nations, 2022b). The UNDHR has inspired the enactment of over 80 international human rights treaties and declarations worldwide (United Nations, 2022c).

The social work profession has been closely aligned with the human rights tradition, and universal human rights influence several national associations and accreditation agencies' codes of ethics (Mapp et al., 2019). In the Ethical Principles of the International Federation of Social Workers, the first and foundational principle is human rights and human dignity (IFSW, 2018). Of importance, the UDHR and professional ethics not only advocate for equal treatment and nondiscrimination under the law on the basis of race, nationality, gender, age, and so on but also assert positive or affirmative rights, such as access to housing, health care, food, adequate income, and employment (Mapp et al., 2019). In addition, the UDHR affirms the collective cultural and political rights of communities, peoples, and indigenous groups (United Nations, 2022a).

Decolonization

More recently, and perhaps belatedly, social workers have come to recognize the historical legacy of colonialism on peoples and nations in the modern era. Imperial colonialism is the economic, geographic, and cultural domination of a territory by an external nation through force. It is a coercive model of international development that benefits the colonizer nation by affording cheap access to primary goods, natural resources, and labor. It is accompanied by the imposition of the colonizer's language, culture, traditions, religion, and economics and by the suppression of indigenous and national cultures, traditions, languages, customs, and economic relations. Empires are built on colonies through mercantilism – an economic model that builds wealth in the dominant society by maximizing exports of finished goods and products while relying on external natural resources and labor as a subsidy. Colonialism is maintained through military strength and occupation, control of internal security and justice systems, slavery and indentured servitude, state terrorism, repression of indigenous cultures and society, restrictions on freedom of expression, and an ideology of racial superiority and hierarchy.

During the early stages of colonialism from the beginning of the occupation of the Americas up to the wars of independence that transferred power to local elites, nearly all of Africa, the Americas, and South Asia were under the control of imperial monarchies. Even by the mid-twentieth century, much of the planet's land mass continued to be comprised of territories that were governed by imperial powers in Europe. In 1945, there were still 750 million people, about a third of the world's population, living in colonial territories (United Nations, 2022d). The process of decolonization accelerated after World War II when the British Empire receded and independent governments began to rule at the local national level. Japan lost its colonies in the war. By 1960, most African nations were independent. The Soviet Union (empire) began to disintegrate in the 1980s, and in 1991, it collapsed completely, and most of the states it controlled ceded from Russia and became independent states. Since the founding of the United Nations, 80 territories have become independent states and members of the UN (United Nations, 2022d).

That being said, political decolonization is incomplete. China continues to occupy Tibet and is committing cultural genocide and carrying out a program of massive repression in Xinjiang. Russia is in the throes of a neo-imperialist effort to take back territories it once controlled as is evidenced by its illegal war against Ukraine and its civilian noncombatant population. It is also important to mention its collusion with allied authoritarian states in Syria, Saudi Arabia, Belarus, Georgia, Chechnya, and Montenegro, among others, and clandestine campaigns to disrupt elections in the United States and other democracies. To complicate the postcolonial world, a number of emerging democracies have been taking definitive steps toward authoritarian nationalism such as Turkey and Poland, and there are retreats from pluralistic inclusive democracy toward authoritarian nationalism in established democracies such as the United States and India.

Political decolonization, the national independence of territories, either by wars of independence or peaceful succession, does not necessarily result in economic or cultural independence. Thus, there are two phases of decolonization, the initial exit from political control by the imperial power and the process of achieving full economic and cultural independence – our primary concern in human rights at this stage of global development.

Postcolonialism

The extent to which much of the world has been dominated by Western modes of thought, culture, and political philosophy has been widely unrecognized in the Western world. The Eurocentrism of the west has created a chronic myopia about the lived experience of the vast majority of the planet who now live in a postcolonial world but are still subject to its paradigm. Looking at the world through a Western lens not only distorts how the rest of the world is organized but also misrepresents how a huge portion of those who reside in the West experience the postcolonial aftermath. Colonialism erased local history, submerged regional cultures, and ignored or discounted established local knowledge. Postcolonialism seeks to restore and valorize historically subjugated indigenous and regional knowledge, wisdom, and tradition.

Postcolonialism is an effort to alter the distorted relations between Western and non-Western people (Young, 2020). Rather than looking at the East or the Global South through the assumptions and perspectives of the West, postcolonialism seeks to understand other cultural realities outside of the West on their own terms – through their languages, cultures, representations, and politics. Postcolonialism critiques the racist and condescending perspectives of colonizers, who perceived the colonized other as exotic, inferior, backward, traditional, and ignorant, thus requiring paternalistic assistance. In the postwar era, this guidance and oversight from "developed" nations has been through international economic and social technical assistance by agencies such as USAID and the World Bank (McEwan, 2008).

A key idea in postcolonialist thought is "decolonization of the mind," a concept that is particularly pertinent to the professions. The term, originally coined by Ngũgĩ wa Thiong'o, has been used to analyze the way that colonialism has distorted the use of and appreciation for indigenous languages by the hegemonic lingua franca of colonizers, such as French or English. His work forms a basis for the critical study of the interconnectedness of cultures and languages and how imperialism disrupts the linkage by creating a colonial alienation that separates peoples from their identity, language, and ways of knowing (Wa Thiong'o, 1992). As with decolonization theory, the concept of "decolonizing the mind" has been used beyond its initial application to address other projects such as race, gender identity, migration, and border thinking (Young, 2020). And the Eurocentric and paternalistic traditions of the "helping professions," such as social work, are also a fair game. Indeed, social work is based on a power differential between workers and clients and is replete with "practice wisdom" and projected cultural representations of the poor that subordinate those with whom they work. To decolonize the minds of social workers requires a reorientation that recognizes the importance of non-Western knowledge and transfers insurgent knowledge from the periphery to the center. Social workers are tasked to stop looking at the world from privileged perches above to adopt a peripheral bottom-up orientation to be on equal footing with those they serve.

Revisiting Neocolonialism and the Legitimization of the North-South Divide

How can social work as a human rights profession engage in a process of localized decolonization? The process of decolonization starts when social workers become aware of how complex social problems affecting people's lives today are rooted in a history of systemic injustice and oppression. It can begin by recognizing the legitimacy of an existing pain over past wrongs. Centuries of colonial rule and enslavement of peoples continue to impact societies because the structures of oppression are still in place. We see this in the destruction of territorial resources and the damage committed against peoples' culture and collective identity (Escobar, 2012; Tauli-Corpuz, 2006; Young, 2016).

When coming to terms with history, communities can determine specific ways of dealing with painful events. It can begin by recognizing the legitimacy of an existing pain over past wrongs. Communities can decide to act in an organized manner to construct ways redeeming the past by envisioning a collective future. These processes move in complex ways of recovering forgotten or lost legacies in both material and ideational cultures. It calls for the recovery of knowledge systems that promote indigenous practices compatible with community values (Smith, 2012; Werbner & Modood, 1997). Social work with its human rights mandate has to learn from history in order to create and integrate decolonizing approaches within its own professional body of knowledge and practice. In this way, decolonizing approaches in social work are acts of restorative justice intent at confronting the remaining vestiges of colonialism and subverting any attempt to perpetuate or legitimize its existence in our present history.

The decolonization process as restorative justice is also reconciliatory. Together, we acknowledge that colonization as a reality in human history is a shared legacy regardless of where we are positioned geographically and politically. And because of this, we are all passive or active actors in the decolonization project. Social work can bring different people in their different positionalities to a thoughtful analysis over the systemic causes of human suffering (Smith, 2012). The task of addressing human suffering is momentous, and it has to be carried out with the reminder that the errors in history need not be repeated in our contemporary times. Decolonizing approaches in social work are as complex as people's subjective experience of history. So that today, we bear witness to global problems that generations from now will still struggle to resolve.

The process of decolonization addresses the various manifestations of historical wrongs. This could not be undone only in the present because restoration is an intergenerational task. It is imperative for social work to engage in dialogue with those who carry markings of individual and collective histories that need retelling in the light of truth. There are symbolic and material structures in the lives of many people that consigned them to the oppression of intergenerational poverty. It can be a social work practice to professionally advocate for a deeper understanding of the systemic causes of problems. It takes commitment to engage in discourse, to reflect on various standpoints, and to seek actionable channels of advocacy within our present-day decolonization movements.

The process of localizing the decolonization process starts with a professional commitment to investigate the systemic causes of social problems as these exist in our interconnected world (Ife, 2000). Such awareness and desire for action will coalesce with other equally motivated groups, communities, and political movements. The decolonization project is after all a justice movement propelled by equally impassioned people who believe that the future can be redeemed by acknowledging past wrongs so as to break away from the cycle of oppression. History is replete with lessons, and social workers are studious learners who, from time to time, succeed at imparting and acting on these lessons.

In the following section, we will briefly focus on the example of international development aid and describe how social work as a human rights profession can draw insights from history in order to understand the systemic rootedness of global inequalities.

Development Aid and Neocolonialism

Social work, as a human rights profession, addresses social problems that cut across populations and geographic locations. Social work is strongly associated with international development aid programs, which countries in the Global North have initiated as a postwar commitment. Global crises such as poverty, wars and conflict, hunger, and environmental exploitation can all be traced to a history of oppression as experienced by people living in countries that have been subject to the yoke of colonialism for centuries (Gandhi, 2019). As mentioned earlier in this chapter, the once-colonized people waged bitter wars of resistance against colonial powers to liberate themselves from slavery (Fanon, 2021; Memmi et al., 2016). The shifting balance of global power after World War II compelled colonial empires the opportunity to retreat from expensive wars of liberation by "granting independence" to countries where nationalist movements were in protracted struggles to win territorial sovereignty. Even as the once-colonized countries in Latin America, Asia, and Africa had established their own national governments, they were made to submit to the onerous conditions of global free trade that their once-colonial masters imposed on their economies (Gandhi, 2019; Gardner & Roy, 2020).

When empires relinquished their colonial territories, it is not for certain that economic, political, and structural institutions were strongly established to ensure a smooth transition from colonies to independent states. For centuries, empires were primarily concerned with amassing great wealth from the territories of enslaved people, leaving them in abject poverty (Gardner & Roy, 2020). Hardly were institutions for self-governance and independent statehood put in place to ensure that the handover of power was successful. World War II was even more ruinous for newly independent countries or colonies because their territories were the vicious battlefield of warring superpowers, as in the case of Southeast Asia and North Africa.

The Allied Powers had known that subjugating the Axis enemy at war did not guarantee long-term victory if former colonies were not able to recover from the ruins of the war. The capitalist free enterprise economy can only thrive in a global order where the position of the ruling elites is securely maintained. They knew how a devastated global economy would drastically impact everyone, including their own people (Bello, 1982; MacEwan, 2009). Proactive measures have to be enacted to maintain a global status quo where the empires and the emerging superpower in the United States will continue benefitting from a renewed form of colonial relations.

So in 1945, the United States convened a meeting among Allied Powers and their supporters to formulate the Bretton Woods Agreement. It was meant to ensure the continuance of a global order that would protect the gains derived from the war, as well as to secure the capitalist interest of empires. For newly independent states and colonies, significant decisions with enduring social and economic consequences were promulgated in the agreement (Hancock, 1989). The Bretton Woods Agreement bolstered the United States' position as a rising military and global economic power. It saw the establishment of the International Monetary Fund (IMF) and the International Bank of Reconstruction and Development, otherwise known as the World Bank (WB). At the behest of the United States, all circulating monetary currencies were pegged to the value of the US dollar. These financial institutions functioned as the global gatekeepers in social and economic programs for postwar recovery efforts, which eventually became known as development aid. The World Bank proceeded to position itself as the "knowledge bank" in development politics (MacEwan, 2009).

By the end of World War II, emerging states had to deal with the momentous challenge of political transition from colonies to independent governance while contending with populations ravaged by disease, hunger, and poverty (Bello, 1982). Governments had no recourse but to turn to the WB or IMF in the recovery process of reconstituting national institutions in education and culture, economy, and governance. Development aid, in actuality, was a misnomer because aid packages were delivered in borrowing programs that compelled cash-strapped countries to accept onerous loan conditions, including the submission to structural adjustment policies (SAP). Development aid came in the form of loans issued to the so-called developing countries under a system of interest payments known as debt servicing. Recipients of development aid were compelled to confine national spending according to the conditionalities issued by the IMF/WB (Bello, 1982; Hancock, 1989; Kothari, 2019; MacEwan, 2009). Under the SAP, borrowing countries must appropriate external debt servicing in their annual budgets and confine all forms of spending in the economic and social sectors along with conditions set by global lending institutions. Furthermore, receiving countries have to agree to free trade and open-market policies, which allow foreign investors unregulated access to the country's human and environmental resources.

Nations receiving development aid from the WB and IMF in the form of external debts were under the stranglehold of policies designed to keep them as economic and political clients of the world's most powerful financial institutions and the governments they represented, including the United States and other capitalist industrialized countries. Aid was the political tool that reduced former colonies into the third-world category of developing or underdeveloped countries. While third-world countries were nominally independent with their own system of governance, their dependence on foreign loans and acquiescence to global economic policies of free trade and open markets rendered them neocolonies of their former masters. The vestiges of colonialism still existed in a global economy where capitalist countries invested in manufacturing and extractive industries taking advantage of cheap labor, open access to raw materials, unlimited repatriation of profits, and untrammeled flow of financial capital from the developing to the developed world (Bello, 1982; Kothari, 2019).

Colonial dependence was kept intact by the mandate that development aid comes not only with a package of economic and political reforms but also with directives on how institutions of education, culture, and social services carry out their work. In essence, the colonial arrangement has not changed; only this time, political and economic powers are redistributed in their disparate spheres of influence. The creation of the WB and IMF further deepened the wedge between the Union of Soviet Socialist Republics and the United States as they competed in expanding their global interest among satellite nations within their respective spheres of interest. The cold war period saw the world divided into three spheres of political influence (Escobar, 2012; Mignolo & Walsh, 2018). The first world are countries with capitalist industrialized economies in Europe, North America, New Zealand, and Australia. The second world are countries within the orbit of the USSR. The third world are the former colonies orbiting around the free market democratic ideology of their former colonial rulers.

The designation of countries into numerical categories was eventually abandoned in the 1980s when assigning developing countries as the third world was considered a pejoration. The terminology Global South was preferred for countries with emerging economies, and Global North referred to leading capitalist powers with highly industrialized economies.[1]

Revisiting the manner the world was subdivided into spheres of influence could explain how former colonies to this day reel under the weight of poverty, political conflict, and social inequalities. Development aid was instrumentalized to establish a neocolonial relationship that lasted insofar as governments were pliant to the demands of the WB and IMF. Political dynasties in the third world were condoned, if not propped into office insofar as they were seen as friendly to the Western democratic ideology of global free trade and open market. Postwar development efforts were undertaken in neocolonies mired in massive indebtedness to the World Bank. There was no stopping to the issuance of unsustainable loans in the guise of development aid despite corruption, military dictatorships, human rights abuses, and widespread poverty as the eve present denominator among developing countries.

[1] The Global North-South terminology is attributed to German Chancellor Willy Brandt who led a commission to study international development in the 1980s. The demarcating line between North and South was also known as the Brandt Line.

The Search for Decolonized Alternatives

Decolonial practice will be the rewriting of history and the creation of new realities marked by struggle, resistance, and subversive movements. New stories will be written about the refusal to submit to any continuing representation of power by colonialists (Mignolo & Walsh, 2018). Social work in the Global South is set against this history, and it is for this very reason that Eurocentric social work will not find a location there. The decolonization of social work calls for a global movement that will interrogate present knowledge systems because there will be challenges in evolving new forms of knowing, thinking, and doing.

The social work profession transcends local borders because social inequalities and injustices do not recognize localities when permeating the lives of people in the Global North and South. There are geographic and historical connectedness in the lives of all people today as we confront issues of climate justice, disparities in wealth and access to resources, widespread hunger, conflicts, and wars. When deeply analyzed, these structural issues trace back to a North-South political order set in place by corporate interest and expansionist governments (Kleibl et al., 2020). The politics behind development aid illustrates the systemic causality of problems, but there are many other areas where social work can continue interrogating the causality of human suffering. From these investigations, we may yet proceed in creating knowledge and evolving professional tools in decolonizing practice.

The decolonization of social work is a process of professional self-interrogation as we acknowledge complicity in colonial acts of racism and exploitation as evidenced in various points of history, including the support given to the forcible institutionalization of indigenous children to disconnect them from their communities and culture, the condoning of genocidal acts in Nazi Germany, the support given to patriarchal policies in modern times, and even the current collusion with governments bent at the expulsion of desperate migrants. On our watch, knowingly or unknowingly, our disengagement will allow human rights violations to go unchecked and the perpetuation of colonizing values to be normalized.

Decolonizing practice in social work finds a location in the body of postcolonial theory, which is inclusive of the worldviews and cosmic visions valued by people who have been and continue to be affected by colonization (Tamburro 2013). Postcolonial theory interrogates historical experiences so as to capture the perspectives, concepts, and lived realities that colonized people share in common. It includes representations of neocolonial tendencies in present-day power structures to expose the recolonization of the Global South. Postcolonial theory is not all but a linear interpretation of history where the prefix "post" is in reference to that chronological period after empires nominally relinquished colonies. Postcolonial theory is a political stance that acknowledges colonialism's legacies by subjecting these to the critical interrogation of those affected by historical forces so that decisions in redeeming the past could lead to a collective determination of their own society's future (Mignolo & Walsh, 2018; Young, 2016). Postcolonial theory moves away from Eurocentric colonial knowledge structures by presenting opposition to hegemonic worldviews in the educational system that reproduce images of the othered as inferior and deserving of their subordinated status. Given that all social problems interact on both local and global levels and that all forms of social work are international social work (Ife, 2000), it is imperative that postcolonial theory and decolonizing approaches are integral components of social work education.

Decolonized social work education is respectful of the existence of other traditions and practices that indigenous societies evolved in caring for their vulnerable members. There are traditions of care, respect, equality, and justice obtained in traditional societies long before social work was institutionalized in Eurocentric educational curricula and exported to the colonies. The philosophical underpinnings in Ubuntu or Sumak Kawsay held communities together in an intergenerational system of care because every community member may claim a sense of belonging as a vital component of convivial living (IFSW Global Summit 2022). It is inherently present in communities where mutuality, care, and respect are not only the tacit underpinnings of social interaction but, more importantly, an encompassing cosmological understanding of the human relationship with an entire ecological system. An understanding that human life can only be viable when elements in the natural world, such as land, water, air, flora, and fauna, are respected as equals. This comes with the acceptance that the Western-inspired anthropocentric worldview of putting the narrow interest of humankind above all other forms of life is a violation of the rights of nature. Social work employs decolonizing approaches as it challenges the notion of humankind's hegemonistic right to have dominion over the Earth and sky. Indigenous values in social work are compatible with ecological justice in respecting the rights of nature as equally important to the rights of humankind.

When borrowing from environmental studies, social work education moved into interdisciplinary approaches to enrich our own discipline. Indigenous communities have long recognized that a collective life of dignity and worth can only be achieved when interconnected reciprocities among all who draw sustenance from the Earth's resources can pursue this in a social and physical environment of peaceful coexistence. These knowledge systems and value orientations which are inherent in many traditional communities are renamed as green social work (Dominelli, 2014), environmental sustainability, environmental citizenship, and corporate social responsibility (Gray et al., 2013b).

Transcending the limits of green social work is the expanded postcolonial concept of ecological justice which takes into account the extractive character of North-South relations. It takes into account carbon emissions stacked in the Earth's atmosphere from the time of Europe's industrial revolution, for which low-lying vulnerable countries in the South are made to pay the highest price in climatic disasters (Mount & O'Brien, 2021; Walker, 2021). Postcolonial analysis indicts the Global North's hegemonistic extraction of environmental resources from neocolonies, the destruction of natural habitats, and the loss of cultural heritage when people are forcibly dislocated from forest homes and ancestral land. Multinationally owned extractive industries proliferate in once-unexplored territories in the Global South, where they operate to supply raw materials needed in the production of every consumer item required by citizens in the Global North to maintain an acceptably modern quality of life. Postcolonial social work is confrontative, as it is militant in denouncing injustice committed against our interconnected life system in a shared human ecology.

Decolonization Theory and Practice

Decolonized approaches in social work can range greatly from perspectives that focus on a person's individual situation applying autoethnography (St-Denis & Walsh, 2016) and decolonization of the mind using mindfulness (neurodecolonization) (Yellow Bird, 2013), through indigenous family-based research (King, 2022) and anti-oppressive community work practice (Hölscher & Chiumbu, 2019), to broader, decolonizing perspectives of social work lineages (Clarke, 2022), eco-spiritual approach (Gray et al., 2013b), indigenous perspectives (Ibrahima & Mattaini, 2018), through postcolonial theory/approach (Tamburro, 2013) to the development of critical thinking and critical consciousness (Cook, 2020). This overview of decolonization perspectives in social work raises several issues, including the use of local knowledge or, more broadly, local perspectives on the conceptual and practical underpinnings of decolonization processes. This also raises the question of universal values and decolonization principles that will drive the process.

What can be expected in decolonizing approaches to social work is a plethora of individualistic concepts centered on the process, at first (a journey) leading to reclaiming indigenous heritage and identity through awakening, exploring, indigenizing, reclaiming, belonging, and finally nurturing the emerging warrior (St-Denis & Walsh, 2016). The process includes phases described as an *awakening* that begins with the recognition of a self as an "indigenous woman" and its expression via recollections, thoughts, and dialogues. *Exploring* emerging identity is the second phase that occurs during the ceremony guided by elders. Indigenization is part of this process involving indigenous ways of knowing, being, and doing. The fourth phase, *reclaiming*, involves the *reconciliation* of indigenous and Western worldviews and is connected to *belonging* that is based on the reconstruction of an indigenous community. The *emerging warrior* is the final stage based on the integration of personal and professional identity as a social work practitioner (St-Denis & Walsh, 2016).

A broader approach includes indigenous family-based research embedded in indigenous methodology aiming at preserving, remembering, and engaging the power of knowing one's stories, history, gifts, and responsibilities. The self, family, and relationships are highlighted as critical sites of resistance and resurgence in this approach. Though the method sometimes takes the form of family narratives focusing on close family members, it is intended to be the type of research that involves broader contexts allowing knowledge to be recognized, valued, and developed, as well as a much broader concept of "relatives" comparing to Western perspectives (St-Denis & Walsh, 2016). This type of approach emphasizes personal transformation and engages spiritual and affective fields as essential sites of resistance and resurgence. Wilson (2015) describes that type of research activity as a love in action that is "a very contemporary political expression of old knowledge" (p. 256).

As a type of relational activity, indigenous family-based research focuses on the micro level, an individual change that affects mezzo and macro levels that in the end include collective empowerment, indigenous self-determination, and the well-being of a group. Very close to this practice is anti-oppressive social work that assumes anti-oppressive theory, and the resulting community work practices are crucial for understanding the location of the Global South and enhancing our understanding of the process of decolonizing social work.

Another conceptual framework used in the decolonization process is neurodecolonization, which builds on identifying how the brains and cognitions of those living under colonial rules are affected and assists individuals in avoiding the cognitive and emotional consequences of colonial trauma and oppression (Yellow Bird, 2013). This perspective is compatible with the concept of mindfulness, which, according to Yellow Bird, draws not only from indigenous traditions but also from more universalistic traditions such as Buddhism and aids in mitigating the negative effects of colonialism. Interestingly, Buddhist philosophy is recognized as consistent with indigenous worldviews assuming the interconnectedness of all beings. As Yellow Bird (2013) puts it, "neurodecolonization seeks an understanding of how mind and brain function are shaped by the stresses of colonialism and compromise the well-being of Indigenous Peoples" (p. 300). According to this viewpoint, decolonization should include curriculum changes that include traditional mindfulness practice as well as social work practice with indigenous people, which should articulate an "enlightened" understanding of oppression that allows overcoming it. Neurodecolinization has been widely used in the recovery of traditional practices and their contribution to youth resilience (Sasakamoose et al., 2016). This approach incorporates not only Buddhism but also yoga and meditation as triggers for understanding how the mind and cognition interact with the negative effects of colonialism.

Other proposals for decolonizing social work include approaches that criticize colonial epistemic frameworks that reinforce colonizing epistemologies and focus on broadening the social work field of ancestors and relatives. This shift is based on extended recognition of ancestors and relatives who are part of multifaceted lineages of social work and rewrites its origins and history through the postcolonial lens (Clarke, 2022). This approach is intended to better understand indigeneity, local contexts, and diverse social work epistemologies capable of decentering social work lineage from its English-speaking core to include its forgotten non-English ancestors. Some include the concept of public history that is based on the mode of understanding the past in the process of collaborative co-creating of histories (Dean, 2018). Clarke assumes that this kind of public history creates an opportunity for universities, social work professionals, service users, and communities to come together to explore memory, professional traditions, and social work history, thereby challenging the hierarchical boundaries between experts and amateurs through creative methods (p. 273).

Another approach that exemplifies how social work can be decolonized is *eco-spiritual decolonization*, which recognizes the relationship between a person and the natural world, inquires about it, and includes it in its assessment of what matters to the people for whom services are designed (Ferreira, 2010). It is based on the premise that people's futures must be supported by awareness of the interconnectedness of all beings and life and future lives to lessen the negative effects of late capitalism (Coastes, 2013). This process has been broken down by Coates into six steps, which are as follows: acknowledging the diversity of cultures and manifold worldviews, recognizing the fact that a person has been subjected to the process of decolonization, developing the historical perspective that explains entanglement of an individual into the current power relations, understanding how discourses and power relations shape individual's identity and conceptual frameworks, critical self-reflection that examines how individual lifestyle and choices frequently support "oppressive ideology," and a discursive shift in language from the dysfunction language to "sacred vitality." The eco-spiritual approach is based on interdisciplinary research that integrates indigenous knowledge, social and environmental history, and modern science. As a result, it is a very comprehensive and encompassing approach that integrates different viewpoints and philosophical stances.

A different strategy known as "indigenization" has emerged in response to criticism of the Western model of social work and the presumed significance of local customs and traditions. According to this theory, social work knowledge "arise from within the culture, reflect local behaviors and practices, and should be interpreted within a local frame of reference and thus becomes locally relevant, that is, it should address culturally relevant and context-specific problems" (Gray & Coates, 2010, p. 615). One of the concerns related to indigenous approaches is that they fail at addressing structural and contextual issues and need to be supplemented with more universalistic approaches that promote partnership with existing community-based systems (Ibrahima & Mattaini, 2018). They also have limited application to non-indigenous populations that have also experienced colonization. Others recognize the risks associated with adopting ethnocentric viewpoints that confine indigenous knowledge to local contexts and prevent it from having broader cultural relevance (Gray & Coates, 2010). Indigenous social workers search for a fundamental commitment to shared values and recognition of cultural relevance that calibrates the memory of indigenous peoples' unfair colonial relations of power because indigenous social work is by no means a political process framed within the discourse of human rights and social justice. It's interesting to note that some support discipline-based indigenization by using pragmatism, holism, and phenomenology, which are more compatible with indigenous worldviews and concerned mainly with local perspectives (Gray & Coates, 2010).

When working with indigenous peoples, methods based on the postcolonial theory essentially encourage social workers to consider the effects of colonization in their practice. Since postcolonial theory offers a conceptual framework capable of explaining the experiences of colonized people that they share globally, they employ more general approaches and, as a result, make more universal claims (Tamburro, 2013). According to this perspective, the theory serves as a guide for decolonizing social work practice by bringing attention to the negative effects of colonialism and encouraging less oppressive practices. This shift in thinking not only offers social workers a different viewpoint from Western but also "raises the possibility of creatively drawing upon the knowledge from…the diversity of Indigenous cultures…or creating new Indigenous knowledge applicable to contemporary social challenges" (Baikie, 2009, p. 56).

Interestingly there is an approach combining postcolonial and indigenous perspectives called indigenous postcolonial theory framework for decolonizing indigenous education and establishing educational sovereignty not biased by the "colonial abyss" and capable of designing the future. The emphasis of Battiste (2013) is on indigenous humanities that discuss the similarities and differences that all peoples who develop from their ecological origins share and that are the foundation of resilient humanity. She promotes alternatives (in balance with Eurocentric discursive categories) and new understandings of humanity that start with ecological teachings and practices of what it means to be a human in a particular ecology. The concept of indigenous humanities is a kind of universal claim for bringing together the "core capacities" of all cultures that are abilities to "communicate through language and art, to mark our place and progress across time and space, and to locate ourselves reflectively and spiritually in relation to each other, to the world we all share, and to the forces that lie beyond our understanding or control" (Battiste, 2013, p. 114). This knowledge approach stems from the thrive for cognitive pluralism, self-determination, and identity reclamation and results not in ethnic elitism but in inclusive and encompassing universalist claims where the urge for decolonizing science is the common denominator.

Probably the most known indigenous, local, and non-Western approaches include *Sumak Kawsay* (Buen vivir) and Ubuntu which are a part of the anti-colonial tradition and in opposition to capitalist modernizing development. *Sumak Kawsay* is a South American indigenous (Incan) social movement that advocates for a way of life and a development model in which social, cultural, environmental, and economic concerns are balanced and function together rather than individually and hierarchically as they do at the moment. *Sumak Kawsay* is defined both as a concept and as a lived experience that seeks to promote social harmony through the concepts of reciprocity, complementarity, and relationality. As a creation of Andean indigenous people, it is actually a comprehensive decolonial strategy focused on opposing the prevalent Western, liberal, and anthropocentric ideologies of development (Jimenez et al., 2022). The concepts and ideas of *Sumak Kawsay* which include the communitarian economy, the food sovereignty, and the rights of nature founded on the lived experiences of indigenous peoples. The communitarian economy views labor as an expression of sociocultural and communitarian ties, as well as a right to work with dignity, whereas the food sovereignty concept focuses on establishing the rights of a community to develop protective laws in front of the global trade system. On local terrains, it is expressed as a right of peasants and indigenous peoples to be given the freedom to choose an agricultural system that goes beyond the extractivist or productivist paradigms (Calderón Farfán et al., 2021). The foundation of rights of nature is the idea that nonhuman organisms possess rights, can't be endlessly commodified and exploited, and need to be treated with respect as human beings. It focuses on interactions' ability to improve interactions' potential for enhancing relations between human beings and nature as a whole since it is based on the collective way of life. This enables the development of networks of reciprocal, complementary, and solidaristic social ties as it retrieves traditional, suppressed, and popular knowledge. Because it advocates for a way of life and social structures free of social hierarchies based on class, race, gender, and sexual orientation, *Sumak Kawsay* becomes a significant force in decolonizing social work. It has been proven to be successful in different context of Latin American societies (Pimentel, 2014).

Another important approach to decolonizing social work is *Ubuntu*, based on indigenous knowledge, which represents the diverse philosophical directions of the Global South. As a broad philosophical approach, Ubuntu is basically about perceiving individuals through the lens of community, spirituality, and environment. It refers to a set of beliefs and practices that black people of African descent perceive as defining what it is to be an authentic human being. Some advocate for Afrocentric social work that incorporates Ubuntu as the core of African life (Kurevakwesu & Maushe, 2020). It consists of a collection of ideas about how people relate to one another: person becomes a human being through other people, through compassion and empathy; on this principle, a community is built and given dignity. Ubuntu connects humans to the natural environment through its values assuming the environment, as a living being capable of thoughts, feelings, and emotions, is perceived as an inseparable part of humanity.

Interestingly, Ubuntu is seen as a promising theory for decolonial social work (Van Breda, 2019), and as an indigenous knowledge system, it becomes important in social work theory and practice as they inform sociocultural differences in line with the principle of individualization.

Critical theory and critical consciousness in social work are stated in many of the approaches already mentioned above as a means of decolonizing social work (Cook, 2020). Green and Baldry (2008) go into greater detail about the potential for developing indigenous critical social work and highlight four concepts that are relevant to indigenous knowledge related to social work, including social justice, emancipation, anti-oppressive practice, and self-determination. Additionally, they discuss the potential of indigenous Australian social work and the drawbacks of critical approaches in social work that lack indigenous worldviews such as collective self-determination, interdependence, reciprocity, obligation, and the question of land and family, which are understood differently. Rowe et al. (2015) developed a decolonizing framework to educate non-indigenous social workers about the practice of social work research that becomes a part of a fight against forces of dominance that are hostile to the healing of not only indigenous peoples but also everyone who shares the legacy of colonization.

This tension between theories and practices of decolonization may be characterized by the continuum of perspectives ranging from local, individualistic, through group-related, approaches operating on the level of family and community to more broad ideas focusing on eco-spiritualism or indigenous perspective, and abstract and universal approaches, less sensitive to local settings, such as postcolonial theory or critical theory (Coastes, 2013). The development of new ways to knowledge (respectively, education, worldviews, ontologies, etc.) and the identity of a person making knowledge claims (the role of subjects of practices related to knowledge creation, reconstruction, or use) are the fundamental justifications for social work decolonization theories and practices. The important role of indigenous, local, traditional or Western, modern, or universal knowledge forms and their use in the process of decolonization is the focus of decolonization theories that should be conceptualized in order to map the whole range of approaches and identify possibilities. At the first, there is a significant role for the person (who speaks) and its location (from which position or perspective speaks) in the spectrum of possibilities between indigenous, traditional and modern, and Western.

The issues are how decolonizing approaches are legitimized by which practices and who can be the subject of these practices. There is another possible dimension that characterizes these approaches which is context dependency. Therefore, we can say that some knowledge practices related to decolonizing social work can be more context-dependent or context-independent, as in this case the context may depend on the localization of a person, subject, or author making knowledge claims for decolonization. This localization may be considered in a broad sense, being part of Global North or Global South societies, or, in a narrower understanding, being a part of local, indigenous, traditional or modern, Western, or global societies. We can also ask about the rules of integrating different forms and traditions of knowledge into the body of decolonization of social work. Therefore, we can expect a tendency to separating traditions and approaches; building on local contexts and developing them according to the internal, local rules (Ubuntu, *Sumak Kawsay*); or building approaches on the principle of integration (neurodecolonization, eco-spiritual) where, in line with the needs, different traditions and worldviews can be possibly combined within the different approaches to decolonize social work.

Let us see the way of decolonizing social work through the lens of *Legitimation Code Theory* (henceforth, LCT) which primarily focuses on the field of knowledge production and introduces elements that allow for the analysis of the forms of knowledge that are prevalent in particular sets of knowledge (programs), disciplines, or subjects (Maton, 2015). We will use the so-called *specialization* dimension that supports the idea of practices as knowledge-knower structures whose organizing principles can be investigated in terms of epistemic relations, to other knowledge and study objects, as well as social relations, to ways of knowing and knowers. The notion that every practice is focused on or directed at something and by someone, to put it simply, is the basis for specialization. Maton (2015) analytically separates social relations (SR) between practices and their subject, author, or actor from epistemic relations (ER) between practices and their object or focus – in other words, area of the world toward which practices are oriented and who is enacting those practices. Both epistemic (between knowledge and its declared object of study) and social relations (between knowledge and its subjects, creators, or authors) relate to the question of *what* (what can be defined as "legitimate knowledge") and *who* (declare oneself as "legitimate knower").

LCT relies on the underlying assumption that every social practice, including decolonization in various contexts and regions, has its own underlying code (organizing principles of knowledge practices), which is conceptualized as legitimate in this specific field. In this project, we focus on specialization, a dimension that views social fields of practice as knowledge-knower structures with specialization codes as their organizing principles.

It is possible to independently emphasize each of these relations either more strongly (+) or weakly (−) that would generate *specialization codes*: ER+/− and SR+/−. These can be visualized through topological space of infinite positions within four modalities marked on the *specialization plane* that consists of (i) *knowledge codes*, which are characterized by strong epistemic relations and weak social relations (ER+, SR–), when the basis of achievement is the acquisition of specialized knowledge, principles, or procedures specific to particular objects of study and the characteristics of actors are minimized; (ii) *knower codes*, which are characterized by weak epistemic relations and strong social relations (ER–, SR+), whereby specialized knowledge and objects are minimized and the qualities of actors are highlighted as indicators of achievement, whether these characteristics are considered as social (e.g., being member of colonized people), learned (e.g., "being critical thinker"), or innate (e.g., "natural ability stemming from being member of indigenous community"); (iii) *élite codes*, which are characterized by strong epistemic relations and strong social relations (ER+, SR+), where being the appropriate type of knower and having specialized knowledge are conditions for legitimacy; and (iv) *relativist codes*, defined through weak epistemic and social relations (ER-, SR-), where anything is legitimate; neither expert knowledge nor knower characteristics are relevant. These broad concepts need to be "translated" in order to be applied in the field of decolonizing social work. In the words of LCT, an external language of description for specialization codes needs to be identified. As mentioned, ER refers to the part of a world that practice is pointing to, and as such, they refer to an emphasis on principles or procedures that in the context of decolonization means ways, methods, approaches, and procedures to decolonize particular context. ER indicates that the content of knowledge is prioritized as valid and legitimate as decolonized, decentered, non-Western knowledge, whereas SR indicates the relation between the author and the actor of the practice of decolonization: its experience, opinions, and background. To analyze the principles and assumptions of the decolonization approaches, we developed the following structure relating to *specialization plane* and its modalities (see Table 1.1).

The measures of achievement conceptualized by specialization codes are one aspect of the actors' dispositions, contexts, and behaviors. What matters in the four codes above is either "what you know" or "the sort of knower you are, "…both, as in the case of élite codes, or neither as in the case of relativist codes. What is observable in research based on the specialization codes or more generally LCT is the so-called 'code' clash" (Maton, 2015; Maton & Chen, 2020), the situation where different approaches within an intellectual field or practices can be identified and create the spectrum of possibilities as in the case of decolonization approaches. The way different approaches can be characterized by codes indicates that there are different forms of knowledge and authors'/actors' dispositions at stake and the underlying principles. What is particularly striking in this perspective is the absence of a relativist code that would prevent publications on decolonizing social work from taking an "anything goes" stance. This is presumably the result of the presumption

Table 1.1 Specialization codes of decolonizing social work

Specialization codes	Summary	Examples
Knowledge code (ER+, SR-)	The emphasis is on specialized knowledge, principles, or procedures, and the qualities of actors are unimportant (in the context of decolonization means impersonal ways, methods, and approaches to decolonization of social work)	Critical theory, postcolonial theory, social work lineages
Knower code (ER-, SR+)	The emphasis is on specialized knowledge, principles, or procedures that are minimized, and the qualities of actors are highlighted as indicators of achievement (in the context of decolonization means that the main role play qualities of actors that are highlighted as indicators of achievement, whether these characteristics are considered as social, e.g., being a member of colonized people; learned, e.g., being successor of local, indigenous knowledge; or innate, e.g., natural ability stemming from being a member of indigenous community)	Autoethnography, indigenous family-based research
Élite code (ER+, SR+)	The emphasis is on being the appropriate type of knower and having specialized knowledge. These are conditions for legitimacy of practice called decolonization of social work (it means having knowledge, principles, or procedures to decolonize and at the same time being appropriate *person* that is part of colonized communities, having traditional *knowledge*, knowing the ways of transforming of personal identity, etc.)	Ubuntu, *Sumak Kawsay*, indigenous critical theory, indigenous postcolonial theory, neurodecolonization, eco-social approach, indigenous approach
Relativist code (ER-, SR-)	Anything can be legitimately accepted, neither expert knowledge nor knower characteristics are relevant, "anything goes" stance	

that the process should involve at least some level of knowledge or personal disposition – in each case or approach, social or epistemic relations play a role in the process.

While mapping approaches, we notice possible scenarios and guiding principles for decolonizing knowledge in social work: from a local, isolated, individual, or local community-based conceptions of knowledge relevant to social work emerging from the local context, they can take the shape of ethnic elitism, ethnocentric views, or universalistic, abstract, and context-independent such as Marxism, critical theory, or postcolonial theory (see Fig. 1.1). The question may be formulated as follows: What are the guiding principles for how knowledge may be applied to decolonize social work? There are at least two ways to be applied: integrative universalistic approaches or separating localized essentialisms. The struggle to establish methods and approaches of decolonization oscillates between essentialism and universalism, where the former would focus on the content of knowledge and related

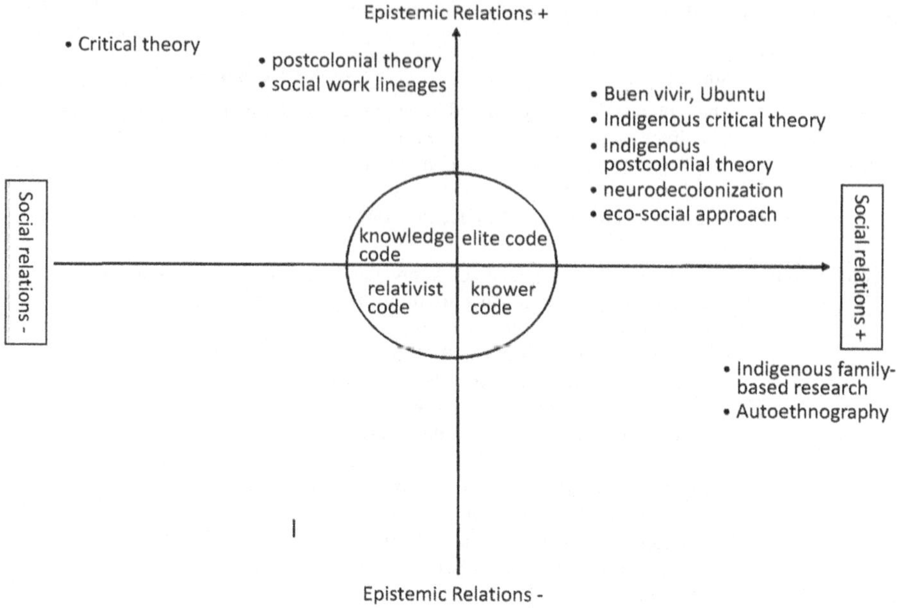

Fig. 1.1 Mapping positions of social work decolonization within specialization code framework

practices of the "local," in this case, the traditional and more or less culturally dependent body of knowledge that in some contexts may be referred to as indigenous and letter could be possibly based on decolonized dialectics – new decolonized universal – that escapes Eurocentric universalism as continually displaced universalism that was described by Ciccariello-Maher as the following: "What may seem a contradiction, however, is only resolved temporally through the constant and open-ended struggle that defines our decolonized dialectics: there can be no unity until after combat, and it is in the assertion of the need for such 'future combat' that the universal is continually displaced" (2017, p. 136). The nature of universalism – whether it be "continually displaced" or "temporary" – remains an unsettled topic. From the theoretical and practical point of view, the only possible universalism is the universalism "which is not one": "it is not a matter of weighing each particular claim to the universal against some transcultural or transhistorical universal, or of deciding which claim will be authorized as the 'true universal' according to some preexisting normative, ethical, or cognitive criteria. It is a matter, rather, of mediating the relation between the particular and the universal in a public space, with every mediation remaining open to further universalism" (Zerilli, 1998, p. 18). The idea of universalism "which is not one" expresses the possibility of retaining imperfect and obviously temporary universalisms. We believe that the way social work is being decolonized reflects this process of mediation creating temporary pluriveralisms and open conceptual frameworks for non-Western perspectives.

There are several examples of the movement toward acknowledging the importance of local, indigenous knowledge and practices in the decolonization of social work:

- Actions taken by the International Federation of Social Workers, such as creating structures for integrating indigenous knowledge and skills in the delivery of services, that led to the appointment of the Indigenous Commission of IFSW.
- The global movement for equality and sustainability – the People's Summit "Co-building a New Eco-social World: Leaving No One Behind" – created by trade unions, health sectors, Faith Invest network, global student bodies, international social work, United Nation's agencies, social movements, academic networks, etc. that share global ideas and principles with the core tenets of Ubuntu and *Sumak Kawsay* (The People's Charter for an Eco-Social World, 2021).
- Momentum in the global arena, particularly after being highlighted in the Global Agenda of the social work profession by the IFSW and became global social work main theme on the occasion of World Social Work Day in 2021.
- As social work develops into a worldwide academic and practice profession, there is an acknowledged need to broaden this Western focus to accommodate different viewpoints. Frequently, one of the sources cited in the literature is Ubuntu, which has philosophical characteristics that can improve social work theory, practice, and education (Mayaka & Truell, 2021; Mungai, 2021; Van Breda, 2019).

There is little doubt that theories within the framework of decolonizing social work will develop in accordance with the integrative principle, moving toward a knowledge code and elite code (according to LCT), where epistemic and social relations will become more relevant. It is reasonable to predict that a patchwork of many traditions will result an integrative interplay of possible localized ways of decolonizing social work or that the new local universalist movements like Afrocentric Ubuntu or South American *Sumak Kawsay* would change the situation while becoming partially global.

Conclusion

The following chapters of this book will provide discussions on human rights instruments in greater detail. It is helpful to note that the seminal instrument United Nations Universal Declaration of Human Rights (UN-UDHR) was proclaimed by the UN in 1948, paving the way for the adoption of several other human treaties. The economic interest of colonial empires coupled with the ambitions of a rising global superpower in the United States was well ensconced in the Bretton Woods Agreement in 1944. The significance of Bretton Woods and the UN-UDHR are polar events in development politics. The UN-UHDR was meant to protect individual rights. However, it fell short of sanctioning governments from installing mechanisms meant to perpetuate neocolonial relations and hegemonic power structures for recolonization purposes (Gardner & Roy, 2020).

Through time, the community of nations advocated for the recognition of collective and community rights, which are articulated in instruments such as the International Covenant on Civil and Political Rights (United Nations). With us today are various other UN conventions and declarations aimed at safeguarding the rights of women, indigenous peoples, children, and many other vulnerable groups.

As a human rights profession, social work can rely on these instruments to advocate for decolonization and restorative justice. A decolonized human rights movement pursued in many parts of the world is an interrogation of historical injustice. Such interrogation aligns social work to the many truths that people living in a plurality of worlds have known for centuries.

In themselves, human rights instruments bolster arguments in contentious debates in the decolonization project (Burke, 2010). Upholding human rights in social work is an anti-colonialist political stance that recognizes how individual and community rights are achieved within a global order that is structured around the principle that the inherent worth and dignity of all forms of life must be upheld.

Discussion Questions

1. In our present global interaction, how does the legacy of colonization impact the lives of people living in the Global South and the Global North?
2. Are there traces of colonization left behind in our social work profession? How do we engage in a process of decolonizing social work education?
3. How did colonization and neocolonization amass so much land and other resources from the non-Western world – known today as the Global South?

References

Baikie, G. (2009). Indigenous-centred social work. In R. Sinclair, M. A. Hart, & G. Bruyere (Eds.), *Wicihitowin: Aboriginal social work in Canada*. Fernwood Publishing.

Battiste, M. (2013). *Decolonizing education: Nourishing the learning spirit*. Purich Publishing.

Bello, W. (1982). *Development debacle: The World Bank in The Philippines*. Institute for Food and Development Policy/Philippine Solidarity Network.

Burke, R. (2010). *Decolonization and the evolution of international human rights. Pennsylvania studies in human rights*. University of Pennsylvania Press, Inc. http://www.sehepunkte.de/2013/06/17799.html

Calderón Farfán, J. C., Dussán Chaux, J. D., & Arias Torres, D. (2021). Food autonomy: Decolonial perspectives for indigenous health and buen vivir. *Global Health Promotion, 28*(3), 50–58. https://doi.org/10.1177/1757975920984206

Ciccariello-Maher, G. (2017). *Decolonizing dialectics*. Duke University Press.

Clarke, K. (2022). Reimagining social work ancestry: Toward epistemic decolonization. *Affilia, 37*(2), 266–278. https://doi.org/10.1177/08861099211051326

Coastes, J. (2013). Ecospiritual approaches: A path to decolonizing social work. In M. Gray, J. Coates, M. Yellow Bir, & T. Hetherington (Eds.), *Decolonizing social work*. Routledge. https://doi.org/10.4324/9781315576206

Cook, S. (2020). *If social work knowledge is still based on western values, can practice really be anti-oppressive?* https://www.communitycare.co.uk/2020/02/03/social-work-knowledge-still-based-western-values-can-practice-really-anti-oppressive/

Dean, D. M. (2018). *A companion to public history*. John Wiley and Sons, Inc.

Dominelli, L. (2014). *Green social work: From environmental crises to environmental justice*. Polity Press. https://ebookcentral.proquest.com/lib/kxp/detail.action?docID=1524246

Escobar, A. (2012). *Encountering development: The making and unmaking of the Third World* (paperback reissue). Princeton University Press. https://ebookcentral.proquest.com/lib/kxp/detail.action?docID=767225

Fanon, F. (2021). *The wretched of the earth*. Black Cat.

Ferreira, S. B. (2010). Eco-spiritual social work as a precondition for Social Development. *Ethics and Social Welfare, 4*(1), 3–23. https://doi.org/10.1080/17496531003607891

Gandhi, L. (2019). *Postcolonial theory: A critical introduction* (2nd ed.). Columbia University Press.

Gardner, L., & Roy, T. (2020). *The economic history of colonialism*. Bristol University Press.

Global Summit. 2022. *The People's Charter for an Eco-Social World: Leave no one behind*. International Federation of Social Workers. https://newecosocialworld.com/the-peoples-charter-for-an-eco-social-world/

Gray, M., & Coates, J. (2010). 'indigenization' and knowledge development: Extending the debate. *International Social Work, 53*(5), 613–627. https://doi.org/10.1177/0020872810372160

Gray, M., Coates, J., & Hetherington, T. (Eds.). (2013a). *Environmental social work* (1st ed.). Routledge.

Gray, M., Coates, J., Yellow Bird, M., & Hetherington, T. (2013b). *Decolonizing social work*. Routledge. https://doi.org/10.4324/9781315576206

Green, S., & Baldry, E. (2008). Building indigenous Australian social work. *Australian Social Work, 61*(4), 389–402. https://doi.org/10.1080/03124070802430718

Hancock, G. (1989). *Lords of poverty: The power, prestige, and corruption of the international aid business* (1st Atlantic Monthly Press ed.). Atlantic Monthly Press.

Hölscher, D., & Chiumbu, S. (2019). Anti-oppressive community work practice and the Decolonization Debate. *Community Practice and Social Development in Social Work*, 1–20. https://doi.org/10.1007/978-981-13-1542-8_2-1

Horowitz, M. C. (1974). The stoic synthesis of the idea of natural law in man: Four themes. *Journal of the History of Ideas, 35*(1), 3–16. https://doi.org/10.2307/2708739

Ibrahima, A. B., & Mattaini, M. A. (2018). Social work in Africa: Decolonizing methodologies and approaches. *International Social Work, 62*(2), 799–813. https://doi.org/10.1177/0020872817742702

Ife, J. (2000). Local and global practice: Relocating social work as a human rights profession in the new global order: Voices of social work. International Association of Schools in Social Work. The Eileen Younghusband Lectures, Montreal.

IFSW. (2018). *Statement of ethical principles and professional integrity*. International Federation of Social Workers.https://www.ifsw.org/wp-content/uploads/2018/06/13-Ethics-Commission-Consultation-Document-1.pdf

Ishay, M. R. (2008). *The history of human rights: From ancient times to the globalization era*. University of California Press.

Jimenez, A., Delgado, D., Merino, R., & Argumedo, A. (2022). A decolonial approach to innovation? building paths towards buen vivir. *The Journal of Development Studies, 58*(9), 1633–1650. https://doi.org/10.1080/00220388.2022.2043281

King, J. (2022). Decolonizing social work education through indigenous family-based research. *Intersectionalities, A Global Journal of Social Work Analysis, Research, Polity, and Practice, 10*(1), 37–49.

Kleibl, T., Lutz, R., Noyoo, N., Bunk, B., Dittmann, A., & Seepamore, B. (Eds.). (2020). *The Routledge handbook of postcolonial social work*. Routledge.

Kothari, U. (Ed.). (2019). Development essentials. *A radical history of development studies: Individuals, institutions and ideologies* (2nd ed.). Zed Books.

Kurevakwesu, W., & Maushe, F. (2020). Towards Afrocentric social work: Plotting a new path for social work theory and practice in Africa through Ubuntu. *African Journal of Social Work, 10*(1), 30–35.

Lloyd, G. (2005). *Human nature and human rights. Ancient worlds, modern reflections: Philosophical perspectives on Greek and Chinese science and culture*. Oxford University Press. https://doi.org/10.1093/0199270163.003.0011

MacEwan, C. (2009). *Postcolonialism and development. Routledge perspectives on development*. Routledge.

Mapp, S., McPherson, J., Androff, D., & Gabel, S. G. (2019). Social work is a human rights profession. *Social Work, 64*(3), 259–269. https://doi.org/10.1093/sw/swz023

Maton, K. (2015). *Knowledge & knowers: Towards a realist sociology of Education*. Routledge.

Maton, K., & Chen, R. T. H. (2020). In J.R. Martin, K. Maton, & Y.J. Doran (Eds.), *Accessing academic discourse: Systemic functional linguistics and legitimation code theory*. Routledge.

Mayaka, B., & Truell, R. (2021). Ubuntu and its potential impact on the International Social Work Profession. *International Social Work, 64*(5), 649–662. https://doi.org/10.1177/00208728211022787

McEwan, C. (2008). *Postcolonialism and development*. Routledge. https://doi.org/10.4324/9780203887387

Memmi, A., Sartre, J.-P., & Gordimer, N. (2016). *The colonizer and the colonized* (H. Greenfeld, Trans.). Independent Voices. Souvenir Press.

Mignolo, W., & Walsh, C. E. (2018). *On decoloniality: Concepts, analytics, praxis*. Duke University Press.

Mount, D., & O'Brien, S. (2021) Postcolonialism and environment. In *Oxford handbook of postcolonial studies* (pp. 521–539).

Mungai wa, N. (2021). Adopting Ubuntu in teaching social work. In: *Teaching and learning in higher education: The context of being, interculturality and new knowledge systems*, pp. 223–236. https://doi.org/10.1108/978-1-80043-006-820211017

Pimentel Marañón, B. (2014). *Buenvivir y descolonialidad. Crítica al Desarrollo y la racionalidad instrumentales*. Universidad Nacional Autónoma de México.

Rowe, S., Baldry, E., & Earles, W. (2015). Decolonising social work research: Learning from critical indigenous approaches. *Australian Social Work, 68*(3), 296–308. https://doi.org/10.1080/0312407x.2015.1024264

Sasakamoose, J. L., Scerbe, A., Wenaus, I., & Scandrett, A. (2016). First Nation and Métis youth perspectives of health. *Qualitative Inquiry, 22*(8), 636–650. https://doi.org/10.1177/1077800416629695

Smith, L. T. (2012). *Decolonizing methodologies: Research and indigenous peoples* (2nd ed.). Zed Books. https://ebookcentral.proquest.com/lib/kxp/detail.action?docID=1426837

St-Denis, N., & Walsh, C. (2016). Reclaiming my indigenous identity and the emerging warrior: An autoethnography. *Journal of Indigenous Social Development, 5*(1), 1–17.

Stearns, P. N. (2019). *The Industrial Revolution in world history*. Routledge. https://doi.org/10.4324/9780429494475

Tamburro, A. (2013). Including decolonization in social work education and practice. *Journal of Indigenous Social Development, 2*(1), 1–16.

Tauli-Corpuz, V. (Ed.). (2006). *Good practices on indigenous peoples' development*. Valley Printing.

The People's Charter for an Eco-Social World. (2021). *World leaders invited to join global mass movement for eco-social change – Co-Building a New Eco-Social World*. https://newecosocialworld.com/2021/11/01/world-leaders-invited-to-join-global-mass-movement-for-eco-social-change/

United Nations. (1945). *International covenant on civil and political rights*. https://www.coe.int/en/web/compass/the-international-covenant-on-civil-and-political-rights#

United Nations. (2022a). *History of the UN*. https://www.un.org/un70/en/content/history/index.html

United Nations. (2022b). *The core human rights instruments and their monitoring bodies*. https://www.ohchr.org/en/core-international-human-rights-instruments-and-their-monitoring-bodies

United Nations. (2022c). *The foundation of international human rights law*. https://www.un.org/en/about-us/udhr/foundation-of-international-human-rights-law

United Nations. (2022d). *Decolonization*. https://www.un.org/en/global-issues/decolonization

Van Breda, A. (2019). Developing the notion of ubuntu as African theory for Social Work Practice. *Social Work*, 55(4). https://doi.org/10.15270/55-4-762

Wa Thiong'o, N. (1992). *Decolonising the mind: The politics of language in African literature*. East African Publishers.

Walker, G. (2021). *Environmental justice: Concepts, evidence and politics: Concepts, evidence and politics*. Routledge. https://www.taylorfrancis.com/books/9781136619243, https://doi.org/10.4324/9780203610671

Werbner, P., & Modood, T. (Eds.). (1997). *Debating cultural hybridity: Multi-cultural identities and the politics of anti-racism*. Zed Books.

Wilson, A. (2015). Afterword: A steadily beating heart: Persistence, resistance and resurgence. In E. Coburn (Ed.), *More will sing their way to freedom: Indigenous resistance and resurgence* (pp. 255–264). Fernwood.

Yellow Bird, M. (2013). Neurodecolonization: Applying mindfulness research to decolonizing social work. In M. Gray, J. Coates, M. Yellow Bir, & T. Hetherington (Eds.), *Decolonizing social work*. Routledge. https://doi.org/10.4324/9781315576206

Young, R. (2016). *Postcolonialism: An historical introduction* (Anniversary edition). Wiley Blackwell. http://onlinelibrary.wiley.com/book/10.1002/9781119316817

Young, R. J. (2020). *Postcolonialism: A very short introduction*. Oxford University Press.

Zerilli, L. M. (1998). This universalism which is not one. *Diacritics, 28*(2), 3–20. https://doi.org/10.1353/dia.1998.0013

Marcin Boryczko is an Associate Professor at the University of Gdańsk, Poland, where he teaches Social Work on bachelors' and masters' levels. He serves in the board of several international and national associations such as the Polish Federation of Social Workers and Social Service Employees Unions (Polska Federacja Związków Zawodowych Pracowników Socjalnych i Pomocy Społecznej), the European Social Work Research Association, and the International Advisory Board of the *European Social Work Research Journal* and serves as the Polish Representative in the International Federation of Social Workers (IFSW). His main research interests include social work education, critical social work theory, human rights, decolonization, neoliberal governmentality, and populism in Central Europe.

Mark Lusk is a Faculty Member in the School of Social Work at New Mexico State University. He was Senior Fulbright Scholar at the Catholic University of Peru in Lima and also a Fulbright Research Scholar at the Catholic University of Rio de Janeiro in Brazil. He currently works with forced migrants and refugees from Central America and Mexico and related human rights issues. He was the Founding Director of the School of Social Work at Boise State University (Idaho) and has served as Associate Provost at the University of Georgia.

Melinda Madew is Professor in International Social Work at the Protestant University of Applied Sciences Ludwigsburg, Germany, and a Research Associate of the University of Johannesburg, South Africa. She serves as Board Member of the European Social Work Research Association. Her teaching and research are in the areas of gender politics, postcolonial social work and indigenous knowledge, and practice in community organizing. She has served as Education and Research Consultant for international development organizations. She conceptualized and implemented international projects under the auspices of European Union educational programs for North-South university collaboration.

Chapter 2
Relativism, Universalism, and Pluriversality in Human Rights

Marcin Boryczko, Jason M. Leung, and Melinda Madew

Introduction: On the Nature of Human Rights: Between Radical Relativism and Universalism

When analyzing the spectrum of possible positions within the debate on the validity and nature of human rights, we may distinguish between two fundamentally opposed stances: radical relativism and radical universalism. The first one considers culture as a source of the legitimacy and validity of moral principles and ideas, which indicates that since rights are an inherent element of culture, they cannot be justified by cases outside of that culture and there are no universally accepted standards. The opposing view is predicated on the idea that human rights, *ex definitione*, are inherent to every human being that shares the same inalienable rights. This is a common approach used by theorists dealing with human rights who agree on the fact that all people have human rights based on having a status of a human (Freeman, 2022).

M. Boryczko (✉)
Department of Social Work, Faculty of Social Sciences, University of Gdańsk, Gdańsk, Poland
e-mail: marcin.boryczko@ug.edu.pl

J. M. Leung
Department of Environmental Studies, Benguet State University, La Trinidad, Benguet, Philippines

Philippine Department of Science and Technology Research – Extractive Mining and Indigenous Communities, Baguio City, Philippines
e-mail: j.leung@bsu.edu.ph

M. Madew
Department of Social Work, Protestant University of Applied Sciences Ludwigsburg, Ludwigsburg, Germany

Department of Social Work, University of Johannesburg, Johannesburg, South Africa
e-mail: m.madew@eh-ludwigsburg.de

M. Madew et al. (eds.), *Decolonized Approaches to Human Rights and Social Work*, https://doi.org/10.1007/978-3-031-33030-8_2

It is also agreed that not all human rights are universal since some of them belong to specific categories of people, such as women, children, and minorities. But some rights are basically concerned as universal (prohibitions on torture and slavery), whereas others are perceived as potentially universal: firstly when they are evoked in extraordinary situations (the right to a fair trial) and secondly when certain criteria of subjects of those rights are met (rights of minorities) (Freeman, 2022).

However, what does universalism entail in terms of human rights? There are three types of universalism, which should be mentioned in order to better comprehend the dispute: (i) descriptive universalism asserts that there are fundamental differences between conventional norms, but there is a set of norms that are shared by all human beings; (ii) normative universalism regards some norms as universal irrespective of factual disagreements on the justification of those norms as long as moral norms are universal; and (iii) epistemological universalism is based on the assumption that the process of justifying valid norms exceeds contextual differences and every valid norm has to be universally reasonable. It should come as no surprise that the relativist critique of universalism reflects all three forms of universalism: descriptive relativism recognizes conventional norms as strongly bound to certain contexts (such as human rights supposedly depending on the cultural context), normative relativism holds that we should not accept any norm as legitimate universally (justification of norms is context-dependent), and epistemological relativism argues that there are no grounds for justifying norms that merely depend on the settings of their occurrence (Namli, 2018). These three types of arguments are often at the core of the critique of human rights. Although the most typical example of critique that assumes the distinction between Islamic and liberal human rights traditions indicates the inability to translate conceptions of human rights, which results in the conclusion that trans-contextual dialogue is impossible (Bonnet, 2015). The descriptive, normative, and epistemic aspects of human rights are typically the subject of relativist critique. Therefore, it is claimed that since human rights rely on the context in which they are produced, their justification depends on a certain set of beliefs or cultural norms; they are justifiable in a certain context that cannot be legitimately justified in other contexts.

Most importantly, there is no common acceptance of the idea of the universal character of all human rights. Some human rights can be called absolute in their obligatory level of protection which means that limiting these rights by balancing their applicability against the achievement of a legal objective is not permissible, such as the prohibition of torture or slavery. Most of the time, people do not view rights as absolute; therefore, they can sometimes be limited for good reasons by entities like states. The treaty clauses, which frequently identify the so-called reasons like public order or national security, occasionally specify the criteria for restricting the rights. Another type of limitation is described as an inherent limitation that is not specified in treaties and developed by national and international courts depending on the context, for instance, the right to be tried without "undue delay" (Klein, 2021). However, the most obvious assumption about the universal character of human rights stems from the liberal ideology that is based on "the myth of Enlightenment" that created the possibility of becoming an ideological legitimization for power and violence (Horkheimer & Adorno, 1988).

Criticisms and Objections

It should come as no surprise that the universalist approach to human rights has drawn harsh criticism from ideologies other than liberalism and religious or cultural views. On a general level, the tension within human rights can be identified by the distinction between global perspective (often called global justice) and community-based particularisms of norms and principles stemming from "natural" cultural life-worlds. This inherent conflict is reproduced by differences in understanding of human rights, which is expressed in the relationship between universalism and relativism, replicating this underlying contradiction: the first, requires a minimal set of principles and values that must be preserved, and the second is claiming for the need of reconciliation of different principles that enable coexistence of culturally different communities that recognize human rights and international law as a universal regulatory framework but not as a universal ethical model to be followed unconditionally.

The following waves of criticism of universalistic claims of human rights can be described as (i) criticism of Western imperialism based on liberal and democratic principles of human rights and (ii) criticism based on the celebration of cultural differences (Freeman, 2022). The first criticism equates universalism to imperialism arguing that the dominant version of human rights is based on the Enlightenment project of European philosophical rationalism and old-fashioned modernism. The counter-imperialist criticism of human rights engages two sound arguments: everyone has the same right to respect, and therefore respect toward a person entails also respect toward that person's culture. These rules obviously contradict relativist concepts because they are universalist in nature, asserting that there are rules that are relevant in situations independently as we cannot assume that there are no cultures that apply them.

There is another problem with anti-imperial criticism of liberal universalism. As proceeding criticism, often in the name of liberty, relativism requires common if not universal rights to freedom. On one hand, it criticizes universalist ramparts of liberal theories of rights, but on the other, it cannot put forward any argument against its own culture that may be oppressive and hegemonic toward its members as collective and individuals (Gawin et al., 2016). This contradiction that relativists fall into is accompanied by the instrumentalization of human rights that play a vicious role in the realization of particular and often egoistic interests of a community or a nation. Relativism often neglects the fact that local cultures are often oppressive toward individuals as in the case of women often subsumed by patriarchal assumptions of cultural relativism. On the other hand, the cultural relativist argument should be also considered valid in the context of tribal and indigenous struggles around the world. In times of globalization and neo-colonization, cultural difference should be a part of valuing those cultures and identities in terms of the dignity of populations living in the "peripheries" of the modern world.

This relationship between human rights and culture is developing in the field of anthropology where discussions revolve around ways of translating human rights into different cultural contexts (Messer, 2002) and middle-ground theories or developing critical anthropology approach as promising stances in the discussion on human rights (Goodale, 2021). In spite of the fact that middle-ground theories appear to be viable strategies for bridging the gap between universalist and relativist perspectives, in fact, they should be perceived as mutually dependent. As a result, we shouldn't consider middle-ground theories to be a resolution to the relativism vs. universalism debate because both are essential for our comprehension and moreover application of human rights in different cultural settings. As Johansson Dahre (2017) assumed, middle-ground theories "often speak in general normative terms about the need to strike a balance of immersion between relativism and universalism as these antipodes are fundamental social factors to consider" (p. 9). In the realm of practice, the issue is still up for debate if a medium ground is indeed possible to find.

Anthropological criticism of universalist versions of human rights stems from the assumption that culture is equally important as in Herskovitz's statement on behalf of the American Anthropological Association on human rights saying "respect for the cultures of differing human groups is equally important" (American Anthropological Association, 1947) and importance of cultural values and local context that was always in the center of the anthropological approach. According to the anthropological tradition, if human rights are to be put into practice, they must be linked to people's experiences, local values, political institutions, and cultural identity. Middle-ground theories seem to be a way to avoid the allure of cultural relativism fostered by the anthropological appreciation of local cultures. If universalist approaches to human rights are to have meaning in people's lives, they must be translated, understood, and modified to various local contexts.

Though the middle-ground theory makes an intriguing claim, one can wonder if there truly is a middle ground between relativism and universalism. The issue to be addressed here can be characterized slightly differently whether rights are just cultural or contextual manifestations or whether they come ahead or beyond culture. As some state, "rights talk has produced powerful ideas which interrogate culture: equality, feminism, social justice" (Deng et al., 2009, p. 113) that would lead us to the conclusion that rights discourse transcends culture. The issue with human rights relativists' conception of culture is that they see it as static and monolithic, but in reality, its primary characteristics are the ability to disseminate, diffuse, and reproduce (Pedersen & Cliggett, 2021). The nationalist notion of cultural unity, which is conveyed by forcing the high culture on society, is often articulated by states that are actively involved in upholding the vision of cultural homogeneity based on an idea of common culture (Gellner & Breuilly, 2008). Furthermore, it is feasible to claim that human rights do not necessarily require culture because it is possible for human nature to act as a bearer of human rights values and ideas.

Let us refer to Kymlicka's example of the problem of moral justification by a Muslim woman saying "sexual discrimination is wrong," as it is interpreted by Kymlicka (1989): "she does not mean 'We don't do that around here.' On the contrary, she is saying this precisely because it is done around there, and has always been done, and is very firmly embedded in all the myths, symbols, and institutions of their history and society" (p. 65–66). This example shows that often the allegation of sexual discrimination requires more than simply a culture that often justifies the oppression of its members. In her culture, she would not find any allegations supporting her claim; therefore, we could reasonably ask about where could we find the justification of criticism of cultural wrongs of our own. Collective cultures may be repressive to their members, and because every society is composed of individuals, thinking about human rights necessarily includes thinking about individual rights, especially in social work practice. In actuality, this is frequently the case for social workers who assist victims of human rights abuses and who also support the ideologies, cultures, and religions that justify such abuses and are repressive to such individuals from birth.

Returning to Nussbaum's (2000) claim that the perspectives of victims of abuse cannot justify the standards they are subjected to and cannot provide ethically compelling evidence about access to basic needs, such as food, education, healthcare, etc., therefore, it is crucial to consider if the presumed consent ignores fundamental needs and whether oppression is a result of a deliberate decision or a strong devotion to cultural tradition. It should be evident that social work practice transcends cultural and local factors and circumstances. This raises the question of whether it is possible at all to place oneself outside of culture. It could be argued, following Rorty's (2011) argument, that adopting the position of radical relativism assuming that all cultural traditions and values have equal status could only be possible when expressed by some kind of God that possesses the proper perspective. The only position we have is situated in a particular cultural setting, ethno- and culture-centric claims, and therefore ethnocentrism in some way is unavoidable. Does this mean that our cultural entanglement is inevitable? From this standpoint, relativism is indefensible as it would require God's perspective, whereas the positions we have are culturally dependent.

In order to defend universal claims of human rights, it might be claimed that in addition to the relativists' premise of the equality of all cultures, the presumption of European origins of human rights should also be reexamined. We frequently take the Eurocentric assumption for granted that the majority of contemporary concepts, including human rights, originated in Europe, whereas, according to Bhambra (2007), the entire concept of modernity is too often recognized as a uniquely Western trait disseminated to the rest of the globe. One may speculate that human rights and the idea of modernity were founded on a failure to take into account the reality of people and non-Western societies. From this perspective, one could wonder if the critique of alleged Eurocentrism of human rights is still valid. Bhambra (2007) makes the historical argument that the abolition of slavery was only incorporated in the *French Declaration of Human Rights* after a committee from the colony of Saint Domingue travelled to France in 1794 and made the point to the Constituent Assembly. Interestingly, Eurocentrism can be recognized at the core of criticisms stating the arbitrability of Western perspectives on human rights. This mental trap is similar to Chakrabarty's (2008) notion that in postcolonial reality, we cannot see ourselves outside of Western concepts and everything that may be conceived separately from the Western perspective necessarily reflects Western development. We may ask this question: If human rights are not particularly Western, the problem at hand is why we claim human rights as exclusively Western conception.

Donnelly (1982) distinguished between human rights and human dignity, claiming that the latter is central to non-Western cultural traditions and that Western ideas of human rights (based on special entitlements of person) are foreign and do not align with Islamic, African, Chinese, and Indian traditions. Baxi (2006) makes the interesting claim that only specific types of human rights emerged in the West. The debate over the origins of human rights reflects the ways in which they are criticized and justified: Eurocentric criticism assumes that the human rights regime lacks equality and balance, whereas a non-Western perspective on the genesis of human rights will justify the human rights regime as inclusive and equal (Mende, 2021). Three significant sorts of justifications are offered by Mende (2021) for the non-Western origins:

(i) Time: The current human rights regime is fundamentally different from the Western human rights tradition.
(ii) History: Non-Western movements and revolutionaries contained very radical (at the time of being) ideas, such as anti-slavery, anti-colonialism, anti-racism, etc..
(iii) Tradition and philosophy: There are many non-Western philosophies and thoughts that contributed to the development of human rights.

It seems that the research on the origins of human rights should be continued, but what is sure is human rights did not originate from one source: religion, value system, culture, or tradition. It has not only emerged from various and heterogeneous, but as we see later, most of them are pluriversalist in nature. Future justifications and legitimization of humanitarian law and human rights will be impacted by the debate over the purported origins of those; as Baxi (2006) puts it, "When, if ever (given the present mode of production of knowledge about human rights), the originalist history of human rights is written from non-Euro-enclosed perspectives, the future of human rights will be more secure than it is now" (p. 42). Whatever the future holds for human rights, one thing is for certain: they cannot be defended only in terms of legal requirements of the Western global system or exclusively by skepticism and critique from non-Western perspectives. In our opinion, the human rights equinox is drawing near, and unprecedented calls for new universalism will emerge from both local and global contexts rather than dismissing its universal claims. The space seems open for a pluriversal world where we may observe the negotiation between universal and local values.

Can Universal Human Rights Find Location in a Pluriversal World?

The concept of pluriversality evolved among Latin American intellectuals who espoused the possibility of a world consisting of many worlds (Mercier, 2019). Notable among them is Walter Mignolo who argues that the concept of universality dismisses other known cosmologies. Writing on *The Darker Side of Modernity: Global Futures, Decolonial Options* (2011), he cites how every known civilization is built on its own cosmology. As there are many known civilizations, there are sources of knowledge obtained from ontological and epistemological systems prevailing among people rooted in their own cosmological understanding of relationships and visions of a future (Escobar & Frye, 2020). Western thought attempts to argue, explain, prescribe, or even control the sources of knowledge and arrogate the prerogative to interpret them. This epistemological and hermeneutical practice is a self-proclaimed Western entitlement (Mignolo, 2011).

Pluriversality is a system of thought that critiques the limitations of a universal pattern of thinking in terms of its tendency to prescribe an epistemology of knowledge sourced from Western superiority. Plurversality proceeds from an awareness that in as much as civilizations began and proceeded according to the many cosmological interpretations, there is not just one world but a multiplicity of worlds. The task of ontological world making should not proceed from the prescribed vision of a world contoured according a unified Western totality (Escobar & Frye, 2020).

The bodies of knowledge that find place and congruence in a multiplicity of worlds are the epistemological moorings of pluriversality. It is acting beyond the borders of any claim that there exists a one-world perspective that advances the thought of a Western universal that is superior over all others. Pluriversality is a decolonizing engagement in reacquiring knowledge and recreation of meanings. It is an attempt to push epistemological limits and transcend the hermeneutics of the Western universal (Escobar & Frye, 2020; Mignolo, 2011; Querejazu, 2016).

The exponents of pluriversality contend that while the West has its own cosmology, it cannot be indorsed as either superior or encompassing (Mignolo, 2018). The Western concept of universality with its own cosmological underpinnings is significant in its tendency to claim a superior position for itself. The pluriverse does not arrogate this position to itself because pluriversality promotes the actuality of a world where many other worlds can coexist (Marcos, 2022). The ontology of the pluriverse is obtained through principles of knowledge in all its diversity. The multifaceted aspects of knowledge systems exist in a pluriverse of interpretation and meanings. As such, Western hermeneutics of universality prevents the rich possibilities of the pluriverse to assert the existence of many equal truths from the rich possibilities of discovering and rediscovering meaning.

Universalizing the manner by which knowledge is distilled, processed, and interpreted can only be possible if one was to resort to the notion that there are owners of hermeneutical and epistemological imperatives who demand compliance, whereas pluriversality is a universal project that has no singular owner because every culture, every civilization, has an ontological task of changing or building new worlds (Querejazu, 2016). Therefore, there is not one singular way of envisioning the future in an established notion of one world.

As such, there is a contention that the universalization of knowledge is a hegemonic exercise that needs decolonization. Pluriversality is the decolonial vision of a world in which many other worlds could coexist. The imagined universal utopia belonged to the colonizer who built upon the notion of an enlightened world where the white men's notion of what constitutes humanity reigns supreme. It is embracive of the modern enlightened thought that men (Mignolo, 2011) imbued with reason are therefore entitled to the exercise of rights by virtue of being human. The question Mignolo further ask is as follows: Who speaks for the human in the universality of human rights?

Who Defines the Human in Human Rights?

Pluriversality is a critique to universality. The incompatibilities have to be acknowledged and the polarities accepted. The meanings are irreconcilable when the universal is the dominant Eurocentric or Western notion on what constitutes our world (Escobar & Frye, 2020; Mignolo, 2018).

The pluriversal project is to know how multiple worlds coexists on the basis of respect and equality. We respect and acknowledge difference by bringing the richness of other epistemologies by asking the following: How do human rights become compatible to the many realities existing in a pluriversal world? The ontology of the pluriverse is in the truth that it exists (Kothari et al., 2019). The epistemology of the pluriverse lies in its theoretical underpinnings within its own scope and methodical source of knowledge. The dismissal of pluriversal ontologies and epistemologies created by those who live in pluriversal worlds is not new in this time and age. Indeed, there are many contending regimes of knowledge, and the universal knowledge regime has had the gatekeeping position (Mignolo, 2018).

It can be argued therefore that the universal human rights knowledge regime could yet accept that there are still many worlds to be known. This is a project that calls for more than just respecting difference among people in the application of human rights. Advocates of pluriversality argue that human rights discourse is often grounded on monopolar ontologies, which means that the existence of what is true and valued as desirable as a human condition rests on a singular paradigm. The manner by which universally desired values are achieved becomes the epistemological process prescribed and promoted within that singular paradigm (Mignolo, 2018). That singular paradigm is protected against any counter-thought by elevating it to a universalized unquestioned status. It is against monopolar ontologies that proponents of pluriversality raise the impossibility of a unipolar world where there are many forms of knowledge as there as also many forms of acquiring them. The process of unitary knowing is an imperialistic imposition which by itself is an act of violence (Querejazu, 2016).

The negation of other people's ways of knowing can still be suppressed by effective campaigns that overtly promote a universalized one-world perspective, and that world is defined by unipolar knowing shaped by Western paradigmatic claim that theirs is where the enlightened world began. The decolonization of human rights must also address the question of the legitimacy of universalizing human rights.

The act of defining the human in human rights does not rest on a homogenized reality. The practice of human rights is all about enacting new political realities attuned to the existence of those who abide by them. We all choose to live in a world when lived reality is not homogenized. The rejection of other ontologies, especially those coming from the global south, rendering them as irrelevant is a continuing exercise of colonization. The dismissal of the once colonized people's epistemologies as unscientific and based on mythical narrations (Marcos, 2022) can only be the tool of the colonizer who negated the truth as experienced by those it had wanted to subjugate.

Advocates of pluriversality subscribe to that radical worldview that espouses a world where many other worlds fit. When many worlds can coexist on equal terms, it is then possible for human dignity to be inherent in all. The acknowledgment that all forms of life are imbued with dignity, and this attribute is inherent to all, is a long-standing project in decolonization. It is a response to the hegemonic universality of one world where the paradigms of Western imperialism are the normative imperatives putting humankind above all other forms of life. And the humans are the harbingers of wisdom processed and refined through the age of enlightenment.

Pluriversality rests on the assertion of wisdom derived from the many life-sustaining archetypes people themselves nurtured and promoted as viable in their envisioning of a multifaceted futures (Kothari et al., 2019). In so doing, peoples around the word claim a human right to self-determination over the directions their collective lives are pursued.

The Meaning of Dignity in a Pluriversal World

A pluriversal expression of worldviews flourishes in many parts of the world. Pluriversality as it exists allows us to enter into the richness of other epistemological framework that testifies to a plurality of worlds (Reiter, 2018). People representing a diversity of cultures have distinctive ways of determining the purpose and meaning of either their individual or collective existence. In a pluriversal world, there are many different ways of knowing which cannot be dismissed as inferior and therefore invalidated. The question remains that knowledge and wisdom sourced from other places other than the West do not elicit the same respect accorded to those expressed in a dominant language in a structure that is easily recognizable as belonging to a cosmopolitanized system.

Human right discourse is entangled not only with the relativist or universalist duality but also with the epistemology of pluriversality as advanced by the Global South communities. The pluriversal epistemology of human right is an invitation to a multipronged dialogue on how human dignity is framed in different cultures. This is special critical because human dignity has its own colonial attributions. The human in human rights is defined, measured, and weighed from the perspective of those who have written it from their own normative prescriptions, with the assumption that theirs is the one true perspective that represents a unitary universal world.

Awareness over the multiplicity of worlds expressed in the richness of diverse cosmologies bring cognizance to the existence of a pluriversal world that acknowledges how human beings conduct themselves in relation to other existing lifeworlds where the human is not the center of creation but one among the many whose existence intertwines with other life forces existing in nature. This epistemological outlook promotes how human dignity is not held separate from the dignity accorded to life forces present in rivers, mountains, seas, land, and air (Kothari et al., 2019). The dignity of human life which is protected and promoted by a human rights regime can only be realized through the recognition that it is the entire ecosystem that upholds and protects the dignity of human life. In turn, a dignified human life is one which accords care and respect for an ecosystem from which human life depends. The violation of life forces innate in nature is corollary to the violation of human dignity. Therefore, protecting the dignity and rights of nature is inseparable to the protection of human dignity and rights.

Conclusion

Pluriversality exists in a world with a capacity to embrace many other worldviews. It is a world where many other worlds fit. It is a world where the rights of humankind is as valued as the rights of nature (FitzGerald, 2022a).

Pluriversality does not create hierarchies in life-forms because there is a purposive intertwining of all that is meant to coexist in equally important manner. Human rights in pluriversal world cannot be confined to a hierarchical elevation of the human life for above all others (FitzGerald, 2022b). Pluriversality stands as a critic to a human right regime that presupposes a universality of worldviews that is unitary and all encompassing. If human rights is all about human dignity, pluriversality offers many constellations by which this is conceived (Williams & Bermeo, 2020).

Human dignity is all about the capability of all to live as long and as naturally possible without the unnatural interruption of disease, war, and climatic catastrophe. Human dignity is achieved when there is a certainty in the envisioning of a future where everyone, especially the young, is assured that it can only be better than the present. The decolonization of human rights has still to acknowledge that achieving human dignity is more than just a declaration. Human dignity within a human rights regime has been historically pursued in unrelenting sacrifice and struggle by those whose worldviews need not necessary be homogenized in a universalized hegemonistic constellation.

Discussion Questions

1. Can you outline possible viewpoints in the debate over the relevance of human rights in various cultural contexts?
2. What aspects of the universal nature of human rights do relativists disagree with?
3. How is the universalist position on human rights defendable?
4. What best describes the project of pluriversalism?
5. What does a pluralist approach add to our understanding of human rights?

References

American Anthropological Association. (1947). Statement on human rights. *American Anthropologist, New Series, 49*(4), 539–543.

Baxi, U. (2006). *The future of human rights* (3rd ed.). Oxford University Press.

Bhambra, G. (2007). *Rethinking modernity, postcolonialism and the sociological imagination*. Palgrave McMillan.

Bonnet, S. (2015). Overcoming eurocentrism in human rights: Postcolonial critiques – Islamic answers? *Muslim World Journal of Human Rights, 12*(1), 1–24. https://doi.org/10.1515/mwjhr-2014-0010

Chakrabarty, D. (2008). *Provincializing Europe: Postcolonial thought and historical difference*. Princeton University Press.

Deng, F., An-Na'im, A., Ghai, Y., & Baxi, U. (2009). *Human rights: Southern voices*. Cambridge University Press.

Donnelly, J. (1982). Human rights and human dignity: An analytic critique of non-Western conceptions of human rights. *American Political Science Review, 76*(2), 303–316. https://doi.org/10.2307/1961111

Escobar, A., & Frye, D. L. (2020). *Pluriversal politics: The real and the possible*. Duke University Press.

FitzGerald, M. (2022a). *Care and the pluriverse: Rethinking global ethics* (1st ed.). Bristol University Press.

FitzGerald, M. (Ed.). (2022b). Bristol studies in international theory. In *Care and the pluriverse: Rethinking global ethics*. Bristol University Press. https://doi.org/10.2307/j.ctv2rh2c37

Freeman, M. (2022). *Human rights* (4th ed.). Polity.

Gawin, M., Markiewicz, B., Nogal, A., & Wonicki, R. (2016). *Prawa człowieka i obywatelaw zglobalizowanym* świecie [Human and citizen rights in a globalized world]. Wydawnictwo Uniwersytetu Warszawskiego.

Gellner, E., & Breuilly, J. (2008). *Nations and nationalism*. Cornell University Press.

Goodale, M. (2021). After international law: Anthropology beyond the "Age of human rights". *AJIL Unbound, 115*, 289–293. https://doi.org/10.1017/aju.2021.42

Horkheimer, M., & Adorno, T. W. (1988). *Dialectic of enlightenment*. Continuum.

Johansson Dahre, U. (2017). Searching for a middle ground: Anthropologists and the debate on the universalism and the cultural relativism of human rights. *The International Journal of Human Rights, 21*(5), 611–628. https://doi.org/10.1080/13642987.2017.1290930

Klein, E. (2021). On limits and restrictions of human rights: A systematic attempt. In J. David, Y. Ronen, Y. Shany, & J. Weiler (Eds.), *Strengthening human rights protections in Geneva, Israel, the West Bank and beyond* (pp. 10–39). Cambridge University Press. https://doi.org/10.1017/9781108973069.002

Kothari, A., Salleh, A., Escobar, A., Demaria, F., & Acosta, A. (2019). *Pluriverse: A postdevelopment dictionary*. Tulika Books.

Kymlicka, W. (1989). *Liberalism, community, and culture*. Clarendon Press.

Marcos, S. (2022). *Zapatista stories for dreaming another world.* PM Press.
Mende, J. (2021). Are human rights Western—And why does it matter? A perspective from international political theory. *Journal of International Political Theory, 17*(1), 38–57. https://doi.org/10.1177/1755088219832992
Mercier, C. T. (2019). Uses of "the pluriverse" - Cosmos interrupted - or the others of humanities. *Ostium, 15*(2). https://ostium.sk/language/sk/uses-of-the-pluriverse-cosmos-interrupted-or-the-others-of-humanities/
Messer, E. (2002). Anthropologists in a W\world with and without human rights. In J. MacClancy (Ed.), *Exotic no more: Anthropology on the front lines* (pp. 319–335). Chicago University Press.
Mignolo, W. D. (2011). *The darker side of Western modernity: Global futures, decolonial options.* Duke University Press.
Mignolo, W. D. (2018). *On decoloniality: Concepts, analytics, praxis.* Duke University Press.
Namli, E. (2018). Critique of human rights universalism. In M. Stenmark, S. Fuller, & U. Zackariasson (Eds.), *Relativism and post-truth in contemporary society: Possibilities and challenges.* Palgrave Macmillan.
Nussbaum, M. C. (2000). *Women and human development.* Cambridge University Press.
Pedersen, L., & Cliggett, L. (2021). *The sage handbook of cultural anthropology.* Sage.
Querejazu, A. (2016). Encountering the pluriverse: Looking for alternatives in other worlds. *Revista Brasileira De Política Internacional, 59*(2). https://doi.org/10.1590/0034-7329201600207
Reiter, B. (Ed.). (2018). *Constructing the pluriverse: The geopolitics of knowledge.* Duke University Press.
Rorty, R. (2011). *Objectivity, relativism, and truth.* Cambridge University Press.
Williams, H. M., & Bermeo, M. (2020). A Decolonial Imperative: Pluriversal rights education. *International Journal of Human Rights Education, 4*(1). https://repository.usfca.edu/ijhre/vol4/iss1/1

Marcin Boryczko is an Associate Professor at the University of Gdańsk, Poland, where he teaches Social Work on bachelors' and masters' levels. He serves in the board of several international and national associations such as the Polish Federation of Social Workers and Social Service Employees Unions (Polska Federacja Związków Zawodowych Pracowników Socjalnych i Pomocy Społecznej), the European Social Work Research Association, and the International Advisory Board of the *European Social Work Research Journal* and serves as Polish Representative in the International Federation of Social Workers (IFSW). His main research interests include social work education, critical social work theory, human rights, decolonization, neoliberal governmentality, and populism in Central Europe.

Jason M. Leung is the Department Head of the environmental studies program at the Benguet State University, Philippines. His areas of teaching and research are in human ecology, food regimes, and sovereignty and community rural development. He has published in Germany where he completed his master's studies in environmental science. He spent years of teaching in Korea and did research work on food sovereignty in Germany. He is currently undertaking a nationwide research with the Philippine Department of Science and Technology on the impact of extractive mining industries on indigenous communities.

Melinda Madew is Professor in International Social Work at the Protestant University of Applied Sciences Ludwigsburg, Germany, and a Research Associate of the University of Johannesburg, South Africa. She serves as Board Member of the European Social Work Research Association. Her teaching and research are in the areas of gender politics, postcolonial social work, and indigenous knowledge and practice in community organizing. She has served as Education and Research Consultant for international development organizations. She conceptualized and implemented international projects under the auspices of European Union educational programs for North-South university collaboration.

Part II
History of Social Work as a Human Rights Profession

Chapter 3
Interrogating the Colonial Past: The Conflicting History of Social Work as a Human Rights Profession

María Inés Martínez Herrero and Prospera Tedam

Introduction

Accounts of the histories of both human rights and social work tend to present these as neat, linear, and emancipatory, marked by key milestones and the legacy of historical pioneers and leaders. In the field of human rights, the signature by worldwide leaders of the United Nations Declaration of Human RightsHuman rights (UNDHR) (United Nations, 1949) in the aftermath of World War II and the subsequent development of international human rights legal instruments are justly celebrated among "the greatest achievements of the twentieth century" (Ife, 2009, p.79), as "nothing short of a revolution in thought" whose unprecedented scope and adherence exceeded any previous efforts to establish rights and the basis for cooperation beyond borders (Reichert, 2011, p.18).

Social work, on its part, is claimed to be a "human rights profession" (Healy, 2008; IFSW-Europe, 2012, p.5; United Nations, 1994; Wronka & Staub-Bernasconi, 2012, p.70) with a human rights tradition "of more than 100 years" (Staub-Bernasconi, 2016, p.40). While not always consistent, the connections between human rights and social work have been made explicit and underscored by global social work organizations throughout social work's history. The following statement of the International Federation of Social Workers in 1988 may serve as an example.

M. I. M. Herrero (✉)
Department of Social Work, UNED, Madrid, Spain
e-mail: inesmartinezh@outlook.com

P. Tedam
Department of Social Wellbeing, United Arab Emirates University,
Abu Dhabi, United Arab Emirates
e-mail: p.tedam@uaeu.ac.ae

M. Madew et al. (eds.), *Decolonized Approaches to Human Rights and Social Work*,
https://doi.org/10.1007/978-3-031-33030-8_3

Social work has, from its conception, been a human rights profession, having as its basic tenet the intrinsic value of every human being and as one of its main aims the promotion of equitable social structures, which can offer people security and development while upholding their dignity (IFSW, 1988, cited in Healy, 2008, p.737).

In this vein, the most recent global social work definition (IFSW & IASSW, 2014) paves the way for a human rights-based, decolonizing social work practice:

> Social work … promotes social change and development, social cohesion, and the empowerment and liberation of people. Principles of social justice, human rights, collective responsibility and respect for diversities are central to social work. Underpinned by theories of social work, social sciences, humanities and indigenous knowledges, social work engages people and structures to address life challenges and enhance wellbeing. The above definition may be amplified at national and/or regional levels.

However, intertwined with this emancipatory, even "triumphant" history of social work and human rights, there is another, much less known, history of social work and human rights which needs to be brought to the fore in the discussion of social work, human rights, and decolonization. This is that of the dark histories of the profession which unfortunately include a track record of complicity with colonialism and human rights violations.

We believe both histories, or these two sides of social work history, are important for this chapter to address fairly and in-depth social work's historical contributions to human rights and decolonizing struggles. Historical awareness is a key avenue for understanding the present (including the ramifications of past harms and social work's potentially emancipatory and oppressive nature) as well as for imagining ways forward for decolonizing social work practice, education, and research drawing on human rights.

Defining Key Concepts

It is important to outline a few of the key terms and concepts to aid understanding. Terms such as decolonization, racism, and indigenization, while contested and without a universal agreement of what they mean, are briefly defined here to contextualize the discussion. These terms have also been explained elsewhere in this book (see Chaps. 5, 7, and 9).

Decolonization

Decolonization is broadly understood as undoing colonialism and is not a swappable term for other things we want to do to improve our societies and schools. Decolonization does not have a synonym (Tuck & Yang, 2012). According to Clarke and Bird (2020), decolonization may be defined as "undoing the effects of colonization by consciously considering to what degree we and the world we live in have been manipulated, controlled, misled, and silenced by the processes and structures of colonialism" (p. 4).

Racism

Karl Marx argued that racism is a social construct and a by-product of capitalist systems of economic exploitation proposing the idea that in order for the labor market to function the interaction between Black workers and White employers was often one which perpetuated racism (Ashiagbor, 2021).

In its simplest form, racism is the conscious or unconscious processes where actions, attitudes, policies, and systems create and maintain inequitable experiences and outcomes for people based on race.

Indigenization

According to Gray (2005), indigenization refers to the extent to which social work practice fits local contexts. Social work practice is, in turn, shaped by the extent to which local sociocultural, political, economic, and historical factors. Local and/or indigenous voices have been known to shape and inform social work theoretical and practice responses.

Social Work's History of Contributions to Human Rights and Decolonization Struggles

According to Connerton (2014), the way in which we narrate our past represents our understanding of the present and hopes for the future. Social work as a profession has contributed to human rights and decolonization efforts in many parts of the world; however, as Bent-Goodley (2006) argues, more needs to be written about the diversity of people considered to be trailblazers of social work. For the purposes of this section, we will discuss events, individuals, and their contributions to human rights and decolonization.

Healy (2008) asserted that social work's involvement in human rights can be traced from "official documents indicating the compatibility of the profession's mission and values with human rights; the contribution of social work leaders to human rights causes; official professional representation and action on human rights; and social work involvement in critical incidents or major human rights movements" (p.737).

It is argued that pioneer social workers were clearly influenced by ideas of universal human rights that were contributing to the social and intellectual climate in Europe by the time of the profession's emergence at the end of the nineteenth century. This influence became particularly prominent in relation to the atrocities of World War I at the beginning of the twentieth century (Reichert, 2011). In this climate, they saw the need to establish a common knowledge and value base for an international social work profession and to establish mechanisms and organize for international, national, and regional cooperation among social workers. These developments included the creation, during the first decades of the twentieth century, of the International Conference of Social Welfare (current ICSW), the International Committee of Social Work (current IASSW), and the International Permanent Secretariat of Social Workers (now IFSW) (Dominelli, 2010; Reichert, 2011; United Nations, 1994).

Social work founders and leaders were involved in human rights movements and international organizations including the League of Nations, the Red Cross, and Save the Children (Healy, 2008; Reichert, 2011). Widely known social work pioneers such as Jane Addams (the USA, awarded the Nobel Peace Prize in 1931), Eglantyne Jebb (the UK), Alice Salomon (Germany), and Bertha Reynolds (the USA), as well as many other social work pioneers and activists from across the world who are less known or have been made invisible due to power dynamics of coloniality class and race in mainstream social work history made very important contributions to the struggles for human rights. These included struggles for women's rights, education, children rights, peace, and so on.

Some of the social work pioneers whose human rights legacy is being reexamined and brought to the fore are Birdye Henrietta Haynes (1886–1922), who was the first African American graduate of the Chicago School of Civics and Philanthropy and became head of settlement houses that attended racialized people or African American social welfare reformer Elizabeth Ross Haynes (1883–1983) (Clarke, 2021). More attention is also starting to be paid globally to the human rights contributions of social work leaders from diverse countries, for example, to the legacy of Japanese radical social worker, Hiroshi Urabe (1905–2002), who resisted the authoritarianism of the Japanese Empire countries and supported social justice movements (Ito 2017, cited in Clarke, 2022), or to that of Spanish social work pioneer Concepción Arenal (1820–1893), who was a tireless advocate of women's rights and played a key role in reclaiming prisoner women's rights and denouncing unfair social conditions leading to crime and social suffering (Idareta Goldaraena, 2020). Considering why some of these social work pioneers are less known is an important yet largely pending task.

Throughout the twentieth century, many social work leaders showed a familiarity with the term human rights and related ideas in their work and speeches. Bertha Reynolds, for example, called on US Social Workers in a National Conference of Social Work in 1940 to "join hands with every honest fighter for peace and human rights" and to "not be moved" from this position (Reynolds, 1940, as cited in Healy, 2008, p. 739).

However, it is argued that as these human rights ideas and values were formally expressed in social work codes of ethics and teaching materials, an explicit human rights language became increasingly lost, leading to a generalized lack of attention to the links between human rights and social work practice, theory, and teaching (United Nations, 1994; Dominelli, 2007).

Healy (2008) argues that with the huge milestone in the advancement of international human rights brought about by the UNDHR of 1948, some specific references to human rights slowly started to reenter the profession, but these tended to be rare for decades. She attributes one of the causes for this to the fact that despite social work's interest in human rights, social workers "have usually paid more attention to human needs than to human rights" and "focused on emergency, action oriented human needs efforts, leaving human rights policy to others" (Healy, 2008, p. 745). For example, she highlights that when the UNDHR was drafted and adopted, the profession's interest and involvement in international human rights developments focused on war relief programs in Europe and China and on initiating emerging UNICEF child welfare programs.

There are nevertheless documented accounts of social workers and social work leaders' involvement in the Civil Rights movement in the USA, the anti-apartheid movement in South Africa, the nonviolent tradition of Gandhi, campaigns for the rights of indigenous people, and other forms of activism with a clear reference to human rights in different parts of the world (Staub-Bernasconi, 2016; Healy, 2008; Ife, 2016). Moreover, it is claimed that given the interdisciplinarity of the human rights field, many important contributions by social workers to human rights struggles will never have been linked to the profession (Healy, 2008).

However, it is argued that since the establishment in 1988 of an IFSW International Commission on Human Rights, human rights started to be explicitly addressed and have become increasingly prominent in international social work (Healy, 2008; IFSW, 2012). Other reported milestones in that direction are the publication by the UN in 1994 of a guide on human rights and social work (as a result of a collaboration between the UN, IFSW, and IASSW) and the assertion in the IFSW (2000) definition of social work that "principles of human rights and social justice are fundamental in/to social work." Subsequent statements and policy developments by international social work organizations have drawn on this. These include the 2014 Global Definition of Social Work (IFSW & IASSW, 2014) as well as other IFSW and IASSW joint and separate social work ethics statements and global agendas.[1] Alongside this, there has been an increased involvement of social workers and social work academics globally in the development of human rights-based social work theory and practice models (IFSW, 2012).

[1] More detailed information and documentation can be accessed through the organisations' websites (links provided at the end of the chapter's list of references).

Social Work's History of Complicity with Colonialism

It is well known that the emergence of social work as a profession is linked to the global "social question" brought about by capitalist industrialization, urbanization, and mass migration of the nineteenth century. Among the responses to widespread poverty and social unrest of the time, one particular approach to helping the poor in the slums of London in the late nineteenth century became formalized and soon achieved recognition as the new profession of social work. This new profession aspired to use and develop scientific knowledge and specific methods of intervention in order to deal with individuals' and families' poverty and lack of education as well as to organize and rationalize charitable and beneficence initiatives.

The new profession quickly expanded in England to the USA and to other Northern and Central European countries. Parallel and mutually influential developments in the USA and England followed two main approaches facing the task to address social problems related to poverty and lack of education: (1) The Charity Organisation Societies' (COS) psychosocial casework approach (Richmond, 1917) with a focus on therapeutic relationships with individuals and families in order to help them overcome the "individual malfunction" leading to their problems (Higham, 2006, p. 21) (2) The settlement house movement (Addams, 1912) oriented toward community action and education, and more concerned with understanding and addressing the societal origin of the social problems of the poor. Despite the clear differences between the COS and settlement house movement approaches, it is important to highlight a key common feature of pioneer social work: led, mainly, by privileged White women of the time, this was founded on a classist Victorian morality and a philanthropic, liberal worldview alongside an unquestioned belief in Protestant individualism and work ethic which would mark the profession's values, principles, and ethics up until today.

Social work was quickly "spread" (by or with assistance from experts) to the rest of the world in several waves, notably to Middle East, Latin American and Caribbean, Asian, and African countries in the 1920s and to Central and Southern Europe in the 1940s, with the last of these waves introducing modern social work in former Soviet Union and Eastern Bloc countries. Even if social work had developed in some kind of political vacuum, a first issue emerges when considering the history of social work's complicity with colonialism: As social work became institutionalized as a profession across the way, any other "social working" – "the vastly diverse interventions into the social world that are found in all times and all places, which include caring, sharing, community work, and activism" (Chapman & Withers, 2019, p.3) – was placed outside the social work's professional legitimacy boundaries and knowledge base.

Nevertheless, social work did not emerge and spread in political vacuums but in colonial and capitalist contexts where the profession acquired key roles related to the commercialization and government control of social relations (Jordan, 1984; Ferguson et al., 2018) and where truly dangerous doctrines on how to eliminate social problems posed by "problem populations" (poor, disabled, ethnic minorities, migrants, etc.) who did not conform with governments' political projects and deviated from dominant social norms counted on widespread moral and scientific authority and support. Chapman and Withers (2019) document how US social work pioneers and leaders upheld, promoted, and/or failed to challenge assimilationist and eugenic views regarding the motivations and means for social intervention. Perhaps shockingly, these were often the same leaders who were advocating and working hard for human rights and social justice-oriented political reforms.

Social work's "dark" histories of complicity with structural violence and human rights violations have taken different shapes and directions. Seeking to categorize these, Ioakimidis and Trimikliniotis (2020) analyze on the one hand the histories related to family social work in the context of oppressive political regimes (from Nazi Germany to Francoist Spain) where social work's priorities revolve around reproducing the dominant political ideology and ensuring the "perpetuation "of working-class families as a disciplined unit of production and consumption" (p. 1894). On the other hand, they explore the social work's troubled histories related to "colonial social work," including the colonial history of South African social work (see Harms Smith, 2014) and some infamous assimilationist policies and social experiments in Canada, Greenland, and Australia involving the systematic removal of indigenous children from their communities and their placement in "White" families and settings.

Chapman and Withers (2019) offer a most thorough analysis of social work's "violent history," bringing to the fore the origin and developments of many deeply rooted problematic aspects of the profession. These include the professions' histories of "White supremacy" and moral imposition, "the erasure of racialized social workers," and key roles played in the advancement of eugenics and assimilation.

When analyzing social work's history of complicity with colonialism, we can consider two fields: the first of these relates to the *roles played by the profession in relation to historical and ongoing settler colonialist oppression*, whereas the second links with the *professional imperialism underpinning many of the expansive efforts of the profession itself*. In order to delve into the first field, we will next follow Chapman and Withers (2019) and explore this through the notorious example of Canadian social workers' roles in applying assimilationist policy established by the 1920 Canadian Indian Act amendment. In the following section, we will then consider the second of the fields.

The 1920 Canadian Indian Act Amendment dictated the compulsory removal of all indigenous children who could not attend Indian day schools (as was often the case) to remote state-sponsored Indian residential schools. As Canadian Prime Minister Harper's 2009 public apology acknowledged, the objective of such state-sponsored Indian Residential Schools was to "remove and isolate children from the influence of their homes, families, traditions and cultures, and to assimilate them into the dominant culture" (CBC, 2008). In this regard, the Truth and Reconciliation Commission of Canada established in 2015 that the schooling system "was always more than simply an educational program: it was an integral part of a conscious policy of cultural genocide" (The Truth and Reconciliation Commission of Canada, 2015, pp. 54–55), a policy designed to "kill the Indian, save the man" (Churchill,

2004). It is estimated that at least 139 residential schools of this type were run by the Catholic, Anglican, and united churches during most of the twentieth century in Canada (Voce et al., 2021). 150,000 indigenous children are estimated to have attended these (ibid). As part of this system, social workers took active roles, as they "were tasked to accompany Indian agents onto reserves to remove children to residential schools" and, as a profession, would advocate for their continuous operation (Sinclair, 2009, p.20).

The violent, genocidal act of forcibly transferring children from the target group to another should have been enough to raise serious concerns within a profession concerned from its inception with promoting the inherent dignity and worth of every person and pursuing social justice, but it did not. As Chapman and Withers illustrate (2019, p. 288) "decades before the coining of the word genocide, social workers from across Canada and the USA rallied to ensure that White orphans of the 1917 Halifax Explosion were raised by other White Nova Scotians" as they belonged there and had sacred rights to safeguard, but they did not express this kind of zeal about indigenous children's dignity, worth, and rights. However, the violence suffered by the children at the schools went far beyond separation from their families and lifeworld, as, within their walls, they were also victims of neglect, physical and psychological abuse, and cruel treatment in all kinds of forms.

Documented traumatic experiences and punishments at the Indian schools include being forbidden to speak their languages and having needles pierced through their tongues as a punishment for doing so, segregation of siblings and hindering contact with families, forced haircuts and removal of personal belongings, vilification of home cultures and use of racist and dehumanizing language, imposition of the institutions' religion, forced labor and not being allowed to play with toys, insufficient or spoiled food, exposure to freezing temperatures, exposure to infectious illnesses, withholding medical attention and painkillers, beatings, strapping, scalding, and other different kinds of severe physical punishments (often inflicted in public, humiliating situations) (The Truth and Reconciliation Commission of Canada, 2015).

It is also documented how in addition to the cruel practices and punishments endorsed by the institutions individuals were able to use the system to further physically and/or sexually abuse children with no or little consequence, while those who tried to raise the alarm or protect the children in different ways were punished or fired instead (Chapman & Withers, 2019). The extent of the death rates (as high as 50%) and abuse within the Indian schools is still being unveiled, as survivors and witnesses' stories continue to emerge and remains of children buried in the schools sites continue to be discovered today (Voce et al., 2021).

Returning to the reactions of Canadian social workers of the time, Chapman and Withers (2019) highlight that whereas some of the abuse was covered, much of it was publicly known and raised uproar. However, despite this, according to Blackstock (2009), children aid's societies, established in the earlier 1900s, did not protect indigenous children from the residential schools, and there is no evidence that social work as a profession took any action to address "the problems" of the schools. Instead, Blackstock notes the Canadian Association of Social Workers and the Canadian Welfare Council (CASW and CWC, 1946 cited in Blackstock, 2009, p.29) defended in 1946 that despite "the problems," these had "a place in a well-rounded system of Indian education" and social workers would continue to be active in the placement of children at the schools up until the 1960s.

Analogous colonial systems aimed at assimilating whole generations of indigenous children also existed and converged with the emergence and development of the social work profession in other "colonial territories" like in the USA, Australia, or across the British Empire, without triggering the new "human rights profession's" significant action or outrage. It may appear that pioneer social work human rights vision was to a large extent colonial, as, despite the rhetoric around all human beings being equal, it embraced unproblematically "the Unquestionable Good of Imposing Whiteness onto Others" (Chapman & Withers, 2019, p. 293) as the superior, overarching moral mandate to be achieved.

Professional Imperialism

As stated above, when considering the history of social work's complicity with colonialism, in addition to historical and ongoing settler colonialist oppression, we need to pay attention to the (related and frequently converging) history of professional imperialism which has marked and continues to affect the international expansion of the profession today.

Muñoz Arce (2015, p. 424, authors' own translation) defines professional imperialism as follows:

> The knowledge transfer from an intellectual community (which self-attributes superiority) to another (considered inferior or underdeveloped), with the subsequent adoption and overestimation of the foreign knowledge in relation to the mere fact of having been transferred from that intellectual community, which is also recognised as superior by the colonised one.

Colonization and its damage did not end with political independences, Muñoz Arce (2015) reminds us, or with the abolition or modification of colonial laws (such as the Canadian Indian Act). This is as colonial logic continues to reproduce through internalized colonialism of the political elites that continue to embrace colonial institutions, practices, and power imbalances in the political, legal, economic, cultural, and epistemological fields.

Most frequently, simplistic and politically naïve versions of international social work history present this as a growing unified profession based on the values of human dignity/rights and social justice. These accounts revolve around how professional relationships between social work leaders crossed borders and how social work pioneers collaborated in building a social work's knowledge base and professional status through correspondence, international visits, international conferences, and the formation of international associations. However and notwithstanding the importance and value of many achievements of the young profession and its most widely known pioneers, a more balanced history reveals that social work "spread globally through [both] colonising state agendas and altruistic impulses" (Dominelli, 2012, p.13).

As above, as social work spread from Western, capitalist societies, notably the UK and the USA, to "less developed" parts of the world through the exportation of educational courses and social work literature, their "superior" nature and applicability to very different context was rarely questioned. As Midgley (1981:Xii, own translation) puts it, throughout the world, generations of social work students "are trained to apply social work principles in the same way that western countries' students, read the same literature and are taught the same theories and methods." Motivated by the ideals of "modernisation" (Midgley 1981, p. 60) and a shared international professional identity and instructed in the belief to be learning universal intervention models and be joining superior international organizations, students in these countries tend to reproduce colonial practices and dependency relations among countries (Lavalette & Ioakimidis, 2011; Muñoz Arce, 2015).

Moreover, the social work profession has a history of being used, directly, as a means of enabling, or paving the way, for Western geopolitical interests, notably those of the USA. One large expression of this took place during the rehabilitation period which followed the end of World War II and saw the beginning of the cold war, where "schools of social work funded by the US government and supervised by American academics," in collaboration with international social work organizations, were established globally. During this period, "even in countries where social work existed before the war the profession enjoyed a period of revival and development" (Lavalette & Ioakimidis, 2011, p.145).

It is no coincidence, Lavalette and Ioakimidis (2011) report, that, during this timeframe, considered a "great time" in historical accounts of the development of international work, most of the countries that received attention from US-led international social work were those in the American government "key countries" lists of political and military interests. These included countries such as Greece, Italy, Turkey, or Latin American ones, considered at risk of falling into the influence of Communism and where reconstruction aid was followed by US open military intervention (ibid). In this regard, Healy (2008, p.387–390) developed a "timeline of Milestones in the International History of Social Work Around the World" (1856–2007), which can be explored critically to illuminate how social work's histories of struggle for human rights and decolonization coincide in time with dark histories and imperialist expansions and interests.

In relation to the above and returning again to the present time, Mutis and Ong'Wen (2011) and Muñoz Arce (2015, p. 431) highlight the importance to bear in mind that across Latin America, as well as in other countries of the Global South, most of the intervention programs carried out by social workers continue to be financed by supranational organizations (notably the World Bank which in Latin America monopolizes poverty relief programs) that "reproduce their colonial logics' in the territories they establish their aid programs. Hence, they bring attention to the utmost importance for social work education in these countries to prepare students to navigate and disrupt the colonization of their knowledge base and contexts of practice through a critical, culturally sensitive social work, focused on seeking social justice through respect, dialogue, and power sharing with social work diverse service users.

Thinking about social work practice in the "West," evidence continues to show that people from Black, indigenous, and racially minoritized groups continue to be overrepresented in social work services. For example, in Australia (Harms et al., 2011), in Canada (Antwi-Boasiako et al., 2022), and in Britain (Bernard & Harris, 2016; Keating, 2020), these overrepresentations can be found in child welfare, criminal justice, and mental health sectors. Writing from an Australian perspective, Briskman (2020) argued that social workers' role in offshore asylum seeker detention centers reveals a connection between social workers and colonialism. She argues that this connection can be seen through the following processes:

1. Social workers' practices are not scrutinized in the same way in these "offshore" sites as well as, consequently, practice standards and principles, for example, empowerment is impossible to uphold.
2. Social workers contributed to the trauma experienced by asylum seekers rather than work in trauma-informed ways.
3. Institutionalized racism existed in these offshore detention centers, yet social workers were expected to work in environments where excessive control was normalized.

As social workers practice in the front line and forefront of these services, it is evident that they have been and are complicit in these overrepresentations. Consequently, it is critical for students to understand and acknowledge the evidence of ongoing coloniality in social work academic and practice contexts which Waaldijk (2011, p.234) articulates thus:

> Social workers have in different circumstances behaved differently, some resisted, other assisted racist political regimes. Some were cogs in a machine of repression; others combined social work with struggles for survival, liberation and freedom. The remains of these choices continue to play a role in professional ideals – we'd better address them.

Human Rights: Lights, Shadows, and Their Connection with Decolonization

The problematic nature of the colonial histories of social work we have discussed resonates with criticisms of human rights Western hegemony, which highlight the fact that grandiose humanistic traditions and ideals have coexisted throughout history with exploitative practices such as colonization, slavery, and subordination of women to men. And that expressions of many of these exploitative mechanisms continue to be embedded in contemporary Western philosophies and uses of human rights.

These criticisms have unraveled and brought to light important biases in the humanistic traditions underpinning Western human rights understandings. These include individualistic and anthropocentric biases that artificially separate human beings from one another and from the natural world (Ife, 2008, 2009; Dominelli, 2010); the difficulties of Western philosophy and culture in understanding, respecting, valuing, and incorporating diversity (Moosa-Mitha, 2005); and the limitations of Western thought and morality in dealing with the holism and complexity of the world and experiences of human lives (Banks, 2006; Dominelli, 2010; Ife, 2008; Sen, 1999). Evans and Ayers (2006, p.289) further argued that the pervasiveness of neoliberal ideology is such that "the triad of human rights, free markets, and democracy" is accepted as the desirable and attainable political target worldwide, even when readjustments for the advance of free market involve severe transition costs to some groups.

Indeed, as highlighted by Salil Shetty, Secretary General at Amnesty International, in a speech in 2018 (p.3), "the essence of human rights and decolonisation are basically the same thing: the struggle for freedom against the abuse of power." But "human rights themselves have always been subject to efforts at colonisation: misappropriation and being manipulated for political ends. We need to recognise this for what it is, and in this sense the fight to decolonise human rights is a permanent one."

The similar thing could be said, we argue, about social work, especially as we embrace the claim for this to be in essence a human rights profession aimed at promoting human rights, social justice, and greater well-being for all. As Harms Smith and Rasool (2020) argue, social work has faced throughout its history a paradox of coloniality and hope and is well placed to engage with the interrogation and disruption of coloniality, "drawing on a complex history of both oppressive and domesticating, as well as radical and liberatory practice" (Harms Smith & Rasool, 2020, p. 148). Moreover, Ife (2009, p.80) claims human rights discourses seem to constitute "one of the few legitimate alternatives to the dominant discourses of neoliberalism, unbridled capitalism, economic globalization, individualism and the free market" which legitimate the primacy of market interests against the interests and well-being of societies and their citizens. Hence, despite the vulnerabilities of human rights, these become a key framework for disrupting coloniality, including within social work.

Looking Forward

Waaldijk (2011) argued that as part of their role, social workers often ask service users about their past so as to inform the intervention and support needed in the future. Consequently, "social work must be accountable to telling the complete story of institutional racism and how it has placed people of colour into downcast roles since the inception of the discipline" (Wright, Carr & Akkin, 2021, p. 289). This accountability includes recognizing the role of social workers in, for example, the more recent global Black Lives Matter protests, discussions about systemic racism which rewarded colonialists with ownership of artifacts, and revenue acquired through colonialism and slavery. For students of social work, understanding that the legacy of colonialism has helped to perpetuate oppression and exploitation is the first step toward being able to truly understand concepts such as anti-racist, anti-oppressive, and anti-discriminatory practice. It is important that social work students are introduced to a range of perspectives and experiences and are able to challenge overrepresentation and disproportionality in the various areas of social work and social care services for specific minoritized groups. Research by Tedam and Cane (2022) found that some newly qualified social workers in England did not feel that their training had provided them with sufficient knowledge and skills to work with racially minoritized service users, thereby putting them at risk of oppressive practice. The authors recommended a review of curriculum content to ensure that adequate attention is paid to exploring race, diversity, and intersectional issues within placements and in the classroom.

Freire (1996) proposed that in order to develop critical consciousness and transform the world, students need to question knowledge and ideas given to them in spaces of learning and not simply absorb and accept these as sacrosanct. These spaces of learning are varied and diverse and should enable students to develop their understanding of justice/injustice, equality/inequality, inclusion, and marginalization.

Concluding Thoughts

This chapter has outlined the contributions made by early framers of human rights in the decolonizing struggles and also highlighted their history with colonialism making them complicit with oppression and racism. As academics and researchers, our priority is in supporting epistemic decolonization by making available less told histories of colonization and the role of social work within that context. The aim is to ensure that graduating social workers can better understand the source of the knowledge base underpinning their current practice and demand broader and more diverse representations of history and knowledge.

Discussion Questions

1. Can you describe the contributions of early human rights framers to decolonization struggles?
2. What role did social work play in the colonial system of oppression? What is its role today?

References

Addams, J. (1912). *Twenty years at hull-house: With autobiographical notes*. Macmillan.

Antwi-Boasiako, K., Fallon, B., King, B., Trocmé, N., & Fluke, J. (2022). Understanding the over-representation of black children in Ontario's child welfare system: Perspectives from child welfare workers and community service providers. *Child Abuse & Neglect, 123*, 105425. https://doi.org/10.1016/j.chiabu.2021.105425

Ashiagbor, D. (2021). Race and colonialism in the construction of labour markets and precarity. *Industrial Law Journal, 50*(4), 506–531. https://doi.org/10.1093/indlaw/dwab020

Banks, S. (2006). *Ethics and values in social work*. Palgrave Macmillan.

Bent-Goodley, T. B. (2006). Oral histories of contemporary African American social work pioneers. *Journal of Teaching in Social Work, 26*(1–2), 181–199. https://doi.org/10.1300/j067v26n01_11

Bernard, C., & Harris, P. (2016). Introduction in Bernard C and Harris P (eds) Safeguarding Black Children: Good Practice in Child Protection. London: Jessica Kingsley Publishers.

Blackstock, C. (2009). The occasional evil of angels: Learning from the experiences of aboriginal peoples and social work. *First Peoples Child & Family Review, 4*(1), 28–37.

Briskman, L. (2020). Social work co-option and colonial borders. In T. Kleibl, R. Lutz, N. Noyoo, B. Bunk, A. Dittmann, & B. Seepamore (Eds.), *The Routledge handbook of postcolonial social work*. Routledge.

CBC. (2008, June 11). *Prime Minister Stephen Harper's statement of apology*. https://www.cbc.ca/news/canada/prime-minister-stephen-harper-s-statement-of-apology-1.734250

Chapman, C., & Withers, A. J. (2019). *A violent history of benevolence. Interlocking oppression in the moral economies of social working*. University of Toronto Press.

Churchill, W. (2004). *Kill the Indian, Save the Man*. City Lights Books.

Clarke, K. (2022). Reimagining social work ancestry: Toward epistemic decolonization. *Affilia, 37*(2), 266–278. https://doi.org/10.1177/08861099211051326

Clarke, K., & Yellow Bird, M. (2020). Decolonizing Pathways towards Integrative Healing in Social Work (1st ed.).Routledge. https://doi.org/10.4324/9781315225234

Connerton, P. (2014). *How societies remember*. Cambridge University Press.

Dominelli, L. (2007). Human rights in social work practice: An invisible part of the social work curriculum? In E. Reichert (Ed.), *Challenges in human rights: Social work perspective* (pp. 16–43). Columbia University Press.

Dominelli, L. (2010). *Social work in a globalizing world*. Polity Press.

Dominelli, L. (2012). Globalisation and indigenisation: Reconciling the irreconcilable in social work. In K. Lyons, T. Hokenstad, M. Pawar, N. Huegler, & N. Hall (Eds.), *Sage handbook of international social work*. Sage.

Evans, T., & Ayers, A. J. (2006). In the service of power: The global political economy of citizenship and human rights. *Citizenship Studies, 10*(3), 289–308. https://doi.org/10.1080/13621020600772081

Ferguson, I., Ioakimidis, V., & Lavalette, M. (2018). *Global social work in a political context: Radical perspectives*. Policy Press.

Freire, P. (1996). *Pedagogy of the oppressed*. Penguin Books.

Idareta Goldaracena, F. (2020). *Concepción Arenal: Reformadora moral y social desde la compasión*. Consejo General de Trabajo Social.

Gray, M. (2005). Dilemmas of international social work: paradoxical processes in indigenisation universalism and imperialism International Journal of Social Welfare 14(3) 231–238. https://doi.org/10.1111/ijsw.2005.14.issue-3 https://doi.org/10.1111/j.1468-2397.2005.00363.x

Harms Smith, L. (2014). Historiography of South African social work: Challenging dominant discourses. *Social Work/Maatskaplike Werk, 50*(3). https://doi.org/10.15270/50-3-402

Harms Smith, L., & Rasool, S. (2020). Deep transformation toward decoloniality in social work: Themes for change in a Social Work Higher Education Program. *Journal of Progressive Human Services, 31*(2), 144–164. https://doi.org/10.1080/10428232.2020.1762295

Harms, L., Middleton, J., Whyte, J., Anderson, I., Clarke, A., Sloan, J., Hagel, M., & Smith, M. (2011). Social work with aboriginal clients: Perspectives on educational preparation and practice. *Australian Social Work, 64*(2), 156–168. https://doi.org/10.1080/0312407x.2011.577184

Healy, L. M. (2008). Exploring the history of social work as a human rights profession. *International Social Work, 51*(6), 735–748. https://doi.org/10.1177/0020872808095247

Higham, P. (2006). *Social work: Introducing professional practice*. Sage.

Ife, J. (2008). *Human rights and social work: Towards rights-based practice*. Cambridge University Press.

Ife, J. (2009). *Human rights from below: Achieving rights through community development*. Cambridge University Press.

Ife, J. (2016). Human rights and social work: Beyond conservative law. *Journal of Human Rights and Social Work, 1*(1), 3–8. https://doi.org/10.1007/s41134-016-0001-4

IFSW. (2000). *International definition of social work*. http://www.ifsw.org/f38000138.html

IFSW. (2012). *Standards in social work practice meeting human rights*. https://www.ifsw.org/wp-content/uploads/ifsw-cdn/assets/ifsw_92406-7.pdf

IFSW & IASSW. (2014). *Global definition of Social Work*. http://ifsw.org/get-involved/global-definition-of-social-work/

Ioakimidis, V., & Trimikliniotis, N. (2020). Making sense of social work's troubled past: Professional identity, collective memory and the quest for historical justice. *The British Journal of Social Work, 50*(6), 1890–1908. https://doi.org/10.1093/bjsw/bcaa040

Jordan, B. (1984). *Invitation to social work*. Martin Robertson.

Keating, F. (2020). Black men's conversations about mental health through photos. *Qualitative Social Work, 20*(3), 755–772. https://doi.org/10.1177/1473325020922293

Lavalette, M., & Ioakimidis, V. (2011). International social work or social work internationalism? Radical social work in global perspective. In M. Lavalette (Ed.), *Radical social work today. Social work at the crossroads* (pp. 135–151). Policy Press.

Midgley, J. (1981). *Professional imperialism: Social work in the third world*. Heinemann.

Moosa-Mitha, M. (2005). A difference-centred alternative to theorization of children's citizenship rights. *Citizenship Studies, 9*(4), 369–388. https://doi.org/10.1080/13621020500211354

Muñoz Arce, G. (2015). Imperialismo Profesional y trabajo social en América Latina. *Polis (Santiago), 14*(40), 421–438. https://doi.org/10.4067/s0718-65682015000100020

Mutis, P. A., & Ong'Wen, O. S. (2011). *Strategies against poverty: Designs from the North and alternatives from the South*. Consejo Latinoamericano de Ciencias Sociales (CLASCO).

Reichert, E. (2011). *Social work and human rights: A foundation for policy and practice*. Columbia University Press.

Richmond, M. E. (1917). *Social diagnosis*. Sage Publications.

Sen, A. (1999). *Development as freedom*. Oxford University Press.

Shetty, S. (2018). *Decolonising human rights speech*. Amnesty International. (2021, May 20). https://www.amnesty.org/en/documents/doc10/8463/2018/en/

Sinclair, R. (2009). Bridging the past and the future: An introduction to indigenous social work issues. In R. Sinclair, M. A. Hart, & G. Bruyere (Eds.), *Wícihitowin: Aboriginal social work in Canada* (pp. 19–24). Fernwood Publishing.

Staub-Bernasconi, S. (2016). Social work and human rights—linking two traditions of human rights in social work. *Journal of Human Rights and Social Work, 1*(1), 40–49. https://doi.org/10.1007/s41134-016-0005-0

Tedam, P., & Cane, T. (2022). "We started talking about race and racism after George Floyd": Insights from research into practitioner preparedness for anti-racist social work practice in England. *Critical and Radical Social Work, 10*(2), 260–279.

The Truth and Reconciliation Commission of Canada. (2015). *Honouring the truth, reconciling for the future. Summary of the Final Report of the Truth and Reconciliation Commission of Canada The Truth and Reconciliation Commission of Canada*. https://ehprnh2mwo3.exactdn.com/wp-content/uploads/2021/01/Executive_Summary_English_Web.pdf

United Nations. (1949). Universal Declaration of Human Rights : adopted and proclaimed by the General Assembly of the United Nations on the tenth day of December 1948 : final authorized text, [New York]: United Nations Department of Public Information.
United Nations. (1994). *Human rights and social work: A manual for schools of social work and the social work profession*. Center for Human Rights.
Voce, A., Cecco, L., & Michael, C. (2021, September 6). 'Cultural genocide': The shameful history of Canada's residential schools – mapped. *The Guardian*. https://www.theguardian.com/world/ng-interactive/2021/sep/06/canada-residential-schools-indigenous-children-cultural-genocide-map
Waaldijk, B. (2011). Social work between oppression and emancipation. Histories of discomfort and inspiration in Europe. *Social Work & Society. International Online Journal, 9*(2), 232–247.
Wright, K. C., Carr, K., & Akkin, B. A. (2021). The whitewashing of social work history: how dismantling racism in social work education begins with an equitable history of the profession. *Advances in social work, 21*, 274–297.
Wronka, J., & Staub-Bernasconi, S. (2012). Human rights. In K. H. Lyons, T. Hokenstad, M. Pawar, N. Huegler, & N. Hall (Eds.), *The Sage handbook of international social work*. Sage.

Resources

International Federation of Social Workers (IFSW) website: https://www.ifsw.org/
International Association of Schools of Social Work (IASSW) website: https://www.iassw-aiets.org/. [object HTMLSpanElement][object HTMLSpanElement][object HTMLSpanElement][object HTMLSpanElement][object HTMLSpanElement][object HTMLSpanElement]

María Inés Martínez Herrero is a Lecturer at the UNED University (National University of Distance Education) in Spain. Her research addresses historical and present-time human rights and social justice issues in relation to social work.

Prospera Tedam is an Associate Professor and Chair of the Department of Social Wellbeing at the United Arab Emirates University, where she has been since 2018. Her research interests are around anti-racist and anti-oppressive practice, relationship-based practice, and culturally sensitive approaches in social work.

Chapter 4
The Postcolonial Present and a Decolonized Future for Social Work

Samuel Terrazas

Introduction

The social work profession has failed to acknowledge the conflict between the historical collusion with and acceptance of a paradigm of knowledge dominated by theoreticians embedded in a Eurocentric worldview who themselves ascribed to and promoted views that today would be considered racist, oppressive, and colonial. The Eurocentric hegemony by which social workers understand human behavior and social welfare problems is the result of the colonization of knowledge and spaces.

Social work knowledge is influenced by colonialism, unearned racial power, and classism but arguably is unintentionally proliferated implicitly and explicitly through the latent and acknowledged values of social workers who throughout history have benefited from the privilege gained from advantaged ancestries.

Social work struggles to make significant strides in the elimination of racism and oppression because of a failure to acknowledge and separate the colonial past from the postcolonial present. At a conscious and intellectual, yet superficial, place, social workers recognize the importance of efforts to change the sociopolitical influence of racism and oppression; however, from what perspective is this effort being mounted? Is it through the viewpoints of people who face the violence of racism and the barriers of oppression or the socially, economically, politically, and racially privileged who see the oppressed through a lens of their advantaged position and colonized bias? Contemporary intellectual efforts to explain colonization are through the unconscious or implicit bias construct, suggesting that people can hold bias in any of its forms beyond their cognitive awareness (Rogerson et al., 2022).

Social workers holding implicit biases may find alignment and comfort in the values, ethics, knowledge, and practice of social work; however, their worldview

S. Terrazas (✉)
Department of Social Work, University of Texas Permian Basin, Odessa, TX, USA
e-mail: terrazas_s@utpb.edu

M. Madew et al. (eds.), *Decolonized Approaches to Human Rights and Social Work*, https://doi.org/10.1007/978-3-031-33030-8_4

paradigm creates conflict and clouds their understanding of the lived realities of the oppressed, marginalized, discriminated, and othered or those attacked because of their race, sexual orientation, migration, or economic status. Privileged White or White-passing social workers and other professionals may question the validity of pain and suffering of clients caused by racism and oppression as the result of colonization, because Eurocentric and White supremacy-rooted beliefs and values have survived and permeate our understanding of human behavior. For example, nurses and physicians have been found to deny or believe pain levels of African American patients especially women believing their expression of pain as histrionics (Green et al., 2003). Social workers from receiving countries of migrants fleeing war or famine may also lose sight of the physical and psychological trauma of many migrants suffer avoiding focused attention on their trauma because they are focused more on the challenges of acculturation and assimilation into the host country.

Social workers tend not to examine social welfare problems in the context or the history of pain and suffering but as needs, barriers, goals, and objectives. The reality that poverty is painful may infrequently cross the minds of the most well-intentioned social workers because most do not understand poverty as it is experienced by the poor but from an intellectual empathic perspective, influenced with the dogma of Christianity and colonial values that view poverty as a character deficiency and the poor must suffer as long as it takes for them to pull themselves out of poverty. They fail to recognize the historic and racial trauma that exists within the collective narratives and experience of indigenous people, the descendants of slaves, and how the past plays out in the present among the poor, othered, marginalized, oppressed, and discriminated.

This belief system allows for racist and discriminatory practices, beliefs, and attitudes to become so ingrained in an understanding of the world that it has become an intrinsic element of contemporary social work. Cultural relativism explains that truth exists in our understanding of the world; however, it is culturally located (Olteanu, 2019). I argue that social workers' cultural location influences their worldview beyond what research and evidence have confirmed. This cultural influence, in this case privilege of White males and colonial White supremacy, strongly binds social workers' understanding of the world beyond what is known through science to the influences of colonization resulting in the colonization of the mind (Dascal, 2009).

A counter and decolonized perspective of this idea of a linear history and how knowledge, values, and beliefs continue to propagate what Dascal calls a "colonization of the mind" comes from Navajo people who understand their histories referenced not by time but by geographic sites that represent an important event or experience (Dascal, 2009). A collective narrative is created with an understanding of life events from an evolving story that allows all who visit or experience the place and to have their own encounter with the space adding to rather than removing from and creating a history biased by power holders. This way of understanding is not a part of what is known because it has been deleted through cultural genocide and devalued by the scientific and professional communities. The idea that a singular science must exist is rooted in residual power left over from colonial rule that strove to dominate the world through conquest.

We have no choice but to be influenced by colonization given the all-encompassing influence of a known history written from a Eurocentric perspective while indigenous and other histories have been hidden, destroyed, demonized, and reduced to myths and fables. The ideas, narrative, science, and cultures of colonized peoples have limited influence or significance in the "common world." The common world does not exist but is understood through a limited perspective of those who hold power – the power of race.

It is not my intent to devalue the positive impacts of post-positivism, but to offer a critique of this dominant view, which has also limited other modes of understanding – an understanding that includes the sciences and knowledge of First Nations, indigenous societies, and knowledge from colonized populations. This examination of social work and human rights is a critique and historicism of social work past and present to:

1. Explore the failings of social work profession to address the dominance of Western European, affluent White male philosophy of science, values and,
2. critically examine social work in a postcolonial context as a human rights profession, and
3. offer suggestions to decolonize social work practice toward human rights.

Colonial imperialism is the deliberate process of human migration by powerful states to a land that to which they hold no rights and become permanent settlers who hold strong political allegiance or obligation to their home nation. Postcolonialism is defined as a place that has cut all formal allegiance, rule, or obligation to the imperial power; however, the cultural, political, religious, values, and power structures remain indistinguishably entrenched within those people who racially and ethnically identify with their nation of origin.

The remnants of the alignments with Europe, for instance, are strongly represented in colonized nations today in language, religion, government, and education. The tragedies and suffering caused by the genocide of indigenous people and the slavery in the USA, for example, have been "whitewashed" yet continue to cause pain and suffering. These atrocities have been manifested into systems of oppression fueled by racism and discrimination perpetuated today by mutated belief systems brought to the Americas from Europe. Arguably, the imperialist influences have survived more than cultural views. For instance, contemporary European views are much more liberal than in the USA. European laws are very strict on gun control, and Europeans are provided with universal health care, while in the USA mass shootings have become daily occurrences and no recent American administration has made significant progress in establishing universal health care.

A postcolonial stance and critical examination of the known world is a consciousness of its situationality or what Sandra Harding (1998) refers to as a "strong objectivity." Understanding the world by purposely accessing and including diverse narratives that expand on what is known moves us closer to a fuller understanding of the world and its inhabitants. Social work, like all academic and professional disciplines, has only recently actively included the narratives of people with diverse views, knowledge, and experiences, leaving much of what is known about human behavior influenced by men from mostly European ancestry. The idea of understanding the "client" from the client's perspective is relatively a recent innovation in the world of social work practice. This shift in perspective has led to the understanding of the client biased toward the perceptions and a philosophy of science created by colonizing White men. The voice of the client is reconstructed to align with the science of time not by the events and experiences of the client but by the biased lens of privileged people with the power to conduct research, leaving the client responsible for their oppression, while oppressors write the oppressed out of history supported by the scientific method.

Postcolonial theory's central claim is that what is known about this world cannot be understood without a critical understanding of the history of imperialism and colonial rule (Go, 2018). What is "known" or believed about human beings and the world in the USA is based on a Western European paradigm that includes the view that native or aboriginal and non-Europeans are inferior to Europeans. Throughout history, this belief has justified the global genocide of indigenous and aboriginal people and the enslavement of African and other people of color. In contemporary times, we see the manifestations of historical global proliferation of Christianity that has replaced indigenous spiritual beliefs and customs, resulting values, and policies that attack the rights of women, sexual minorities, and indigenous people. These beliefs have evolved into a political and social structure of a ruling class that can be seen in democratic systems of government, policies, and laws that protect and promote ruling class or elite people's interests and oppress others. The profession of social work's mission has been to address the problems of racism, oppressive systems, and symptoms of these forces. The core values of the profession include social justice, yet many social work programs have minimized the place of macro practice in the curriculum. This movement away from macro practice allows for a shift away from social justice and human rights practices.

Social justice and human rights can be placed in the contexts of social work education in textbooks and discussion; however, without a focus on the theoretical, practice, and ethical accountability to macro practice, these terms are simply a *wish list* or *bucket list* for social workers. Social work education is focused on micro practice due to its seemingly less complex nature and unfortunately driven by the market of social work students (Krings et al., 2020) – a market set in a context that promotes a historical worldview that is rooted in Christianity and American values and the need to civilize the "savages" through the righteous work of kind-hearted people willing to leave the comforts of their privileged lives. I argue that the ties to Western European worldview paradigm need to be placed into historical context that allows social workers and students to compare this perspective with a wider array of knowledge and narratives. This critical analysis can produce new lines of thought, theory, and practice allowing an opportunity to develop and balance the power of knowledge to include distant sources of wisdom and the silenced voices of the present.

The stance and mission of social work speak to the tragedy and systems of racism, institutionalized oppression, and the elimination of poverty and a focus on human rights. That mission requires that social workers acknowledge and understand that all people have intrinsic human rights. A global perspective on human rights is beyond the scope of this chapter, but social workers might find tension or confirmatory perspectives on human rights that may place limits on how human rights are defined and operationalized in practice. The tension of human rights at the practice level comes from the lingering and pervasive influences of colonization of thought, Christianity, White supremacy reinforced by institutionalized racism, and oppression. It is difficult for even the most well-intentioned social worker or social work students to recognize the basic human rights of people who are existentially different, leaving them no other option but to resort to the lingering and pervasive stereotypes and biases.

The profession of social work has evolved since its inception and while there has been significant movement toward a profession that not only claims to support human rights but also promotes practices and efforts to advance human rights. On balance, social work has moved in a progressive direction, but there has also been regression. For example, some schools of social work are embedded in sectarian universities that require its faculty to promote their religious views in class and in their lives. Social work schools with religious affiliations that promote the othering of people rooted in the dogma of their religions arguably influence the perspectives of human rights by their students. For instance, the LGBTQ community may not be perceived as having the same human rights as others or women who believe they have the rights over their bodies.

A critical issue in that stance is the practice of social work, which is primarily practiced by women based on a foundation of knowledge created by and for the ancestors of Europeans. Vodde (2000) suggests that social work education is failing to address the issue of power and oppression because of White male privilege. While people who face the burden and trauma of oppression and racism tend be the ancestors of slaves, indigenous, or non-Europeans, they have had minimal impact on the creation of social work knowledge and thus on practice methods. Social work professional values provide the intellectual formation of professional ethical practice; however, the practice is not as strongly correlated to professional values and more correlated to personal values (Spano & Koenig, 2007). This can lead social workers away from the professional mission and focus on an intellectual imperialism that requires social workers to align with social work values and knowledge. In practice, social workers rely on more on personal versus professional values and knowledge in intervention.

Western social work is a value-laden profession that is partly rooted in Judeo-Christian values centered on the ideals of human rights, social justices, dignity, and societal responsibility for its failings to meet the needs of all people and its purposeful efforts to marginalize and gain from the suffering of people perceived to be less valuable. The advent and inclusion of evidence-based practice moved the social work profession toward a stronger alliance with positivism in the application and use of interventions and practice approaches that were supported by evidence. The limitations of evidence-based practice have been that many of the interventions produced and supported were not designed for the very people the social work mission claimed to be focused (Drisko & Grady, 2015). In research courses, I assign students the task of finding evidence-based practices for indigenous people, Latinos, African Americans, or persons with disabilities. They are frustrated because they find very little in the research literature. Social workers are at an intellectual level seeking to ameliorate social welfare problems and to understand the associated social determinates of those problems but are critically behind in a focused effort to address these problems. The significant weight of problems that are pressing on people living with a disability, sexual minorities, migrants, poverty, and discrimination is poorly understood by social workers because the voices of the affected are muffled by the colonization of the mind. Dascal (2007) coined this idea which suggests that through formal public education and social structures a focus on a colonial narrative is propagated. Social workers strive to use practice methods and skills that assess and understand the client's problems as they experience it; however, the methods and skills being used have not been developed to truly hear the words of the client.

The social work profession must acknowledge that it is not immune to nor has it recovered from its oppressive and racist beginnings and that its knowledge and values are based on colonization and its manifestation of a Eurocentric worldview and philosophy of science. Social workers, educators, and leaders must learn to move past the intellectualized, elitist quasi-liberal views toward an authentic self-examination of their unearned power and privilege. This will allow the voices, narratives, knowledge, and influences of people who have historically been dismissed as barbaric, mythical, savage, and nonscientific to be heard and added to how social workers understand human behavior. In essence, the power of what is known to be social work evidence-based knowledge must be challenged as one element of what needs to be known to promote human rights and resolve social welfare problems: not in competition with but in addition to.

Social work, like other professions, is grounded in language, and the behavioral expression of values and theory that drive social work practice occur at the cognitive level but expressed in words and actions of the social worker. Is the unperceivable influence of a colonizer apparent through the education and practice of social work? Can an overriding paradigm of what is known of the world and its inhabitants be reformed by education and knowledge? Can Eurocentric values and colonization be tested and challenged as part of an intellectual discourse without being labeled as unprofessional or nonscientific? Can "othered" people who have not historically been able to add to the social work knowledge base and narrative be heard in the space of understanding human behavior? There is a polarization of experiences between people who experience the world as oppressive and racist who understand their experiences as trauma and harm, while colonized social workers perceive the world from the perspective of power and privilege. They are unaware and angered when made to take notice of their privilege, colonial, imperialist past and collusion with racism. Othered people who enter the professional world are subjugated to be accepted and suppress the internal psychological turmoil fueled by experiences of traumas. People who are characterized with "isms" and survive the power of system racism are harmed and expected to experience harm and resulting pain in silence.

Critical theory has been used to expand an understanding of how power structures and power disparities impact people. Critical theory cannot be effectively applied to American Indian, social work education and practice. While critical theory has provided an intersection between philosophy and social science through empirical social research, it fails to provide adequate explanation of the wrongs with current social reality or to identify the actors to change the wrongs or practical goals for social transformation of the emancipation of oppression and racism of people (Bohman, 2005).

A major weakness in critical theory is its genesis, which is from a colonial reality that has influenced every element of what is known in Western societies. Critical theory offers a basis to identify the domination and oppression of specific people; it fails in the use of Eurocentric language to accurately define the lives of the oppressed and dominated. Eurocentric language is biased toward the justification of colonization leaving the reader struggling to hear the voices of the oppressed because the historical voices of their ancestor have been eliminated from what is known; therefore, there is no context to allow the reader to gain true understanding. Consequently, social reality is blurred about the oppressed and dominated, leaving them responsible for their own oppression and domination because only they can hear their own realities. The social worker and client are both trying to understand each other but in an echo chamber canceling out others' voice leaving each finding meaning in the social constructs.

We also see this in the lack of understanding and bias propagated about the oppressed and dominated people who refuse to follow Euro-Anglo/colonizer cultural norms. The words and descriptions of non-Euro Anglo people are rooted in the beliefs that they are *savages*. A social reality of people of color or sexual minorities, for instance, the stereotype in the USA, for example, that African American men are intrinsic threats because of the belief that they are violent and criminals, is propagated by messaging through every form of social media. The racist or discriminatory language used to describe oppressed and dominated people is so embedded in the colonial lexicon that it is virtually impossible to accurately define colonized people and to give them the power of respecting their cultural ways and traditions. Social workers are thus forced to understand cultural from a biased colonized science versus from the truth of the oppressed and dominated people themselves.

A second critique of critical theory is that while it does provide an explanation of the structures of oppression, it leaves the perpetrators and actors who maintain oppressive systems unabated or held accountable for the harm they cause. The remedy for social workers is policy advocacy and social action if a democratic political system exist that would allow such action. In nations ruled by dictatorships or totalitarian regimes, the idea of political action may not be an option – leaving the voices and human rights of oppressed people silenced. In nations where social workers are present, the political context influences the methods and approaches to address human rights critical theory that offers a discourse to understanding social and political determinants of health, poverty, education, and human rights versus placing blame on the oppressed for their poverty.

Decolonized Social Work and Social Justice

The effort to decolonize social work requires a realignment of the skills, methods, and textbooks to inform social work practice (Swepaul & Henrickson, 2019). Alternatives to Western Eurocentric cultural historic perspectives and education and postcolonial thinking raise the possibility of creatively drawing on the knowledge from the diversity of indigenous cultures and incorporating indigenous knowledge applicable to contemporary social challenges. A dialectical, deconstructive process using critical historicism can provide social workers with a process to examine social work's record from a perspective that questions it and allows for the oppressive and colonial influence to be identified and labeled within the biased narratives. Social work has failed to critically examine its own history a process to challenge colonial influence, leaving social work knowledge deeply embedded with Christian male Eurocentric views. The issue becomes the following: Is there enough motivation within the profession to deconstruct social work literary products when so many in the profession benefit from the intrinsic power and privilege many social workers possess? Is there enough awareness with the social work professions of these perspectives to support a movement toward a decolonized social work profession?

The theoretical and practice evolution of social work away from the pathologizing of social welfare problems such as poverty and the use of the medical model to diagnose individual problems can be replaced with the use of the strength-based and person-in-environment perspective. There is a movement in social work education to add decolonization and anti-fascism, diversity, inclusion, and equity content into social work undergraduate and graduate curricula. This movement appears to have some momentum in social work education and may have a beneficial effect at the practice level – how social workers realign their practices to include decolonization, antiracism, diversity, inclusion, and equity. Malcolm Payne suggests that the prominence of theories is not their value in understanding human behavior but the political appeal they have to the profession (Payne, 2021).

Historically, American social workers have aligned with the moderate Democratic Party agenda and have opposed many of the conservative to reactionary Republican agenda of fiscal conservatisms, prolife, progun, anti-migrant, and small government. In a Supreme Court case, the rights to access an abortion in the USA was overturned by the court after Speaker of the House Mitch McConnell strategically supported the installation of arch-conservative justices Brett Kavanaugh and Amy Coney Barrett to side with radical reactionary judges such as Justice Clarence Thomas to overturn the precedent. A lead up to this Supreme Court ruling was an uprising of racist organizations like the Proud Boys and neo-Nazi organizations, which historically pushed to the fringe of society found an ally who promoted their racist views in Donald Trump. Trump and his allies attempted to overthrow the government and arguably change a democratic system of government into a formal patriarchy. This attempt failed; however, this form of government, values, and beliefs is supported by his constituents and the majority of the Republican Party. One could argue that given these events and the efforts by Republicans to promote Trumpian political views, postcolonialism may have been a transitory part of US history. Additionally, the fact that these political views where so swiftly moved from the political fringes to the mainstream suggests they were quietly entrenched within the social political subsurface of some significant portion of the population versus what was considered politically incorrect and found only in distant past of the country.

The nationalist and conservative agendas are on the rise around the world. Eastern Bloc countries reacted to the fall of the Soviet Union by adopting liberal democratic systems; however, the early 2000 has seen an uprising of right-wing nationalism in Eastern Europe. For instance, in 2022, the right-wing Vox Party of Spain was one of the top three parliamentary parties in the country. I do not want to enter in the elitist political fray of judgment of other countries' political processes. I want to make the point that these views and beliefs are on the rise in countries all over the world. Arguably, if there are enough social workers who align with prolife, nationalism, and ultranationalist views, this movement could hinder and slow the process for the profession to move beyond its colonial history and its influences on modern-day policy, practice, and theories.

In group work, Yalom suggests that the group is a microcosm of each member's ecosystem and each member brings their own experiences and influences back into the group (Yalom & Leszcz, 2005). This process allows each member of the group to gain personalized growth because they are learning about themselves in the context of their other people's lives and experiences. Social workers are similarly part of their respective environments and systems and bring with them those influences into the social work learning and practice space. Presumably, professors strive to teach social workers to understand their biases and to integrate professional values, ethics, and an understanding of human behavior in the social environment. It has been my experience teaching students about poverty and the like and is such a departure from many student's worldviews, knowledge, and values that it's shocking to many students the fact that poverty is the result of systemic racism not laziness or character flaws as suggested by societal stereotypes. In contrast, students generally do not challenge when they learn about gravity or photosynthesis or genetics or economics. The contrast between the physical sciences and social sciences is rooted in the political and religious implications of the social sciences. The social sciences include disciplines such as anthropology, sociology, ethnic studies, social work, and psychology, which examine politics, religion, and the social problems.

In the USA, the Republican Party launched an attack on critical race theory and efforts to eliminate racism by creating laws such as the "Don't Say Gay Law" in Florida, and in 2022, Governor DeSantis created the civics literacy excellence initiative designed to influence teachers to emphasize American exceptionalism, patriotism, and Christian conservative ideologies. The question and concern become to what degree do these beliefs and political views enter into the social work knowledge base, values, ethics, and practice.

The fact that the religious and political groups are organized to deconstruct civil rights laws and human rights laws, promoting White supremacy and legalizing discrimination, suggests that while these groups do not include all groups, these messages play into and reinforce colonization of thought which arguably will influence the beliefs and values of large groups of people. These groups argue their positions as issues of social justice as attacks on religion, White heritage, and political views. These groups are often characterized as fringe groups; however, many in Republican political discourse is supportive of these groups or do not speak out against them for fear of losing political power. The power of these groups cannot be argued given their voting power and power over the Republican Party. Kathy Morris conducted an analysis of data on campaign contributions by job title and found the 10% of American clinical social workers supported the Republican Party. Lusk and Terrazas (2015) found from a sample of Texas LCSWs that 22% believed that race impacted their professional supervision.

The primary mission of the social work profession is to enhance well-being and to meet the basic human needs of all people, with particular attention to the needs and empowerment of people who are vulnerable, oppressed, and living in poverty.

If a social worker interprets the social work mission and values as a menu to select from or a profession that does not require its members to strongly align with the profession's mission, values, and professional practice, then the profession devolves into a technical occupation designed to provide a services void of values or professional standards. Services are designed to meet some need of its consumers and its workers motivated by reimbursement not by the mission of the profession. A profession with professionals who do not abide by the profession's value system, who focused on a fee for service provided by technicians, or who are motivated by the profit of the credentials is not meeting the basic needs of people. The focus on micro practice is one of the pitfalls of the profession since it has the strong allure of economic gain for social workers and universities.

Social work's social justice efforts are tied closely to the macro practice and policy advocacy, and this area of practice is declining in popularity (Austin, 2019). Accreditation agencies require social work programs to include macro practice in social work curriculum; however, social work programs that offer specialized practice in macro have dwindled, while micro or clinical practices have proliferated. If social justice is such a foundational and important social work value, then why is it not a prominent feature in social work education and less featured in social work research? There is no clear answer to this question; however, we do know that the influence of conservatives, Christian nationalism, and political views that are in conflict with social work values are on the rise. Is the social justice issue promoted by White supremacy groups, Christian Nationalist, and the so-called prolife groups going to be recognized by professional societies if enough social workers promote the values of these groups? Who will hold the mission and intellectual line and maintain the definition of social justice as it is described in the code of ethics, and will it matter if social workers conform their views and practices to the powers of the politic and personal beliefs? Sociologist Max Weber spoke to the influence that economic power has had on the sciences and suggested with enough money the laws of nature could be bent toward the views of those who had the financial power. Has social work practice entered into realm of for-profit technologies that corporation can take advantage of as they did with health care?

Will the corporations who have developed virtual platforms and ease of process for social workers to offer their services online to the select people who can afford Internet services and computers drive research to influence social work mission, values, and standards to best fit their business model? Will these corporations respect or reinforce social work ethics and professional standards or focus on the mechanics of the practice to increase productivity? The issue is not if virtual- or face-to-face-centered practice is of value, but which becomes a standard of practice and how does this process occur? What does this have to do with decolonized social work and social justice? The power of corporate influence on social work practice exemplifies a colonization of the profession. Social work has historically not been able to produce anything to generate profit. With the advent of computer technology and the Internet, corporations found a way to profit off of the suffering of others. Social workers who find the practice of social work not to their liking enter private practice with ease and moving away from the mission and values of the profession.

A *decolonized future for social work as a human rights profession* is not a forgone conclusion. As social work is realigned with a decolonization agenda, it will require the profession to critically examine social work from a historical lens. As sociologist Chibber (2018) suggests, one of the key elements of postcolonial theory is that it critically discloses the cultural logics attendant with empire. In fact, it must examine all types of discourses, epistemology, cultural schemas, representations, and ideologies that were part and parcel of Western imperialism (Tomicic & Berardi, 2018).

The profession of social work and social work education, researchers, journal editors, and peer reviewers must come to terms with our colonizing past, postcolonial present, and decolonized future. Volunteering to enter into the social work profession and completing a degree in social work do not automatically mean alignment and commitment with the ethics, values, and mission of the social work profession. It also does not mean that social worker's racist and discriminatory beliefs, values, and affiliations will in every case be replaced with antiracist, diversity, inclusion, and equity practices and values. Minimizing these influences will require a strong commitment by the profession and social work educators to hold the line on attacks on human rights.

Students and social workers must agree, believe, and understand that *all* people deserve dignity and have worth. How does a social worker make a paradigm shift away from the perspective that indigenous, decedents of slaves, forced migrants, or people of color are not "savages" and be complacent in the othering of people, discriminated against or oppressed? The belief is that through social work education, exposure to social workers, and professional trainings, a person will evolve into a social worker and will come to terms with their racism and privileged position and come to value all people. I believe this is possible and have had the privilege to work with many social workers who practice ethically and are guided by our professional values and mission founded on social justice, but it is not a forgone conclusion.

Decolonized Approaches to Human Rights

1. Social work education must acknowledge its failings to include the voices of the oppressed, delegitimized, and unpopular and language beyond mainstream English. Beyond the social work profession's alignment with the popularized and repackaged movement of antiracism, equity, diversity, and inclusion, social work must deconstruct and correct the historical collusion with colonization. Social work education must include a critical examination of social work history and allow the voices of all oppressed people to inform social work practice theory, research, and practices.

   Voices of the Oppressed: Practice and research skills and theories must include the voices of the oppressed; the standards of client self-determination; the self-reported psychosocial assessment and the ethics related to human subjects, ensuring processes are not coercive; and the avoidance of dual relationships. In practice, I would argue that some portion of social workers do not abide by these standards and ethics and resort to their personal values and beliefs about human behavior and the social environment. Additionally, I contend that because there has been a paucity of the voices of the oppressed, most social workers struggle to hear their messages, views, feelings, and experiences because the language required for social workers creates barriers to communication and understanding. This lack of understanding creates a void in communication that is filled in with colonizing thoughts, generalizations, and biases in an effort by the social worker to feel competent and powerful.

   People who do not ascribe to because of cultural identity or who do not fit the ideal cultural type face the isolation, discrimination, oppression, and delegitimization of their existence through the power of linguistic construction of opposites in what Franz Fanon described as the "one and the other" defined as a term that holds a subrogate status because it is believed to be inferior (Fanon, 1952). The oppression of indigenous people and other oppressed and discriminated groups is mirrored in linguistic constructions where preferred linguistic constructions of White males are the mechanism that reduces othered people linguistics as primitive. This dynamic forces the othered to adapt to colonizers' language and syntax and to clearly understand its morphology. Othered people face being labeled as less than with every word they speak because their syntax and style of language are perceived as inferior. The language of migrants does not fit with what is considered as proper, good, or articulate language of the host nation, which provided the hearer the proof that they are not part of the deserving Americans. We often hear a person who holds majority status offer a person of color the micro aggression "you are so articulate" feeling that this statement is a compliment; however, the meta message is "Wow! How did you learn to speak like us?"

2. Social workers must learn to accept diversity of language, expression, and thought along with race and ethnicity and recognize their language is not superior or common but one of many within the dialectic of human verbal interactions. We do not teach social work students language as the primary interface with the client and to respect and appreciate the wider-ranging diversity of language. We focus on the counseling skills developed for the majority population forcing these complex processes on the client who often must accommodate to the social workers' intervention and language to benefit to the intervention.
3. Social work as a profession must strive to reconstruct its identity to remove the colonial past and move toward a decolonized future where social workers are not bound by their past but informed by it and strive to seek an inclusive truth. This requires the approach of historicism to critically put into context social work theory, practice, ethics, and understanding of human behavior.
4. Critically examine the social work and social justice ideology and move it to a form of practice that centers all social work practice.
5. Examine social work education and avoid the pitfalls of becoming social work technicians instead of supporting the development of social work professionals.
6. Train social workers to accept and appreciate critical review of their work as students and as practitioners as it relates to their racist and discriminatory beliefs. Move away from the passive language of implicit and explicit biases and name inappropriate behaviors as such. Move away from White fragility, and allow the intellectual discourse of the classroom to directly examine racists and discriminatory beliefs. Recognize the harm and violence of racism that occur in classroom, agencies, conferences, and all spaces where social work and social work education exist.
7. Include mandatory coursework in social justice and field placement experiences.
8. The social worker can invest in the intellectual and often emotional process of learning to hear the voices of people who they have long believed are inferior or belonging to groups who have been stigmatized, discriminated, oppressed, and intentionally segregated to benefit the privileged.

A Balanced Approach to Generalist Practice

Micro Social Work

The center of micro social work practice relies on the capacity of the social workers to develop and maintain professional relationships with their clients. It is this space that I want to focus attention on because it is at the engagement stage where the client determines the legitimacy of the professional relationship. This is where the social worker works to develop trust through nonjudgmental, warm, and thoughtful communication. The social worker must include in their understanding of human behavior social welfare policy, research methods, and social work practice that the client's knowledge and expressions of the world may be beyond their ability to understand and perceive. This will require the social worker to include in their social work practice that it is, at its core, biased toward a Eurocentric worldview. The social worker will have to allow the language, views, and knowledge of their clients to be as much a part of the truth about human behavior as is what is known from science.

Mezzo Social Work

I believe that group work and family social work face the most challenges in the influence of Eurocentric and colonial ideologies and personal biases of social workers. It has been my experience that many students are not interested in group work or family social work because of its complicated and messy practice approaches. These practices were well recognized and researched during the 1970s and 1980s; however, since the 1990s, these have come into less favor and interest, research, and advancements in practice. Arguably, the popularity of micro practice has been the mechanism to push mezzo practices aside.

Group Work

Some of the power of group work lies in what William Schwartz (1994) called mutual aid and the process of group member cohesion as Yalom and Leszcz (2005) has suggested. What group workers have failed to recognize is that the group can also deconstruct biases through the process of group work. Corrigan has extensively researched the phenomena of stigma and has found that direct exposure to people living with mental illness reduces stigma (Corrigan, 2007). The human process of interaction in a safe environment can be the genesis for insightful understanding of self with dissimilar people. The group worker provides the safety and methods to allow for differences among group members to develop into healthy respectful interactions, relationships, and social movements in essences decolonizing the client interactional process.

The group is a microcosm of each member's lived experiences, and these truths are directly or indirectly expressed in the group process. The social worker must be trained and have insight on how colonization has influenced their perspectives of systems, people, and power structures to hear and allow to be heard these truths. Removing the colonized perspective, the conflicts of opinions especially among different races or classes must be ended. The center of this reaction is White fragility and the anxiety that comes from the fear of the uprising, anger, and violence of people of color. Instead, the group worker must lean into the depths of differences and allow the group members to find their common humanity.

Family Social Work

Social work borrows much of its practice and theory from family therapy theoreticians and practitioners such as Bowen, Satir, and Minuchin who developed various family therapy approaches such as structural family therapy and strategic and systems family therapy. The role of social workers in practice often includes the family; however, third-party pay systems and auspices of care create barriers for the social work to engage the family, as does the social worker who is indoctrinated into the singular and popularized micro-practice models of social work. Social workers must pay particular attention on how colonization influences how we understand the family. The basic definition of family has been based on a structure influenced by Christianity, middle classism, gender role, and the politics of women's oppression and objectification. The realties of women of color in the work force, such as Black women's historical trauma of rape by White men and losses of family, Latinas' sexualization and stereotype and value as domestic workers and the abduction and murder of indigenous women and the targeting, hate crimes and murder of transwomen and the power and control that men hold of women must be included in the descriptions and definitions of family. This will allow the social worker to include in their human rights interventions for women as a central feature of family social work.

Macro-Social Work

Macro practice is the area of practice that must be brought back to life and relevance in social work if the future of social work will include social justice as a mechanism to ensure that all people experience human rights. The focus on the present and future such as suggested in symbolic interactionism must be challenged to include the cyclical historical experiences of indigenous and oppressed people. The realities of historic and ongoing trauma and systemic racism must be part of macro-practice approaches if they are to ameliorate the human injustice in societies across the world. Social work students must be exposed to the ideas, experiences, insights, and understanding of the human behavior for the silenced and dismissed. This will require social work educators and university departments of social work to examine their curricula and include more indigenous content and challenges to Eurocentric worldviews into the learning space of students. It will also require social workers to expand their own worldviews and reflect on different voices and recognize that difference does not equate to wrong or deviant.

Macro practice must be part of each social worker's practice and that practice must include working to protect human rights. Social workers must come to terms with colonization and their individual alignments and willingness to shift their practice and self-improvement efforts toward decolonization of the profession. I believe macro practice is the intellectual and practice space that can raise social workers' attention, understanding, insight, and practice to include human rights as a central perspective in macro practice. We cannot allow the unbalanced and micro-focused social work of today to maintain its momentum, but we can disrupt this momentum by infusing the philosophical perspectives of colonization and decolonization into the intellectual discourse of social work. This will allow the distillation of our work to focus on the basics of human rights for all and to refocus micro practitioners to the importance of macro practice as a method to eliminate and reduce problems caused by systemic racism rooted in colonization versus colluding with human rights violators.

Summary

The global social work profession has promoted human rights in its mission, but has not accounted for how social work knowledge has been heavily influenced by a Eurocentric paradigm of knowledge. The issue is not the value and quality of this knowledge, but its applicability to the client whose worldview and experiences do not fit the paradigm of knowledge that was developed to help. The social worker brings with them into the helping space the bias rooted in the colonization of their land. A colonized mind is unable to see the truth of their clients' experiences, views, traditions, language, expressions, oppression, and violence. This results in changing their client's words to better fit the lens of the colonizer whose Eurocentric perspective cannot understand the value and worth of people who were perceived to be savages and less than human. This may sound hyperbolic, but one only need to look into our history and daily accounts of people of color or people with different religious views who are murdered by police in the name or some religion or in genocides as the result of a political coup.

Social work practice, theory, or research was not developed taken into consideration the influence colonization has had on social welfare problems or oppressive systems. This has resulted in less effective social work practice methods and approaches, because they have been developed with the privileged, educated, and detached social worker as the focus versus the client. The social worker must learn the language of the colonizer and to deconstruct and separate the oppressive messages from their worldview to allow the client's truth to be heard and acted upon, which requires an authentic appreciation for the client's strengths, value, and human rights. Social work is moving in the direction of decolonizing; however, this is not a forgone conclusion because this process will require the profession to move past its colonized mind.

Discussion Questions

1. Who will hold the mission and intellectual line and maintain the definition of social justice as it is described in our code of ethics, and will it matter if social workers bend their views and practices to the powers of the politic and personal beliefs?
2. If human rights are important social work values, then why is it not a prominent feature in social work education and less featured in social work research?
3. How can the colonized mind be identified and, if needed, changed?

References

Austin, M. J. (2019). Pathways for promoting macro practice in social work education: A commentary. *Human Service Organizations: Management, Leadership & Governance, 43*(4), 241–257. https://doi.org/10.1080/23303131.2019.1666764

Bohman, J. (2005). Critical theory. *Stanford Encyclopedia of Philosophy*, https://plato.stanford.edu/entries/critical-theory/

Chibber, V. (2018). *Iconoclasia: Investigaciones sobre y desde Marx, 1*, 341–351.

Corrigan, P. W. (2007). How clinical diagnosis might exacerbate the stigma of mental illness. *Social Work, 52*(1), 31–39. https://doi.org/10.1093/sw/52.1.31

Dascal, M. (2009). Colonizing and decolonizing minds. *PhilPapers*. https://philpapers.org/rec/DASCAD

Drisko, J. W., & Grady, M. D. (2015). Evidence-based practice in social work: A contemporary perspective. *Clinical Social Work Journal, 43*, 274–282. https://doi.org/10.1007/s10615-015-0548-z

Fanon, F. (1952). *Black skin, White Masks*. Grove Press.

Go, J. (2018). Postcolonial possibilities for the sociology of race. *Sociology of Race and Ethnicity, 4*(4), 439–451. https://doi.org/10.1177/2332649218793982

Green, C. R., Anderson, K. O., Baker, T. A., Campbell, L. C., Decker, S., Fillingim, R. B., Kalauokalani, D. A., Lasch, K. E., Myers, C., Tait, R. C., Todd, K. H., & Vallerand, A. H. (2003). The unequal burden of pain: Confronting racial and ethnic disparities in pain. *Pain Medicine, 4*(3), 277–294. https://doi.org/10.1046/j.1526-4637.2003.03034.x

Krings, A., Trubey-Hockman, C., Dentato, M. P., & Grossman, S. (2020). Recalibrating micro and macro social work: Student perceptions of social action. *Social Work Education, 39*(2), 160–174. https://doi.org/10.1080/02615479.2019.1616686

Olteanu, A. (2019). Cultural relativism and politics of recognition. In *Multiculturalism as multimodal communication. Humanities – arts and humanities in progress* (Vol. 9). Springer. https://doi.org/10.1007/978-3-030-17883-3_2

Payne, M. (2021). *Modern social work theory*. Red Globe Press.

Rogerson, C. V., Prescott, D. E., & Howard, H. G. (2022). Teaching social work students the influence of explicit and implicit bias: Promoting ethical reflection in practice. *Social Work Education, 41*(5), 1035–14046. https://doi.org/10.1080/02615479.2021.1910652

Schwartz, W. (1994). *Social work: The collected writings of William Schwartz*. F.E. Peacock.

Spano, R., & Koenig, T. (2007). What is sacred when personal and professional values collide? *Journal of Social Work Values and Ethics, 4*(3), 4–19. https://jswve.org/download/2007-3/JSWVE-Volume-4-Number-3.pdf

Swepaul, V., & Henrickson, M. (2019). The (r)evolution and decolonization of social work ethics: The global social work statement of ethical principles. *International Social Work, 62*(6), 1469–1481. https://doi.org/10.1177/0020872819846238

Tomicic, A., & Berardi, F. (2018). Between past and present: The sociopsychological constructs of colonialism, coloniality and postcolonialism. *Integrative Psychological & Behavioral Science, 52*(1), 152–175. https://doi.org/10.1007/s12124-017-9407-5

Vodde, R. (2000). De-centering privilege in social work educations Whose job is it anyway? *Race, Gender & Class, 7*(4), 139–160. https://www.jstor.org/stable/41955731

Yalom, I. D., & Leszcz, M. (2005). *The theory and practice of group psychotherapy*. Basic Books.

Samuel Terrazas has 17 years of professional social work practice experience in South Florida in the areas of community mental health and community organization in both rural and urban settings. He holds an LCSW in Florida and has held similar licensure in Texas. As a Social Worker, he has written and implemented a variety of program grants in the areas of community mental health, community development, culturally competent mental health care, school-based social work, and mental health services for farmworkers. He is currently a Professor and Chair of the Department of Social Work at the University of Texas Permian Basin. He has conducted research and published in the areas of Latino farmworker mental health, secondary trauma, LGBTQ foster youth, professional social work supervision, and migration.

Chapter 5
Kinship Care, Responsibility, and Self-Determination: Exploring African Individual and Community Rights in Decolonized Social Work

Ndangwa Noyoo and Tanja Kleibl

Introduction

When we look at human rights in the African context, we must first note that we are dealing with a very Western-oriented discourse, the foundations of which can be found in the European Enlightenment, during which the intensity of colonization efforts increased. During this period, the population of the continent was portrayed by the West as uncivilized and inhuman.

Many of those who influenced the early debates on human rights and the Enlightenment in Europe, such as Hegel, Kant, and de Tocqueville, legitimized the colonial project of their time while also elaborating some of the philosophical foundations for the later Universal Declaration of Human Rights after World War II. In discussing human rights in the African context, it is therefore important to link this concept to the continent's past and to see how the Western-influenced concept of human rights has placed the people of Africa on the margins or even, as Hegel says, outside of humanity. This, of course, ignores Africa's people's rich pre-colonial practices and values of kinship care, community responsibility, and respect for and dependence on the environment, among others. These practices and values, it could be argued, also existed in the Global North, but they were largely destroyed with capitalist expansion, while they still exist in many regions of Africa.

N. Noyoo (✉)
Department of Social Development, University of Cape Town, Cape Town, South Africa
e-mail: ndangwa.noyoo@uct.ac.za

T. Kleibl
Social Work Department, Technical University of Würzburg-Schweinfurt, Würzburg, Germany

Department of Social Development, University of Cape Town, Cape Town, South Africa
e-mail: tanja.kleibl@thws.de

M. Madew et al. (eds.), *Decolonized Approaches to Human Rights and Social Work*,
https://doi.org/10.1007/978-3-031-33030-8_5

According to Mann and Deap (2020) in the context of social rights, it is primarily important to mention that kinship care is embedded in the lives of children and families across sub-Saharan Africa as evidenced by the near universality of the practice, its long-standing use in rural and urban communities in manifold settings, and the vast array of different forms it can encompass. Thus, when we refer to kinship care, we mean the protection and nurturing of individuals by relatives or friends of families (Mann & Delap, 2020). On the other hand, when we examine the notion of community responsibility in this context, we are guided by Ikuenobe's (2018) analysis, which points to the fact that there is no conflict between individuals and the community in African societies or, to be precise, communalism. Furthermore, from a decolonial perspective, our argument is as well rooted in the basic collective human right to self-determination, in relation to which the African Charter on Human and Peoples' Rights is the only regional convention on the protection of human rights which "enshrines the peoples' right to self-determination" (Przetacznik, 1990). In this sense, the three are mutually supportive, and people are required to have the moral attitude of contributing to the community for their own well-being and self-determination. This attitude creates the priority of duty, which is for the fundamental goal of creating a self-determined community, in order to provide the material conditions for actualizing individuals' and group's substantive right and well-being (Ikuenobe, 2018).

Essentially, Africa's past is rooted in the pre-colonial era, which predates European colonization, intrusion, and bastardization of its peoples and institutions. Crucially, pre-colonial Africa was anchored in community-based approaches to social and political organization as opposed to individualism. It is important to note that in contemporary times, institutions, policies, and legal frameworks, among others, which African countries rely on to govern themselves, are derived from Europe. They form part of the colonial relics, which continue to plague and define Africa's so-called modernization project in the postcolonial era. In fact, Africa continues to be extremely vulnerable and susceptible to Western capitalist exploitation. In addition, Western-dominated institutions such as the World Bank and the International Monetary Fund (IMF) continue to direct institutional reform in Africa, further complicating the efforts being made by Africans to reconstruct their societies (Gaye, 1998) and even contributing to new conflicts and wars. Consequently, we see new forms of extreme human suffering and forced displacement. Again, the former can be traced back to the IMF, and the World Bank promoted structural adjustment programs after the Cold War. It can be exemplary observed in countries such as Mozambique where levels of conflict, inequality, and environmental destruction have increased massively over the last years (Hanlon, 2022).

Conversely, it looks as if "modernization" in Africa is a caricature of European societies' experimentations and their trial-and-error efforts over the centuries and seems to be premised on the modernization myth which assumes that all people desire to "modernize" and that it is necessarily beneficial (Klinghoffer, 1973). However, this perspective overlooks the side effects such as the weakening of the extended family, growing urban unemployment, increasing depersonalization, dismemberment of a system based on subsistence farming, environmental protection of sacred forests and lands, and mutual self-help as well as the increasing challenge of forced human displacement because of capitalist resource exploitation and so forth (Klinghoffer, 1973). Furthermore and by extension, postcolonial states, which emerged after African countries became independent, look as if they are merely scions of colonial states and arguably products of colonialism (Olowu, 1994; Noyoo, 2014). While we may refer to the postcolonial era as a time when African countries are independent, in all its intents and purposes, this period has mostly served and continues to shore up the interests of the West. Many African states continue to be neocolonial outposts (Nkrumah, 1965; Fanon, 1963; Hanlon, 2022). Due to this situation, Africa's epistemic paradigms, among others, continue to be tainted by the West's worldviews, positionalities, as well as social and economic policies. It is within the above-cited context that we explore how the notion of human rights and the practice of social care could further be embedded in an African way of life. Also, this backdrop provides us the rationale to call for the decolonization of human rights and social work discourses in Africa while arguing that wide-ranging culturally embedded values and practices should find expression in human rights and social work endeavors in Africa. However, it would be remiss of us to discuss issues such as human rights in Africa without first recognizing the content-rich diversity, delving into its pre-colonial era, and shedding some light on this period and its impact on social development so far.

Africa: A Diverse Continent

Tucci and Akey (2019) point out that Africa is home to considerable cultural and linguistic diversity. Indeed, more than 2000 ethnolinguistic groups are known to exist in Africa at present. The majority of languages spoken in Africa belong to four linguistic groups and are known to exist in Africa at present. Also, Jackson and Rosberg (1998) point out that most African countries are multiethnic societies with populations that are sharply divided along ethnical, cultural, linguistic, religious, and similar cleavages. Most are composed of several, and some, of many different traditional societies, each with distinctive institutions to which members of other traditional societies are not only detached but also disinclined, if not actually opposed (Jackson & Rosberg, 1998). What this evidence is pointing to is a period in Africa's past which is rarely factored into contemporary discourses, and yet it still has indelible marks on Africa's sociopolitical and economic structures. This past was rudely interrupted by colonialism and put a stop to Africa's state formation when the colonialists drew arbitrary boundaries lumping various pre-colonial nation-states into colonial territories. These forerunners of the present-day postcolonial states were diverse and unique in their own ways while defining their citizens in particular ways.

Similarly, the economic system, which came with colonization, was dislocating to the Africans in that it clashed with their value systems, which extolled the sharing of wealth as opposed to the exploitation of people and maximization of profit.

Arguably, economic "alienation" is the specific form of capitalism, which governs the reproduction of society in its totality and not only the reproduction of its economic system. The law of value governs not only capitalist economic life, but all social life in this society (Amin, 2014). Prior to colonization, Africans had relied on the barter system, where they exchanged goods and other products based on need and not the profit motive alone. After resisting this form of economic system in the early stages of colonial rule, Africans were forcibly incorporated into it by taxing them on what they already had or owned, for example, their huts or heads (hut tax, head tax, and so forth) (Gann, 1958). Thus, when we later shine a light on pre-colonial Africa, we want people to understand the fact that there are still few examples of non-Western and non-European forms of social organization. Despite forceful incorporation into Western constructs and institutions, indigenous systems have withstood colonial corrosion and Europeans' deliberate, conscious, and pernicious efforts to completely obliterate anything that had existed in the pre-colonial period. Even the way human rights were presented to Africans as something totally alien to their way of life by Westerners remains a total fallacy to date.

Defining Human Rights

According to the Office of the United Nations High Commissioner for Human Rights (OHCHR) (2018), human rights are rights we have simply because we exist as human beings – they are not granted by any state. These universal rights are inherent to us all, regardless of nationality, sex, national or ethnic origin, color, religion, language, or any other status. They range from the most fundamental – the right to life – to those that make life worth living, such as the rights to food, education, work, health, and liberty. In certain instances, a distinction is often made between civil and political rights, or first-generation rights, and economic, social, and cultural rights, or second-generation rights. Although it is clear that the modalities of their implementation are different, their interrelationship is far more complex than a simple statement of categories of rights would lead one to suppose (Conte & Burchill, 2016). Furthermore, it might also be assumed that the term civil and political rights implies a distinction between two, different but related, sets of rights, which are strongly associated with group or collective rights, as discussed already earlier. While civil rights are those rights which are calculated to protect an individual's physical and mental integrity, to ensure that they are not the victims of discrimination, and to preserve their right to a fair trial, political rights are those which ensure that individuals are able to participate in the public life of the state, freedom of expression and assembly, and freedom of thought, conscience, and religion (Conte & Burchill, 2016).

For Taylor-Gooby (2008), the notion of "rights" is essentially a juristic concept referring to the legitimacy of an individual's claims. However, rights can be extended to other contexts, for example, social policy. Here, the question would be whether claims to social benefits and services should be backed by state force, so that social rights become an element of citizenship in the modern state. While taking the above definitions of human rights, we are again guided by Hansungule (2010, p. 28) who emphatically states that the notion of human rights, therefore, is not purely a Western invention. It cannot be. Neither did the concept of human rights originate from any particular part of the world. Arguably, all peoples of the world do not assent to the same values and beliefs, but what is certain is that every society has been concerned with the notion of social justice, the relationship between the individual and his/her political authorities, and indeed their right to self-determination and development as a collective right. Given the foregoing, it can be speculated that social work's inclusion into the human rights narrative seems to follow the highlighted pattern above which removes Africans from the human rights narrative, thus cementing the erroneous notion that there were no human rights or perspectives related to the aforementioned before colonial intrusion. This notion is also foregrounded in an individualist understanding of human rights, which ignores the African tradition of kinship care, community responsibility, as well as communalism as a widely accepted ideology orientating the identity of many African people.

Examining Human Rights in an African Context

From time immemorial, all human societies have been guided by moral codes which clearly delineate good and evil or what can be deemed just or unjust. African pre-colonial societies were not an exception. Nmehielle (2001, p. 7) opines that the debate on the existence of human rights as a concept in pre-colonial African legal thought is a very controversial one and is hinged on another controversial subject: whether law existed in pre-colonial Africa. Some Western scholars have questioned the notion of law in pre-colonial Africa. This stems from the historical obscurity given to Africa by early Western historians. Hegel in his *Lectures on the Philosophy of History* positioned Africa out of history and civilization. However, both law and human rights existed during this period. The interpretation of human rights now may not have been the same in this period before colonial domination, but the practice was embedded in the pre-colonial societal practices (Nmehielle, 2001). For Hansungule (2010), the evolution of human rights in Africa should be viewed as three cascading levels, i.e., pre-colonial, colonial, and postcolonial phase. The colonial phase of development, as the term suggests, is the period when Africa like various parts of Asia was under alien rule. This is the time when Africa got into contact with the outside world and therefore international law. Furthermore:

> Colonialism brought Africa onto the international stage even though only as colonies represented by European masters. An important feature of international law then is that it legalised both slavery and colonization itself. This is a period in which, under the 'watchful eye of Christianity,' human rights of the local people were grossly violated. Local people were denied basic rights like participation and, therefore, the right to vote solely on the grounds of their skin-colour. (Hansungule, 2010, p. 13).

Debates and discussions pertaining to human rights seem to mostly tilt toward Eurocentric notions and understandings regarding this concept, as if other societies did not have such ideas in their cultures. Notwithstanding this, the year 1948 is taken as a milestone, when the Universal Declaration of Human Rights (UDHR) was adopted by the UN General Assembly. It was the first legal document to set out the fundamental human rights to be universally protected and continues to be the foundation of all international human rights law. For the first time, individual rights were pronounced at an international level with the objective of making them binding within nations globally (OHCHR, 2018). Its 30 articles provide the principles and building blocks of current and future human rights conventions, treaties, and other legal instruments. The UDHR, together with the two covenants – the International Covenant on Civil and Political Rights and the International Covenant on Economic, Social and Cultural Rights – makes up the International Bill of Rights (OHCHR, 2018).

Human rights perspectives in Africa seem to neatly fit into such a Eurocentric template and continue to be informed by Northern Global concepts of individual responsibility and not of the community, as in the case of Africa. This anomalous situation continues to reinforce itself in postcolonial Africa despite the fact that many of the continent's countries have been independent for more than five decades or more. Arguably, African legal statutes, academic analyses, and political documents, such as the African Charter on Human Rights, among others, seem to mirror those of the continents' former colonizers and are not sufficiently rooted in Africa's pre-colonial value systems. The African Charter on Human and Peoples' Rights (ACHPR) (also referred to as the Banjul Charter) was adopted in late 1981 and entered into force in 1986. Robertson (2004) observes that it took its emphases from the Organization of African Unity's (OAU's) (forerunner of the African Union (AU)) own Charter, the United Nations (UN) Charter, and the UN Universal Declaration of Human Rights. According to the said author, the African Charter is one of a series of regional human rights documents encouraged by the UN as part of a general strategy for enforcing human rights worldwide, the most effective of which is the European Convention on Human Rights. Mutua (2002, p. 71) highlights some misgivings regarding the African Charter:

The African Charter has attracted criticism because it departs from the narrow formulations of other regional and international human rights instruments. In particular, it codifies the three generations of rights, including the controversial concept of peoples' rights, and imposes duties on individual members of African societies. While a number of scholars have focused attention on apparent tensions between human and peoples' rights, there has been little discussion of the notion of individual duties in the context of the African Charter. Yet a thorough understanding of the meaning of human rights, and the complicated processes through which they are protected and realized, would seem to link inextricably the concepts of human rights, peoples' rights, and duties of individuals. Individual rights cannot make sense in a social and political vacuum, devoid of the duties assumed by individuals. This appears to be truer of Africa than any other place. The individualist, narrow formulation of human rights is ill-suited for the African political and cultural universe.

The abovementioned seems to suggest there was no understanding or conception of human rights in Africa prior to colonialism. However, the difference between Africa and the West was the prism used to interpret human rights. Chigangaidze et al. (2022) argue that Western ethics are rooted in the individual – the autonomous and responsible decision-making individual – but African morality relies on the community. Hansungule's (2010, p. 14) lucidly drives this point home:

> This unit provided for all the individual's material, social and emotional needs. Such kin-based societies are characterised by the overriding emphasis placed on loyalty to the family, and the stress placed on duties rather than rights. In Africa, individualism would not be valued as in the West. Rather, a person would be expected to compromise his or her interests for the good of the larger unit; to stand on one's rights would be thought anti-social. It follows that whenever rights were in issue, they would be the concern of the family or group. The foregoing point has special relevance for the welfare of children. In the African tradition, children's rights were not seen as burden but rather a welcome addition to any household, it would be assured of food, shelter and support. There were no formal mechanisms to protect children, but then none would have been necessary. Abundant land, a subsistence economy, and the highly developed sense of generosity due to all family members, underwrote the support obligations. African law had no concern with a child's rights to a proper upbringing; its interest was in a family's right to claim the child as one of its members.

Notwithstanding the above critical analyses and as mentioned earlier, the basic collective human right to self-determination became a strong pillar in the African Charter on Human and Peoples' Rights. Furthermore, it is important to appreciate how the human rights discourse is gaining ground in Africa. For example, the ACHPR is increasingly entering into the debate on how environmental and socioeconomic rights are interdependent. The ACHPR has in the recent past recognized the importance of a clean and safe environment and links this issue to human rights. Informed by challenges in the Niger Delta in Nigeria, around oil exploitation, the ACHPR recognizes that there is a nexus between socioeconomic rights and to the extent that the environment affects the quality of life and safety of individuals and groups (Ebeku, 2003). However, it can be argued that this debate has not sufficiently included public policy-makers, who still have to embrace this right in practice. For instance, how could we otherwise explain the seeming inability to fundamentally revise Western structural policy application, on the one hand, and political elite complicity with the West, on the other, in several African states, as well as minimal anti-colonial reforms? Indeed, the political economy of resource exploitation has by now provoked massive levels of human rights abuses, inequality, poverty, and environmental destruction on the African continent, a dynamic driven mainly by the World Bank and the IMF in alliance with a small number of oligarchs residing on the African continent – both sides ignoring the basic right of self-determination of human and people's rights (Hanlon, 2022). According to Franciscans International (2003, p. 16), implementing this right as part of a human rights-based development and social work agenda would indeed require a new value system:

> ...whereby human rights are not the residual of other values and belief systems. But rather, an integral part of it. This implies a major cultural shift, or a return to societies' original human values. The humanization of economic systems is necessary.

Africa's Pre-colonial Past and Its Relevance to Present-Day Human Rights Discourses

As mentioned earlier, the pre-colonial period is an important phase of development because it explains Africa in its original sense (Hansungule, 2010). According to Taylor (2018), pre-colonial Africa had a wide diversity of politics and government, which were all related to the type of economic systems in existence at the time. Hunter-gatherers were engaged in a form of nascent communism, while elsewhere three broad systems may be identified: large centralized kingdoms and empires, centralized mid-sized kingdoms, and widely scattered chiefdoms. Political and social identities were generally more related to affiliations, such as sharing a common language, than to being an inhabitant of a particular territory (Taylor, 2018). To understand and appreciate the pre-colonial era, we should cast a glance at the pre-colonial state, which seemed to have been at the center of most human activities. This will also enable us to come to grips with some of postcolonial Africa's political and economic development challenges, among others. More importantly, we will grasp the fact that some of the aspects that undergirded the pre-colonial era continue to endure in the postcolonial era, albeit peripherally. For instance, Olowu (1994) asserts that in spite of the efforts to distort, supplant, and suppress it, the pre-colonial state formation remains the institution which serves the needs of the majority of the African peoples especially in the rural areas, although elements of the pre-colonial state can be discerned even in Africa's largest metropolitan centers (Olowu, 1994). This situation let scholars such as Peter Ekeh (1975) argue that societies in Africa are constituted of two publics: one can be considered as the primordial public, closely identified with primordial groupings, sentiments, and activities, and the other as the civic public, influenced by colonial and postcolonial nation-state building, which is often seen as amoral, lacking the generalized imperative operative in the private realm, and in the primordial public. This distinction is an important one when it comes to decolonizing the Western concept of civil society in Africa and provides us with a necessary reflection when it comes to constructing more self-determined and culturally sensitive social work in postcolonial African countries (Kleibl, 2021).

Emanating from the former, among other things, is gender relations in Africa. Arguably, one distinct feature of pre-colonial Africa, which is rarely factored into contemporary analyses of the continent, is how female-based African pre-colonial societies were constituted. In fact, we would argue that patriarchy is a by-product of colonialism, which was solidified by the political elite after African countries became independent. This is not to say that there was no patriarchy in pre-colonial Africa. Indeed, Ogbomo and Ogbomo (1993) somberly remind us that men have almost everywhere in Africa dominated politics and thus the oral narrative focuses almost exclusively upon political and military affairs omitting other vital contributions women made to their societies in the pre-colonial period. Despite this, however, it was the manner in which patriarchy was elevated in the colonial society and instrumentalized by the colonialists which was alien to Africa.

According to Saidi (2020), in pre-colonial Africa, relations between women and men were varied, changing, and culturally specific, yet there were some common themes. Most African societies attempted to attain forms of heterarchy, which meant they often created several centers of authority and aspired to establish communities where gender relations between women and men were equitable. Additionally, throughout history, most Africans determined status by the amount of labor a group or individual could control, and in a historically underpopulated continent, this meant that motherhood and giving birth to children were very important. The result is that women, both as biological and social mothers and as grandmothers, were highly respected throughout the history of the continent (Saidi, 2020). It has been said that pre-colonial societies were mostly matrilineal (Semwaza, 2013), and this seems to be the case in present times (see, for instance, Chemhuru, 2022; Robinson & Gottlieb, 2021), even though patrilineal societies now dominate where matrilineal ones once existed. Matrilineal in this case relates to societies being anchored in the maternal lineage and not referring to matriarchy (Chemhuru, 2022). In the same vein, there is ample evidence, which suggests that women were not merely spectators of pre-colonial history but actively shaped and defined it. Even though there are regional variations, the common strand, when it comes to pre-colonial African women's roles and responsibilities, was their prominence in almost all the societies or communities across the continent. For instance, Amoah-Boampong and Agyeiwaa (2019) observe that women in pre-colonial West Africa were not a homogenous group that lived static lives relegated to the domestic sphere. Women contested, negotiated, complemented, and transformed their societies through their diverse roles in the political, social, religious, and economic realities of pre-colonial life in West Africa.

In another part of Africa, Moagi and Mtombeni (2020, p. 1113) posit that the women in southern Africa were not restricted to the domestic sphere or oppressed; instead, they played important roles in production, religion, and politics. Women were very active in the public domain: in politics as princesses, queen mothers, and regents and in religion as prophets, diviners, and rainmakers (Moagi & Mtombeni, 2020). Furthermore, it can be argued that the gender division of labor was not rigid in pre-colonial southern Africa as women could cross over to male-type duties and sometimes the sexes complemented each other (see also Jaji & Kleibl, 2020). The social, economic, and political domains were therefore not exclusively for men; they were for both sexes. In short, women in pre-colonial southern Africa were independent; they controlled their bodies, owned their labor, and determined their destinies argued by Moagi and Mtombeni (2020).

We might therefore further argue that by extension, women probably had more rights in the pre-colonial than in the colonial era. Specifically, if we talk about equality and equity, in

> pre-colonial era, there was equilibrium in accessing privileges and chances between men and women; such equal balance was defined by division of labor and specialization. In the colonial phase, however, colonialists favored men and infused the concept of Victorian women in all colonial projects; subsequently, the patriarchal system started to have its hold on African lives. Consequently, the modern African communities have entered into an independence era while incorporating the colonial patriarchal structures into their modern communities. Surprisingly, researchers on the topic under discussion continuously find African cultures' guilt as they still offer patronage to such inequalities as it was in the pre-colonial epoch. Henceforth, its obliteration is essential in a long walk to gender equalities on the continent (Mikidady, 2022, p. 1).

The gender relations in some pre-colonial and contemporary regions of Africa described above illustrate the importance of a deeper understanding of societal structural determinants and how ignorantly Western social work has so far looked at the continent, negating its human progress and failing to address economic relations of exploitation with which it is intertwined. To discuss this situation further, we now delve a little deeper into the developments of social work in the Global North and link them to the developments of the profession on the African continent.

Social Work as a Human Rights Profession in Africa

According to Kleibl and Xypolytas (2020), since its origin, social work was closely associated with the emerging Western capitalist industrial society of the late nineteenth century. While its history can be tracked in different ways and from various perspectives, the confrontation with the "social question," which became more and more urgent at the time, was always central to social work's ambition. In Britain, the Charity Organization Society (COS) tried to respond to the increasing misery of large parts of its population with distinguishing between the "deserving" and "undeserving" poor based on a scientific "case-by-case" analysis, hence, displaying all of the prejudices of the English middle classes of the time, while ignoring large sections of the workers' movement which tried to make the social question obsolete by fighting for a socialist overthrow of capitalism. The COS approach was later significantly challenged from the "settlement movement," which arose around 1880 (Ferguson, 2009).

The settlement reformist social movement aimed to directly support the increasingly struggling urban poor, often immigrant, workers' communities. At its high point around the 1920s, in particular British and American social workers, inspired from the work of Jane Addams, an American sociologist, feminist, and peace activist, followed the broad vision of the movement, which was to bring the rich and the poor, as well as the various cultural influences from immigrant communities together, in physical proximity and social interconnectedness. Through the establishment of the so-called settlement houses in poor urban areas, services such as day care, education, and healthcare were provided for the marginalized poor, alongside community organizing and support for the unification of exploited workers (Wade, 2004). These social work strategies, in a Gramscian (1971) sense, could be viewed as a temptation to create a new "common sense" linked to a multitude of cultural worldviews. They were also part of a political social work response to the structural barriers poor immigrant families were facing in their spatially segregated neighborhoods. From this contradictory mix, it was, however, primarily the individual and charity-orientated social work that was exported to the Global South, specifically Africa, during colonial rule. Ironically, social work's role in supporting community organizing, respecting cultural diversity, and supporting political consciousness building was clearly neglected, or in other words, those involved into community and political social work in Europe did not extend their views beyond their own contexts and nation-states and never even attempted to learn from the rich African experience of kinship care, community responsibility, and movements of self-determination. Furthermore, with the transition from colonial rule to formally independent African nation-states, the development of social work in Africa can be specifically associated with the narrative of civilizing the poor, white charity, and aid programs for the supposedly underdeveloped. This in turn can be traced back to the work of Christian missionaries and the colonial authorities' agenda of using the civilization narrative and its false moral underpinning for exploiting the colonies for the benefit of Europe (Noyoo & Kleibl, 2020).

Above all, it is important to note that missionaries were the forerunners of colonialism. Thus, alongside their preaching, missionaries began to introduce some social welfare services such as schools and clinics and later social work. Colonialism provided the sociopolitical context and general environment in which social work in Africa was initiated. The introduction of social work in Africa was characterized by case work and community mobilization, especially through rural development projects (Mwansa & Kreitzer, 2012, p. 398). Due to the cited European origin of the profession, Mwansa (2011) argues that social work has not been the product of a progressive social metamorphosis, but rather that of foreign methodologies imposed on African societies. Consequently, the essence of social work education lacks relevance in terms of its philosophical, value, and ideological base. That being said, some African scholars still regard social work as still in its infancy. For example, Chitereka (2009) is of the view that social work in Africa is a relatively young profession, which was introduced on the continent in the 1960s. Although the first school of social work – the Cairo School of Social Work in Egypt – was established in 1937, the profession did not take root until the 1960s. This is because most African countries were once colonized and then they attained independence in rapid succession in the 1960s. Nevertheless, in his discussion, Chitereka (2009) does not include South Africa which had earlier centers of social work education and training.

When we talk of social work's supposedly natural affinity to human rights, we cannot be guided by this paradoxical history of its origins, but perhaps by its evolution, whereby at a certain juncture it had to arrive at some principles. According to the International Federation of Social Workers (IFSW) (2014), the principles of social work are social justice, human rights, collective responsibility, and respect for diversities central to social work. Moreover, we concur with Ife (2012, p. 6) who notes that a human rights perspective from below (rather than imposed from above) can strengthen social work and that it provides a strong basis for an assertive practice that seeks to realize the social justice goals of social workers, in whatever setting, providing space for oppressed and marginalized people and communities to voice the injustices they experience on a day-to-day bases in an exclusionary capitalistic global system. Human rights, however, are also contested and problematic when they are applied in a selective and purposive way from above, as it is very frequently the case in many African and Global South contexts. Hence, to develop a human rights basis for social work requires that the idea of human rights, and the problems and criticisms associated with it, be carefully and critically examined. According to Reynaert et al. (2022), human rights are foundational to social work, as recognized in the global definition, leading many to consider social work a human rights profession. Although the idea of human rights has become an important compass and theoretical approach for social work, comprehensive frameworks for understanding the "practice" of human rights in social work are still limited. Only recently, attempts have been made to fill this gap. Therefore, for human rights and social work to resonate with African realities and practicalities, we call for their radical and urgent decolonization.

Decolonizing the Discourse and Future Prospects: Linking Individual, Community, and Collective Rights to Human Rights and Social Work in Africa

Due to Arica's colonial heritage, there have been resounding calls made by some African and other scholars to reconceptualize, indigenize, and decolonize social work on the continent. For example, Osei-Hwedie (1993) observes that the need for indigenization is based on the realization that social work in Africa failed to respond appropriately to the major social problems confronting the continent. In his view, the social work profession is heavily influenced by Western theory, and no meaningful attempts have been made to ensure that the profession fits into the social, economic, and practical environment in which it operates. Rwomire and Raditlhokwa (1996, p. 15) seem to echo Osei-Hwedie and express their skepticism when it comes to the adoption of radical social work in Africa, which in many instances is taken as proxy for indigenization or decolonization:

> Although some academic social workers in Africa adopt a radical posture in their writing, we are aware that none of the schools of social work in Africa offers a progressive or radical educational programme. This observation applies even to educational curricula of schools in the so-called democratic states…

Further afield, scholars such as Kleibl (2019, p. 9) weigh in on the issue of decolonizing social work:

> The language of decolonization is nowadays used by many indigenous, Afro-diasporan and other social activists and scholars. It is driven by a profound critique in relation to the process and structural discrimination that emerged out of colonialism and the impact colonialism has until today. Many of the scholars and activists involved in the discourse of, and

actions aimed at, decolonization demand deep changes within postcolonial national, transnational, and international state - society relationships, the transformation of the global capitalist economy, and a revaluing of cultural and collective rights as well as feminisms within the international debates about sustainable development.

We argue that not only was the conception of human rights intrinsic to the African way of life, prior to colonial oppression, but it is in synch with the value systems of most African communities and ethnic groups which are underpinned by the philosophy of *Ubuntu* (a word derived from Nguni groups of southern Africa) or *botho* (as expressed by the Sotho/Tswana groups of southern Africa) or *butu* (by the Lozi or Barotse people of Western Zambia or Barotseland). Chigangaidze et al. (2022, p. 320) go further and show the universality of *Ubuntu* in Africa:

> Ubuntuism is an African philosophical framework that is characterised by interconnectedness of all things and beings; the spiritual nature of people; their collective/individual identity and the collective/inclusive nature of family structure; oneness of mind, body, and spirit; and the value of interpersonal relationships. The philosophy is known in different languages in Africa including *bomoto* (Congo); *gimuntu* (Angola); *umunthu* (Malawi); *vumutu* (Mozambique); *vumuntu*, *vhutu* (South Africa); *humhunu/ubuthosi* (Zimbabwe); *bumuntu* (Tanzania); umuntu (Uganda) to mention but a few…

Ubuntu is a concept which is the principle of caring for each other's well-being and acknowledges the fact that people are people through other people. It also recognizes both the rights and the responsibilities of every citizen in promoting individual and societal well-being (Department of Welfare & Population Development, 1997, p. 9). Wherever one goes in sub-Saharan Africa, the notion of *Ubuntu* abounds, and even though it may be expressed in different names, it still refers to the same spirit of human solidarity that has protected African communities against social dislocation for thousands of years. Therefore, for social work to be decolonized and human rights to have meaning in Africa, they must incorporate kingship care and other forms of indigenous solidarity and all together a political momentum calling for the urgency of dismantling the current system in order to let something new emerge.

When we mention kingship care, we allude to those pre-colonial institutions that survived colonial assaults and postcolonial neglect (Noyoo, 2022) which responded and continue to meet the needs of the vast majority of Africans who are not incorporated into the so-called modern sector. Some examples of the former are Indigenous Social Security Systems, which can be defined as:

> Mechanisms of care and organic safety-nets emanating from Africa's pre-colonial past, which survived colonial onslaughts and post-colonial State neglect, which are employed by Africans to support each other in times of need and during social and economic crises, and which assist the most vulnerable, marginalised and excluded members of African societies to sustain their livelihoods. They are naturally occurring and intrinsic to particular communities across Africa and are characterised by strong bonds of solidarity and buttressed by value-systems, philosophies, cultures and traditions, which enjoin all members to relate to each other in a mutually obligatory and reciprocal manner. (Noyoo, 2022, p. 2)

What need to be underscored in the above definition are the notions of *mutual obligation* and *reciprocity and hence social and relational accountability*. The idea of mutual obligation in pre-colonial Africa was part of family and community responsibilities, and there was no need to enforce them. Therefore, decolonizing human rights in Africa would involve transformation from human rights organized around a state-determined practice to one that is focused on a people-centric approach that empowers individuals and collectives to decide how human rights would be understood and integrated into their communities (An-Naim, 2021).

Conclusion

In this chapter, we explored how the notion of human rights and the practice of social care could further be embedded in an African way of life. We argued that even though there seemed to be a broad acceptance of social work as a human rights profession in many African societies, social work was still at variance with the deeply rooted cultural practice of kinship care and community responsibility on the continent. The chapter was also able to bring to light the discrepancy between cultural practices in kinship care, community responsibility, and ongoing need for self-determined social development in Africa, on the one hand, and social work education and practice, on the other. Furthermore, the chapter was able to illuminate the divide between Africa's kinship care and community responsibility, which still needs to be bridged through more collective, participatory, solidarity-based, and resistance-experienced social work approaches, defined on the continent with its people and communities. In the final part of the chapter, we call for the decolonization of human rights and social work discourses in Africa through supporting human rights "from below." Among other things, we advocate for indigenous systems of care and indigenous social security systems to be at the center of a decolonized human rights and social work agenda in Africa. We also propose, in the case of Africa, that the African philosophy of *Ubuntu* should undergird the foregoing approach. This should certainly include joining the decolonizing movement building efforts of more independent local political groups, which are gaining momentum through the multitude of resistances against the ongoing neocolonial practices of resource exploitation. The latter should certainly be a specific matter of concern for social work in the context of Africa and be supported by global social work attempts to re-politicize the discipline and profession, reminding itself to its "old" linkages with more progressive movements such as the settlement movement in the 1920s, as well as the women and worker's movements prior and after World War II.

Discussion Questions

1. How can an African perspective help us better understand non-Western-oriented human rights?
2. Can you explain how the African concepts of kinship care, responsibility, and self-determination are compatible with social work practice?

References

Amin, S. (2014). Understanding the political economy of contemporary Africa. *African Development, 19*(1), 15–36.
Amoah-Boampong, C., & Agyeiwaa, C. (2019). Women in pre-colonial Africa: West Africa. In O. Yacob-Haliso & T. Falola (Eds.), *The Palgrave handbook of African women's studies* (pp. 1099–1112). Palgrave Macmillan. https://doi.org/10.1007/978-3-319-77030-7_126-1
An-Naim, A. A. (2021). *Decolonizing human rights*. Cambridge University Press.
Chemhuru, M. (2022). *Environmental justice in African philosophy*. Routledge.
Chigangaidze, R. K., Matanga, A. A., & Katsuro, T. R. (2022). Ubuntu philosophy as a humanistic -existential framework for the fight against the COVID-19 pandemic. *Journal of Humanistic Psychology, 62*(3), 319–333. https://doi.org/10.1177/00221678211044554
Chitereka, C. (2009). Social work practice in a developing continent: The case of Africa. *Advances in Social Work, 10*(2), 144–156.
Conte, A., & Burchill, R. (2016). *Chapter 1 – Introduction*. https://www.google.de/books/edition/Defining_Civil_and_Political_Rights/DgcpDAAAQBAJ?hl=en&gbpv=1&dq=Defining+human+rights&printsec=frontcover
Ebeku, K. S. A. (2003). The right to a satisfactory environment and the African commission. *African Human Rights Law Journal, 3*(1), 149–166.
Ekeh, P. (1975). Colonialism and the Two Publics in Africa: A Theoretical Statement. *Comparative Studies in Society and History. 17*(1), 91–112.
Fanon, F. (1963). *The wretched of the earth*. Grove Weidenfeld.
Ferguson, I. (2009). Another social work is possible! Reclaiming the radical tradition. In V. Leskosek (Ed.), *Theories and methods of social work, exploring different perspectives* (pp. 81–98). University of Ljubljana.
Franciscans International (2003). The Right to Development: Reflections on the First Four Reports of the Independent Expert on the Right to Development. Geneva: Franciscans International.
Gann, L. H. (1958). *The birth of a plural society*. Manchester University Press.
Gaye, M. (1998). Western influences and activities in Africa. *Journal of Third World Studies, 15*(1), 65–78.
Gramsci, A. (1971). *Selections from the prison notebooks*. International Publishers.
Hanlon, J. (2022). How the IMF and World Bank caused a resource curve and civil war in Mozambique. In *LSE working paper series* (pp. 22–209).
Hansungule, M. (2010). The historical development of international human rights. In A. R. Chowdhury & J. H. Bhuiyan (Eds.), *An introduction to international human rights law* (pp. 1–28). Brill.
Ife, J. (2012). *Human rights and social work: Towards rights-based practice* (3rd ed.). Cambridge University Press.
Ikuenobe, P. (2018). Human rights, personhood, dignity, and African communalism. *Journal of Human Rights, 17*(5), 589–604. https://doi.org/10.1080/14754835.2018.1533455. ISSN 1475-4835.
International Federation of Social Workers (IFSW). (2014). *Global definition of social work*. https://www.ifsw.org/what-is-social-work/global-definition-of-social-work/
Jackson, R. H., & Rosberg, C. G. (1998). Personal rule: Theory and practice in Africa. In P. Lewis (Ed.), *Africa: Dilemmas of development and change* (pp. 17–42). Routledge.
Jaji, R., & Kleibl, T. (2020). Women's empowerment: Unravelling the cultural incompatibility myth in Zimbabwe. In T. Kleibl, R. Lutz, N. Noyoo, B. Bunk, A. Dittmann, & B. Seepamore (Eds.), *The Routledge handbook of post-colonial social work* (pp. 233–244). Routledge.
Kleibl, T. (2019). Part I: Postcolonial social work perspectives and approaches. In T. Kleibl, R. Lutz, N. Noyoo, B. Bunk, A. Dittmann, & B. Seepamore (Eds.), *The Routledge handbook of post-colonial social work* (pp. 9–11). Routledge.
Kleibl, T. (2021). *Decolonizing civil society in Mozambique*. Bloomsbury/ZED Books.

Kleibl, T., & Xypolytas, N. (2020). Oppression or liberation? The function of social work in migration management. In R. Munck, T. Kleibl, M. C. dos Santos Goncalves, & P. Dankova (Eds.), *Migration and social transformation: Engaged perspectives* (pp. 285–306). Machdohnil.

Klinghoffer, A. J. (1973). Modernization and political development in Africa. *The Journal of Modern African Studies, 11*(1), 1–19.

Mann, M., & Delap, E. (2020). *Kinship care in Sub-Saharan Africa: An asset worth supporting*. https://www.adamfoghana.com/wordpress/wp-content/uploads/2021/05/kinshipcareinsubsaharanafrica6final12_2020.pdf

Mikidady, M. M. (2022). Gender inequality: An alien practice to African cultural settlement. *Universal Journal of History and Culture, 4*(1), 1–15.

Ministry of Welfare & Population Development. (1997). White paper for social welfare. *Government Gazette, 386*(18166). Government Printer.

Moagi, A. L., & Mtombeni, B. (2020). Women in pre-colonial Africa: Southern Africa. In O. Yacob-Haliso & T. Falola (Eds.), *The Palgrave handbook of African women's studies* (pp. 1113–1132). Palgrave Macmillan. https://doi.org/10.1007/978-3-319-77030-7_125-1

Mutua, M. (2002). *Human rights: A political and cultural critique*. University of Pennsylvania Press.

Mwansa, L.-K. (2011). Social work education in Africa: Whence and whither? *Social Work Education, 30*(1), 4–16. https://doi.org/10.1080/02615471003753148

Mwansa, L. K., & Kreitzer, L. (2012). Social work in Africa. In K. Lyons, T. Hokenstad, M. Pawar, N. Huegler, & N. Hall (Eds.), *The SAGE handbook of international social work* (pp. 389–393). SAGE Publications.

Nkrumah, K. (1965). *Neo-colonialism: The last stage of imperialism*. Thomas Nelson & Sons, Ltd.

Nmehielle, V. O. O. (2001). *The African human rights system: Its laws, practice, and institutions*. Martinus Nijhoff Publishers.

Noyoo, N. (2014, May). *Indigenous systems of governance and post-colonial Africa: The case of Barotseland*. Presented at the conference on African indigenous knowledge systems. Johannesburg, South Africa. https://www.international-arbitration-attorney.com/professor-ndangwa-noyoo-comments-barotseland-issue/

Noyoo, N. (2022, November). *Incorporating indigenous social security systems into post-colonial social policy formulation in Africa*. Conference on International Comparative Perspectives to Social Security. Engagement Global gGmbH and GIZ, November 2022, Berlin, Germany.

Noyoo, N., & Kleibl, T. (2020). Introduction: Setting the scene for critical new social work approaches in the neoliberal era. In *The Routledge handbook of postcolonial social work* (pp. 1–8). Routledge.

Ogbomo, O. W., & Ogbomo, Q. O. (1993). Women and society in pre-colonial Iyede. *Anthropos, 88*, 431–441.

Olowu, D. (1994, January). *The nature and character of the African state*. Paper presented at the African Association for Public Administration and Management (AAPAM) 15th Roundtable, January 1994, Banjul, Gambia.

Osei-Hwedie, K. (1993). The challenge of social work in Africa: Starting the indigenization process. *Journal of Social Development in Africa, 8*(1), 19–30.

Przetacznik, F. (1990). The basic collective human right to self-determination of peoples and nations as a prerequisite for peace. *NYLS Journal of Human Rights, 8*(1), 3.

Reynaert, D., Nachtergaele, S., De Stercke, N., Gobeyn, H., & Roose, R. (2022). Social work as a human rights profession: An action framework. *British Journal of Social Work, 52*, 928–945.

Robertson, D. (2004). *A dictionary of human rights* (2nd ed.). Routledge.

Robinson, A., & Gottlieb, J. (2021). How to close the gender gap in political participation: Lessons from matrilineal societies in Africa. *British Journal of Political Science, 51*(1), 68–92. https://doi.org/10.1017/S0007123418000650

Rwomire, A., & Raditlhokwa, L. (1996). Social work in Africa: Issues and challenges. *Journal of Social Development in Africa, 11*(2), 5–19.

Saidi, C. (2020). *Women in precolonial Africa*. https://oxfordre.com/africanhistory/display/10.1093/acrefore/9780190277734.001.0001/acrefore-9780190277734-e-259;jsessionid=8AB44EFEA90649617798F6C2B9BF0524

Semwaza, F. (2013). Surveying epistemology: Discursive impacts on the African understanding of childhood stories. *Childhood in Africa: An Interdisciplinary Journal, 3*(1), 1–11.

Taylor, I. (2018). *African politics: A very short introduction*. Oxford University Press.

Taylor-Gooby, P. (2008). Equality, rights and social justice. In P. Alcock, M. May, & K. Rowlingson (Eds.), *The student's companion to social policy* (pp. 34–41). Blackwell Publishing.

Tucci, S., & Akey, J. M. (2019).The long walk to African genomics. *Genome Biol, 20*, 1–3. https://doi.org/10.1186/s13059-019-1740-1

United Nations Human Rights Office of the High Commissioner (OHCHR). (2018). *What are human rights?* https://www.ohchr.org/en/what-are-human-rights

Wade, L. C. (2004). *Settlement houses*. http://www.encyclopedia.chicagohistory.org/pages/1135.html

Ndangwa Noyoo is a Professor at the University of Cape Town (UCT) in South Africa. He holds a Doctor of Philosophy (Ph.D.) from the University of the Witwatersrand, Master of Philosophy (MPhil) in Development Studies from the University of Cambridge, and Bachelor of Social Work (BSW) from the University of Zambia. He was also a Postdoctoral Fellow at the Fondation Maison des Sciences de l'Homme (FMSH) Paris, France.

Tanja Kleibl is Professor in Social Work, Migration, and Diversity at the Technical University of Würzburg-Schweinfurt (FHWS), Germany, and Research Associate at the University of Johannesburg, South Africa. She is also Director of the Master's Program "International Social Work with Refugees and Migrants." She served as Professor for Scientific Foundations of Social Work at the University of Applied Sciences Augsburg and Associate Professor for Social Work at the Catholic University of Applied Sciences Munich. Her research and teaching focus on discourses and concepts in development, migration and mobility, civil society, as well postcolonial theory and governance in the Global South. She currently holds a 3-year research chair in participatory action research in Northern Mozambique. She brings together 15 years of extensive practice and research experience in development cooperation and migration.

Part III
Human Rights Mandate in Social Work

Chapter 6
Mapping Basic Human Rights Instruments

Mark Lusk and Nicholas D. Natividad

Introduction

While the term human rights is of recent origin, having emerged in the post-World War II context as a set of ideas and principles that supersede national and local laws and norms, the concepts that undergird contemporary human rights are rooted in long-held religious concepts as well as in ancient philosophy. It has to be said that the unprecedented international catastrophes of the two world wars of the twentieth century created a historical moment when existing ideas about the law of nations simply failed as an organizing structure for preventing the genocide, industrial warfare, and mass destruction of protracted conflict on a global scale. The existence of places like Auschwitz and Buchenwald affirmed that for civilization to be preserved, a new way of looking at each other was crucial to human advancement and to avoid repeating anything like the Holocaust. Yet, there was no preexisting vocabulary to articulate the inherent principles that would put human dignity at the center of an international structure of thought that would guide nations and peoples in their treatment of human beings. Thus, we see the emergence and flowering of human rights and the covenants, treaties, and international instruments that codify them.

M. Lusk (✉)
School of Social Work, New Mexico State University, Las Cruces, NM, USA
e-mail: marklusk@nmsu.edu

N. D. Natividad
Department of Criminal Justice, Department of Borderlands and Ethnic Studies, New Mexico State University, Las Cruces, NM, USA
e-mail: ndn@nmsu.edu

M. Madew et al. (eds.), *Decolonized Approaches to Human Rights and Social Work*,
https://doi.org/10.1007/978-3-031-33030-8_6

Background

Most religious traditions have at the core of their beliefs an idea about the inherent worth and dignity of persons, but theological traditions can be seen as giving greater emphasis to the duties, obligations, and responsibilities of persons, rather than rights. Notwithstanding, all of the global great religions include humanistic ideals that anticipate contemporary conceptions of human rights (Ishay, 2004). The concept of human rights has entered the vocabulary of contemporary theology as modern conditions have challenged traditional beliefs. With their emphasis on marginalized populations, human dignity, and the fundamental equality of all people, theologies of liberation exemplify this development (Lusk & Corbett, 2021).

Ancient philosophy provides the foundation for contemporary human rights ideas. Over 2000 years ago, Confucius developed an ethical system that anticipates human rights ideals. Notably, he argued that all people, including the so-called commoners, had equal human qualities and sensibilities of reason and awareness that could be developed through education and the role of the state is to develop and cultivate these qualities by providing for the moral welfare of its citizens (Ishay, 2004). Ancient philosophers in the Western world further laid a foundation in the ethical systems elaborated by the Stoics who argued that humans are rational beings subject to natural law by which all are equal under the law and must be given fair treatment and a guarantee of justice regardless of nationality or identity (Horowitz, 1974).

Prior to the Renaissance and Enlightenment when the foundations of modern democracy and what was called the rights of man were fully developed, King John of England was forced to sign the *Magna Carta Libertatum* (Great Charter of Freedoms). This document, which established that the king was subject to the rule of the law, ended absolute monarchy. It elaborated the basis for habeas corpus rights against false arrest and imprisonment and laid the groundwork for due process. Although the charter was later repealed, it had a lasting influence on the development of English common law and shaped later documents such as the American constitution (Klug, 2015). The Magna Carta, while it did advance the concept of rights, extended those rights only to property-owning men. In contrast, human rights are universal and belong to all persons.

The emergence of universal rights as an intrinsic entitlement for all people solidified during the Enlightenment. This largely European intellectual movement of the seventeenth and eighteenth centuries established the centrality of human freedom, choice, tolerance, reason, science in human affairs, and governance. A key Enlightenment idea that persists today is the notion that societies continuously *progress* forward toward higher levels of freedom and inclusion, especially when they are organized as democracies. Echoing that sentiment today, US Chief Justice Sonia Sotomayor states, "…I truly believe in the magical words, the arc of the universe bends toward justice" (Marcus, 2022).

A series of groundbreaking texts provided the philosophical and moral basis for rights in a democracy. John Locke's *The Second Treatise of Civil Government* (1689) introduces several key ideas that continue to inform political philosophy today. The concept that laws exist to benefit the "public good" departs from monarchist views and forms a central idea in modern democracy. Locke also discusses the concept of the "laws of nature" by which human freedom is regulated by universal laws based on reason that govern humans who are born as equals under natural law and in which there is no inherent and preexisting natural hierarchy among people. The state of human freedom is mediated by a social contract wherein citizens enter an unwritten mutual contract and agree to a common consent to conform to a government that enforces the laws of nature – a government that applies the law equally and without favor or prejudice.

The contractual relationship of humans to their government is fully developed in Jean-Jacques Rousseau's *The Social Contract* (1762). He argues the laws in a state of nature were corrupted as a result of the primacy of private property and the development of class hierarchy and social and economic inequality. To resolve the inequality and resulting subserviency that shaped human society, Rousseau contends that the social contact restores inherent equality and moral dilemmas of modern society – one based on competition, conflict, and property. Legitimate political power, he argued, was only possible in a society where people organize themselves under democratic rule in which the government exists and functions with the consent of the governed, thereby guaranteeing that the rights of the individual are not overridden by the powers of the propertied classes or by a tyranny of the majority. These ideas were at the core of the French Revolution.

Thomas Paine was a British-American who provided much of the rationale for the American revolutionary secession from Britain. His brief essay *Common Sense* (1776), like Rousseau, argued that by nature, men are born into equality and that monarchy is an unnatural form of government because it denies citizens their inherent rights. Failing as a government to serve its people, British rule was to be expelled to pave way for representative democracy in which the colonies united as one nation in a federal union. In the *Rights of Man* (1791–2), Paine proposed universal suffrage for men over 21, progressive income-based taxation, universal public education, and pensions for the elderly, poor, and unemployed. Against the backdrop of the French Revolution, he contended that to ensure liberty and security, each citizen must be given political power through the right to vote and in the event that a government ceases to be representative, citizens have the right and obligation to overthrow it. He contends that with rights come responsibilities, notably the obligation to protect the rights of others. As he succinctly phrases it, "A Declaration of Rights is, by reciprocity, a Declaration of Duties also. Whatever is my right as a man is also the right of another; and it becomes my duty to guarantee as well as to possess" (Paine, 1792).

Key Documents: Constitution of the United States

Several notable documents reflect the Enlightenment in practice, which is the application of the concept of natural rights in the organization and administration of government. One of the most remarkable and influential documents was the Constitution of the United States (1787) and the Bill of Rights (1789), which amended the original document and specified the rights of citizens in a federal republic. The Constitution has influenced governments around the globe and has served as a model for emerging democracies as they transitioned from colonial rule to independence. The document elaborates a tripartite form of government that functions as system of checks and balances, in which each branch of government (the executive, legislative, and judicial) carries out complementary functions that act to balance power and to limit executive overreach or despotic rule. While recent events in the United States have severely challenged the integrity of the balance of power, to date, no single branch of government has monopolized power under a single division.

In addition to organizing government into three branches, the Constitution articulates a sharing of power between individual state governments and the federal government. This shared division of power, known as federalism, allows for state-level priorities to be decided at that level subject to congressional and judicial oversight. It could be argued that these two systems of shared governance work to protect the rights of the individual. This was clearly not the case under the original document for either women or slaves. Once slavery was outlawed and women were granted suffrage, problems with state's rights have persisted. Historically, states have been in multiple standoffs in America's past to deny individual rights through racist voting requirements, racial segregation, and gerrymandering. State barriers to voting persist today.

The most important legacy of the Constitution is the elaboration of a set of rights that comprise the first ten amendments to the document, which were adopted simultaneously in 1789 and are known as the *Bill of Rights*. These include freedom of speech, the press, religion, assembly, and petition. Also included are the rights of *due process* for accused persons – trial by jury, freedom from self-incrimination, legal representation, fair and speedy trial, and freedom from cruel or unusual punishment. Three notable amendments further advanced individual rights – the 13th Amendment abolished slavery (1865), the 15th Amendment prohibits the denial of the right to vote based on race or color (1869), the 19th Amendment prohibits the denial of the right to vote based on sex (1919), and the 24th Amendment prohibits revocation of voting rights due to no payment of a poll tax (1962).

In retrospect, it may be too easy to dismiss the significance of the Constitution, yet we must acknowledge that there were no truly representative democracies in the mid-eighteenth century. By the separation of powers and establishment of the rights of citizens, the Constitution had a profound historical global impact (Rosenthal & Henkin, 1990). As other European colonies secured independence, many, if not most, modeled their own governments on the principles of the American Constitution as it decolonized itself from British rule.

That being said, the influence of the US Constitution today is in decline as two global trends have emerged. The first is a distinct shift toward authoritarian nationalism in established and emerging democracies (the United Kingdom, Hungary, Serbia, Poland, the Philippines, Poland, Tunisia, Brazil, Turkey) and as authoritarian states become more hard line (Russia, China, North Korea, Iran, Myanmar, Belarus) (Repucci & Slipovich, 2022). According the Freedom House, an independent research organization that monitors political rights and civil liberties, democracy, and freedom is in a 16-year decline in which attacks on liberal democracy and self-government based on human rights have accelerated by authoritarian movements that promote hatred, patriarchy, violence, and unrestrained power (Repucci & Slipovich, 2022).

Over 60 countries have experienced democratic declines during the past decade, including in major Western democracies such as the United States, where democratic institutions are under attack by far-right groups as exemplified by the insurrection and violent assault on the US Capitol on January 6, 2021 (Repucci & Slipovich, 2022). Countries with advanced and mature democracies, such as Germany, have been challenged by white nationalist movements and neo-Nazi organizations. Western democracies have experienced efforts to undermine election, attack freedom of the press, discriminate in the treatment of immigrants and refugees, repress the rights of LGBTQ persons, and subvert the rule of law. In the meantime, established authoritarian countries have consolidated central power under the rule of a single authoritarian ruler. Vladimir Putin, seeking to reestablish the former Russian Empire, invaded Ukraine (the so-called Little Russia) to be reunited and restore it to its "rightful place" as part of Mother Russia, an effort to recapture former subordinate states and subject them to neo-imperial rule (Putin, 2022). China, which has long since subjugated neighboring Tibet, has increasingly rattled sabers over Taiwan and openly expressed its intent to dominate the Asian region (Schuman, 2022; Cheng-Hin Lim & Cibulka, 2018).

In the context of the rise of authoritarian nationalism and antidemocratic movements, the influence of key documents like the US Constitution is in decline, even in the nation governed by that same document. A second trend has also shaped the movement away from a hegemonic constitutionalism based on an American model, notably the emergence of a global constitutionalism that is based more on human rights instruments. A global consensus has emerged since the founding of the United Nations that national documents governing the rights of citizens should be modeled more closely to current global instruments such as the Universal Declaration of Human Rights (Law & Versteeg, 2012). At the same time, recent US Supreme Court rulings have been shaped by a historically conservative court, thereby giving rise to rulings that grant corporations the same rights accorded to persons and upholding radical interpretations of the second Amendment which details the right to bear arms – a "right" that is hardly part of the human rights tradition.

Key Documents: Declaration des Droits de l'Homme et du Citoyen

Another critically important document that laid the foundation of contemporary human rights is the French Declaration of the Rights of Man and of the Citizen (1789). This charter of human liberties was compromised of 17 articles that paralleled the US Bill of Rights. The document, which reflects French Enlightenment thinkers such a Rousseau, Voltaire, and Montesquieu, became part of the Constitution of 1789 and was the foundation of the French Republic.

The French charter sets out "the natural, unalienable and sacred rights of man" and includes the right of equality by which "Men are born and remain free and equal in rights. Social distinctions may be based only on considerations of the common good" (Élysée, 2022, p. 1). Among natural rights are liberty, property, safety, and resistance to oppression. Liberty is defined as being able to do anything that does not harm others. The document also guarantees rights of due process, free speech, and freedom from unlawful punishment. It also prescribes the separation of powers in government and asserts that taxes are to be paid by all in proportion to their means (progressive taxation). The effect of the declaration was effectively to end the privileges of the aristocracy and to bring an end to feudalism in France. By virtue of its universalist claim that all men are born and remain free and equal in rights, the document is a precursor to the United Nations Universal Declaration of Human Rights (1948) and the European Convention on Human Rights (1950) (Élysée, 2022).

The French declaration, like its American counterpart, did not revoke slavery nor did it extend the rights it elaborated to women. The document had influence on the Haitian Revolution of 1791–1803 and that nation's abolition of slavery in 1793, the first colonial nation to do so (Moyn, 2018; Blackburn, 2006). The French declaration granted rights to male "active citizens" who held property and excluded women, servants, and slaves, although slaves were not permitted in European France. The Jacobins outlawed slavery in the French colonies in 1794, but it was reinstated by Napoleon in 1802.

Pioneers: Mary Wollstonecraft

Before turning to contemporary human rights documents, it is important to name at least two less well-known human rights pioneers. Drawing from the ideas of the Enlightenment and liberal humanism, Mary Wollstonecraft, a groundbreaking English feminist, made the case that women have a fully rational understanding of the world and argued against the "tyranny of men." She appealed for equal access of women to education and the professions and denounced the gendered organization of society. In her powerful monograph on the rights of women, she rebelled against notions of feminine docility and frailty (González, 1997). She made the case for a revision of the French Constitution to grant equal rights to women and contended that men were in no position to decide what is best for women (Clapham, 2015). Wollstonecraft asserted that women gave the appearance of inequality and superficiality only because of their limited access to schooling. Her work was a counterpoint to Rousseau who had argued on behalf of personal rights, but did not believe in liberty for women. Given the time and place, her statements were groundbreaking. "I do not wish them [women] to have power over men; but over themselves" (Wollstonecraft, 1792). Wollstonecraft was among the very first feminists and in many ways laid the foundation for women's suffrage (Rowlatt, 2015). Her legacy was felt in the post-Enlightenment international women's rights movement and directly influenced Europe's first suffragists (Botting, 2006). Her book *A Vindication of the Rights of Woman: With Strictures on Political and Moral Subjects* (1792) built the foundation of modern feminism and gender quality and was a precursor to the suffrage movement.

Notwithstanding the influence of early European feminism, universal suffrage advanced through Europe and the colonies slowly. The Australian colony granted women the right to vote in 1902. Women obtained suffrage in the Grand Duchy of Finland in 1906 and Norway followed in 1913. Great Britain granted the right to vote to women in 1918 under the Representation of the People Act. The United States amended its constitution in 1920 to guarantee women's right to vote. France was a bit of an outlier in Europe awarding women suffrage in 1944.

Pioneers: Bartolomé de las Casas

Born in Sevilla, Bartolomé de las Casas migrated to Hispaniola where he taught catechism and was later ordained as a priest, perhaps the first Catholic to be ordained in the Americas. He witnessed the brutality of the Spanish conquest firsthand and became a strong advocate for the rights of the indigenous Americans, who were murdered en masse and stripped of their land through the establishment of *encomiendas*, Spanish estates on indigenous lands that subordinated Amerindians to forced labor. A Dominican, de las Casas was appointed bishop and served in Guatemala. Over the course of his life, he prolifically wrote and advocated for reform in the treatment of indigenous people and argued on their behalf in Madrid where he was successful in moderating the encomienda system and the means by which Amerindians were evangelized. His book, *A Short Account of the Destruction of the Indies* (1542), tells the gruesome story of the mass slaughter, torture, and enslavement of the indigenous peoples by the Spanish. Notably, he also chronicled the lives of the indigenous people by transcribing their oral traditions into written *testimonios*, thereby giving them voice in a system that had regarded them as less than fully human. Terms such as human rights had not yet entered the vocabulary, but de las Casas was a radical humanitarian who was perhaps the most significant advocate for justice and freedom for indigenous people in the sixteenth and beyond (De la Resilla, 2019).

Pioneers: Mahatma Gandhi

Mahatma Gandhi, the founder of the modern state of India, is known for his major contributions to the concept of human dignity and the importance of nonviolence. Although Gandhi did not specifically align himself with the Universal Declaration of Human Rights, his thought has had a powerful influence on contemporary notions of political, civil, and cultural rights. Gandhi notably rejected a key idea of the UDHR that human rights were inherent to all humans simply because of their humanity but instead saw human rights as entailing unilateral duties of humans to each other based on human dignity (Puri, 2015). Gandhi developed and practiced the principle of *Satyagraha* – a philosophy that resists tyranny and requires nonviolence. Satyagraha emphasizes "holding on to truth" through the pursuit of harmony by way of correct daily living that confronts evil and builds economic and political institutions that promote peace and equality.

Satyagraha was born with Gandhi's struggle, as a young attorney, on behalf of the Indians and South Asians in South Africa (Gandhi, 1928). His work to end racial injustice and prejudice on South Africa appealed less to the idea of the inherent rights of people as it did to a philosophy that pursued social justice through individual sacrifice and suffering to break the cycle of violence (Mayton, 2001).

Gandhi's approach to human rights was not centered on individualism, but tended to emphasize the duties that humans have to each other. His ideas had a significant influence on the authors of the UDHR, especially the Indian delegation, who sought to end colonialism, promote the international struggle for freedom, and establish the rights of colonized people to self-determination (Kothari, 2018).

Human Rights Instruments

Universal Declaration of Human Rights

The Universal Declaration of Human Rights (UDHR) was adopted by the General Assembly of the United Nations (UN) in December 1948 after 2 years of work by the UN Commission on Human Rights chaired by Eleanor Roosevelt and which included representatives from around the world representing numerous regions, cultures, and religious traditions. The commission was tasked to craft international instrument that would guarantee the rights of every person in the world – a *Magna Carta* for all humanity (Klug, 2015). Its core principle, as stated in the Preamble, was grounded in "…recognition of the inherent dignity and of the equal and inalienable rights of all members of the human family is the foundation of freedom, justice and peace in the world" (UNHCR, 2022).

As is well known, the development of the document was spurred by the disasters associated with global conflict and genocide before and during World War II. Massive crimes against humanity included the genocide of European Jews, Roma, people with disabilities, LGBTQ persons, and the imprisonment, torture, and murder of journalists, intellectuals, socialists, union leaders, clergy, and others.

The document is comprised of 30 articles that detail inalienable and universal political, civil, social, and cultural rights. These include the right to life, freedom from torture and slavery, due process rights, freedom of movement, and core constitutional liberties and freedoms of speech, thought, religion, association, conscience, and the press. It also extends economic rights such as an adequate standard of living and access to health care, food, housing, and social services. The charter was adopted by a vote with 48 of 58 nations voting in favor with no nation voting against it, although there were ten nations that either abstained or did not vote.

Although the original UDHR was widely supported at a global level, it has met with criticism and some opposition regarding its claims of universalism due to its Western origin and presumed cultural bias (Mende, 2021). It has also been criticized for its perceived overall ineffectiveness in preventing human rights violations (Dolinger, 2016).

It was indeed radical to state that the UDHR represented one universal family of all peoples and all nations, and it is unlikely that the authors sought equality of outcome but rather aimed at equality of legal and civil status before the law. Even that was controversial among some nations. The Soviets claimed that "brotherhood" was not possible in a world that includes capitalist societies. Saudi Arabia contended that freedom of religion violated the principles of Islam, particularly those related to marriage, family, and free expression. The South African government at the time of the adoption of UDHR could not abide with declarations on racial discrimination (Gjelten, 2018). The UDHR is not enforceable by the United Nations, and there are no sanctions available apart from UN resolutions, so the document calls on nation-states to fulfill its promises. Hannah Arendt, while an advocate for human rights, expressed skepticism that it was plausible that the universal rights of humans would be guaranteed by humanity itself (Klug, 2015, p. 53). The UDHR forbids servitude, forced marriage, arbitrary arrest, and suppression of speech, yet many of the signatory nations routinely flaunt these norms. By that reason alone, some contend that the UDHR is a "total failure" (Dolinger, 2016).

Our view is that such cynicism fails to acknowledge the degree to which the UDHR has changed the global narrative in the near 80 years since the end of World War II. Recent events do give one pause. The undeclared war by the United States against Iraq; the imprisonment of "insurgents" in Guantanamo without due process; the Russian invasion of Ukraine; the continuing Stalinist dictatorship in North Korea; the repressive regimes in Iran, China, and Myanmar; the mass deportation of asylum seekers and refugees in the Western world; the exclusion of girls from schools; and the many other human rights concerns do not invalidate the purpose and ideals of the Universal Declaration of Human Rights. On the contrary, they point to the urgency of human rights and the need for an ongoing global commitment to their preservation. "Despite routine breaches, it is impossible – even unconscionable – to imagine a world without a strong commitment to basic principles of humanity" (Pantuliano, 2022).

Covenant on Civil and Political Rights

A number of treaties, conventions, and legal instruments have emerged that amplify, extend, and focus the tenets of the Universal Declaration of Human Rights. The UDHR declaration identifies general principles of human rights, and subsequent covenants contain binding human rights commitments which each signatory nation agrees to enforce. In addition, international human rights instruments may also include conventions, international treaties and agreements, and declarations made by international and regional professional societies and associations.

The Covenant on Civil and Political Rights was adopted by the General Assembly of the United Nations in December of 1966. It entered into force in March of 1976 and has been ratified by 167 nation-states upon which it is legally binding. It is grounded in the first Article, which states that nation-states are committed to promote the right of self-determination for individuals and must have legal recourse when that right and any of the others specified in the document are violated. These individual rights include equality among women and men; right to life and survival; freedom from degrading treatment or punishment; freedom from servitude; due process rights (arbitrary detention and imprisonment due to debt, equality before the law, impartial trial); liberty of movement and residency; freedom of opinion, expression, and religion; prohibition of propaganda advocating for war or hatred based on race, nationality, or religion; right of peaceful assembly; freedom of association; right to marry and form a family; rights of children (status, nationality, residency, and name); right to vote; and right for religious, ethnic, or linguistic minorities to practice their religion, enjoy their culture, and use their language (Council of Europe, 2022).

The document amplifies the UDHR by expanding on the rights of women, minorities, children, and people who move or migrate. The prohibition of hateful propaganda is novel. Two optional protocols were introduced: the first aimed at establishing a mechanism for individuals to complain to the Human Rights Committee regarding violations of the covenant and a second optional protocol to abolish the death penalty with exception made for serious crimes committed during a war.

The Covenant on Civil and Political Rights has 74 signatories and 173 parties. Numerous nations stated official reservations, understandings, and declarations about particular items in the covenant. For example, regarding the rights of the child, the United States stated its reservation that it "…reserves the right, in exceptional circumstances, to treat juveniles as adults" (United Nations, 2022a).

Covenant on Economic, Social, and Cultural Rights

The United Nations General Assembly adopted the Covenant on Economic, Social and Cultural Rights in December 1966, and it entered into force a decade later in January 1976. This covenant extends and clarifies that the rights identified in the Covenant on Civil and Political Rights are granted to *peoples*, rather than just *individuals*.

Civil and political rights are *negative* rights, which means that they protect an individual from being subjected by a person, group, or government; they limit the powers of others toward individuals. Social, economic, and cultural rights are *positive* rights that provide individuals or peoples with a claim against another person or government and the right to services or protections that ensure their rights (Foldvary, 2011). Examples of negative rights are the rights to free speech or freedom of association in that another person or government cannot restrict what you say or believe or with whom you choose to associate. Examples of positive rights are the right to education, the right to health care, the right to employment, or the right to housing, in that one may claim that they are owed a place to live and access to health care and schooling and pensions for old age or disability. Positive rights require action. Negative rights require inaction or restraint. Most national constitutions include negative rights, but few grant positive rights.

The Covenant on Economic, Social and Cultural Rights details positive rights among signatory nations including education, fair and just conditions of work, an adequate standard of living, the highest attainable standard of health, and social security. The rights identified in the document can be divided into four spheres: the *economic sphere* (right to work and right to strike), the *social sphere* (right to social security, protection of the family, protection to mothers, and an adequate standard of living, including housing, and right to enjoy the highest possible standard of health), and the *cultural sphere* (the right to education and the right to participate in cultural life) (Federal Department of Foreign Affairs, 2022). The convention also centers on the sphere of the rights of *collectives, peoples, and nationalities* to equally share the benefits of economic, social, and cultural rights.

As with other UN covenants, signatory nations were able to note reservations about articles and provisions, and many nations posted such reservations. Iran, for example, declared that "...the entry of the Republic of Iraq as a party to the International Covenant on Economic, Social and Cultural Rights and the International Covenant on Civil and Political Rights shall in no way signify recognition of Israel nor shall it entail any obligation towards Israel." India declared that "...the right of self-determination'appearing in [this article] apply only to the peoples under foreign domination and that these words do not apply to sovereign independent states or to a section of a people or nation" (United Nations, 2022a).

The Universal Declaration of Human Rights (UDHR), the International Covenant on Economic, Social and Cultural Rights (ICESCR), and the International Covenant on Civil and Political Rights (ICCPR) together comprise the *International Bill of Rights.* Although international covenants and treaties are binding, these international instruments are subject to the precedence of national sovereignty, and there are limited mechanisms by which the rights which are elaborated in these covenants can be enforced as such (Strydom, 2019). One mechanism is to refer complaints and inquiries to UN committees, such as the Human Rights Committee or the Committee on Social, Economic and Cultural Rights, for example, where representatives can consider individual complaints, conduct country inquiries, adopt general comments, and engage conflicting parties in a constructive dialogue (United Nations, 2022b). Each UN covenant, treaty, or convention has a particular "committee of experts" to monitor implementation and conformity to the treaty's articles and provisions.

Convention on the Elimination of All Forms of Discrimination Against Women

The Convention on the Elimination of All Forms of Discrimination Against Women (CEDAW) was adopted by the General Assembly in 1979 and has been ratified by 189 of 194 member countries. Although the Covenant on Civil and Political Rights and earlier international agreements prohibited discrimination against women and girls, no previous treaty document spoke to the positive rights of women, by which they would achieve *substantive* equality or "equality of results" in economic and social life (Khanna & Kimmel, 2022).

Among the 30 articles of the instrument are general provisions of standard rights such as nondiscrimination, equality under the law, equal pay, and access to education and health. Others specifically address human trafficking, girl's education, access to sports and recreation, family planning, and equal rights in marriage, such as the right to freely choose a husband, the freedom of movement within the family, and the same rights as the husband with regard to the property, the choice of profession, spacing of children, and the dissolution of marriage.

The document requires signatory nations to eliminate gender discrimination in both the *public sphere* (political, civil, and educational rights) and the *private sphere* (including the home, marriage, and family). The inclusion of women's rights in the private areas of life, such as the family, made this document the most comprehensive treatment of women's rights to date. It presupposes that the oppression of women can no longer be left solely to remediation by nation-states and in fact requires international remedies (Zoelle, 2000).

The United States, along with Sudan, Somalia, Iran, Tonga, Palau, and the Holy See, is among the few governments that have not ratified CEDAW – countries that have more traditional views on gender equality (Verveer & De Alwis, 2021). In the case of the United States, it could be asked if this is a result of patriarchy and religion or is it the country's supposed *exceptionalism* – the manner in which the country has historically perceived itself as different and better than other nations especially with respect to international law. It is argued that such hubristic exceptionalism in the case of CEDAW has morphed into an *exemptionalism*, whereby Americans have no obligation to engage in international institutions which might diminish the country's sovereignty and "uniqueness." But underneath such rhetoric lies the simple fact that the US Senate cannot muster the votes to ratify women's equality due concerns such as preserving the so-called family values, protecting traditional family structure, maintaining strict gender roles, and invoking religious notions of natural law (Schalatek, 2019). It is ironic that the nation that imagined and enacted the original Bill of Rights will not ratify CEDAW – the global women's bill of rights.

Convention Against Torture and Other Cruel, Inhuman, or Degrading Treatment or Punishment

The Holocaust and the Nuremberg Trials had a major influence on the UN Charter, the UNDHR, and the Genocide Convention of 1951, which together form the foundation of the modern international human rights regime (Mende, 2021). A central idea that unites the rights regime has been that the "…recognition of the equal and inalienable rights of all members of the human family is the foundation of freedom, justice and peace in the world…" and that such rights are derived from inherent human dignity (United Nations, 2022a).

The UN Convention against Torture and Other Cruel, Inhuman or Degrading Treatment or Punishment (CAT) was adopted by the General Assembly in 1984 and following ratification came into force in 1987. It extends and clarifies the core human rights documents by declaring that torture is forbidden in any and all circumstances, including war. Article 1 of the convention offers a clear and concise definition of torture: the causing of "…severe pain or suffering, whether physical or mental, is intentionally inflicted on a person for such purposes as obtaining from him or a third person information or a confession, punishing him for an act he or a third person has committed or is suspected of having committed, or intimidating or coercing him or a third person, or for any reason" (United Nations, 2022c). It does not include pain and suffering due to lawful sanctions or acts of torture inflicted by private individuals who are not public officials or acting on behalf of a government or state. It also clearly states that persons are not exempt from the covenant when acting under the order of a superior officer or public authority, a commonly invoked false rationale that a person was "just following orders."

Another important element of the covenant includes the principle of *non-refoulement* – the tenet that those who seek asylum may not be returned to a country in which there are reasonable grounds to believe they will be subjected to persecution or torture. This rule was established by the UN Convention Relating to the Status of Refugees. In a time of increasing global migration, much of which is motivated by escape from persecution, the convention has particular relevance today.

The Convention against Torture and Other Cruel, Inhuman or Degrading Treatment or Punishment (CAT) requires that signatory states criminalize torture and subject grave penalties on all parties involved. It established a Committee against Torture, representing signatory member states, that is empowered to monitor, investigate, and issue reports on violations of the convention. However, absent any authority to take concerns to an international tribunal, the enforcement mechanisms for the CAT amount to little more than "naming and shaming" which may marginally change public opinion but which can be countered by government messaging (Greenhill & Reiter, 2022).

One provision of the CAT in Article 5 states that the convention covers "offenses are committed in any territory under its jurisdiction or on board a ship or aircraft registered in that State" and does not specifically outlaw torture outside the national jurisdiction. This creates a potential loophole for the use of black sites or secret offshore detention facilities, and many such sites exist outside of international scrutiny where unlawful interrogations, renditions, and detentions continue to take place under inhumane conditions (Tayler & Epstein, 2022).

Convention on the Rights of the Child

In November 1989, rather late in the era of the modern international human rights regime, the UN General Assembly finally adopted a convention exclusively aimed at the human rights of children and "...proclaimed that childhood is entitled to special care and assistance" (United Nations, 2022). The convention has become the most ratified human rights document in history (UNICEF, 2022).

The Convention on the Rights of the Child (CRC) established the principle that all children are not objects, or mere property of their parents, nor are they "adults in training," and while deserving of special protection, have full rights of expression (UNICEF, 2022). The convention specifies that children have full and fundamental human dignity, which requires that they have the right to education, health care, and an adequate standard of living. They have freedom of association, privacy, speech, conscience, assembly, due process, and religion. They are protected from discrimination; forced separation from their parents; unlawful detention; illicit transfer or trafficking; physical, sexual, or mental abuse; neglect; unlawful adoption; forced labor; conscription into armed conflict; economic exploitation; torture; or unlawful deprivation of their freedom (United Nations, 2022).

The guiding principles that underlie the convention are the idea that children have the right to develop to their fullest potential, deserve special protection from harm and exploitation, must be free from discrimination in any form, and may express their views fully and freely and the state has an obligation to ensure their survival and development. The nation-state is to act in *the best interest of the child.*

The implementation of the convention has led to longer life expectancy for children, reductions in child mortality, and an increase in vaccination rates for key infectious diseases (Reinbold, 2019). Measures of child well-being have improved since the convention was adopted, and the prevalence of stunting and malnutrition has also declined (UNICEF, 2020),

The Convention on the Rights of the Child has been ratified by 198 countries. The only nation that has not ratified the convention is the United States.

The Refugee Convention

In the immediate environment of post-World War II, there were around 40 million refugees and displaced persons in Europe. These included former prisoners, concentration camp survivors, war widows, slave laborers, prisoners of war, and those who were dislocated due to loss of their homes, destruction of cities, and relocation after their home country was occupied by new powers. The division of Europe by the Allied nations and the Soviet Union led to deportation, incarceration, and forced migration. Left behind in the twilight of war was a vast population of stateless, homeless, and jobless persons in desperate circumstances (Marrus, 2022).

The United Nations Relief and Rehabilitation Administration (UNRRA) was created in 1943 to organize economic assistance, relief assistance, and repatriation to refugees and displaced persons in parts of Europe under Allied control. The massive challenge overwhelmed the organization and after the surrender of Axis powers and the UNRRA was replaced by the International Refugee Organization (IRO) in 1946. The IRO, which was under United Nations administration, assisted displaced persons and refugees to return to their countries or to relocate those who could not return or did not wish to return to their home country for political reasons. European and global refugee assistance were consolidated in 1951 with the adoption of the UN Convention on Refugees.

The Convention Relating to the Status of Refugees, as it is if formally known, entered into force in 1954. The treaty, ratified by 145 nations, defines refugees as persons with a "well-founded fear of being persecuted for reasons of race, religion, nationality, membership of a particular social group or political opinion, is outside the country of his nationality and is unable or, owing to such fear, is unwilling to avail himself of the protection of that country; or who, not having a nationality and being outside the country of his former habitual residence as a result of such events, is unable or, owing to such fear, is unwilling to return to it" (United Nations, 2022e). A core principle is non-refoulement, which is the tenet that refugees shall not be returned to their country of origin if there is a threat of harm, including loss of life and/or freedom. The convention details numerous rights and responsibilities that refugees hold in host countries. Rights under the convention include *access to* public relief, social security protection, education, equal taxation, employment, legal documents, and housing. Their rights include freedom of movement, equal treatment in the courts, religious expression, equal taxation, and freedom from discrimination. The duties of the refugee "…require in particular that he conform to its laws and regulations as well as to measures taken for the maintenance of public order" (United Nations, 2022e).

The Convention on Refugees led to the creation of the UM High Commission on Refugees (UNHCR) in 1951. The organization, formed to assist WW2 refugees, was expected to complete its work in 3 years, but international refugee displacement continued globally, and the agency now takes the international lead in coordinating refugee policy, relief, relocation, and assistance. Over 70 years since its foundation, the agency now works in over 130 countries with an annual budget of $8.6 billion. The UNHCR has received two Nobel Peace Prizes (1954 and 1981) and has helped over 50 million refugees (UNHCR, 2022).

UN Declaration on the Rights of Indigenous Peoples

The Declaration on the Rights of Indigenous Peoples (UNDRIP) was adopted by the General Assembly in 2007 with 144 signatory nations. At the time of adoption, four nations with colonial histories and sizable indigenous populations (Australia, Canada, New Zealand, and the United States) voted against the UNDRIP (United Nations, 2022f). Subsequently, these nations later changed their position in support of the convention.

The purpose of the declaration is to establish minimum standards related to the dignity, survival, and well-being of indigenous people and to expand upon the rights and freedoms of First Nations groups and individuals. The declaration departs from previous UN human rights documents by emphasizing the protection of *collective* rights as well as the individual rights of indigenous people. The UNDRIP was developed after more than two decades of discussions among member states and representatives of indigenous groups around the world. As a declaration, rather than a convention, the document is nonlegally binding and reflects aspirational goals of member nations. As a document of "soft law," it asserts indigenous rights rather than claims and, as such, was the first universal document for the comprehensive protection of the rights of indigenous people globally (Barelli, 2009). The UNDRIP departs from a centuries-old history of exploitation, genocide, and cultural destruction of indigenous peoples and cultures by emphasizing that indigenous nations have a right to independent recognition and existence with the authority of self-governance and autonomous control of cultural resources and the right to be recognized as indigenous peoples or nations, rather than as ethnic minorities.

Specific provisions of the declaration include rights of self-determination, freedom from discrimination, and full equality with other citizens. It also asserts the recognition of the property rights of indigenous nations over their cultural resources including language, religion, cultural practices, artifacts, and intellectual property. The declaration affirms the importance of land property rights and authority over environmental assets. The 45 articles of the declaration also specify that indigenous people may not be forcibly relocated or be subjected to compulsory military service. The authority of indigenous people over their education, cultural resources, and juridical customs is strongly emphasized.

The Declaration on the Rights of Indigenous People is one of the most powerful and significant international statements on the importance of decolonization as it pertains to indigenous people and First Nations.

Discussion

Many, but not all, of the human rights documents emerged from the Western tradition – from those of classical Ancient Rome and Greece through to the Renaissance and to the defining documents of the post-World War II era. Notwithstanding, Western human rights thinking has been influenced by multiple traditions and major non-Western civilizations, including Buddhism, Confucianism, Mandarin, and Brahmin cultural traditions (Mende, 2021). More recently, contemporary ideas have been included, such as those generated by the former European colonies after Western empires dismantled following global restructuring after World War II. Nearly all of the former colonized states of the Global South, as well as a wide variety of nongovernmental organizations, activists, and interest groups participated in the discussions and deliberations that led up to the adoption of contemporary international human rights declarations and conventions (Mende, 2021).

The international human rights regime is universal and not divided into dichotomous value systems because it fundamentally states that human rights are for everyone everywhere – a vision that is pluralistic and all-inclusive. Contemporary human rights documents have evolved from an emphasis on the rights of the individual to include community-based human rights, cultural rights, and collective values, such as those affirmed in the Declaration on the Rights of Indigenous Peoples. The shift from seeing human rights solely through the lens of individual persons toward understanding that such rights also inhere to identities, nationalities, tribes, and peoples.

Importantly, human rights documents can be used by any individual, group, or nation irrespective of location in the Global South or elsewhere. Too often, however, critiques of the human rights canon emerge from totalitarian states and serve to disguise or distract from human rights abuses in those authoritarian states.

Ubuntu

A recent development that has been promoted by the International Federation of Social Workers (IFSW) has been the integration of Ubuntu as a central idea in thinking about social work, social justice, and social development from a postcolonial framework (Mayaka & Truell, 2021). Ubuntu is an African philosophy of social development that aims to support community systems in social protection and human rights. Recognizing that the Western perspective on human rights focuses primarily on the rights of the individual, Ubuntu centers the concept of rights on communities and their responsibility to prevent poverty, vulnerability, and insecurity through collective action based on traditional learning. By vesting the community as the central organizing unit, the model moves away from the traditional Western emphasis on individuation in social work and social justice. Rights inhere not just to the person but to the community culture and natural environment in which they are positioned. The community, in this sense, has guardianship over the well-being of its members. This is realized through shared community gatherings around key life events that strengthen and unify relationships and in which the shared responsibility of community members toward each other is reinforced. Social protection is also ensured through economic empowerment where community members come together to collectively offer social and economic care and support grounded in indigenous traditions.

Ubuntu seeks also to repair broken relationships and community imbalances not through retributive justice, but by way of restorative justice that rehabilitates all parties involved using peaceful reconciliation and restoration. Thus, the concept of rights emphasizes a culture of mutual care in which people take responsibility for each other and work to realize everybody's rights. Under Ubuntu, communities themselves are a form of social protection – natural organic systems that provide mutual support for people while protecting the culture and natural environment that sustains them (Mayaka & Truell, 2021).

Meta Human Rights

The next steps in the evolution of human rights will expand their scope to living ecosystems of which humans are an integral part and without which they would become extinct. Ecocide, the extermination of living environments, is at the core of current global economic systems, which are based on uncontrolled growth and massive natural resource consumption, accompanied by unrestrained pollution of the atmosphere, oceans, soils, and water resources. Current models of development do not account for environmental externalities in measuring economic growth, and contemporary approaches to resource utilization are unsustainable. A failure to implement self-restorative sustainable models will harm the health and well-being of human beings over future generations. Short-term development models ignore environmental effects and their damage on both current and future human beings and the ecosystems that sustain them and all other living things.

Within a rights system that accounts for the environment, it follows that human conscience and morality will also come to embrace animal rights. It is hard to imagine that a near-term future generation of human beings will not look back with shock and disgust at the mass cultivation and ongoing daily destruction of millions of animals for human food consumption.

Conclusion: Social Work and Human Rights

Social workers have engaged in social justice and human rights work from the beginnings of the profession. Working to improve conditions for immigrants in low-income neighborhoods and tenements, securing access to sanitary water systems for public health, advocating for the end of child labor, organizing against unsafe and arduous work conditions, establishing child protection laws, working with and on behalf of injured war veterans, waging a war on poverty, regularizing adoption practices, promoting gender equality, and combating human trafficking are all examples of the ways in which social work has been intrinsically enmeshed with the work of human rights.

The International Federation of Social Workers defines social work as "…a practice-based profession and an academic discipline that promotes social change and development, social cohesion, and the empowerment and liberation of people. Principles of social justice, ***human rights,*** collective responsibility and respect for diversities are central to social work" (International Federation of Social Workers, 2022).

While the work of early social work practitioners was grounded in human dignity, the primordial social work model was rooted in charity or assistance to the needy to relieve suffering. It was an itinually a profession largely made up of privileged white women who engaged in philanthropic work that essentially preserved the status quo (Mapp et al., 2019). Little attention was given to addressing the underlying causes of hunger and human suffering. A second stage in social work was waylaid by psychiatry wherein social workers assisted in attending to those with mental illness, primarily working with middle-class anomie and angst – a tradition that is still alive and well within the clinical social work community. This line of work does little to advance social justice and human rights and is firmly in the camp of maintaining the status quo. The global civil rights movements of the 1960s birthed activism, political social work, and macro efforts to address structural poverty and racism. As the profession evolved, it has turned to an explicit preoccupation with human rights (Witkin, 1998).

As Susan Mapp and her colleagues have noted, social work evolved from a charity-based profession to a needs-based occupation and is now increasingly centering on a rights-based paradigm (Mapp et al., 2019). The goal of the profession should be less focused on addressing the immediate deficits faced by individuals and groups and instead seek to rectify structural inequalities that deny people or groups of their human rights.

The international human rights regime and its documents form the foundation of social work ethics, practice, and policy.

Discussion Questions

1. What was the Enlightenment, and how did it influence the concepts of civil and human rights?
2. What is meant by the idea that the Universal Declaration of Human Rights is the *Magna Carta* for the world?
3. What parts of the Universal Declaration of Human Rights are most relevant to the profession of social work?
4. Who are some of the pioneers of contemporary human rights, and what were their ideas?
5. How has social work been influenced by the Human Rights Movement?
6. What is Ubuntu and how are community rights integrated into social work?

References

Barelli, M. (2009). The role of soft law in the international legal system: The case of the United Nations declaration on the rights of indigenous peoples. *International and Comparative Law Quarterly, 58*(4), 957–983. https://doi.org/10.1017/S0020589309001559

Blackburn, R. (2006). Haiti, slavery, and the age of the democratic revolution. *The William and Mary Quarterly, 63*(4), 643–674. http://www.jstor.org/stable/4491574

Botting, E. H. (2006). Mary Wollstonecraft's enlightened legacy: The "modern socialimaginary" of the egalitarian family. *American Behavioral Scientist, 49*(5), 687–701. https://doi.org/10.1177/0002764205282213

Cheng-Hin Lim, A., & Cibulka, F. (2018). *China and Southeast Asia in the Xi Jinping era.* Lexington Books.

Clapham, A. (2015). *Human rights: A very short introduction.* Oxford Press. https://doi.org/10.1093/actrade/9780198706168.001.0001

Council of Europe. (2022). Covenant on civil and political rights. *Manual for human rights Education with young people.* https://www.coe.int/en/web/compass/the-international-covenant-on-civil-and-political-rights

De la Resilla, I. (2019). Bartolomé de las casas: A radical humanitarian in the age of the great encounter. In K. McCall-Smith, J. Wouters, & F. Gomez Isa (Eds.), *The faces of human rights* (pp. 13–21). Hart Publishing. https://doi.org/10.5040/9781509926947.ch-002

Dolinger, J. (2016). The failure of the universal declaration of human rights. *The University of Miami Inter-American Law Review, 47*(2), 164–199. https://www.jstor.org/stable/26788283

Élysée. (2022). Declaration of the rights of man and of the citizen. *The Website of the President of France.* https://www.elysee.fr/en/french-presidency/the-declaration-of-the-rights-of-man-and-of-the-citizen

Federal Department of Foreign Affairs. (2022). *The international covenant on economic, social and cultural rights.* Confédération. Suisse. https://www.eda.admin.ch/eda/en/fdfa/foreign-policy/international-law/un-human-rights-treaties/international-covenant-economic-social-cultural-rights.html

Foldvary, F. E. (2011). Positive rights. In D. K. Chatterjee (Ed.), *Encyclopedia of global justice.* Springer. https://doi.org/10.1007/978-1-4020-9160-5_359

Gandhi, M. (1928). *Satyagraha in South Africa.* Navajivan Publishing House. https://www.vidya-online.org/dl/gandhisouthafrica.pdf

Gjelten, T. (2018, December 10). *Boundlessly idealistic, universal declaration of human rights is still resisted.* National Public Radio. https://www.npr.org/2018/12/10/675210421/its-human-rights-day-however-its-not-universally-accepted

González, M. M. (1997). Mary Wollstonecraft and the "vindication of the rights of women": Postmodern feminism vs. masculine enlightenment. *Atlantis, 19*(2), 177–183. http://www.jstor.org/stable/41055470

Greenhill, B., & Reiter, D. (2022). Naming and shaming, government messaging, and backlash effects: Experimental evidence from the convention against torture. *Journal of Human Rights.* https://doi.org/10.1080/14754835.2021.2011710

Horowitz, M. C. (1974). The stoic synthesis of the idea of natural law in man: Four themes. *Journal of the History of Ideas, 35*(1), 3–16. https://doi.org/10.2307/2708739

International Federation of Social Workers. (2022). *Global definition of social work.* https://www.ifsw.org/what-is-social-work/global-definition-of-social-work/

Ishay, M. R. (2004). *The history of human rights: From ancient times to the globalization era.* University of California Press.

Khanna, P., & Kimmel, Z. (2022). *Convention on the elimination of all forms of discrimination against women – for youth.* United Nations. https://www.unwomen.org/sites/default/files/Headquarters/Attachments/Sections/Library/Publications/2016/CEDAW-for-Youth.pdf

Klug, F. (2015). *A Magna Carta for all humanity: Homing in on human rights.* Routledge. https://doi.org/10.432magna4/9781315689968

Kothari, M. (2018, December 20). *India's remarkable contribution to the Universal Declaration of Human Rights (UDHR): A lecture by Miloon Kothari*. United Nations in India. https://in.one.un.org/event/indias-remarkable-contribution-to-the-universal-declaration-of-human-rights-udhr-a-lecture-by-miloon-kothari/

Law, D. S., & Versteeg, M. (2012). The declining influence of the United States constitution. *New York University Law Review, 87*(3), 762–858.

Lusk, M., & Corbett, D. (2021). Liberation theology and international social work. *Journal of Religion & Spirituality in Social Work, 40*(1), 92–107. https://doi.org/10.1080/15426432.2020.1848750

Mapp, S., McPherson, J., Androff, D., & Gabel, S. G. (2019). Social work is a human rights profession. *Social Work, 64*(3), 259–269. https://doi.org/10.1093/sw/swz023

Marcus, R. (2022, June 17) The soul-crushing lot of a supreme court liberal. *The Washington Post*. https://www.washingtonpost.com/opinions/2022/06/17/court-liberals-years-in-minority/

Marrus, M. R. (2022). *The unwanted: European refugees from the first world wat through the cold war*. Temple University Press.

Mayaka, B., & Truell, R. (2021). Ubuntu and its potential impact on the international social work profession. *International Social Work, 64*(2), 649–662. https://doi.org/10.1177/00208728211022

Mayton, D. M. (2001). Gandhi as a peace builder: The social psychology of Satyagraha. In D. J. Christie, R. V. Wagner, & D. A. Winter (Eds.), *Peace, conflict and violence: Peace psychology for the 21st century*. Prentice Hall. https://cpb-us-w2.wpmucdn.com/u.osu.edu/dist/b/7538/files/2014/10/Chapter-25-Gandhi-as-Peacebuilder-Mayton-2d4ranc.pdf

Mende, J. (2021). Are human rights western - and why does it matter? A perspective from international political theory. *Journal of International Political Theory, 17*(1), 38–57. https://doi.org/10.1177/1755088219832992

Moyn, S. (2018). *Not enough: Human rights in an unequal world*. Harvard University Press.

Paine, T. (1792). *The rights of man*. Printed for J. S. Jordan.

Pantuliano, S. (2022). *Why the universal declarations of human rights is still relevant, 70 years on*. ODI. https://odi.org/en/insights/why-the-universal-declaration-of-human-rights-is-still-relevant-70-years-on/

Puri, B. (2015). The rights of man: A Gandhian intervention. In A. Peetush & J. Drydyk (Eds.), *Human rights: India and the West*. Oxford University Press. https://doi.org/10.1093/acprof:oso/9780199453528.003.0009

Putin, V. (2022, July 12). *On the Historical Unity of Russians and Ukrainians*. Speech. President of Russia. http://en.kremlin.ru/events/president/news/66181

Reinbold, G. W. (2019). Effects of the convention on the rights of the child on child mortality and vaccination rates: A synthetic control analysis. *BMC International Health and Human Rights, 19*, 24. https://doi.org/10.1186/s12914-019-0211-9

Repucci, S., & Slipovich, A. (2022). *The global expansion of authoritarian rule*. Freedom House. https://freedomhouse.org/report/freedom-world/2022/global-expansion-authoritarian-rule

Rosenthal, A. J., & Henkin, J. (Eds.). (1990). *Constitutionalism and rights: The influence of the United States constitution abroad*. Columbia University Press.

Rowlatt, B. (2015, October 5). The original suffragette: The extraordinary Mary Wollstonecraft. *The Guardian*, https://www.theguardian.com/lifeandstyle/womens-blog/2015/oct/05/original-suffragette-mary-wollstonecraft

Schalatek, L. (2019, December 10). *CEDAW and the USA: When belief in exceptionalism becomes exemptionalism*. Heinrich Böll Stiftung (Foundation). https://www.boell.de/en/2019/12/10/cedaw-and-usa-when-belief-exceptionalism-becomes-exemptionalism

Schuman, M. (2022, June 21). China's very dangerous trajectory. *The Atlantic*. https://www.theatlantic.com/international/archive/2022/06/China-xi-jinping-power-zero- covid/661228/

Strydom, H. (2019). The protection of economic, social and cultural rights in international law. *Constitutional Review, 5*(2), 222–247.

Tayler, L., & Epstein, E. (2022, January 9). *Legacy of the "dark side": The costs of unlawful U.S. detentions and interrogation's post-9/11*. Brown University Watson Institute. https://watson.brown.edu/costsofwar/papers/2022/DetentionandTorture

UNHCR. (2022). *History of UNHCR*. United Nations High Commission on Refugees. https://www.unhcr.org/en-us/history-of-unhcr.html

UNICEF. (2020). *UNICEF-WHO-World Bank: Joint child malnutrition estimates*. https://data.unicef.org/resources/jme-report-2020/

UNICEF. (2022). *Convention on the rights of the child*. UNICEF. https://www.unicef.org/child-rights-convention

United Nations. (2022a). *United Nations treaty collection: International covenant on civil and political rights*. https://treaties.un.org/Pages/ViewDetails.aspx?src=TREATY&mtdsg_no=IV-4&chapter=4&clang=_en

United Nations. (2022b). *Treaty bodies: Committee on economic, social and cultural rights*. Office of the High Commissioner on Human Rights. https://www.ohchr.org/en/treatybodies/cescr#:~:text=The%20Committee%20on%20Economic%2C%20Social,Rights%20by%20its%20State%20parties

United Nations. (2022c). *Human rights instruments: Convention against torture and other cruel, inhuman or degrading treatment or punishment*. Office of the High Commissioner on Human Rights. https://www.ohchr.org/en/instruments-mechanisms/instruments/convention-against-torture-and-other-cruel-inhuman-or-degrading

United Nations. (2022d). *Human rights instruments: Convention on the rights of the child*. Office of the High Commissioner on Human Rights. https://www.ohchr.org/en/instruments-mechanisms/instruments/convention-rights-child

United Nations. (2022e). *Human rights instruments: Convention relating to the status of refugees*. Office of the High Commissioner on Human Rights. https://www.ohchr.org/en/instruments-mechanisms/instruments/convention-relating-status-refugees

United Nations. (2022f). *United Nations declaration of the rights of indigenous peoples*. UN Department of Economic and Social Affairs. https://www.un.org/development/desa/indigenouspeoples/declaration-on-the-rights-of-indigenous-peoples.html

Verveer, M., & De Alwis, R. (2021, February 18). *Why ratifying the convention of the elimination of discrimination against women (CEDAW) is good for America's domestic policy*. Georgetown Institute for Women, Peace and Security. https://giwps.georgetown.edu/why-ratifying-the-convention-on-the-elimination-of-discrimination-against-women-cedaw-is-good-for-americas-domestic-policy/

Witkin, S. L. (1998). Human rights and social work. *Social Work, 43*(3), 197+. https://link.gale.com/apps/doc/A20748786/HRCA?u=txshracd2603&sid=bookmar

Zoelle, D. G. (2000). The convention on elimination of all forms of discrimination against women. In *Globalizing concern for women's human rights* (pp. 31–52). Palgrave Macmillan. https://doi.org/10.1057/9780312299699_3

Mark Lusk is a Faculty Member in the School of Social Work at New Mexico State University. He was Senior Fulbright Scholar at the Catholic University of Peru in Lima and also a Fulbright Research Scholar at the Catholic University of Rio de Janeiro in Brazil. He currently works with forced migrants and refugees from Central America and Mexico and related human rights issues. He was Founding Director of the School of Social Work at Boise State University (Idaho) and has served as Associate Provost at the University of Georgia.

Nicholas D. Natividad is an Associate Professor in the Department of Criminal Justice and affiliated Faculty in the Department of Borderlands and Ethnic Studies at New Mexico State University. He obtained his master's degree in International Human Rights Law from the University of Oxford and doctorate in Justice Studies from Arizona State University. His research interests focus on transnational and local community practices of human rights that are informed by indigenous and decolonial methodologies. He is the Co-creator of the museum exhibit Pasos Ajenos: Social Justice and Inequalities in the Borderlands, an art and cultural exhibit that focuses on regional issues of justice as they pertain to identity, environment, history, immigration, human rights, and law.

Part IV
Situating Human Rights in the Global North-South Divide

Chapter 7
Postcolonial Europe and Its Premises for Decolonization

Marcin Boryczko, Tomasz Nowicki, and Emilio Jose Gomez Ciriano

We Need Central and Eastern Europe to Think About Decolonizing Europe

In early 2022, amid ongoing conflict brought on by Russia's invasion of Ukraine, the Polish Federation of Social Workers and Social Service Employees Unions began offering humanitarian aid by safely evacuating social workers, families, and children from conflict zones. The federation decided to assist social workers who are providing aid to Ukrainian refugees entering Poland. Many social workers around Europe, especially in Ukraine's neighboring countries, have actively participated in support by offering their own homes and residences as well as needed humanitarian supplies. One of the powerful, but still uncommon, messages delivered by professional social workers who decided to both provide bottom-up and professional humanitarian aid and participate in policy-making processes was this civic participation in political and humanitarian aid. The International Federation of Social Workers also responded to the crisis in Ukraine by establishing a Community Social Work Centre and Social Work Hub to help Ukrainian citizens and social workers. These international acts of solidarity by social workers demonstrated the significance of civic and professional organizations in the face of humanitarian crises.

M. Boryczko (✉) · T. Nowicki
Department of Social Work, Faculty of Social Sciences, University of Gdańsk, Gdańsk, Poland
e-mail: marcin.boryczko@ug.edu.pl; tomasz.nowicki@ug.edu.pl

E. J. G. Ciriano
Faculty of Social Work, University of Castilla-La Mancha, Cuenca Campus, Ciudad Real, Spain
e-mail: emiliojose.gomez@uclm.es

M. Madew et al. (eds.), *Decolonized Approaches to Human Rights and Social Work*, https://doi.org/10.1007/978-3-031-33030-8_7

But what exactly happened in Ukraine in 2022, and why has the power balance in Eastern Europe changed so rapidly? Both rhetoric used by Russian leaders ("historical unity," artificial separation of Ukraine from Russia, Ukrainians as a bunch of tribes bereft of national identity) and practices related to this armed conflict (incorporation of the Eastern Ukrainian regions, efforts to humiliate Ukrainians, mass destruction of nonmilitary targets including schools and hospitals) indicate that the conflict in Ukraine is another colonial war paradoxically happening in Europe. According to Грабовський (*Gladotsky*) (2013), depending on their historical legacy, Ukrainian regions are colonies with varied statuses that are symptomatic of Central and Eastern Europe (henceforth, CEE). He calls the Ukrainian SSR (Soviet Socialist Republic) a "colony" and cautions that the legacy of colonialism is much more complicated and hazardous for an independent postcolonial country like Ukraine. When compared to the empires of Western Europe, Eurocentrism has not only supported the marginalization of Russia in the history of contemporary empires but also distorted the perception of its imperialist practices and experiences and a combination of historically unique practices that can be used to identify imperial formations and "imperial situations" (Turoma & Waldstein, 2016).

According to Timothy Snyder (2022), the conflict in Ukraine is a colonial war in which Russian colonialism is manifested through the so-called resolution of the Ukrainian question. This form of subordination strongly relates to Fanon's (1967) concept of creating colonial subjects through political dominance, economic exploitation, and, most importantly, the denial of identity and culture as articulated in colonizing discourse in today's Russia. As a consequence, devastating human rights abuses with thousands of civilians killed or injured, massive destruction of civilian infrastructure and housing, arbitrary detentions and enforced disappearances, torture and ill-treatment, and conflict-related sexual violence are common fare for the Ukrainians today. Violations of international humanitarian law and international human rights law have become commonplace. The City of Bucha became a symbol of Russian barbarism at the start of the war, with the invasion most likely aimed at the genocide of Ukrainians who witnessed the most horrific scenes of Russian aggression. Unfortunately, this situation is blood evidence that colonialism is not dead as a political and CEE is not just a region but a part of a global puzzle game in a capitalist world system (Wallerstein, 2004).

The case of Russia is significant in determining Europe's colonial nature that needs to be identified, situated, studied, and deconstructed through postcolonial lenses. As a "second-class empire" based primarily on indirect colonialism, Russia is still the "condition of global coloniality," non-Western but still crucial for international relations. It has "appropriated and transmuted the basic aspects of the western empires of modernity, then projecting them onto the Russian colonial difference, generating mutant forms of the main vices of modernity – secondary Eurocentrism, secondary orientalism, secondary racism" (Tlostanova, 2012, p. 135). Russia, as one of the "last colonial Empires," on the one hand follows the path of the old Western European empires by extending power or control to other countries primarily through direct conquest or indirect political, military, or economic control, but on the other hand, its uniqueness is based on a long imperial tradition marked by several collapses and excessive aspirations to retain imperial power (Bryc, 2008). After Vladimir Putin took power in 2005, true imperial thinking permeated the country's power elites who saw the fall of the Soviet Union as the greatest geopolitical disaster of the century. Shortly after, in 2008, Russia sent troops to Georgia for the first time since the end of the USSR. When Russia-backed minorities in South Ossetia and Abkhazia broke away from Georgia, the Kremlin launched measures in the region that violated international law to keep Georgia within Russia's sphere of influence. This marked a turning point in understanding Russia's meticulous attempts to prevent former Soviet states from encroaching on Western influence and NATO membership.

At NATO's Edge: Conflicts in the Balkans and the Rise of Populism

Russia views the Balkans as a region where it is simple to sow discord and tries to weaken NATO's eastern edge in order to disrupt the post-Cold War European order. The region seems to be an appropriate environment to take revenge on the United States and the European Union's willingness to expand its influence on the south-eastern NATO flank. Refusal to acknowledge Kosovo's independence, backing for separatist leaders in Bosnia and Herzegovina, and a *coup d'état* in Montenegro are good examples of preventive imperialist strategies taken by Russia against the desire to ally with NATO or the EU. The war against Ukraine increased Russia's interest in the region which can be observable in Kosovo where old tensions have risen due to Serbs enforcing the blockade of border crossing because they were incensed that people entering Kosovo with Serbian license plates were forced to switch them out for temporary "RKS" (Republic of Kosovo) plates or turn around. The conflict between Serbia and Kosovo over identity and sovereignty serves as a warning to the outside world about the dangers of unresolved tensions and possible use as a destabilizing tool for Russia (Stronski, 2022).

The region's various ethnic, political, and social divisions as well as broad discontent with the relatively slow Euro-Atlantic integration appear to be major contributors to the unstable system that Russia may easily exploit shortly. In Bosnia, Russia cultivates strong ties to the country's two federal entities leaders Milorad Dodik (Republika Srpska) and Dragan Čović (Bosnian Croats leader). The Russian Federation supports their policies of undermining the institutions in Bosnia and Herzegovina through the use of the threat of secession, the obstruction of measures that would limit the autonomy of the constituent parts of the country, and the signing of international agreements by Serbian authorities on issues that are under central authorities. Although the West has forgotten the Balkan wars of the 1990s, there is a growing possibility of violent right-wing extremism in the region. Some reports indicate similar patterns identified in the region: illegal funding, religious nationalism, support for Russia, homophobia, militarism, and historical revisionism (Buljubašić, 2022).

Intriguing is the fact of using humanitarianism by right-wing organizations to describe their mission as humanitarian or secure the human rights of certain populations in the region. This so-called "black-clad" humanitarianism is an example of how violent right-wing organizations have used humanitarianism to conceal their true ideological agenda (Pekmez, 2021). For instance, amid the surge of opposition to NATO integration in the Balkans, some organizations in Montenegro emerged as patriotic and humanitarian despite being a right-wing political base in reality (Papović & Kovačević, 2021). Misunderstanding of this situation matches the stereotype of humanitarians who are unaware of the ongoing ethnic, national, and racial conflicts in the Balkans. Not surprisingly, radicals in Russia and the Balkans have used a human rights discourse to justify warfare and war crimes. Similarly, during the War on Terror, the conflict between those who oppose human rights and those who work to advance them was justified politically by using human rights discourse (Jahren, 2017).

Far-right populists in Europe, who have benefited from Russia's financial support, have also polarized European society, not just in the Balkans but also in Western Europe, where numerous far-right politicians successfully cooperate with Moscow, try to legitimize its interests, as well as keep them close to mainstream politics (Roonemaa et al., 2022). Not only far-right movements prey on and exploit ethnic grievances increasing electoral support in CEE but also all kinds of populists, nationalists, and illiberals in Western Europe. The dramatic rise of ethno-nationalism, illiberalism, racism, and authoritarianism seen in Europe and around the world poses a threat not only to human rights but also to EU norms, values, and international treaties protecting the rights of minorities.

Wodak (2019) defines populism in its development in the EU through four dimensions: nationalism/nativism/anti-pluralism, anti-elitism, authoritarianism, and conservatism/historical revisionism. Far-right populists attempt to impose an unjustified vision of blood-related one nation/ethnos, as well as anti-elitism related to Euro-skepticism, or define social order in terms of hierarchical relations with the role of savior and charismatic leader and finally reproduce conservative values for protecting the "homeland" and constructing history into a narrative of betrayals or victories, success, and being the chosen people. This conglomeration of ideas poses a serious threat to human rights as populists by claiming to be the *vox populi*, define rights as an obstacle to expressing the will of the majority, and, as a result, reverse the role of human rights from the historically determined way of protecting people from the wickedness of governments to the instrumentalization of human rights discourse by populists who scapegoat refugees, minorities, immigrants, and any "otherness" that allegedly endangers the welfare, safety, and identity of the presumed majority.

The problem consists not only of populism/authoritarianism/nationalism directly violating human rights but also of its colonization and instrumentalization by those who wish to undermine it. The re-emergence of populism in the EU and the United

States after 2016 became a serious threat to the international protection of human rights (Neuman, 2020). As Roth put it in the context of rising of global populism, "a society's culture of respect for human rights needs regular tending, lest the fears of the moment sweep away the wisdom that built democratic rule" (2017, p. 84). Human rights discourse is being constantly hijacked by populists.

Tale of the Borders: Human Rights and Territories of Europe

We began the chapter by telling the enthusiastic story of the Polish-Ukrainian border, which demonstrated the "welcome culture" embedded in European societies and which is widely supported by the governments at first glance. However, this is only half of the truth about European hospitality. The openness toward the Ukrainian refugees was declared by all CEE governments, including national populists, but this openness has a color, a skin color that distinguishes Ukrainians from non-White refugees entering other EU borders including the Ukrainian side. Despite the wide openness of neighboring countries' citizens, people of color from the Global South have had a very different experience including discrimination, violence, exclusion, and overt racism on the Ukrainian and Polish sides of the border (Cénat et al., 2022). However, this is in contrast to the alarming situation at the EU border with Belarus, where racially motivated segregation of refugees is most disturbing. The Polish, Latvian, and Lithuanian parliaments approved legal amendments that allow migrants to be turned back at the border and ignore asylum claims made by those who entered it illegally. Both international and EU laws require that anyone who declares their willingness to seek international protection apply for it and refrain from returning people to the territories of countries where they are threatened or at risk of retaliation. Despite their tragic situation and the increased risk of human rights violations in Belarus, the Polish, Latvian, and Lithuanian authorities refuse to allow these people to enter the EU or receive basic humanitarian aid. With the excuse of "hybrid war," they declared an exceptional state, dispatched military and territorial defense forces, erected barbed wire fencing, legalized pushbacks, denied people access to asylum, and prevented humanitarian organizations from providing lifesaving aid to those trapped in the no man's land inside the border. This situation addresses concerns about the human rights of migrants and refugees at the European borders.

Human rights at the borders are not respected as a result of the absence of efficient and functional accountability procedures leading to the systemic dismantling of protection-sensitive asylum and border controls, particularly through restrictive legislative changes (European Network of National Human Rights Institutions, 2021). The legality of pushback is not unique to CEE; this common practice in Western Europe will be discussed in the following section of the chapter.

The Energy Crisis

Russia's power is largely built on oil and gas, and it takes advantage of its position as a petrochemical superpower that calls the shots to other international players who finally became energy-dependent states, including a large part of the EU. Russia seeks to monopolize natural gas and oil flow routes, and it pursues its interests to prevent the EU from developing a common energy security policy (Bodio, 2008). This is exactly the strategy that has been used by Russia on Western European and NATO members to undermine the support for Ukrainians during the war. The Russian-caused energy crisis, which cut off gas supplies and halted oil and coal deliveries, may cause millions of Europeans to become even poorer, and it will undoubtedly affect the poor.

To effectively execute regional policies aimed at reducing energy poverty, social workers' roles must be strengthened. They should also advocate for regulations and subsidies that would prevent energy poverty in the future. The human rights perspective includes rights to energy, which entails viewing energy not only as a source of poverty, particularly during and after the war in Ukraine, but also as critical for climate change responses and future human rights. It is critical to emphasize that the energy crisis and energy choices – such as low-carbon or renewable energy options – have a direct impact on everyone's human rights and well-being (Karlssoon, 2013).

Central and Eastern Europe in the Context of Colonization and Colonialism

One of the typical slogans of right-wing populists "We will not be a colony of Europe" characterizes the peculiarity of CEE illiberalism that focuses on subordination and exploitation (Pawlicki, 2012). This narrative resonates with words spoken by Kaczyński in 2020, who affirmed that "Poles decided to enter the EU, did not agree to be anyone's colony, but such subordination would make us and others the colony of so-called most influential EU players" (Państwowa Agencja Prasowa, 2020). In the following sections, we concentrate on the historical developments of CEE, discuss the issue of CEE illiberalism, and address the question: Is Eastern Europe so important in terms of current decolonization thinking? There are indeed similarities between colonialism outside of Europe and how CEE was created in reaction to Western Europe's growing demand for agricultural products during the Industrial Revolution. This led to the phenomenon of "coloniality of labor," a form of serfdom entwined with the global network of production, which ultimately resulted in the region being referred to as a "White periphery" with its ambiguous partial privileges coexisting with the constant oppression (Kalmar, 2022).

From a postcolonial perspective, Europe and Latin America might be the first peripheries of a modern world system; they are both political and economic projects (Europe focusing on agricultural production, South America on delivery of first gold and silver and then sugar, cotton, and tobacco), and both were incorporated into the capitalist world economy defined by forced labor. Decolonization is a historical and political process that ended colonialism and resulted in independence and the foundation of nation-states based on a European model in the former European colonies in Asia, Africa, and Latin America. As a result, the situation in Europe itself is rarely discussed in terms of the colonial matrix of power, even though the CEE region is significant from both a historical and a contemporary standpoint for the logic and practices of colonization – from historical legacies of internal colonization to the current situation in Ukraine being subjected to an attempted recolonization by Russia. At a time when colonial policies and practices are being reinstated by Russia's invasion of Ukraine in 2022, it became evident that colonialism still exists today, even in Europe itself. Along with the relationship between the Global North and the Global South, Europe is a symbol of this system. Ongoing research on "internal European colonization" (Etkind, 2011) stimulates discussion on how to engage in a postcolonial world by finding inspiration from how non-Europeans and Europeans both manage, transform, and work on the colonial past, which is simultaneously present as an indisputable legacy in its policies, institutions, and international relationships. Societies in CEE have experienced similar processes to those living under colonial rule overseas.

The analogy is based on several historical processes (slavery, the "second serfdom" in CEE, international division of labor that still exists taking as an example the second-class foreign labor force such as the Turks in Germany (Wiedner & Giesecke, 2021) and the imperial power balance with its colonizing tendencies: Western European or even global, Eastern European (Russia and later the Soviet Union), and the smaller players with imperial ambitions such as Poland and Hungary (Głowacka-Grajper, 2018). From the beginning of modern history, slavery affecting CEE was part of the global power relation with the significant role of the Ottoman Empire and resulted in over 2.5 million Slavs being enslaved (The Cambridge World History of Slavery, 2011) with the important role of Western Europe acting as intermediaries. Furthermore, slavery persisted during the eighteenth century as a means of maintaining international power balances, developing into the "second serfdom" that is so distinctive of CEE. As noted by Wallerstein (2002, p. 93–177), servitude in CEE was imposed to ensure the supply of grains by combinations of poorly waged and forced labor, often resembling slavery at the time when the power of the nobility was secured. By consolidating its food exports, CEE was incorporated as a semi-peripheral territory into the modern capitalist world system, with the prevailing form of labor exploitation persisting until the start of the twentieth century in some regions despite being officially banned in the nineteenth century (Janicki, 2021). As a result, even though the region was undeveloped by Western standards of economic development, it was assimilated into a capitalist world system, which led to its global integration into a growing colonial-racial system.

The characteristics of "in-betweenness" - (semi)peripheral position referring to the core and in racial terms being a part of 'White Europe' but 'not quite' and trying to 'catch up' to the West (Kalmar, 2022). The West also triumphed in CEE, splitting the region into two spheres of influence for the West and the East following the end of the Cold War, which restored the global system of powers. Neoliberalism, liberal democracy, and untamed market capitalism were the main forces of transition faced by CEE countries: "the neoliberal premises of the Washington consensus and respective advisors shaped the policies aimed at the radical, systematic transformation from non-capitalist regimes to capitalist ones" (Drahokoupil, 2007, p. 408).

Understanding the process of neoliberalization of postcommunist countries is crucial to explain the growth of neoliberalism in the welfare state and social security systems. The region's welfare states have seen a considerable alteration as a result of the growth, which was achieved through policy transfer (Cahill, Cooper, Konings, & Primrose, 2018). It is common to characterize the distinctiveness of CEE as a post-socialist system that had to adapt to the new economic circumstances and reality known as neoliberalism. Some state that in those countries there still exist strong antisocial ideological blocs that use socialism as a disciplinary device, which is a key component of contemporary capitalism in CEE region (Chelcea & Druţă, 2016). In reality, the post-1989 era is a postcolonial one, during which desperate attempts to imitate the West drove out third-way strategies and ideas of grassroots democracy that had been prevalent during the 1989 revolutions and gave rise to an illusion of political autonomy. This illusion of political self-determination, as noted by Fowkes and Hailbronner (2019), was the result of weak civil society, IMF pressures, the need to attract foreign investors, and the haste to join the EU. The region evolved into a colony of the twenty-first century, rich in cheap labor and market capacity that was providing ground for international corporations.

Illiberalism as a Threat to Human Rights

Illiberalism is often associated with populism, nationalism, and racism, but what exactly does it mean? According to Laruelle (2022), illiberalism is characterized by (i) a new type of ideological universe; (ii) being a reaction against liberalism using democratic norms, a response resulting from democratic voting procedures; (iii) proposing solutions that favor majoritarian, nation-centric or sovereigntist, conventional hierarchies and cultural homogeneity, and (iv) assuming shift from politics to culture and asserting its rootedness in a globalized world.

The case of CEE is symptomatic in that it experienced radical neoliberal disruptions that resulted in shrinking civil society and welfare state, as well as the rise of new elites at the expense of enormous inequalities in comparison to other parts of Europe. Krastev and Holmes (2020) assume that the illiberal turn in CEE is a complex reaction against the 1989 transition to Western-style democracy. In the process of shifting from communist socialism to liberal democracy, the region was following the path of "democratic mimicry" and "catch-up revolutions" of 1989, as if the area had no prior history of democracy, despite the West's disregard for CEE democratic norms and customs. It is worth considering that, for example, Poland established the first European constitution; the 1948 revolutions were widely echoed in democratic aspirations of CEE nations, often under internal colonization; and the radical democracy of "first solidarity" in Poland was based on social economy and worker empowerment beyond the political horizon.

Following the 1989 revolutions, in particular Central European semi-periphery, although somewhat privileged, was established as being between former colonizers and colonized (Kalmar, 2022). The illiberal turn in CEE is reactive, yet at the same time its anticolonial rhetoric is convincing in terms of the need for decolonization of the region based on retreat from a false choice between communism and neoliberalism (Appel & Orensten, 2016) to hand over the freedom of choice of a political and economic system. The problem might also be described as self-colonization, in which Western patterns clash with the day-to-day practices and institutional backdrop created within a "communist" framework, producing a "culture of absent standards" as a result of colonial "governmentality," such as the case of CEE (Kiossev, 2011). This implies the interiorization of hegemonies without outright dominance or administrative imposition of colonial discipline, but the scenario generated gaps between public, official, European and private, intimate, and national. The triumphant illiberalism is a reaction to the dominance of Western democratic and cultural standards, which generated the discourse aimed at reversing or, at the very least, changing the "core-periphery" framework that thrives on autochthonous state ideologies.

Surprisingly, the anticolonial rhetoric is mostly used by right-wing populists that instrumentalize it for political reasons. CEE illiberalism is not just a threat to human rights protection as a consequence of nationalism but above all the cry from close peripheries for decolonization. The right wing's utterance of decolonization or anticolonialism in the name of nation-centric identity and shift from politics to the rootedness of culture has led to the situation where the decolonizing discourse was captured by antidemocratic political powers. In the context of the possible development of "Westernized" CEE, this "false consciousness" involves no alternatives other than a return to an imagined community of autochthonous nations. The illiberal shift conquers the space of resistance and alternatives for the development of CEE outside of the nationalist paradigm and limits the critical approach to decolonization by other political forces or stances. The left was devoid of powerful analysis tools of the situation in Europe through decolonial lenses. The ongoing "illiberal revolt," as a consequence of Western European colonization, and the long process of peripheralization of the CEE need to be unpacked.

This is similar to human rights' "hacking" by illiberals and populists who declare the need for revisionism or its rejection. They often use three types of argumentation:

1. Effective protection of population defined in terms of ethnic and cultural identity.
2. Seizure of human rights by particular groups promoting their interests, instead of representing concerns of majority.
3. The majority should influence human rights development; they should not be defined by corrupted elites and alienated institutions (Bílková, 2019).

All of these arguments inflame the illiberal revolt in CEE – from Orbán's and Kaczyński's warnings against losing European identity and accusations that the

European Court of Human Rights is complicit in this process. The part of it is supposed conspiracy theories with elites from Bruxelles attempting to destroy national cultures and creating heterogeneous societies by enshrining new human rights alienated from the will of majority. Good example of this processes are governments justifying criminal measures toward people providing help to migrants and refugees. Also, defending restrictions on the freedom of the press or judges' independence in the name of majority proves complexity of illiberalism. It is compelling evidence that there is a shift in the understanding of human rights that includes the move from universal and abstract to local and political contexts.

The lesson of CEE is that fundamentalists, populists, and liberals can easily appropriate or hijack human rights to serve their interests. As a consequence of a complex history of peoples' struggles and positionality of the region defined as semi-periphery, the abuse of human rights has a different form as they become a part of a discourse legitimizing authoritarian regimes and government actions, and on the hand "elitist," universal, and intangible human rights can be easily violated. The developments in the region should not just increase people's awareness and vigilance in situations involving human rights violations but also increase critical awareness and criticism of "local" and particular instrumentalization, abuse, and "hacking" of human rights in public discourses, legal systems, or social practices. The imperialist and fundamentalist revisionist drive to relativize and instrumentalize human rights has grown to be a serious threat to the idea of being endowed with the same rights as others by virtue of being a human. Given the ongoing attempts by forces opposed to the idea of universal human rights to colonize and instrumentalize them, the situation in CEE demonstrates that decolonization of human rights should be a permanent process rather than creation of a new type of single universalism.

As national populism grows in Europe, we forget how easily fascism, nationalism, and conservatism can undermine human rights as they did in Europe in the 1930s and 1940s. As populist revisionism of human rights advances, it is clear that a part of the illiberal strategy is to instrumentalize and localize concrete but incomplete realizations of human rights for political purposes. This is the power of the illiberals, who made social programs accessible to every potential voter while incorporating ethereal and abstract human rights into daily life. It may explain why so many people who went through difficult times of transformation and severe neoliberalism choose this path. This brings up the topic covered in the second chapter's discussion following the question: Who owns human rights, communities, cultures, institutions, or individuals?

What characterizes CEE is "commodified pseudo-social welfare policies" that result in false "empowerment" based on passive monetary transfers that pacify the working classes to foster political loyalty and to keep illiberals in power. It is backed up by populist rhetoric that justifies the abolition of democratic institutions (Baranowski, 2022). One of the identity issues that has arisen as a result of mimicry processes and "Westernization" of social work in CEE is the lack of moral authority of social workers observed by Zaviršek (2015) who assumes the growing ideological influence of religious organizations. State withdrawal from social policy and "anesthesia strategies" common for the region relied on cushioning the social cost of transition to capitalism by using social policy as a tool for enhancing political order and governing power regimes (Vanhuysse, 2009). It is remarkable that, at the same time, church organizations and institutions became important players in shaping the new welfare state creating a phenomenon of "Catholicization" of neoliberalism or, more deeply, a "Catholicization" of the welfare state as in the case of Poland and Hungary (Boryczko, 2019). When considering the re-emergence of religious authorities on the wave of illiberal, populist revolts that accompany the re-establishment of the economic and moral power of religious institutions, this marriage of religion and illiberalism should come as no surprise. A situation in which the right-wing populists express demands for decolonization or anti-colonialism is destructive for the use of postcolonial theory in the context of analysis of contemporary society and breaking with the colonial heritage of Europe, as the postcolonial discourse has become hijacked by political forces hostile to democracy, human rights, and rights of minorities.

A possible reaction would be CEE self-determination as a catalyst for decolonization, which appears difficult in this case because the region, while colonized, was and still is too close to the Western version of Europe, limiting this possibility. It would also require the development of new types of universalisms beyond the European version, involving a network of universal universalisms or a multiplicity of universalisms (Wallerstein, 2006), including "too close to the West" Central and Eastern European versions.

We should certainly look for alternatives and illuminate possible political paths by learning from sources other than Western history and traditions. A good example is the history of CEE, where at the beginning of the twentieth century some argued for the implementation of a planned economy, self-government, and collegial government in management and production as ways of solving social problems, including the first European constitution in Poland, democratic revolts in the "Eastern bloc" that often led to direct democracy, workers' self-government project, and belief that the state had to ensure social security through universal and just working social security. Simultaneously, they believed that the capitalist state needed to provide social security through universal and just working social security. These are just a few examples, but they should not be overlooked because "like family, like freedom, the case can be made that the post-Cold War trio of markets, democracy, and constitutions are goods everywhere. However, their performance might measure up objectively from case to case, we have to remember that, as with freedom and family, these things are only ever real when we can call them our own" (Fowkes & Hailbronner, 2019).

The Russian invasion of Ukraine and other engagements in CEE and post-Soviet republics contribute to the idea of decolonization, not only in terms of the global North-South divide but also in terms of Europe's self-determination at a time when colonial policy is being reinstated directly in its Eastern part. By replicating neocolonial discourse, the narrative on the war shows the NATO-Russia perspective, which takes on the countries in the region as a force that allows them to decide on themselves. The war altered this viewpoint by demonstrating the vision of CEE in global negotiations between Russia and NATO.

In 2006, Wallerstein (2006) wrote that we are nearing the end of a long era known as European universalism and moving into a new type of universalism or "network of universal universalisms." The question remains open who will be the actors in this process, whose voices will be heard, and how imperial balance of power will be restructured after the war in the Ukraine. The decolonization that Europe as a whole requires is also born in Central and Eastern Europe, as evidenced not only by the conflict in Ukraine but also by the situation on the EU's eastern border and, more broadly, NATO's edge. CEE urgently requires decolonization because, in addition to its geographical proximity to Western Europe, it is the best example of how colonization is still occurring today, and populism endangering democracies and violating human rights is one of the most concerning issues in contemporary Europe.

While both CEE societies and people from the Global South actively participate in the "competitive" low-wage system, we must recognize that illiberalism undermines international worker solidarity by enforcing racism, Islamophobia, homophobia, and nationalism. True decolonization would necessitate acts of solidarity based on political action in recognition of the common interests of excluded Global South and CEE populations, as well as the abolition of postcolonial lobotomy described in Chap. 13, which assumes an "abyssal line" between what is allowed to be co-present or thought and what is not present and unimaginable in contemporary Western thought. It would imply linking metropolitan and peripheral (and semi-peripheral as in the case of CEE) societies, where practices, knowledge, imagination, and other aspects of those societies on the other side of the "abyssal line" could be incorporated into practices and theories available to all. Those acts of solidarity should be seen someday.

Racism, Poverty, and the Postcolonial Condition of the European Roma

Romanian Roma have lived in neglected plots of land in Gdańsk (Poland) since 2010. On Monday, August 4, 2014, officials from the Gdańsk magistrate appeared at the Roma camp and forced the Roma to leave by threatening to demolish the makeshift buildings with people inside. The Roma had 1 hour to pack up and leave their homes and could only take their personal belongings. Then, as part of working off debts, residents of municipal flats rented by the municipal property management board of Gdańsk destroyed five houses with axes. Officials operate illegally without a final eviction sentence. Families are not provided with a Romanian interpreter. Since then, the Roma sleep in tents, hidden in nearby bushes in the neighboring town. Fifteen people were left homeless, including five children. Employees of the

Social Welfare Center claim that they did not know about the eviction. One of the social workers is unofficially involved in the activities to protect the rights of the Roma, but he cannot act officially because the institution he works for implements the policy of displacement of the city authorities (Nowicki, 2015a).

The events described above are not isolated and are part of the policy of the European Union Member States, which after the accession in 2007 of Bulgaria and Romania began to tighten their regulations on internal Roma migration. When these countries joined the EU, the large Roma populations lived on their territory used the right to free movement to improve their economic situation. To restrict and control Roma mobility rights, EU countries began introducing anti-mobility measures. The introduced changes to the regulations entailed consequences for the Roma, whose appearance in the old EU countries was perceived as a problem, financial burden, and source of criminality.

Although officially Roma have the same rights as other EU citizens, their rights to free movement have been limited. Since 2007, the discussion on the criminalization of economic migration has been accompanied by the Roma context perceived through the prism of their alleged nomadism. To this end, states implement policies of Roma sedentarization through registration, forced settlement, and deportation requirements. The most emphatic example of this type of policy is denying Bulgaria and Romania the right to join the Schengen visa-free regime, the main reason of which is their reluctance to allow Roma migration (Memetovic, 2021).

Colonial practices toward the Roma community have existed in Europe for centuries. Only their forms of representation are changing. Some researchers compare the history of the Roma in Europe with that of black people in North America. In postcolonial studies, attention is drawn to how, after the abolition of slavery in the United States in the early 1880s, anti-vagrancy laws were introduced to limit the mobility of emancipated slaves. A similar thing happened in Europe when Romania abolished Romani slavery in the second half of the nineteenth century (Achim, 1998). However, unlike African Americans, Roma mobility rights are restricted to this day. Another common feature of the history of Roma and African Americans was the anthropological and historical research conducted at the turn of the eighteenth and nineteenth centuries, the aim of which was to demonstrate the racial and cultural inferiority of these groups by showing biological and cultural differences to prove that the studied groups did not come from Europe or America. Finally, at the end of the nineteenth century, research into the development and hierarchy of races, supported by linguistic analyses of the alleged linguistic purity of the Roma, allowed them to be assigned an origin to the lowest castes of Indian peoples and to break with the hypotheses about their common ancestry with Europeans. According to the formulated findings, the Roma were representatives of the mixed race responsible for the degeneration of racial purity of Europeans. The need to establish the origin of the Roma was to show the lack of their European roots and justify the inequality (Chang & Rucker-Chang, 2020).

Roma in the European Union: From Displacement Policies to Modern Racism

One of the widely discussed aspects of policies toward the Roma is the issue of compliance by EU countries with the right to free movement, guaranteed by the Directive of the European Parliament of 2004 (Directive 2004/38/EC). Pursuant to Article 6 of the Directive, all EU citizens have the right to stay in the host Member State for a period not exceeding 3 months; they only need an identity card or passport. The European Parliament assumed that during this period citizens can support themselves and not be a burden for the host country. Directive in Article 27 restricts the right to free movement only in the event of a threat to public order, security, and public health. However, this right is not respected toward Roma immigrants. Immediately after Romania and Bulgaria joined the EU in 2007, the Italian government established the so-called a security package with the right to immediately expel other EU citizens who are deemed to be a threat to public order without the need for a criminal investigation. The introduced provisions were mainly applied to Romanian Roma. France reacted similarly, where thousands of Roma were deported in 2007–2010 and around 300 Roma camps were broken up. The rationale for these mass deportations was national security and crime control. In 2010, Sweden deported 50 Roma on grounds of public safety. In the same year, 50 Roma were forcibly displaced from Finland, sending them back to Romania. The reason for deportation was poverty and the risk of putting a burden on the social welfare system. Also in 2012, Norway, referring to the need to counteract trafficking in human beings, took steps to deport the Roma. In all the cases of discrimination against Roma described above, the social background for tightening the control and security regulations was begging and accusations of breaking the law.

All of the activities described above were not in line with EU law on the right to free movement. The French government, defending its policy of displacement against the Roma who lived in begging, referred to Article 27 of the Free Movement Directive, considering that they constituted an unreasonable burden on the social assistance system. However, the United Nations Committee pointed out that the deportations are not in accordance with the Directive, as each expulsion of an EU citizen should be considered individually and the reference to public order and security may only be used in a situation where there are overriding grounds for using such radical measures. Moreover, the measures applied did not comply with the principle of proportionality, which means that the rules apply to specific individuals and not to entire social groups. The aim of the Directive was to strengthen the right of EU citizens to free movement if they do not constitute a burden for the host country. In the provisions on the free movement of persons in Article 6, it stipulated that persons wishing to stay for more than 3 months on the territory of a given state must register their stay, which is possible if they have a livelihood, health insurance, and employment or for the purpose of studying. Articles 6 and 7 of the Directive are based on the distinction between the economic status of EU nationals and the assumption that persons moving within the EU's borders are economically active

(Mäkinen, 2013). From the perspective of the events described, the EU was not prepared for the challenges of expanding its borders to include countries whose ethnic minorities are structurally excluded from access to basic services and experience extreme poverty. Considering the violence and systemic discrimination, some researchers point to the necessity to cover the Roma with the status of humanitarian migrants (Saarinen & Calloni, 2012).

An important element of the described policies to limit the right to migrate Roma was linking crime with begging. It is in this field of social policy that states have engaged in social work to reduce and control begging. As part of the system of gradation of social utility, begging is placed between the legality of work and crime, delimiting the space of transition between these spheres. An example of such practices was the anti-beggar media campaign conducted by one of the social welfare centers in Poland, the effect of which was to turn begging into an ethnic issue (Nowicki, 2015b). In this context, the tasks of the social welfare system are to "extend care" over the activity of citizens and forcing the population capable of working to undertake it (Boryczko, 2018).

In American begging research, some scholars have drawn attention to how the issue of gender and ethnicity influences such practices (Lankenau, 1999; Lee & Farrell, 2003; Snow & Anderson, 1993). Some studies show that for representatives of minority groups, begging can have a negative impact by reinforcing stereotypes of blacks being perceived as lazy, devoid of ambition and diligence (Rosenfield et al., 1982). The same mechanisms and stereotypes apply to Roma whose begging is seen as a cultural practice (Ruggiu, 2016). In Polish research on begging, some researchers go even a step further and describe begging Roma by using skin color and race categories in the encoding of empirical data (Dębski, 2013; Makaruk, 2015).

One of the most notorious cases of racialization Roma was a 2012 ruling by the Italian Supreme Court that stated that begging was a Roma cultural practice. An Italian court was to come to this without any anthropological analysis (Ruggiu, 2016). The example of the shaping of anti-begging provisions in the jurisprudence of Italian, Austrian, and Swedish courts shows that although these provisions were formulated in a culturally neutral language, they began to be introduced after Bulgaria and Romania joined the EU. In Sweden, in response to Roma migrations, some local councils have started introducing anti-begging laws. In response to the changes introduced in 2018, the case of new regulations was dealt with by the Supreme Administrative Court, which considered the bans justified, arguing that introducing restrictions on begging is permissible in places where there are problems with this phenomenon. Austria also began introducing legislation to ban begging altogether. As a result, in 2012, the case of the introduced provisions prohibiting begging was brought to the Constitutional Tribunal, which ruled that such solutions infringe Article 10 of the European Convention on Human Rights. Nevertheless, the Austrian constitutional court reopened begging in 2016, ruling that even passive begging could be prohibited in justified cases. On the other hand, in Italy, in 1995, begging was decriminalized because the Italian Constitutional Court found that it did not pose a threat to public order. However, after opening the union to new countries, Italy began to introduce administrative regulations prohibiting begging.

In November 2008, the mayor of Milan introduced a law criminalizing begging, calling it a disgusting and burdensome activity. The regulation allowed for the imposition of financial penalties on beggars in the amount of 500 euros and the confiscation of property (Marcu, 2018). In 2017, the Supreme Administrative Court declared them illegal. Despite these rulings, in 2018, the Italian government passed new laws banning certain types of begging. In none of the discussed cases of changes in the provisions on begging, it was indicated that they directly concern the Roma, only indicating that migrations carry the risk of new crimes and security (Memetovic, 2021). In turn, Germany has passed laws prohibiting begging with children. Luxembourg has also banned begging when it is organized and carried out in a group, as is often the case with begging Roma immigrants. Similarly, Norway has attempted to criminalize begging, which was recognized by the Norwegian Equality Ombudsman as directed against Roma (Memetovic, 2020). In Poland, in 2017, the Ombudsman made a request to deal with the change in the law on begging. The answer of the Ministry of Justice came after 4 years; the Ministry did not agree with the interpretation of the regulations, pointing out that it is not true that the most frequently imposed sanction for begging is a fine, because, as shown by statistical data, Polish courts most often impose a restriction of freedom against begging people (Bodnar, 2021).

Modern Racism and Discrimination in the Heart of Europe

Even though the Roma have been part of Europe for centuries, it has been believed that they constitute a culturally different social group (Chang & Rucker-Chang, 2020). It is estimated that around 10–12 million Roma live in the countries of the European Union and almost all countries have Roma communities. According to international reports on human rights, the Roma are the most discriminated ethnic minority in Europe. Among all groups surveyed by the Fundamental Rights Agency (FRA), Roma achieves the highest rates of discrimination in the areas of education, employment, health, and housing. Recent studies on the poverty of the Roma show that only 17% of households have sanitary facilities, such as a toilet, bathroom, or sewage connection. Moreover, due to the low level of education, lack of vocational training, and discrimination on the labor market, the Roma are excluded from access to the formal labor market. Among all the countries belonging to the EU, Romania has the highest unemployment rate among the Roma (European Union, 2016).

Some researchers argue that *Romophobia* is the last acceptable form of racism (McGarry, 2017). After the accession of Bulgaria and Romania, many European countries chose to ignore the poverty protection legislation while increasing the number of national or local laws and policies against begging and Roma migration (Memetovic, 2020). In the context of the lack of social policy, the implemented measures should be understood as a manifestation of strategy of displacement and forcing this community to continue migrating.

Market, Race, and Colonial Practice

After the fall of communism, the implementation of the free market economy in the countries of Central and Eastern Europe was the subject of numerous studies. Along with the socioeconomic changes, we were dealing with the introduction of a value system based on social Darwinism. With the development of postcolonial theory, this process began to be described as neocolonialism, understood as the exercise of political, economic, and military advantage and the power of stronger states over the weaker ones (Shohat, 1992). Economic transformation, even though it was a structural process of the transition of economic systems previously based on central planning to a free market economy, sought to justify the inequalities and poverty caused by these changes by individual characteristics of people. Responsibility for pauperization, unemployment, and poverty was translated as immaturity and social maladjustment to the new civilization mission imposed on Eastern Europe by the Western capitalist elites.

The promise of universal prosperity, democracy, and social justice based on inequalities, according to Immanuel Wallerstein, stems from tensions within capitalism and racism. Wallerstein identifies modern racism as a way of disciplining the workforce (1991). Modern racism does not focus on the biological and anthropological search for explanations for inequality but takes the form of cultural racism and the racialization of the excluded. The concept of cultural racism should be understood as the process of reifying, essentializing, and naturalizing cultural features ascribed to a given social group to create specific power relations (Bobako, 2010). Racialization in the context of postcolonial studies concerns the mechanism of legitimizing the position of people with low economic capital, which is previously essentialized and assumes the adequacy of description through categories such as ethnic origin, nationality, crime, or "social pathologies" caused by poverty, to then indicate them as the cause and justification of inequality. Racialization is related to the individualization of material needs and equating them with the biological maladjustment of the individual. It is a mechanism that legitimizes inequalities, consisting in the essentialization of a given set of subjective articulations and needs of groups with low social legitimization, at the bottom of the social ladder as the handicapped. After selecting and segregating the desired social characteristics, those considered undesirable are identified as the cause and justification of inequality. Thus, the mere representations of poverty in an Eastern European context resemble in many ways the concept of "Orientalism" by Edward Said (2018). The split between the backward South and the "advanced" West correlates with the split between a "civilized" White European and cheap labor from the former communist bloc states. This would support the argument that colonial practices also took place in Europe, because not only the territory is colonized but also people and their subjective articulations become the subject of colonization (Ashton-Smith, 2010).

Colonialism and Oppression in the Southern European Border

Introduction

The foundations of the Spanish nation were forged in two myths: on one side, reconquest of the (Christian) territory from the (Islamic) moors who had occupied it for almost eight centuries (from 711 to 1492) and, on the other side, the discovery, civilization, and Christianization of the territories that from the late fifteenth century to the late nineteenth century became the Spanish Empire (part of North America, Central, and part of South America as well as the Antilles and the Philippines). To these two elements and inextricably linked to them, it is the presence of the Catholic religion whose maintenance, reinforcement, and imposition by denying, prosecuting, and criminalizing other religious practices was executed by the Spanish inquisition with mathematical precision.

These three elements are central for understanding the traditional delay that Spain had in opening its economy, commerce, ideas, culture, and art in comparison with its more innovative and progressive neighbors (more particularly France). Only when these myths entered into crisis (because of the independence of the South American Republics), the defeat in the war with the United States (in which Cuba, the Philippines, and Puerto Rico were lost) was when a minority of lucid people could develop their projects of a more open, tolerant, creative, and progressive country. However, these periods didn't last for long because again the conservative-fascist forces (big bourgeoisie, church, and army) took the power by a *coup d'état* or even by provoking a civil war (as the one which took place in Spain from 1936 to 1939) and a 40 years period of neofascist dictatorship.

With this framework, it is understandable why in Spain a proper human rights discourse has never taken deep root among huge sectors of the population that still support the narratives of a Christian Spain that leads the Western world with its model of Christian society based on tradition and family.

The Effects of the Narratives in the Treatment of the Vulnerables in Spain

The Jews

People who could not be controlled in their behavior were considered as deviant people, among them there were Roma, Jewish, and Arabic people. In the case of the Jews, the unification of the country by the union of the Kingdoms of Castile and Aragon brought with it the expulsion of the Jews from the Spanish territory in 1492. They were obliged to convert to Christianity or leave the country. But even the ones who were converted were scrutinized and surveilled (Pérez, 2005, 2013).

The Moriscos (Moors)

Something similar happened with the millions of Spaniards of the Arab religion who had lived in the "reconquered" territories and who expressed themselves in Arabic as well as in Spanish. They were obliged to speak only Spanish and forbidden to practice Islamic religion and traditions. They were stigmatized as untrustworthy people who organized barbaric rituals (such as kidnapping Christian children and young women) and secretly planned a new invasion of Spain from the Kingdoms of North Africa. Certainly, these arguments were fake but were very effective in manipulating the public opinion against them. As a result, more than 300.000 Spanish nationals of the Arab religion were expelled from the Spanish territory from 1609 to 1613. It is not causal that the expulsion of the Moriscos coincided with the lack of popularity of the Spanish Monarchy due to the economic crisis, the pandemics, and the continuous defeat in the European wars. So, the Moriscos were the perfect scapegoat. As a result, many skills and working abilities were lost forever (Cortés, 2016).

The Roma People

Roma population because of their nomadic characteristics; their conception of the family, labor, and tradition; and their customs have been perceived with suspicion by a majority of the Spanish population who could not understand their way of living, working, celebrating, or relating with others. Accusations of vagrancy, delinquency licentiousness, and lack of willingness for integration have repeated throughout the times, and as a result, the Roma have been one of the minorities (if not the most) beaten, punished, and criminalized. This could not only be proved by examining the different laws from 1499 (catholic monarchs) to 1973 (Franco's regime) and the big pogroms of 1749 whose aim was to make this evil race disappear (Rothéa, 2014).

It is noteworthy that some of the narratives against Moors and Roma people still persist in essence although these have changed in their forms (some of them very slightly though) and it is not unusual to hear discourses from far-right leaders preventing the population from the presence of migrants.

Stereotypes and prejudices also informed laws aiming at the eradication of poverty by obliging the ones considered underserved to work against their will in what is considered as useful and necessary to the community or taking the risk of being criminalized.

A New Colonial Encounter and Some Unexpected Results

In his book *Anthropology & the Colonial Encounter*, Talal Asad explains in his introduction that there is:

> An unequal power encounter between the West and the Third World, which goes back to the emergence of bourgeois Europe, an encounter in which colonialism is merely one historical moment. It is this encounter that gives the West access to cultural and historical information about the societies it has progressively dominated, and thus not only generates a certain kind of universal understanding but also reinforces the inequalities in capacity between the European and the non-European worlds (and derivatively, between the Europeanized elites and the 'traditional' masses in the Third World. (Asad, 1973, p. 2)

This reflection has been particularly true in the case of Spain in which the presence of migrants coming from Latin American countries and the Maghreb area does not only mean a question of migration management but most of all a big challenge for Spanish society with its colonial past and its remnants.

This challenge can be simplified into two main ideas: Firstly, Spain was the land of the conquerors, who colonized vast territories in Latin America and exploited their resources and riches, but once the American Republics became independent and impoverished, Spain looked at it as a new promised land, and millions of Spaniards migrated to Latin America for a better future. There they realized that they were not the conquerors anymore. However, in the 1990s, there were millions of migrants coming from Ecuador, Peru Colombia, Bolivia, and Paraguay among others who came to Spain and started working in low-qualified and poorly paid jobs.

Secondly, the closeness of the Spanish territory to the Maghreb countries (14 km through the Strait of Gibraltar and even less if we refer to the Spanish provinces of Ceuta and Melilla) has favored migration coming from Morocco (mainly but also from Algeria) was numerous and significative. As the common European policy makes it really difficult for the nationals of their countries (and even more for the nationals of sub-Saharan European countries) to reach the Spanish shores, they tried to enter by irregular means (by using boats and dinghies), and many of them died in the sea (Caminando Fronteras, 2022). However, some discourses use these images as a pretext to speak of a new invasion from Islamic countries that could put Christian values at risk.

When Narratives Inspire Policies

Spain has used repeatedly its privileged situation as the only member of the EU which has Spanish as its mother tongue and a common shared history with Latin American countries to offer itself as their mediator in the European Union. This has been perceived with a certain suspicion by the government of some countries which don't want to feel colonized again by Spain. In terms of migration, it is true that nationals from Latin American countries, the Philippines, and Equatorial Guinea can get Spanish nationality with only 2 years of residence. And this has changed the phenotype of many Spanish cities as more than two million migrants from this origin have got the nationality. However, in terms of labor mobility, there are still huge differences in salaries and jobs as most of them are stuck in precarious jobs that extend from generation to generation.

The situation is completely different with migrants coming from the Maghreb countries who need 10 years to get the Spanish nationality and the obligation to renounce their previous nationality which does not happen with Latin Americans. The economic crisis (2008–2014) and the COVID-19 effects affected more intensively to migrant populations, most of which became even more vulnerable. The visibility of this vulnerability was used by right-wing parties to depict unaccompanied migrants that were in the streets as a potential danger for security and the arrival of migrants to the South Mediterranean and Canary Islands Shores as an invasion.

Social Work as an Anti-oppressive and Human Rights Profession That Challenges Neocolonialist Discourses

Dominelli (1993) defines anti-oppressive social work as "A form of social work practice which addresses social divisions and structural inequalities in the work that is done with 'client' (user) (…). Anti-oppressive practice aims to provide more appropriate and sensitive services by responding to people's needs regardless of their social status. Anti-oppressive practice embodies a person-centered philosophy, an egalitarian value system concerned with reducing the deleterious effects of structural inequalities upon people's lives; a methodology focusing on both process and outcome; and a way of structuring relationships between individuals that aim to empower users by reducing the negative effects of hierarchy in the work they do together" (p. 24), whereas cultural humility is defined by Tervalon and Murray-Garcia as "a lifelong learning process which goes further than cultural competence as incorporates a lifelong commitment to self-evaluation and self-critique, to redressing the power imbalances in the social worker professional dynamic, and to developing mutually beneficial and non-paternalistic clinical and advocacy partnerships with communities on behalf of individuals and defined populations" (Tervalon & Murray-García, 1998, p.117). It seems a statement above is obvious in that to be decolonized, social work needs to be culturally humble and anti-oppressive. However, the matter of the fact is that at the present moment, Spanish social workers have not been trained in these skills neither in academia nor in the institutions they work for. And this implies the risk of reproducing the views of the colonizer that create oppression and do not transform reality.

The Situation in the Spanish Southern Borders

One of the privileged places in which social workers face ethical dilemmas and are challenged by the different conflicting perspectives and responses existing is the situation on the southern border of Spain regarding migration and asylum seekers.

In this context, it is important to highlight that since 2015, access to European territory through the Spanish shores has been increasingly important in terms of a number of arrivals by the sea and land through the two main migratory routes, known as the Western Mediterranean route (Peninsular Mediterranean coast and the Spanish provinces of Ceuta and Melilla in Northern Africa) and the Western African route (Canary Islands). These two routes, at certain times of the year (particularly when weather conditions are favorable), experience an increase in the number of arrivals many of which take place in deplorable transit conditions, on one side, because of the EU migratory policy obsessed with border externalization and the strengthening of controls of migratory flows and, on the other, because of the circumstances of the journey itself. This all makes the decision of getting to Europe extremely hazardous for migrants that experience great vulnerability and suffering and death.

According to the report *Monitoring the Right of Life* of the NGO Caminando Fronteras (2022), the total number of victims trying to enter Spain in 2022 was 2390, out of which 1784 correspond to the Western African Route and 606 to the Western Mediterranean coast.

However, oppressive responses take place on a daily basis, and social workers are confronted by this reality in their work for organizations or state institutions. Probably, the most recent example, due to its importance and relevance in the media, was the one which took place in Melilla, in the Spanish border with Morocco, in June 2022. This clearly demonstrates that repressive responses are assumed and justified by a government which has been labeled as the most progressive in the history of democracy in Spain.

In June 2022, a group of migrants tried to scale the border fence between Spain and Morocco in the African province of Melilla. In this incident, about 37 people died and 217 were injured. The version of the Spanish Government was that the deaths occurred in the Moroccan territory and that the Spanish police had proceeded with due respect for human rights and always used proportionality in the methods used to repel the incursion. However, this version was questioned by the preliminary report from the Spanish Ombudsman (Defensor del Pueblo, 2022) and the BBC documentary "Death at the Border" (Vanhooymissen, 2022) which depicted how people injured on Spanish territory were pushed back to Morocco and highlighted the compliance of the Spanish forces with the brutality of the Moroccan agents.

The main lessons to be learned from this type of incidents is to which extent colonial thought is still present in the views of the Spanish and Moroccan Governments and the European Union. It is particularly paradoxical how a government like the Moroccan assumes the colonial discourse as part of a contract of the EU migration policy on which borders needs to be externalized in a way that human right violations occur outside of the European territory.

In this context, it is important that social workers develop a critical, anti-oppressive, and culturally humble perspective to challenge these human rights violations.

By Means of Conclusion

Five tips to start a process of decolonization from social work:

1. Be aware of the history of your country through critical eyes putting into question what has been taken for granted and dare to view it from the perspective of the victims.
2. Be critical of the way you are being trained in social work in order to identify which practices are still based on colonialist assumptions.
3. Be aware of human rights developments by following the periodical reports, the work of the rapporteurs of the representatives of the IFSW at the United Nations.
4. Denounce the oppressive practices.
5. Be humble enough to admit that this is a lifelong learning process.

Discussion Questions

1. In what ways is the situation in Central and Eastern Europe compelling in terms of Europe's need for decolonization?
2. What are the main characteristics of modern racism, and how it connects with displacement policies?
3. Can you describe the similarities and differences in the situation of refugees at the EU's southern and eastern borders, using Spain and Poland as an example?

References

Achim, V. (1998). *The Roma in Romanian history*. Central European University Press.

Appel, H., & Orenstein, M. A. (2016). Why did neoliberalism triumph and endure in the post-communist world? *Comparative Politics, 48*(3), 313–331. https://doi.org/10.5129/001041516818254419

Asad, T. (1973). Anthropology and the colonial encounter. .

Ashton- Smith, A. (2010). Colonized culture: The emergence of a Romani Postcolonialism. *JPCS, 1*(2).

Baranowski, M. (2022). The illiberal turn in politics and ideology through commodified social policy of the 'family 500+' programme. *Forum for Social Economics*. https://doi.org/10.1080/07360932.2022.2138936

Bílková, V. (2019). Populism and human rights. In J. Nijman & W. Werner (Eds.), *Netherlands yearbook of international law 2018*. T.M.C. Asser Press. https://doi.org/10.1007/978-94-6265-331-3_7

Bobako, M. (2010). Konstruowanie odmienności klasowej jako urasawianie. Przypadek polski po 1989 roku [Constructing class diversity as a racialization. The Polish case after 1989]. In *Podziały klasowe i nierówności społeczne. Refleksje socjologiczne po dwóch dekadach realnego kapitalizmu w Polsce* (pp. 165–177).

Bodio, M. (2008). *Polityka energetyczna w stosunkach między Unią Europejską a Federacją Rosyjską w latach 2000–2008* [Energy policy in relations between the European Union and the Russian Federation in the years 2000–2008]. Oficyna Wydawnicza ASPRA.

Bodnar, A. (2021, January 21). *Najwyższy czas zlikwidować karalność żebrania. Rzecznik pisze do MS. Resort odpowiada* [It is high time to eliminate the criminality of begging. The spokesman writes to MS. The resort responds]. Rzecznik Praw Obywatelskich. https://bip.brpo.gov.pl/pl/content/najwyzszy-czas-zlikwidowac-karalnosc-zebrania-rzecznik-pisze-do-ms-resort-odpowiada

Boryczko, M. (2018). Governmentality w systemie pomocy społecznej [Governmentality in the social welfare system]. *Miscellanea Anthropologica Et Sociologica, 19*(3), 189–203.

Boryczko, M. (2019). Neoliberal governmentality in social work practice. An example of the polish social security system. *European Journal of Social Work, 23*(2), 191–202. https://doi.org/10.1080/13691457.2019.1617678.

Bradley, K. R., & Cartledge, P. (Eds.). (2011). *The Cambridge World History of slavery*. Cambridge University Press.

Bryc, A. (2008). *Rosja w XXI wieku - gracz światowy czy koniec gry* [Russia in the 21st century - a world player or the end of the game]. Wydawnictwa Akademickie i Profesjonalne.

Buljubašić, M. (2022). *Violent Right-Wing Extremism in the Western Balkans: An overview of country-specific challenges for P/CVE.* Radicalisation Awareness Network. https://home-affairs.ec.europa.eu/whats-new/publications/violent-right-wing-extremism-western-balkans-july-2022_en

Caminando Fronteras. (2022). https://caminandofronteras.org/2-390-personas-migrantes-perdieron-la-vida-en-2022-en-sus-trayectos-hacia-el-estado-espanol/

Cahill, D., Konings, M., Cooper, M., & Primrose, D. (2018). *The SAGE handbook of neoliberalism.* SAGE Publications Ltd.

Cénat, J. M., Darius, W. P., Noorishad, P. G., McIntee, S. E., Dromer, E., Mukunzi, J. N., Solola, O., & Williams, M. T. (2022). War in Ukraine and racism: The physical and mental health of refugees of color matters. *International Journal of Public Health, 67*, 1604990. https://doi.org/10.3389/ijph.2022.1604990

Chang, F., & Rucker-Chang, S. (2020). *Roma rights and civil rights: A transatlantic comparison.* Cambridge University Press.

Chelcea, L., & Druţă, O. (2016). Zombie socialism and the rise of neoliberalism in post-socialist Central and Eastern Europe. *Eurasian Geography and Economics, 57*(4–5), 521–544. https://doi.org/10.1080/15387216.2016.1266273

Cortés, L. M. (2016). El Proceso de expulsión de los Moriscos de España (1609–1614). Universitat de València.

Dębski, M. (2013). Charakterystyka problemu żebractwa w Gdańsku: na podstawie obserwacji ukrytej nieuczestniczącej [Characteristics of the problem of begging in Gdańsk: based on a hidden observation not participating]. *Forum o Bezdomności Bez Lęku, 6*(6), 103–125.

Defensor del Pueblo. (2022). Informe sobre las actuaciones de las fuerzas y cuerpos de seguridad del Estado en Melilla. https://www.defensordelpueblo.es/resoluciones/actuaciones-y-medidas-de-los-cuerpos-y-fuerzas-de-seguridad-del-estado-en-melilla/

Directive 2004/38/EC. (n.d.). *Directive 2004/38/EC of the European Parliament and of the Council of 29 April 2004 on the right of citizens of the Union and their family members to move and reside freely within the territory of the Member States amending Regulation.*

Dominelli, L. (1993). *Social work: Mirror of society or its conscience? 'race', gender and social justice in a profession.* Department of Sociological Studies, University of Sheffield.

Drahokoupil, J. A. N. (2007). Analysing the capitalist state in post-socialism: Towards the Porterian workfare Postnational regime. *International Journal of Urban and Regional Research, 31*(2), 401–424. https://doi.org/10.1111/j.1468-2427.2007.00727.x

Etkind, A. (2011). *Internal colonization. Russia's imperial experience*. Polity Press.

European Network of National Human Rights Institutions. (2021). *Gaps in human rights accountability at Borders. Report.* https://ennhri.org/wp-content/uploads/2021/12/Gaps-in-Human-Rights-Accountability-at-Borders.pdf

European Parliament and of the Council. https://eur-lex.europa.eu/legal-content/EN/TXT/?uri=celex%3A32004L0038

European Union Agency for Fundamental Rights. (2016). Second European Union minorities and discrimination survey Roma – Selected findings.

Fanon, F. (1967). *Black skin, white masks*. Grove Press.

Fowkes, J., & Hailbronner, M. (2019). Decolonizing Eastern Europe: A global perspective on 1989 and the world it made. *International Journal of Constitutional Law, 17*(2), 497–509. https://doi.org/10.1093/icon/moz040

Głowacka-Grajper, M. (2018, November 3). *Internal colonization*. https://keywordsechoes.com/internal-colonisation

Hering, S., & Waaldijk, B. (2003). *History of social work in Europe (1900–1960): Female pioneers and their influence on the development of international social organizations*. Leske + Budrich.

Jahren, K. A. (2017, November 3). Use and abuse of human rights discourse. *E-International relations*. https://www.e-ir.info/2013/10/27/use-and-abuse-of-human-rights-discourse/

Janicki, K. (2021). *Pańszczyzna. Prawdziwa historia polskiego niewolnictwa* [Serfdom. The true story of Polish slavery]. Wydawnictwo Poznańskie.

Kalmar, I. D. (2022). *White but not quite: Central Europe's illiberal revolt*. Bristol University Press.

Karlssoon, G. (2013). A human rights approach to energy, poverty and gender inequality. In C. Holder & D. Reidy (Eds.), *Human rights the hard questions* (pp. 231–245). Cambridge University Press.

Kiossev, A. (2011). *The Self-Colonizing Metaphor*. http://monumenttotransformation.org/atlas-of-transformation/html/s/self-colonization/the-self-colonizing-metaphor-alexander-kiossev.html

Krastev, I., & Holmes, S. (2020). *The light that failed: A reckoning*. Penguin Books.

Lankenau, S. E. (1999). Panhandling repertoires and routines for overcoming the nonperson treatment. *Deviant Behavior, 20*(2), 183–206.

Laruelle, M. (2022). Illiberalism: A conceptual introduction. *East European Politics, 38*(2), 303–327. https://doi.org/10.1080/21599165.2022.2037079

Lee, B. A., & Farrell, C. R. (2003). Buddy, can you spare A dime? *Urban Affairs Review, 38*(3), 299–324. https://doi.org/10.1177/1078087402238804

Makaruk, K. (2015). Żebractwo dzieci w Polsce [Begging of children in Poland]. *Dziecko Krzywdzone. Teoria, Badania, Praktyka, 14*(2), 113–133.

Mäkinen, V. (2013). Are there fundamental rights for Roma beggars in Europe? *Political Theology, 14*(2), 201–218.

Marcu, O. (2018). Do you trust me? Begging as transnational emotional work for migrant Roma. In M. Caselli & G. Gilardoni (Eds.), *Globalization, supranational dynamics and local experiences* (pp. 288–307). Springer International Publishing.

McGarry, A. (2017). *Romaphobia the last acceptable form of racism*. Bloomsbury Publishing.

Memetovic, S. (2020). *Between freedom of expression and discriminatory policies: Is there a right to beg?*

Memetovic, S. (2021). Anti-begging provisions in Europe through the lens of Critical Race Theory [LLM Capstone / Final Thesis]. Central European University Private University.

Neuman, G. (2020). Populist threats to the international human rights system. In G. Neuman (Ed.), *Human rights in a time of populism. Challenges and responses* (pp. 1–19). Cambridge University Press.

Nowicki, T. (2015a). Badanie ku zmianie. Integracja i opór romskich rodzin wobec polityki wysiedleni [Study to change. Integration and resistance of Roma families to displacement policy]. *Pedagogika Społeczna, 1*(55), 207–243.

Nowicki, T. (2015b, May 19). *Dlaczego uczyniono żebractwo w Gdańsku kwestią etniczną? (komentarz)* [Why was begging in Gdańsk an ethnic issue? (comment)]. Infomigrator

Trójmiasto. http://www.trojmiasto.info-migrator.pl/aktualnosci-trojmaisto/1338-dlaczego-uczyniono-żebractwo-w-gdańsku-kwestią-etniczną-komentarz

Państwowa Agencja Prasowa (2020, October 21). *Kaczyński: Polska nie będzie kolonią,* [Kaczyński: Poland will not be a colony]. https://www.pb.pl/kaczynski-polska-nie-bedzie-kolonia-1006055

Papović, P., Kovačević K. (2021, November 3). *Rast desničarskog ekstremizma u Crnoj Gori: Građanska država na ispitu* [The growth of right-wing extremism in Montenegro: Civil state on the test]. Centar za demokratsku tranziciju. https://www.cdtmn.org/wp-content/uploads/2021/03/Rast-desnicarskog-ekstremizma-u-Crnoj-Gori_WEB-Preview-3.pdf

Pekmez, I. (2021, April 5). Black-Clad 'Humanitarians' Promote Pro-Russian Agenda in Bosnia. *Detektor.* https://detektor.ba/2021/04/05/black-clad-humanitarians-promote-pro-russian-agenda-in-bosnia/?lang=en

Pérez, J. (2005). *Los judíos en España* [the Jews in Spain], Marcial Pons Historia.

Pérez, J. (2013). *Historia de una tragedia: La expulsión de los judíos de España* [History of a tragedy: The expulsion of Jews from Spain]. Austral.

Pawlicki, J. (2012, January 22). Marsz poparcia dla Orbána. ''Nie będziemy kolonią Europy'', [March of support for Orban. ''We will not be a colony of Europe'']. *Gazeta Wyborcza.* https://wyborcza.pl/7,75399,11012187, marsz-poparcia-dla-orbana-nie-bedziemy-kolonia-europy.html

Roonemaa, H., Laine, M., & Weiss, M. (2022, November 3). *Exclusive: Russia backs Europe's far right.* https://newlinesmag.com/reportage/exclusive-russia-backs-europes-far-right/

Rosenfield, D., Greenberg, J., Folger, R., & Borys, R. (1982). Effect of an encounter with a black panhandler on subsequent helping for blacks. *Personality and Social Psychology Bulletin, 8*(4), 664–671.

Rothéa, X. (2014). Construcción y uso social de la representación de los gitanos por el poder franquista 1936-1975 [Construction and social use of the representation of gypsies by the Francoist power 1936-1975]. *Revista Andaluza De Antropología,* (7), 7–22. https://doi.org/10.12795/raa.2014.i07.01

Ruggiu, I. (2016). Is begging a Roma cultural practice? Answers from the Italian legal system and anthropology. *Romani Studies, 26*(1), 31–62.

Saarinen, A., & Calloni, M. (Eds.). (2012). *Builders of a "new Europe": Women migrants from the eastern transregions.* Kikimora Publications.

Said, E. (2018). *Orientalism.* Zysk i S-ka.

Shohat, E. (1992). Notes on the "post-colonial.". *Social Text, 31*(32), 99.

Snow, D., & Anderson, L. (1993). *Down on their luck: A study of homeless street people.* University of California Press.

Snyder, T. (2022, April 28). The war in Ukraine is a colonial war. *The New York Times.* https://www.newyorker.com/news/essay/the-war-in-ukraine-is-a-colonial-war

Stronski, P. (2022, November 3). *Russia in the Balkans after Ukraine: A troubling actor.* https://carnegieendowment.org/politika/8795

Tervalon, M., & Murray-García, J. (1998). Cultural humility versus cultural competence: A critical distinction in defining physician training outcomes in multicultural education. *Journal of Health Care for the Poor and Underserved, 9*(2), 117–125. https://doi.org/10.1353/hpu.2010.0233

Tlostanova, M. (2012). Postsocialist ≠ postcolonial? On post-Soviet imaginary and global coloniality. *Journal of Postcolonial Writing, 48*(2), 130–142.

Turoma, S., & Waldstein, M. (2016). *Empire de/centered: New spatial histories of Russia and the Soviet Union.* Routledge Taylor & Francis Group.

Vanhooymissen, S. (2022). *Death on the Border* [Film]. BBC Africa Eye Documentary.

Vanhuysse, P. (2009). Power, order and the politics of social policy in Central and Eastern Europe. In A. Cerami & P. Vanhuysse (Eds.), *Post-communist welfare pathways. Theorizing social policy transformations in Central and Eastern Europe.* Palgrave.

Waldstein, M., & Turoma, S. (2016). *Empire de/centered: New spatial histories of Russia and the Soviet Union.* Routledge.

Wallerstein, I. (1991). The ideological tensions of capitalism: Universalism versus racism and sexism. In E. Balibar & I. Wallerstein (Eds.), *Race, nation, class. Ambiguous identities*. Verso.

Wallerstein, I. (2002). *The capitalist world-economy: Essays*. Cambridge Univ. Press.

Wallerstein, I. (2004). World-systems analysis. In G. Modelski & R. Denemark (Eds.), *World system history* (*Encyclopedia of life support systems*). UNESCO EOLSS Publishers.

Wallerstein, I. M. (2006). *European universalism: The rhetoric of power*. New Press.

Wiedner, J., & Giesecke, J. (2021). Immigrant men's economic adaptation in changing labor markets: Why gaps between Turkish and German men expanded, 1976–2015. *International Migration Review, 56*(1), 176–205. https://doi.org/10.1177/01979183211029903

Wodak, R. (2019). *The Trajectory of Far-Right Populism – A Discourse-Analytical Perspective*. In B. Forchtner (Ed.), The Far Right and the Environment. Politics, Discourse and Communication. Routledge.

Zaviršek, D. (2015). Social work education in Eastern Europe. *Global Social Work*, 271–282. https://doi.org/10.2307/j.ctv1fxm2q.23

Грабовський С. (2013, November 3). Чим же була УРСР у складі Союзу? [What was the Ukrainian SSR in the Soviet Union?]. *Den*, 91 https://day.kyiv.ua/uk/article/podrobici/chim-zhe-bula-ursr-u-skladi-soyuzu

Marcin Boryczko is an Associate Professor at the University of Gdańsk, Poland, where he teaches Social Work on bachelors' and masters' levels. He serves in the board of several international and national associations such as the Polish Federation of Social Workers and Social Service Employees Unions (Polska Federacja Związków Zawodowych Pracowników Socjalnych i Pomocy Społecznej), the European Social Work Research Association, and the International Advisory Board of the *European Social Work Research Journal* and serves as Polish Representative in the International Federation of Social Workers (IFSW). His main research interests include social work education, critical social work theory, human rights, decolonization, neoliberal governmentality, and populism in Central Europe.

Tomasz Nowicki, a graduate of philosophy, is a Doctor of Social Sciences and Assistant Professor at the University of Gdańsk, Poland. He is also an Author of publications and monographs in the field of animal studies, popular culture, migration policy, and new technologies, combining scientific experience with practice, and a Creator and Coordinator of programs in the field of social policies – in particular integration and housing policy – as well as a human rights Expert. Moreover, he is Initiator of pioneering programs in Poland in the area of counteracting social exclusion, Editor of the book *Revenge of Emancipation: Nationalism, Refugees, Muslims*, and Originator and Co-creator of the first common room in Poland for begging children. In his scientific work, he deals with the issue of constructing the subject through cultural practices related to zoos and begging.

Emilio Jose Gómez Ciriano is Associate Professor at Universidad de Castilla-La Mancha (Spain). He teaches social services, human rights, and migration. He has led some research projects related to migration and asylum. He has a background in law, social anthropology, and social work. Before entering academia, he worked for Human Rights and Migration NGOs for 10 years. He does consultancy work at EU level. Currently, he is the Secretary of the European Social Work Research Association.

More info at https://dialnet.unirioja.es/servlet/autor?codigo=321043

Chapter 8
Decolonized Approaches to Human Rights and Social Work in the United States

Erica R. Balderrama, Araceli Garcia, and Eva M. Moya

Introduction

Social work as a profession is founded on the premise of promoting social justice and protecting human rights. At its core, the field focuses on addressing social justice through the development of policies and practices that protect human rights, eradicate poverty, and defend those who are at the margins. To do this, social work tackles "isms" – such as racism, sexism, classism, ableism, ageism, and colonialism – all of which are part of the structure of oppression. However, social work is embedded in and influenced by the structural injustices that it aims to overcome. Western and Eurocentric frameworks are at the heart of the profession's work, values, and practices. Colonization has historically affected the way communities and groups of people expressed their cultures. Colonization entailed the theft of indigenous land and the erasure of cultures with the goal of economic exploitation as well as accommodation and acculturation to the colonizer's culture. The profession is now being challenged by the very same things that built it. While attempting to advance equality, social work has been instrumental in promoting oppressive ideas and imperialist values. Changing the course of the profession will entail reframing the definition of the profession and imagining effective and more inclusive practices, severing its ties to oppressive policies and practices. By looking at the history

E. R. Balderrama (✉) · A. Garcia
Department of Social Work, College of Health Sciences, Univeristy of Texas at El Paso, El Paso, TX, USA
e-mail: erbalderrama@utep.edu; agarcia185@utep.edu

E. M. Moya
Department of Social Work, College of Health Sciences, Univeristy of Texas at El Paso, El Paso, TX, USA

Border Biomedical Research Center, El Paso, TX, USA
e-mail: emmoya@utep.edu

M. Madew et al. (eds.), *Decolonized Approaches to Human Rights and Social Work*,
https://doi.org/10.1007/978-3-031-33030-8_8

of the profession to understand the colonialist roots of the field, we can embark on a new path of anti-oppressive social work.

In this chapter, we describe the history of social work in the United States, from its formation to its current challenges, review the current state of the field, and assess its attempts at becoming more effective and inclusive.

Overview of US History of Colonization: Fifteenth to Nineteenth Century

The history of the United States serves as an example of the concepts of both imperialism and colonialism, both of which are manifested on a global scale. To understand the country's historical roots, one must understand the terms and their differences. Imperialism can be summed up as the expansion of a country's economic and political power beyond its territorial borders. Colonialism is the process by which a country physically exerts its power over another territory, usually by conquering and settling territories by force. The history of the United States began in the late fifteenth century with Europeans forcibly exerting their power and expansion onto land already inhabited by the indigenous tribes of people living in what is now known as North America. Colonialism began with the genocide of more than seven million indigenous people, eradicated from existence by war, conquest, and disease. Modern education systems in the United States would go on to generate their own "creation story or origin myth" (Martinez, 2004) to describe the early history of the founding of the country, a story that would omit and diminish its dark roots. However, the realities, beginning with the genocide of indigenous people and tribes, would initiate a long history of colonial imperialistic practices, all of which directly affect the people social workers work with and the communities in which they work.

Following the domination and the forced removal of indigenous people and tribes, the newly established powerholders of the country would begin their conquest to expand its reach for even more sovereignty. The country has historically been fueled by the desire to expand its reach for economic growth through capitalism, militarism, domination by Whites, and the spread of Christianity. This has been historically influenced by issues of overpopulation, economic depression, and mercantilism. Examples of this lust for power date back to the fifteenth century. However, during the seventeenth through the nineteenth centuries when White Americans believed they were superior to others, the country would begin its efforts to exert more control and power on a local and global scale. Examples of actions taken during this time are common knowledge to those familiar with US history. As the United States' economy was expanding during the agricultural and industrial periods, the need for affordable labor was in high demand. After having rid the lands of indigenous men and women, the alternative to finding affordable labor was to engage in the slave trade. "Enslaved Africans provided the labor force that made the growth of the United States possible" (Martinez, 2004). Levy (2021) as cited in

Janeway (2021) states, "in 1860, the value of property in slaves was three times the value of all U.S. industrial capital," indications of the future of capitalism that the country would experience well into modern times.

In addition to the actions taken against indigenous tribes and enslaved Africans, the United States was colonizing other territories in its pursuit for power and expansion. In hopes of gaining power of land and territory already owned by Mexico, the United States would end up in yet another war, the Mexican American War in 1846 following the annexation of Texas in 1845. Following the victory in this war, the country would begin a time of "aggressive western expansion" (Martinez, 2004). Out of this expansion would come the doctrine of "Manifest Destiny," which justified the colonization of territory that historically was occupied by others. This doctrine stated the "United States was destined by God to take over other peoples and lands" and it was "the right of our manifest destiny to overspread and to possess the whole continent which Providence has given us for the development of the great experiment of liberty and federated self-government" (Martinez, 2004). American ideologies have long contended that Americans were to bring glory to the country and it was the duty of the American people to "civilize" others across the world.

Two notable individuals, social work's "founders," Mary Richmond and Jane Addams, while well-intentioned, participated in the work of "civilizing" immigrants in the United States at the time (Stanley, 2020). These ideas and belief systems are still present today, playing out in various forms of oppression of immigrants and others.

Actions taken because of this ideology during the nineteenth century resulted in the Spanish-American War, which claimed the lives of hundreds of thousands. In addition to the lives lost, more territories were gained, strengthening America's power through colonization. With this power, American men were emboldened to strip the dignity and worth of Filipino individuals, a territory colonized by America in the Spanish-American War, lessening this group to "monkeys" to be on display. Termed the *White Man's Burden*, Americans believed it was the duty of Whites to bring civilization to othered people who were regarded as "backward" (Kipling, 1899). A commonly known fact, which resulted after years of American colonization and expansion, was the purchase of Puerto Rico. Puerto Rico is still only considered a US territory – a territory with no voting rights in federal elections, reflecting the oppressive powers of colonization. Following the Spanish-American War, America embarked on other journeys of "civilizing" and reigning power over countries with populations who were not White or Christian.

White Superiority and White Supremacy

This would pave the way for a long history of White superiority, more commonly termed White supremacy, in early American society, still being felt and experienced in America today. Several Americans during the nineteenth century would ascribe to the ideology and belief system of White superiority. Historical accounts confirm this identity which was adopted by most people living in America at the time. For example, arguments in favor of slavery were rooted in White supremacy views. These same views are key to the Lost Cause myth used to explain the demise of the southern Confederacy and were central to the support for segregation. As Gardiner (2009) defines in his work, a definition of "internalized racist superiority" is a complex multigenerational socialization process that teaches Whites to believe, accept, and practice superior societal definitions of self and to fit into and inhabit dominant social roles. These behaviors define and normalize the race construct and its outcome – White supremacy. White supremacy can be found at the root of oppressive and discriminatory practices that are commonly known as "isms."

A common example of this ideology is the philosophy of social Darwinism. This argument was "another European scientific concept that supported the concept of race" (Gardiner, 2009). The ideas behind social Darwinism as espoused philosophy Herbert Spencer claimed are that natural selection and survival of the fittest were explanations for the differences in races. Spencer (1894) contended that people of color were in a "natural condition" due to their deficits in intellectual and physical capacities, rendering White people "more fit." This aberration of scientific Darwinist theory was used to justify the actions taken against the indigenous people and would influence and support public policy of segregation and outlawing interracial marriages. White superiority and the desire for Whites to exert control have been a driving force behind the colonization of minorities in America. This can be confirmed through the history of slavery in the United States, the separation of indigenous children from their families, exclusion laws targeting Chinese immigrants, and the repatriation and the deportation of Mexicans during the Great Depression. Interestingly, the first European settlers of the British colonies did not refer to themselves as "White" as many of them arrived as indentured servants themselves, which would later influence the development of a class system driven by racist ideologies. After indentured servants together with black slaves recognized the power they had together to combat the oppression they faced, White powerholders responded in a manner that perpetuated racism and established the class system we see today. Classism and racism are two practices that are deeply intertwined.

There are several other events in US history worth mentioning that have either been influenced by or have occurred in response to colonialism. For example, the Civil War was rooted in the conflict over slavery. Additionally, the US Constitution and Bill of Rights were both drafted under the presumption that people had fundamental rights that were to be protected by their government. Paradoxically, these documents were created with the idea that all persons had fundamental rights yet were developed after atrocities such as the colonizing of indigenous tribes or First Nations. Other historical events, such as the rise of industrialization, transformed American society and its economic landscape into one of the largest and most successful in the world at the time. The influx of immigrants who came to America for economic opportunity in the late 1800s and early 1900s, the Progressive Era in which progressives, as they were called, advocated for more democratic processes, and the Great Depression where over a quarter of Americans were out of work and their livelihoods were threatened by the sequelae of the stock market crash of 1929.

Social Work in Early History

How does all of this pertain to social work? How has social work combated or participated in this colonizing imperialistic culture? Late in the nineteenth century, when the nation was going through the Industrial Revolution, a social question began to emerge that sparked the widespread interest. Why were so many people living in poverty while the country's economy was booming? Rates of unemployment were on the rise in urban areas, and higher rates of child abandonment and neglect became an issue of concern. In response, people from religious backgrounds as well as those who aimed to rationalize the situation developed charity groups, the first activity of what would become social work. An area of concern these charity groups aimed to address was the issue of orphans and poor children in urban areas (Stuart, 2013). Historical accounts of orphaned children claim children were abandoned for multiple reasons (i.e., lack of economic stability, children born out of wedlock, death of parents). In response to this issue, the New York Children's Aid Society (CAS), the "orphan trains," implemented one of the early child saving measures. These orphan trains transported poor children from New York to live with Christian farm families in the Midwest – essentially creating the first foster care system (Stuart, 2013). The "Christian family home" was the desired family structure for these children to live in, in hopes of spreading Christian values, even if the children came from different religious backgrounds. Some historical accounts also note "communities and families in western states complained of being dumping grounds for the little criminals in their midst" (Wollons & Wollons, 1993). It can be argued that these early accounts of social work practice reinforced a colonizing imperialistic culture of "us versus them." A prominent idea within imperialism and colonialism is the idea of "individualism" and "picking oneself up by their bootstraps," which has had implications for how the overall society viewed citizens. The "orphan trains" were an example of how poor parents, unable to care for their children, lost them to the state, which believed was a better parent than actual human beings. The idea that parents could not care for their children because they were poor is a historical representation of how people were seen as the problem, not the system – a colonial mindset.

Both Mary Richmond and Jane Addams have been credited for their activist work in Settlement Houses and the Charity Organization Society (COS). However, while their work has been noted as being charitable and kind, the ideology of the country at the time emphasized the need for "civilizing" those who were non-White. The work of both women enforced this push for Whiteness. The work being conducted in Settlement Houses and in the COS focused on "teaching" immigrants of the time to be "respectable" (Velarde, 2008, as cited in Stanley, 2020) and emphasized "temperance, cleanliness, thrift, and religious observance in the home" (Addams, 1899, as cited in Maree Stanley, 2020). All this work, possibly well-intentioned, was imported from the United Kingdom. This only adds to the argument that the colonizer philosophy of ridding people of their culture, behaviors, and thoughts to force these groups to conform to the values and behaviors deemed fit by the colonizer was in fact being reinforced. As stated by On Jin Lee and Ferrer

(2014), "the purpose of the Settlement House Movement was White settlement and nation-state building" (as cited in Maree Stanley, 2020). Both the Settlement House and the COS and other Boards of Charity were founded in religious movements contributing to the teachings provided within them. These included maintaining the nuclear family, patronizingly "teaching" immigrants how to dress, talk, eat, sleep, clean, and make a house and how to exercise personal self-control (Stanley, 2020). This was part of the mission of these early social workers.

However, the American government has historically posed a macroscale barrier to social work and its effectiveness despite the profession's early work to maintain the status quo. Additionally, the government would negatively influence the work being done by early social workers. For example, during the Civil War (1861–1865), the first federal social welfare program, referred to as the Freedmen's Bureau, began aiding newly released slaves (Simmons University, n.d.). However, due to the public's views on slavery at the time, this program was terminated due to a lack of funding and pressure from the federal government.

It is crucial that professional social workers in the United States are aware of the nature of early American society in order to fully comprehend the structures of the society in which they work. The lived experiences of the clients and the communities in which social workers work reflect the consequences of a history of oppression and discrimination influenced by colonialism. Having knowledge of this reality creates an awareness that can then be used to influence the approaches and actions taken when working alongside the communities and people who have fallen victim to these discriminatory practices. Social work, as a profession, prides itself on its call for advocacy and service to others. Advocacy and service are practice principles clearly expected of social workers as explained by the profession's code of ethics.

Social Work Education in America

While social work has had some influence on maintaining a status quo that for some was oppressive in many ways, social workers have historically been the group to advocate for vulnerable populations in America. Social work was first considered an occupation in the United States in the early twentieth century and became a profession by the 1920s (Stuart, 2013). To gain its professional status, educational programs that taught curricula relating to social work emerged throughout the country. Early academic social scientists who were also members of the American Social Science Association (ASSA) also took an interest in the societal issues that were occurring in the country in the late 1800s. Some of these academics believed the problems being experienced were in large part the fault of the individuals experiencing these struggles – "blaming the victim." Others were beginning to recognize that the issues being faced by individuals were largely due to social and economic structures over which people had little control (Austin, 1997). The charity work conducted by early social work pioneers would also influence the education offered in the schools of social work training.

Prior to adopting a more focused curriculum, students were introduced to an array of opinions about social work practice and policy. At times, this became a topic of conflict between advocates for "university-based education" and "agency-based education" (Chaiklin, 2017). Additionally, the roles and responsibilities of researchers, reformers, and agency executives, as well as administrators and policy leaders, were formed in these early years of education (Chaiklin, 2017). Students who were educated with more of a focus on research and who became policy leaders were predominantly men (Austin, 1997).

In the early years of its inception, the structure of social work education was rather informal, moving between the two models of applied social science practices or skills-focused training. Mary Richmond, a social work pioneer, was one of the advocates in favor of a more practice-based education. Richmond is credited for the development of practice-focused social work training programs after presenting staff training programs, which she developed from her time with the Charity Organization Society in Baltimore (Austin, 1997). As a result of her advocacy, the first social work training course would be offered in the summer of 1898 at Columbia University (NASW, 2022) formerly known as the New York School of Philanthropy. By 1904, three schools were offering social work education: the New York School of Philanthropy, Chicago School of Civics and Philanthropy, and the Boston School for Training Social Workers, which would later become Simmons College School of Social Work (Chaiklin, 2017). It is important to mention that training programs for social workers were structured for graduate level studies as opposed to undergraduate – an issue that remains a discussion topic for US social work education programs today.

These early days of social work education did not come without struggles, some of which were oppressive in nature. The early colonial mindset of male settlers influenced the patriarchal belief that women were meant for more "traditional homemaker" or "caregiver" roles, rather than professional roles. Early academic institutions that implemented apprenticeship programs and required faculty research published articles were based on the belief that women were not suited for this style of education and training. Similarly, this mindset influenced the perception of men in the field of social work. As noted previously, men were more likely to be educated as leaders and policy analysts. This division between sexes would create a perceived tension between men and women in the field of social work. In addition to the divisions of labor between men and women, the curriculum models also created friction as leaders of these programs fluctuated in their choice to keep the training models more practice focused versus the more traditional academic approach of applied social sciences. This indicated early conflicts around the environment of social work education and foreshadowed the importance of direct practice as part of the education process – what would later be seen as the field practicum.

Over the next several decades, social work education grew exponentially and changed significantly. In 1913, the first social work training program for black students was added at Fisk University (Austin, 1997). The workforce that hired social workers varied based on the college degree that social workers earned. For example, graduate level students were prepared to work in more specialized settings such as hospitals, child guidance clinics, and child welfare agencies and in psychiatric settings (Taylor-Owen, 1987 as cited in Austin, 1997). Undergraduate students were prepared to work primarily in publicly funded welfare programs in rural and urban areas, focusing mainly on meeting the basic needs of their client base. Into the 1930s, 1940s, and 1950s, discussions about the importance of viewing social work as a profession, mainly because it was dominated by women, became an issue. Out of these discussions came the shift from viewing graduate social work training and undergraduate training as a dichotomy and, instead, influenced the educational structures we see today – undergraduate programs serving as the foundation education in social work training preparing students for entry-level practice and for graduate level social work education. Lastly, during these several decades and after the shift took place between the training levels, the Council on Social Work Education (CSWE) was founded in 1952 (Austin, 1997) as a means for providing an accreditation review process for social work education. In 1982, CSWE began to accredit undergraduate programs as well. These accreditation standards have been the guide for educating competent social workers. CSWE created nine competencies for social work programs to follow in educating students. These competencies have been revised multiple times since 2008 and recently again in 2022.

The process by which the profession of social work and social work education evolved was problematic. The system and structures that contributed to the creation of the United States were driven by colonialism and patriarchy, both of which diminished women and restricted their opportunities. Early American social work, and the charity work it is noted for, was shaped by outspoken women who used their nurturing skills to respond to and support people who had been oppressed by a system that was created for a select few. Social workers became advocates for social reform in a politically and economically conservative society (Abbott, 1995). Early American social work pioneers asserted themselves as professionals in a society where "true professions" were controlled by men (Etzioni, 1969). The education models seen in modern social work training reflect the early ideas that women were best fit for direct practice that focuses on techniques and skills such as individual assessment and treatment through casework (Austin, 1997). In addition, the interactional skills used within these techniques of casework were thought to be skills men lacked; therefore, men were historically viewed as being more appropriate for the academic teaching, administrative, and social research aspects of social work education. This approach and line of thinking were oppressive to women. However, women were at the forefront of providing support, finding solutions, and advocating for people whose voices were not being heard and whose lives were challenging in response to structural violence and inequality.

In reviewing the development of social work education, one aspect is particularly relevant. The individuals who contributed to the formation of the social work training and education system were people who held a high level of status and privilege in early American society. They were academics, scholars, and women from wealthy religious families who believed that it was their duty to "save" people. Missing was how to train social workers to work with oppressed individuals. History's narrative has been elaborated by powerholders, the "visionaries," the privileged men and women who have shaped society and, in turn, created oppressive structures, all the while keeping the voices of the oppressed silenced. Social work education created a call for professionals who had "expertise" in "fixing" people's problems.

Human Rights Issues

World War II shaped American society for the women who entered the workforce in unprecedented numbers as men left for combat abroad. Following the end of the war, America's economy boomed and a middle class emerged that purchased homes, went to college, and began earning livable wages. African Americans, Hispanics, and women lagged in their participation in the postwar boom. Excluded groups "became more aggressive in their attempts at trying to win their full freedoms and civil rights as guaranteed by the Declaration of Independence and the U.S. Constitution" (Library of Congress, 2022a, b). As noted earlier in this text, the US Constitution was influenced by ideologies found in the Magna Carta Libertatum, a document with a long history, asserting people had inherent rights that deserved recognition and protection. Minority groups in American society sought fair treatment as human beings with inherent human rights.

Following World War II, human rights emerged as an issue on a global scale. Human rights are "the set of entitlements held to belong to every person as a condition of being human" (Oxford English Dictionary, 2022). Human rights are "fundamental rights, especially those believed to belong to an individual and in whose exercise a government may not interfere, as the rights to speak, associate, work, etc." (Human Rights Watch, 2022). The belief that a person is entitled to specific rights just because they are human while becoming more mainstream since WWII has historically been assumed by several societies, cultures, and religious beliefs. The "Golden Rule," "do unto others as you would have done unto you," has appeared in myriad cultures and belief systems. Every human has dignity and worth, a core social work value that is central to the concept of human rights. In the United States, the US Declaration of Independence, the US Constitution, and the US Bill of Rights are all examples of declarations of commitment to civil rights for citizens. These rights include the right to life, the right to a fair trial, freedom from torture and other cruel treatment, freedom of speech, freedom of religion, and the right to health, education, and an adequate standard of living (Australian Human Rights Commission, 2022).

Following WWII and the global response to the atrocities of that war, the Charter of the United Nations established an Economic and Social Council (ECOSOC) to address the issues of human rights on a global scale. Out of this council, the United Nations Human Rights Commission was created. Under Eleanor Roosevelt's guidance, the Commission would draft a document that came to be known as the Universal Declaration of Human Rights (UDHR) which was adopted and accepted by the United Nations in December 1948 (United for Human Rights, 2022.). The need for such a declaration was evident on a global level, both before, during, and after WWII.

During the nation's leadership by the most incompetent presidency in its history, the country faced an unprecedented pandemic. A failed response to the COVID-19 pandemic on the part of the 45th presidential administration resulted in over 1.3 million deaths. A disproportionate share of those who died were people of color (United for Human Rights, 2022). In addition to this tragedy, policies aimed at stripping citizens of their basic human rights were pursued. On June 24, 2022, the US Supreme Court ruled in favor of overturning a right gained more than 50 years earlier. In its decision, Dobbs v. Jackson Women's Health Organization (Perry & Jipping, 2021), the highest court determined that the US Constitution does not include the right to privacy and does not protect a right to abortion. As a result, each state was to enact its own laws protecting or outlawing the right to abortion. Several states have enacted some of the strictest abortion bans, many of which do not consider the life of the mother or situations of incest or rape. As a result, social workers in the country have found themselves in an ethical and legal dilemma as they try to abide by laws in their states while providing quality services to clients in reproductive healthcare settings.

This is just one of many examples of human rights violations in US society. In addition to the removal of human rights such as autonomy over one's body, there are other concerns that impact social work professionals' direct practice as well as their policy and advocacy work. For example, issues like racial injustices (specifically related to the impact of COVID-19), poverty and inequality, the criminal legal system, voting rights, rights of noncitizens, and a myriad of other issues all have been brought to the forefront of discussions politically and professionally. Additionally, one might consider how work with military veterans and personnel is impacted by ideologies engrained with imperialistic views. The idea of expansion by force, by colonization, has been proven a tactic used in multiple wars in the last 20 years. Some examples are Iraq and Afghanistan and the idea that we must "save" people from their own communities when really the idea behind all of it is expanded power and expanded wealth. Social workers work closely with veterans who have been in the crossfire of these imperialistic behaviors, posed as "saviorism" by their power-holders. In return, American soldiers are called to "slaughter civilians, plunder oil reserves, and shatter beautiful and ancient civilization" (Rickford, 2018). Imperialism has resulted in the "Global War on Terror," which "…ravaged the planet, engendered ISIS, and spawned a flood of proxy wars, sectarian violence, and refugees" (Rickford, 2018). These wars cost the country trillions of dollars, generating billions of dollars in corporate profits, decimating public program funding, and destroying civil rights.

The International Federation of Social Workers (IFSW) defines social work as "a practice-based profession and an academic discipline that promotes social change and development, social cohesion, and the empowerment and liberation of people. Principles of social justice, human rights, collective responsibility, and respect for diversities are central to social work. Underpinned by theories in social work, social sciences, humanities, and indigenous knowledge, social work engages people and structures to address life challenges and enhance well-being. This definition may be amplified at national and/or regional levels" Sewpaul & Hendrickson, 2019, IFSW, 2022. Per this definition, it is evident professional social workers around the world are called to address issues of human rights as part of their practice.

In their work with individuals, families, groups, communities, and organizations, social workers are faced with addressing problems caused, in large part, by violations of human rights. The profession of social work affords professionals the opportunity to work with a myriad of populations. These populations experience some form of violation of or attack on their most basic human rights. Whether it be the service work provided by social workers to immigrants and/or refugee and asylum seekers (Androff & Mathis, 2021) or direct service to vulnerable populations such a children, adults and families who have been separated upon arrival in the United States, the LGBTQIA+ community, the aging population, and several others, social workers work to address human rights at every level of practice. Social workers would benefit the populations they serve by implementing a human rights framework in practice. "A human rights approach calls social workers to practice in a way that allows for maximum participation of service users in decisions that affect them, addresses power differentials, considers the social context, and privileges an intersectional, strengths based, trauma informed, and recovery-oriented approach" (Villarreal Sosa & Nuckolls, 2018). Applying a framework such as this is a way of approaching the practice from a decolonized perspective. One way in which social workers can adopt a human rights framework into their practice would be to look to colleagues across the globe in their attempts at addressing human rights crises. Additionally, social work accreditation standards for both undergraduate and graduate social work programs have listed the advancement of human rights as a standard of education competencies that is required to be met by social work students. As students in an accredited social work program, students are gaining skills, knowledge, and practice in policies, modalities, techniques, and behaviors that will prepare them for advancing the human rights of the people and communities they will serve.

In addition to adapting accreditation standards of social work education, a curriculum focused on anti-oppressive practices is necessary. Anti-oppressive social work practice meets clients where they are, validates their experience with oppression, and calls for social workers to collaborate with their clients while engaging in critical self-reflection. An example of a collective response to the inequities caused by attacks on human rights is the Grand Challenges for Social Work. The challenges addressed by this project focus on human rights issues related to overall healthy living, strengthening the social fabric by responding to homelessness and the changing environment, as well as eliminating racism, building financial capacity for all, and economic equality. Working to address the issues laid out in the Grand Challenges is a commitment made to human rights and responding to the attacks on these rights.

Contemporary Social Work Education

Too little of the education provided to social work students focuses on training students with the skills to address societal injustices. Most social work programs focus on training social workers at the microlevel. This clinical focus aims to prepare social workers to work directly with individuals facing challenges in life with little or no attention to the underlying structural causes of their personal plights.

The Council of Social Work Education (CSWE) Educational Policy and Accreditation Standards (EPAS) developed nine practice and behavior competencies that social work students should gain while obtaining either an undergraduate or graduate degrees. One of the competencies calls for students to advance human rights and social, racial, economic, and environmental justice (CSWE, 2022a). The practice behaviors associated with this competency have called on students, educators, and professionals to advocate for human rights at the micro-, mezzo, and macro levels of practice. Additionally, this competency calls for professionals to engage in practices that will advance human rights to promote social, racial, economic, and environmental justice. To do so, social work students must be knowledgeable about the injustices experienced on a global scale that are a result of the inequitable distribution of power and privilege within society.

In addition to advancing human rights, which has been included since the development of competencies, CSWE updated the EPAS to include a newly added competency of engaging anti-racism, diversity, equity, and inclusion (ADEI) in practice, reflecting the direction in which the profession is moving – a direction toward a more anti-oppressive practice with the individuals, families, groups, organizations, and communities. This competency, unlike others in previous years, clearly and explicitly references the impact of White supremacy and privilege on society and human experiences in the United States taking a leap forward in being more authentic in discussing topics that might otherwise be challenging. While the country at one point early in its history might have placed influence on early social workers to advance White American ideology, the profession is evolving slowly from its early work to serving and advocating for vulnerable populations. A common discussion in social work curriculum focused on students becoming culturally competent, however, this has evolved into practicing cultural humility. As part of implementing the EPAS competencies, educators encourage students to approach diverse clients and populations from a culturally responsive and humble perspective. A cultural humility perspective calls social workers to hold themselves and the structures in which they work accountable. To do this, social workers engage in constant self-reflection of their own cultural identities, and how these identities might further oppress their clients, as well as advocate for and initiate change in their organizations or communities should they also continue to oppress the populations they serve.

While CSWE competencies guide the content provided to social work students inside the classroom, the "signature pedagogy" of social work education is the application and practice of these competencies in the practicum (CSWE, 2008). CSWE clearly states the "intent of field education is to connect the theoretical and conceptual contribution of the classroom with the practical world of the practice setting" (2008, p.8). Considering this point, social work students are called to perform and demonstrate through their practice an understanding and knowledge of material being provided in and outside of the classroom – material that should be teaching students how to address macroscale issues of oppression, discrimination, poverty, and injustices. The field practicum provides students with direct oversight of a professional social worker who can guide, consult, and problem-solve with students who are beginning their professional practice.

Educating future social workers through the lens of micro practice creates a separation between the macro and microspheres essentially creating a dichotomy in the profession where students overlook the need to create macro level change. A challenge we pose to current social work students to take on is how to make a difference on the macroscale with the current skillset to work with individuals or families?

Decolonizing Social Work in the United States

International social work (ISW) is a practice that improves civil and human rights (Oxford Bibliographies, 2017). This practice was developed to have a more inclusive approach in social work and develop a curriculum that is culturally grounded and diverse. This practice aimed to create a collaborative field with a global perspective to address post-disaster aid, humanitarian assistance, and global development (IFSW, 2022). As the profession becomes more international, it is important to reexamine its values and goals along with its curriculum to reflect a global perspective in which professionals are able and prepared to address complex international challenges. In international work, social workers have the role of becoming the cultural mediators, and this role cannot be fulfilled unless social work moves from Westernized ideals to a more expansive focus. The internationalization of social work will continue to expand the profession, ensure the goals of the profession are being properly and ethically met, and reduce the damage created to traumatized and displaced communities.

A culturally diverse curriculum has been one of the approaches to globalize social work. Teaching students about other cultures and how to interact with them is simply not enough for this curriculum to work. For these efforts to create a more inclusive profession, students are called to address their own power and privilege (Ibrahima & Mattani, 2019). Understanding how individual identity can represent both advantages and disadvantages will give individuals a detailed perspective on where their biases come from as well as how they can relate to other issues and know the limits, and thinking of one's own experiences and identities and reflecting on them greatly impact how to approach clients and their challenges (Caron, 2020). After understanding this power dynamic, it is vital to make a safe space for others to use their own voice to talk about their challenges and possible solutions. Analyzing when it is right for one to create solutions and when it's time to recognize how our own biases and identities do not allow us to understand the issues others face is essential to meeting these goals.

One way to address this in social work curriculum is to move from what some scholars refer to as a "needs-based" approach to a "rights-based" approach (Villarreal Sosa & Nuckolls, 2018). Working from this perspective positions social workers to work with their clients in gaining back their human rights as opposed to addressing or "serving" a need. Doing so requires input from the clients we serve, at all levels of the decision-making process, including gaining insight for the content covered in the field and in the classroom. Exploring diverse voices and underrepresented narratives and integrating them into social work curriculum will create the change needed. The next step after identifying power imbalances would be to ensure that those whose identities are oppressed are granted the opportunity to create change. In the generalist social work practice curriculum, which is the primary focus of social work education in the United States, students are taught that their clients are the experts in their lives. They drive the car and social workers help interpret the map. Before intervening, it is important for social workers to continue to ask what they want to change and whom they are changing it for and with (Caron, 2020). The questioning does not stop here. One must also ask how we can include these individuals in finding the best solution that respects and meets their needs. More specifically, enhancing social work curriculum involves integrating indigenous knowledge and approaches that will enrich social work practice. Due to the nature of the profession and how it has been dominated by Western and colonial ideas, minority groups have been removed or refrained from contributing to the profession in meaningful and important ways. Just as these voices are needed to find solutions to the issues they face, these voices are also needed to develop an inclusive curriculum. Indigenous voices speaking on indigenous needs will ensure that their history is not erased, that the colonial effects on their communities are addressed, and that the curriculum can prepare nonindigenous students and social workers to respectfully respond to these issues (Hendrick & Young, 2018). To globalize social work, students need to be equipped and qualified to properly work with different groups of people. Curricula need to go beyond being culturally inclusive and take on the tasks to highlight the past mistakes in social work that have further reproduced oppression and review the opportunities to continue developing better research, practice skills, and understanding of their own agency. Unfortunately, current pressures on educators to refrain from teaching on topics like critical race theory require creativity in and commitment to enhancing the knowledge and practice social work students gain while in school.

The goal of the profession is to work from an anti-oppressive framework and impart anti-imperialist practice. For social work to be international, it needs to move away from its ethnocentrism and open itself to other cultures. A postcolonial, intersectional, feminist, theoretical framework has been identified as a step toward a solution. However, understanding that this framework does not look the same all over the globe is the key factor that will make it work (Caron, 2020). It is up to the curriculum to evolve and ensure it constantly reflects the changes in the world. Decolonizing social work is not a one-time change but an ongoing effort.

In research, decolonizing social work means considering diversity, history, culture, and the realities of the people participating in studies and understanding the effects of colonization on that population. In education, this requires changing the curriculum to include diverse and underrepresented voices as well as having open sources, making it more responsive to social justice. Understanding historical and political accounts allows social workers to address the issues at hand and encourages self-reflection in understanding historical contributions. Additionally, the social work code of ethics is clear on the roles social workers play in contributing to the knowledge base for future professionals. Collaborating with the clients we serve and understanding the origin and manifestations of their oppression provide knowledge on how to respond appropriately and from a culturally humbled perspective. Doing so will further educate social workers on how to become involved with communities of color and other minority communities without imposing solutions that disrespect these communities and/or cultures.

In practice, current social work educators, scholars, and practitioners are becoming more aware of the need to evolve the profession to ensure it is anti-oppressive in practice and not just in discussions. Additionally, not only is there a need for a shift in practice efforts with clients served but also within the profession itself. Recent data released by the Association of Social Work Boards (ASWB, 2022) on licensure pass rates in the United States has sparked a major debate between social work professionals in the United States. The data, released only after major pressure was placed on the association, reflected discrepancies in pass rates between Whites and people of color who took the licensing exam. This release of information, while discouraging, has also initiated conversations between social workers about the need for change in the way the profession operates and treats its own. Additionally, discussions about the requirement for licensure and whether licenses truly indicate a person's ability to provide services and do social work have also sparked following this data. This issue has highlighted the unfortunate truth of oppressive acts in a profession that has the primary purpose of practicing in an anti-oppressive manner. As with any new information, and with the skills and knowledge social workers have, this serves as an important opportunity to support the profession in its growth toward change and decolonization efforts. According to the results released by ASWB, more than 50% of first-time test takers for master's level licensure were White (Association of Social Work Boards, 2022). This indicates a need for diversity among the professionals who serve minority populations. The representation of minority populations within the profession is a step in the right direction of responding to the needs of minorities who share similar life experiences as their social workers.

Conversely, while there might be issues of oppression within the profession, more and more professionals are becoming aware of the need for more decolonized approaches when working with their client base. For example, a review and reexamination of the medical model and its use in treating mental health has recently been published. This publication is an example of social workers reexamining the theories and practice models most used that reflect Westernized practice approaches that do not take into consideration issues of cultural diversity, racism, and trauma caused by such discrimination (Minsky-Kelly & Hornung, 2022). Suggestions for non-Westernized practices are provided as an alternative approach, practices from other cultures and societies, highlighting the importance of an international focus on social work. Similarly, other professionals are examining the traditional change process in social work and how it, too, does not consider cultures or lived experiences outside of the White experience, validating, once again, a need for reexamination of what current professionals would deem "best practices." This gives hope to future social workers, to become creative in their work with people of diverse backgrounds.

Current Human Catastrophes and Issues

In the United States, a White cisgender heterosexual male continues to be the normative ideal. People outside of these characteristics may be seen as divergent. In one of the most diverse societies on the planet, this "norm," however, is not reflective of the population. An intersectional perspective takes into consideration the ways in which different characteristics are interrelated in systems of inequality. Gender, race, ethnicity, sexual orientation, gender identity, disability, social class, and immigration status are all taken into consideration to understand how one individual could have multiple characteristics and identities and how they all intersect to create a unique experience of inequality. Each of these characteristics comes with its own unique sets of opportunities and disadvantages according to social norms and systemic problems. Addressing the isms (racism, sexism, classism, ableism, and ageism) found nationally is an essential task in the social work profession to protect human rights and promote social justice.

Climate Change

Climate change is *the* defining crisis of our lifetime, and no one is immune. Sea levels are rising, forests are burning, natural disasters keep impacting communities, polar ice caps are melting, the ocean is acidifying, and coral reefs are dying. These changes have huge impacts on quality of life. Food and water insecurity levels are rising, the economy is disrupted and creating international conflict, and environmental degradation accelerates. Climate change is a challenge that has a global impact, but its effects are felt disproportionally in poor countries and communities. Racism and climate change are interrelated. Communities of color are impacted at greater rates and impacted at greater levels. Climate change also has a history of colonialism, slavery, and a capitalist agenda. This leaves people of color at a disadvantage, having to deal with the immediate effects of the exploitation of the environment. From air pollution leading to more chronic health issues to being the ones most impacted by extreme natural disasters, the poor and communities of color are constantly impacted by these systemic issues. Social work has the opportunity, and responsibility, to work within these communities to create awareness, develop short- and long-term solutions, and become involved in the climate change crisis globally.

In 2015, the Paris Agreement, an international treaty on climate change, was adopted by 196 parties. This agreement has the goal of limiting global warming to 1.5 degrees Celsius and having a climate neutral world by 2050. For this agreement to work, economic and social transformations are needed. If carried out properly, the Paris Climate Agreement should have a favorable outcome (Glanemann et al., 2020). Under President Barack Obama, the United States was one of the agreeing parties. However, under Donald Trump's presidency, just at the fifth anniversary, the United States left the agreement. On his first day in office, President Joe Biden signed an executive order to rejoin the agreement, and as of February of 2021, the United States is back on the agreement again. Although back on the agreement, we can see the instability of the climate change support in presidencies and how ultimately this leads to delays in climate change efforts. Social workers can work among communities, be involved in policy change, and continue to create resources toward successful climate change. This will ensure that no matter the current political state of affairs, climate change, one of the biggest human rights crises, is being addressed.

Incarceration

The United States has the highest incarceration rate of any other country in the world. About 1% of the adult population (1.2 million people) is incarcerated at any given time, and there are approximately five million people who are under supervision (probation, parole) (Carson, 2021). Black, Latinos(as), and indigenous people are incarcerated at higher rates than their White counterparts. About 13% of the US population is black, yet they represent 38% of the incarcerated population (18–21% for Latinos(as) and 0.9–2% for indigenous people) (Sawyer & Wagner, 2022). Most of the crimes by which people are incarcerated are nonviolent. These statistics call for criminal justice reform and policy initiatives.

Another issue aside from mass incarceration is solitary confinement. Solitary confinement, often used as a punishment, is when an inmate is secluded from the rest of the prison population and put alone in a different cell. These types of cells are usually dark and windowless and have steel doors with only one small opening where officers drop off their meals. When in solitary confinement, criminally involved individuals will usually stay there for 22–24 hours of everyday. When allowed in a recreation area, it is usually another indoor room alone. During their solitary confinement, individuals usually have restricted to not access to visitation or phone calls. The individuals are placed in inadequate housing, with no access to sunlight, a clear human rights violation. Solitary confinement is used to not only physically punish criminally involved individuals but also mentally. During their time here, criminally involved individuals have reported to hallucinate, have high levels of anxiety, have nervousness, develop severe chronic depression, experience self-mutilation, and overall have lower levels of brain activity that affects their cognition in the long term. This makes it even more difficult when individuals are released and have to reenter society. Social workers need to become more involved in the fight for the inequalities found in the criminal justice system as these pose great challenges to human rights. Expanding social work to be present at every stage of the criminal justice system like courts, rehabilitation services, recovery programs, and reentry programs can create a difference and ensure human rights are being protected.

Health Equity

Health equity is a key right protected by the UDHR and is an inherent right for all. Health equity refers to the individualized attainment of the highest level of health for all people, and it is only achieved when everyone can attain this full potential for health and well-being. Things such as social, economic, demographic, or geographic dimensions are often things that interrupt health equity. The social determinants of health are conditions that influence these group differences in health status and are supported by the UDHR and other human rights documents. These include economic stability (employment, income, expenses, debt, medical bills, support), neighborhood and environment (housing, transportation, parks, walkability, geography), education (literacy, language, early-childhood education, higher education), food (food security, access to healthy options), community safety and social context (social integration, support systems, community engagement, stress, exposure to trauma, policing), and healthcare system (health coverage, provider and pharmacy availability, access to respectful care, quality of care) (Drake & Rudowitz, 2022).

The majority of the population in the United States is discriminated against based on their sex, gender, age, race, ethnicity, disability, and immigration status, among others, and are prevented from attaining health equity (WHO, 2022). Latest statistics reveal that 9.7% (31.6 million people) of the nation is uninsured across all ages (Cohen & Cha, 2022). Due to the nature of data collection, this number could even be higher than reported. Groups more likely to be uninsured are those adults between 19 and 34 years old, non-White Hispanics followed by non-Hispanic black, and families with no or low income (Tolbert & Paulus, 2022). Reasons why individuals may be uninsured include unaffordability and ineligibility (Paulus, 2022).

The US population currently faces significant health challenges. Overweight and obesity – which are linked to chronic health conditions such as hypertension, diabetes, heart/artery diseases, strokes, respiratory problems, and different types of cancers – are common among the population. Research indicates that physical activity and nutrition are the main primary habits to remain healthy and prevent these issues. Tobacco is the single greatest preventable cause of illness in the United States. In 2021, tobacco can only be sold to those 21 and older, and many states in the country are now required to be smoke-free. Substance use of drugs and alcohol also poses a great health impact in the country. Both legal and illegal drugs are often abused for self-medication or knowingly/unknowingly mixed creating even greater impacts on health. Mental health treatment remains inaccessible to many in the United States, with the criminal justice system being the largest treatment provider in the country. Mental health disparities remain a critical healthcare issue. Environmental quality, especially through air pollution, affects people all over the United States. However, as previously mentioned, those with low-income, racial, and communities of color are more likely to live in areas that face greater environmental issues. In general, low healthcare access is a great threat to the population. With high rates of the population being uninsured, having any acute or chronic mental or health disorder can quickly impose a high risk and render to be unable to obtain care. Social workers have the task of caring for those without healthcare access, providing resources, and facilitating the process of public health benefits and continue being involved in healthcare policy reforms.

The COVID-19 Pandemic

In early 2020, the novel coronavirus pandemic generated a public health crisis, and the Centers for Disease Control and Prevention began developing preventive matters by social distancing and isolation. Later, they also implemented face mask requirements, shut down many activities, recommended no social gatherings and constant washing of hands, and even restrained the US and Mexico borders to essential travel. The United States is one of the countries most impacted by the pandemic with 1,070,947 deaths as of November 2022 (CDC, 2022a). Due to the administration and government's reluctance in 2019 to collaborate with the CDC guidelines and follow the steps of other countries in requiring lockdowns, the spread of COVID-19 greatly impacted the United States. Former President Trump's action plan to COVID-19 left much to be desired, as his responses were not empirically based, promoted racism, minimized the actual threat of the virus, and focused on protecting capitalism rather than people (Human Rights Watch, 2020). In 2021, the development of the COVID-19 vaccine did not create a relief response, as many were calling it a hoax, linking it to conspiracy theories, and ignoring empirical research it was developed from. This led to vaccines going unused and trashed and continued the rapid spread of the virus. Once again, communities of color were the ones most vulnerable and impacted by the effects of the pandemic. During the pandemic, the disproportionate risks people of color faced for contagion made themselves evident. As stated previously, it is non-White Hispanics and non-Hispanic blacks that are most likely to be uninsured. These two groups of people are also overrepresented in frontline essential jobs, which put them at higher risk for the virus (University of Washington, 2022).

Today approximately 79% of the US population have received at least one dose, and 68% considered fully vaccinated. However, there is still an average of 45,000 cases of COVID-19 on a weekly average reported (CDC, 2022b). The pandemic was a global manifestation of the current state of affairs and our reactions to imminent threats to human rights. The reactions of the individuals and systems all over the world, and the millions of deaths, highlight the need for a change in response to these crises. COVID-19 left the world with many lessons on health inequities and human crisis. Systems continue to oppress communities of color, placing them at a disadvantage and increasing their vulnerability to disparities. It is important to recognize the inequalities and social determinants of health to acknowledge how they affect individuals in different positions of power. Doing this will identify who needs the change and who can create the change. Community-level work developed by and for the community for long-term sustainable solutions will bridge the gap of inequalities. Social workers have the responsibility to continue working toward health equity by promoting community interventions, policy change, and evidence-based knowledge and continuing work with vulnerable population whose human rights are at higher risk.

Reflections

Historically, there have always been societal and moral issues that have required attention from both governments and individuals within that society. The desire for power and for expansion has negatively impacted people across the world. One would need not look very far to see this in the US history. Unfortunately, at the time, the right to expression and speech is under attack with bans on books that explain this history in its truest context. Efforts to turn away from the true story of US history are the newest method of seeking power and negatively impacting the human rights of citizens in this country.

The current situation in American social work precludes continued complacency on human rights and decolonization. While human rights are mentioned in ethical codes and mission statements, not enough is done to promote human rights in social work education, policy, and, more importantly, practice. The focus on anti-oppressive social work practice indicates the profession's understanding of the need for more action and less discussion. Postcolonial approaches to social work in the United States are minimal and largely limited to addressing the inequities and inclusion of indigenous groups (Gray et al., 2013). Schools of social work in the United States have not focused on the decolonization of the profession, thereby continuing the legacy of Eurocentric social work as developed and practiced by the field's pioneers.

Acknowledging the oppression reproduced along with the missed opportunities for better serving communities is necessary to successfully practice social work in an anti-oppressive fashion. Understanding the true historical development of the United States and its effects on communities of color and other minorities is imperative to enable future social workers to reflect on their own privilege and power and how this privilege and power held by a few have created structures that have maintained oppression. Anti-oppressive social work practice calls for critical self-reflection of oneself, critical assessment of clients' experiences of oppression, empowering clients, working in collaborative partnerships, and intervening as minimally as possible (2020). Developing and implementing inclusive curricula led by indigenous voices and other underrepresented communities will position the profession to begin its process of decolonizing its practices and the profession. Additionally, including indigenous perspectives in the development of curriculum affords students an opportunity to critically examine the experiences of clients' oppression to become skilled in practicing social work from an anti-oppressive perspective. Conversely, and possibly controversially, adding to the curriculum, the perspective of powerholders to better understand the opposing side with hopes of creating community with everyone's perspectives considered.

American social work must challenge and reconfigure the theories it was founded on. Also, social workers must challenge the current form of social work and understand how it can strengthen oppressive systems instead of dismantling them. The kind of work the profession was designed to do needs to be revaluated along with the implications it creates. We are currently at a time where social work can no longer be complacent to these implications and must address the role it plays in this dynamic. A reevaluation of the profession needs to bring with it effective solutions to the challenges it is currently facing. It is the responsibility of higher education in social work to prepare students for a more holistic, inclusive, grassroots, and community-focused approach to social work practice centered in anti-oppressive thought. Without this change, communities will continue to be oppressed, will remain at a disadvantage, and will have their cultures and values further erased. It is important for underrepresented voices to have an active role in the solutions to humanitarian issues and catastrophic events that are currently and directly affecting them. Current catastrophic events such as forced migration, climate disasters, hunger, poverty, and the COVID-19 pandemic have highlighted the impacts that colonization still has on minority groups. Humanitarian efforts to overturn the oppressive impact that imperialism created is the solution to decrease how disparately these communities are being affected.

Maylea (2021) invites social workers to ask themselves if social work is the most effective way to achieve the goals of social work. By questioning the current state of the profession and identifying the challenges, individuals can evaluate the profession, an ethical standard that is stated in the code of ethics. Partaking in research, advocating for policy change, working collaboratively with disadvantaged populations, and giving social work students an opportunity to expand on their education in more macro-focused practicum placements are all opportunities for advancing the profession of social work in a decolonized and anti-oppressive manner. Social workers must continue to change and grow in order to successfully and effectively respond to the attacks on human rights and the oppression faced by many. As a profession, social work has taken the role of being an advocate for human rights and social justice by adopting an anti-oppressive practice. Now more than ever, this practice is needed in the world. Impacts from climate change, social injustices, economic decline, and low access to healthcare, among the many "isms" that are prevalent, are at a point where they can no longer be ignored or mildly responded to.

Social work, then, cannot remain complacent to attacks on human rights. Social workers must continue learning about their history, successes, and failures and ensure they are involved in changing the narrative. Implementing an anti-oppressive, internationally focused, and culturally humble curriculum will ensure that social workers can be found around the globe making efforts to move toward a more just and inclusive world. Reinvigorating social work will give the career the push it needs to expand and be called to action for the social crises that currently surround us. The future of social work requires a macro approach to service delivery; an inclusive, diverse, and anti-oppressive curriculum; and a community-based research guided by the communities themselves and their needs in working toward ameliorating global catastrophes. Additionally, engaging in critical self-reflection and bravery to challenge the systems and stand up against the structures maintaining oppression is essential to successfully approach social work from a decolonized perspective.

We must keep in mind that graduate and undergraduate students are future educators, professionals, and scholars of the profession. It is because of this that it is important that the teaching and experiential learning opportunities selected for the curriculum be based on an anti-oppressive framework and continue to reflect the needs and the protection of human rights. The current political climate poses a great obstacle to this. Ensuring the protection of human rights becomes more salient at a time when some decision-makers and governments are resisting social change.

The call to action then must come from social worker to social worker, social work student to student, and educator to educator. Relying on one another to become aware of our history, understanding the true purpose of the profession specifically as it relates to social justice, engaging in continued self-reflection and learning, and engaging in social action by collaborating with clients, empowering clients, and speaking up against the social and institutional structures are vital. For social workers and future social workers to achieve their profession's goal of social justice and social change, we must evaluate our understanding of how our profession operates. While many of us wish to work within the microsphere of social work, and there is quality work to be done with individuals, it is imperative we comprehend and accept the enormous value of working in the macro arena of social work as well. To respond to the long-standing effects of colonization on a people, social workers have the skillset to bring these people together in solidarity.

A symptom of colonization is the cultural ideology of individualism and taking care of oneself before others. Social work students and professionals alike are called to build strong community with the intention of healing and growth beyond the norms already established, adopting an ideological framework that focuses on liberation – liberation from the effects of a system built to benefit some but not all which creates an environment of oppression.

The benefits of building community as a response to the effects of colonization are immeasurable. When we discuss the need for the voices of indigenous peoples, it is not to omit the perspectives of people from privileged groups. Building community requires, as we have noted throughout this chapter, a critical self-reflection of one's own privilege, oppression, values, and beliefs. Additionally, from a liberatory perspective, it requires working toward a change of heart among people of all walks of life. Social workers are trained to use their innate empathy and to model that empathy for others; with this skill and knowledge, we have what it takes to bring people together, even if they do not agree with one another. It is time for social workers to be courageous in their efforts – courageous to critically self-reflect, courageous when challenging the systems that be, and courageous in their efforts to bridge the divide that we are currently experiencing in our country. These are the steps to decolonizing the work we do and creating equitable living standards for all.

Conclusion

This chapter reviews the history of the United States and the massive effects of colonialism, capitalism, and White supremacy. The beginnings of social work are marked by attempts at creating solutions for poverty and inequality. These first attempts, however, were initiated by White women who took the center stage at "saving" people from their situation and lived experiences. These efforts began creating more inequalities and blamed the individuals over the systems that had originally put them at a disadvantage. Since imperialism and colonialism were the driving force behind social work, many of these solutions for these issues were rooted in ethnocentric values being instilled into black and indigenous people of color. Social workers must acknowledge the impacts that this left in the profession and how some of those same values are still found in the practice of the profession. Decolonizing social work and reinvigorating the theories it has been founded upon are much needed for its continuous success. Integrating more diverse voices and experiences in its curriculum, research, and practice is one of the principal advances. Social work is impacted not only by its past and history but also by the present and future challenges which put human rights at risks. All of the "isms" (racism, sexism, classism, ableism, and ageism) found nationally and globally are the biggest targets for social workers. Other US human rights catastrophes (climate change, incarceration, health inequity, and COVID-19) have continued to impact the profession as well as invite it to change. Awareness of these catastrophes and understanding where social work can make room for itself here are essential for innovation. In the future, social work will continue to be affected by ongoing situations, and new short- and long-term solutions have to be constantly created.

Discussion Questions

1. How are current social work education programs effectively incorporating diversity, equity, inclusion and accessibility examples, and practices in their curriculum?

2. What are three current theoretical frameworks used in social work that could be strengthened or updated by using an anti-oppressive approach?
3. How are current social work educators and social work professionals engaging in self-reflective practices of their privilege and biases?
4. In what ways can social work students use their voices to hold educators, peers, and other social work professionals accountable for the personal growth required for anti-oppressive practices?

Resources

- Advancing Social Change Through Community Practice (ACOSA). https://acosa.clubexpress.com
- Global Social Work Statement on Ethical Practices. https://www.iassw-aiets.org/wp-content/uploads/2018/04/Global-Social-Work-Statement-of-Ethical-Principles-IASSW-27-April-2018-1.pdf
- Influencing Social Policy Institute. https://www.influencingsocialpolicy.org
- International Federation of Social Workers. https://www.ifsw.org
- National Association of Social Workers. https://www.socialworkers.org
- National Association of Social Workers on Diversity, Equity, and Inclusion. https://www.socialworkers.org/About/Diversity-Equity-and-Inclusion
- National Association of Social Workers Anti-Racist Statement. https://www.socialworkers.org/About/Diversity-Equity-and-Inclusion/NASW-Anti-Racism-Statement
- Resources for Social Workers Working with Racial, Ethnic, and Minority Populations. https://socialworklicensemap.com/social-work-resources/toolbox/minority-resources/
- Social Work Organizations. https://socialworklicensemap.com/social-work-resources/social-work-organizations/
- Special Commission to Advance on Macro Practice in Social Work. https://acosa.clubexpress.com/content.aspx?page_id=22&club_id=789392&module_id=335370
- 2022 Educational Policy and Accreditation Standards (EPAS). https://www.cswe.org/centers-initiatives/center-for-diversity/

References

Abbott, A. (1995). Boundaries of social work or social work of boundaries? The social service review lecture. *Social Service Review, 69*(4), 545–562. https://doi.org/10.1086/604148

Addams, J. (1899). *The subtle problems of charity* (pp. 163–178). Atlantic Monthly.

Androff, D., & Mathis, C. (2021, October 26). Human rights–based social work practice with immigrants and asylum seekers in a legal service organization. *Journal of Human Rights and Social Work, 7*(2), 178–188. https://doi.org/10.1007/s41134-021-00197-7

Association of Social Work Boards (SSWB). (2022). *Contributing to the conversation: 2022 ASWB exam pass rate analysis*. Association of Social Work Boards. https://www.aswb.org/exam/contributing-to-the-conversation/

Austin, D. M. (1997). The institutional development of social work education: The first 100 years– and beyond. *Journal of Social Work Education, 33*(3), 599–612.

Australian Human Rights Commission. (2022). *An Introduction to Human Rights*. https://humanrights.gov.au/our-work/education/introduction-human-rights

Caron, R. (2020). Anti-imperialist practice and field placements. A "researcher/educator/practitioner" model for International social work practice. *Journal of Teaching in Social Work, 40*(1), 71–85. https://doi.org/10.1080/08841233.2019.1694619

Carson, E. A. (2021). *Prisoners in 2020 – Statistical Tables*. U.S. Department of Justice. https://bjs.ojp.gov/content/pub/pdf/p20st.pdf

Centers for Disease Control and Prevention (CDC). (2022a). *COVID Data Tracker*. covid.cdc.gov

Centers for Disease Control and Prevention (CDC). (2022b). *COVID-19*. cdc.gov

Chaiklin, H. (2017). History of social work education and the profession's structure. *Social Welfare History Project*. https://socialwelfare.library.vcu.edu/social-work/history-of-social-work-education-and-the-professions-structure/

Cohen, R. A., & Cha, A. E. (2022). Health insurance coverage: Early release of estimates from the National Health Interview Survey, January–June 2022. *National Center for Health Statistics*.

Council on Social Work Education (CSWE). (2008). *Educational policy and accreditation standards*. Council on Social Work Education. https://www.cswe.org/getmedia/52344d5b-9e21-4ce5-b642-c09fa249881e/2008-EPAS-revised-4-0-Aug-2012.pdf

Council on Social Work Education (CSWE). (2022a). *Educational policy and accreditation standards for baccalaureate and master's Social Work Programs*. CSWE. https://www.cswe.org/getmedia/94471c42-13b8-493b-9041-b30f48533d64/2022-EPAS.pdf

Council on Social Work Education (CSWE). (2022b). *Annual survey of social work programs: 2021 annual survey*. Council on Social Work Education. https://www.cswe.org/about-cswe/governance/commissions-and-councils/commission-on-research/research-statistics/annual-survey-of-social-work-programs/

Drake, P., & Rudowitz, R. (2022). *Tracking social determinants of health during the COVID-19 Pandemic*. KFF. https://www.kff.org/coronavirus-covid-19/issue-brief/tracking-social-determinants-of-health-during-the-covid-19-pandemic/

Dictionary. (2022). *Definition of human rights*. Dictionary.com, LCC. https://www.dictionary.com/browse/human-rights

Etzioni, A. (Ed.). (1969). *The semi-professions and their organization: Teachers, nurses, social workers*. Free Press.

Gardiner, W. J. (2009). *Reflections on the history of White supremacy in the United States*. https://www.uua.org/files/documents/gardinerwilliam/whiteness/white_supremacy_us.pdf

Glanemann, N., Willner, S. N., & Levermann, A. (2020). Paris Climate Agreement passes the cost-benefit test. Nature Communications, 11(110). https://doi.org/10.1038/s41467-019-13961-1

Gray, M., Coates, J., Yellow Bird, M., & Hetherington, T. (2013). *Decolonizing social work*. Routledge. https://doi.org/10.4324/9781315576206

Hendrick, A., & Young, S. (2018). Teaching about decoloniality: The experience of non-Indigenous social work educators. *American Journal of Community Psychology, 62*, 306–318. https://doi.org/10.1002/ajcp.12285

Human Rights Watch. (2020). *Human Rights Watch testimony to US House of Representatives ways and means committee: Covid-19 disparities reflect structural racism, abuses*. Human Rights Watch. https://www.hrw.org/news/2020/06/10/human-rights-watch-testimony-us-house-representatives-ways-and-means-committee

Human Rights Watch. (2022). *United States*. Human Rights Watch. https://www.hrw.org/world-report/2022/country-chapters/united-states

International Federation of Social Workers (IFSW). (2022). *Global definition of social work*. IFSW. https://www.ifsw.org/what-is-social-work/global-definition-of-social-work/

Ibrahima, A. B., & Mattani, M. A. (2019). Social work in Africa: Decolonizing methodologies and approaches. *International Social Work, 62*(2), 799–813. https://doi.org/10.1177/0020872817742702

Janeway, W. H. (2021). *The evolution of American capitalism*. Project Syndicate. https://www.project-syndicate.org/onpoint/review-ages-of-american-capitalism-by-william-h-janeway-2021-08?barrier=accesspaylog#:%7E:text=The%20Age%20of%20Commerce,persisted%20until%20the%20Civil%20War

Kennedy, D. (2016). *Decolonization: A very short introduction*. Oxford University Press.

Kipling, R. (1899). *The white man's burden*.

Library of Congress. (2022a). *The Post war United States, 1945–1968*. The Library of Congress. https://www.loc.gov/classroom-materials/united-states-history-primary-source-timeline/post-war-united-states-1945-1968/overview/

Library of Congress. (2022b). *U.S. history primary source timeline*. The Library of Congress. https://www.loc.gov/classroom-materials/united-states-history-primary-source-timeline/

Levy, J. (2021). *Ages of American capitalism: A history of the United States*. Random House.

Maree Stanley, J. (2020). Intersectional and relational frameworks: Confronting anti-blackness, settler colonialism, and neoliberalism in US social work. *Journal of Progressive Human Services, 31*(30), 210–225. https://doi.org/10.1080/1048232.2019.1703246

Martinez, M. C. (2004). Racism: The US creation myth and its premise keepers'. In D. Solnit (Ed.), *Globalize Liberation: Hot to uproot the system and build a better world*. City Lights.

Maylea, C. (2021). The end of social work. *The British Journal of Social Work, 51*(2), 772–789. https://doi.org/10.1093/bjsw/bcaa203

Minsky-Kelly, D. K., & Hornung, B. (2022). Structural Whiteness in mental health: Re-examination of the medical model through a lens of anti-racism and de-colonization. *International Journal of Social Work Values and Ethics, 19*(2), 153–173. https://doi.org/10.55521/10-019-210

National Association of Social Workers (NASW). (2022). *Social work history*. National Association of Social Workers. https://www.socialworkers.org/News/Facts/Social-Work-History

On Jin Lee, E., & Ferrer, I. (2014). Examining social work as a Canadian settler colonial project. *Journal of Critical Anti-Oppressive Social Inquiry, 1*(1), 1–20.

Oxford Bibliographies. (2017). *International social work (ISW)*. Oxford Bibliographies. https://www.oxfordbibliographies.com/view/document/obo-9780195389678/obo-9780195389678-0104.xml

Oxford English Dictionary. (2022). Definition of human rights. Dictionary.com, LCC. https://www.dictionary.com/browse/human-rights

Paulus, N. (2022). *The number of Americans without health insurance*. Money Geek. https://www.moneygeek.com/insurance/health/analysis/americans-without-coverage/

Perry, S., & Jipping, T. (2021). Dobbs v. Jackson Women's Health Organization: An opportunity to correct a grave error. *Heritage Foundation Legal Memorandum, 293*, 1–31.

Rickford, R. (2018). *On War, imperialism and racism*. African American intellectual history Society. https://www.aaihs.org/on-war-imperialism-and-racism/

Sawyer, W., & Wagner, P. (2022). *Mass incarceration: The whole pie 2022*. Prison Policy Initiative. https://www.prisonpolicy.org/reports/pie2022.html

Sewpaul, V., & Henrickson, M. (2019). The (r)evolution and decolonization of social work ethics: The global social work statement of ethical principles. *International Social Work, 62*(6), 1469–1481. https://doi.org/10.1177/0020872819846238

Simmons University. (n.d.). *The evolution of social work: Historical milestones*. Simmons Online. https://online.simmons.edu/blog/evolution-social-work-historical-milestones/

Spencer, H. (1894). *The inadequacy of "natural selection"*. D. Appleton.

Stanley, J. M. (2020). Intersectional and Relational Frameworks: Confronting Anti-Blackness, Settler Colonialism, and Neoliberalism in U.S. Social Work. Journal of Progressive Human Services, 31(3), 210-225. https://doi.org/10.1080/10428232.2019.1703246

Stuart, P. H. (2013). Social work profession: History. In Encyclopedia of Social Work. https://doi.org/10.1093/acrefore/9780199975839.013.623

Taylor-Owen, S. J. (1987). The history of the profession of social work: A second look (Doctoral dissertation, Brandeis University, 1986). *Dissertation Abstracts International, 47*(7), 274A2A.

Tolbert, J., & Paulus, D. (2022). *Key facts about the uninsured population*. KFF. https://www.kff.org/uninsured/issue-brief/key-facts-about-the-uninsured-population/

United for Human Rights. (2022). *The story of human rights*. United for Human Rights. https://www.humanrights.com/what-are-human-rights/brief-history/

United for Human Rights. (n.d.). *Universal Declaration of Human Rights*. United for Human Rights. https://www.humanrights.com/what-are-human-rights/universal-declaration-of-human-rights/

University of Washington. (2022). *COVID-19 unequal impacts*. University of Washington. https://www.washington.edu/populationhealth/covid-19-inequality/

Velarde, M. (2008). *The age of light, soap and water: Moral reform in English Canada, 1885–1925* (pp. 139–142). University of Toronto Press. https://doi.org/10.3138/9781442689268

Villarreal Sosa, L., & Nuckolls, R. (2018, December 8). School social workers: A call to action in support of human rights. *International Journal of School Social Work, 3*(1). https://doi.org/10.4148/2161-4148.1038

Wollons, R., & Wollons, R. L. (Eds.). (1993). *Children at risk in America: History, concepts, and public policy*. SUNY Press.

World Health Organization. (2022). *Health equity*. https://www.who.int/health-topics/health-equity#tab=tab_1

Erica R. Balderrama is the Bachelor of Social Work Program Coordinator and a Clinical Instructor with the University of Texas at El Paso Department of Social Work. She obtained both her Bachelor and Master of Social Work from the University of Texas at El Paso. She has experience working with the Title IV-E child welfare project providing training for both foster parents and child welfare workers while supporting child welfare workers while they obtained their Master of Social Work degree. Her research interests are on the LGBTQI population and their lived experiences, mental health, child welfare, and diversity, equity, and inclusion in the workplace and classroom. She holds a micro-credential in inclusive and equitable teaching.

Araceli Garcia is Research Assistant of the Social Work Department in the College of Health Sciences at the University of Texas at El Paso. She obtained her Bachelor of Arts degree in Psychology and Philosophy from the University of Texas at El Paso in December 2021. Her research interests are in mental health treatment disparities in underserved populations (Latinx, criminally involved individuals, home-free), and she is interested in pursuing a Doctorate degree in Psychology in the future. She is currently involved in the Behavioral Project at the Border Biomedical Research Center which assesses HPV-related knowledge, attitudes, and practices in a Hispanic community sample to identify barriers and facilitate HPV vaccine uptake.

Eva M. Moya is the Interim Chair and Associate Professor of the Social Work Department in the College of Health Sciences at the University of Texas at El Paso. She obtained her Master of Social Work from the University of Texas at Austin and her Doctorate in Interdisciplinary Health Sciences from the University of Texas at El Paso. Dr. Moya is a specialist in border health, with more than 40 years of professional experience in the US-Mexico border region. Her expertise includes border health, tuberculosis and stigma, HIV/AIDS, experiences of the home-free, HPV, community health workers, food security, and the photovoice method of research. She is currently the Principal Investigator of the Behavioral Project at the Border Biomedical Research Center which assesses HPV-related knowledge, attitudes, and practices in a Hispanic community sample to identify barriers and facilitate HPV vaccine uptake.

Chapter 9
Challenging Coloniality in Social Work Theorizations on Human Rights

Kris Clarke

We live in the midst of a cataclysmic crisis. All life forms are endangered as capitalist extractivism continues to ravage the planet through the relentless pursuit of ever decreasing fossil fuels, wreaking havoc on social systems and ecosystems while inflaming conflicts over resources. The existential threat of climate change is so profound that the limitations of our ways of thinking in social work, immersed as they are in coloniality, provide little imaginative power to envision what must be done. Certainly, ecocide has been part and parcel of the modern colonial project from the very beginning, and concerns about the environment are nothing new in territories that have long been subject to invasion, land theft, ecological devastation, cultural annihilation, genocide, and colonial domination. Early colonial invaders brought the notion of land and nation as white possession, which demanded the erasure and elimination of the Indigenous, and uplifting the notion of land as commodity (Dunbar Ortiz, 2014; Moreton-Robinson, 2015, 30; Wolfe, 2006). While Europe is 8% of the world, its colonial invasions pillaged the natural, animal, and human resources of over 80% of the world (Hoffman, 2015; Rodney, 2018). Historian Om Prakash (2006, 699) documents the vast colonial slaughter of animals by pointing to the 80,000 tigers, 150,000 leopards, and 200,000 wolves that were killed during the British Raj. Historian Muchaparara Musemwa (2016) discusses the continuity between colonial and postcolonial ways of mismanaging the once verdant forest of Zimbabwe through "sustainable" methods. Anthropologist Jack Weatherford (1988) documents how knowledge of natural resources was transferred from the colonies to the metropole. This knowledge in the hands of colonizers became predatory commodifying natural resources into raw materials for the burgeoning industries of Europe and fundamentally altering the relationship

K. Clarke (✉)
Department of Social Work, Faculty of Social Sciences, University of Helsinki,
Helsinki, Finland
e-mail: kris.clarke@helsinki.fi

M. Madew et al. (eds.), *Decolonized Approaches to Human Rights and Social Work*,
https://doi.org/10.1007/978-3-031-33030-8_9

between humans and the nonhuman (Pratt, 2022). The massive ecological loss creeping across the globe, the logical consequence of colonialism, is perhaps so vast that like the unspeakable stories of trauma, we often have no words to express our grief.

Human rights are central to the profession of social work (International Federation of Social Workers, 2014). Social work has even been described as a human rights profession due to the congruency in values and advocacy for social justice (Reisch et al., 2013). The teaching of human rights is deeply embedded in global social work curricula and constitutes a significant element of professional identity. Toward the end of the twentieth century, several international social work associations launched initiatives to coincide with the 60th anniversary of the Universal Declaration of Human Rights to highlight the links between the profession and body of legal principles that have defined the post-World War II era (Healy, 2008; Witkin, 1998). This essay explores the limitations of human rights theorizations in social work, especially in the face of climate crisis. Following the critique of Bonaventura de Sousa Santos (2007), this chapter argues that prevailing notions of human rights are limited through their rootedness in coloniality and Eurocentric concepts. It explores how epistemic injustice has erased and ignored significant Indigenous and decolonial knowledge that could expand social work ways of thinking about justice, relationality, and the value of life, and the more-than-human. It proceeds by positioning myself as a white settler author writing on this topic and then opens up how human rights have been theorized in social work. The concept of epistemic justice is introduced, and some central commonalities of Indigenous ways of knowing in relation to climate change as a societal challenge are discussed.

Positioning Myself

I approach this topic as a person with white settler roots in North America. I grew up in the traditional territories of the Yokuts and Mono peoples in what is now called Central California. Growing up, I knew nothing of the traditional stewards of this land because as schoolchildren we were indoctrinated into the history of Spanish missions and white settlers as foundational to our history. Central California is one of the most manipulated landscapes on the planet due to the twentieth-century development of intensive industrial agriculture, which is dependent on massive quantities of imported water. Indeed, I grew up near Tulare Lake, what was once the largest freshwater lake west of the Mississippi, at over 1800 square kilometers. Tulare Lake supported extensive wetlands that were home to a myriad of migratory birds and fish. The Tachi tribe lived on the shores of the lake for thousands of years until the first Spanish colonizers appeared in the seventeenth century. When California became a US state, white settlers launched a campaign of genocide against the Indigenous peoples while refusing to ratify treaties and stealing their land (Fenelon & Trafzer, 2014). White settlers also implanted systems of racial capitalism in the nineteenth century that continue to define how labor relations and social structures operate in the region (Middleton Manning & Gayle, 2022).

As the agricultural economy grew in Central California in the twentieth century, the need for water increased exponentially. The majestic power of the mighty five rivers that filled Tulare Lake from the annual Sierra snowpack was eventually stilled by dams that were constructed between the 1930s and 1950s diverting water to large agricultural fields and growing population centers. Tulare Lake became a "vanished landscape" where the abundant wildlife and sustainable practices of the Yokuts and Tachi people in the lake basin were plowed under cotton fields (Preston, 1981). In the latter part of the twentieth century, global warming began to significantly reduce the snowpack. Drought and the overpumping of the aquifer caused many wells to go dry making it difficult to access running water in small impoverished rural towns. In 2023, large parts of Tulare Lake have roared back to life as a barrage of atmospheric rivers of rain flooded the Central Valley, threatening vulnerable communities.

I relate this long story about my place of origin because its historical erasures and ideology of dominion over the land have shaped me as much as the manipulated landscapes I traversed. The destruction of the native ecosystem was considered a by-product of progress and celebrated in local histories of the region. Our social work curriculum in Central California in the early twenty-first century used concepts of human rights and systems of oppression but did not tackle the multifaceted slow violence of environmental injustice that impacted all forms of life (Nixon, 2011). Though the lack of running water can be seen as a reason for California child protection workers to remove a child from a home, for example, our social work epistemology did not provide a framework for more complex understandings of how such circumstances emerged, how to understand them as human rights violations, or how to challenge them. Just as traces of the long-vanished lake continue to reemerge, diverse knowledge systems are still living among us and can provide insight if we pay attention.

Theorizing Human Rights in Social Work

Several competing origin stories of human rights coexist that range from Judeo-Christian religions to the Enlightenment to the United Nations General Assembly (Roberts, 2017). There are certainly no straight lines from the eighteenth-century broadsides on the Rights of Man to the enclosure of the commons to the end of slavery and the development of international treaties on human rights (Marks, 2020). A common theme of origin stories is the premise that human rights are grounded in modernity and Eurocentric epistemologies, which continue to shape how these rights are conceptualized and adjudicated. Modernity places Europe at the center of the epistemological discovery. Sociologist Aníbal Quijano (2007) has pointed out that the project of modernity is inseparable from coloniality, meaning that modernity as an epistemological framework is intrinsically linked to the coloniality of the modern world system. Ways of thinking about human rights are thus chocked full of contradictions that demand interrogation from diverse epistemological perspectives. Human rights are often viewed as universal, self-evident, and timeless. Considered the bedrock of modern liberal democracy, the body of international legal texts developed since World War II constitutes an internationally recognized yardstick seen as measuring how societies live up to fulfilling the essential freedoms of all human beings. The driving force to create the Universal Declaration of Human Rights Universal declaration of human rights (UDHR) proclaimed by the United Nations in 1948 was the horror of the mass extermination of the Nazi death camps. Yet, as Swedish author Sven Lindquist (2021, p. 160) noted: "Auschwitz was the modern industrial application of a policy of extermination on which European world domination had long rested." In other words, the narrative of shock that "barbarity" could exist in the very heart of Europe belied the willful ignorance of well-documented genocidal colonial population techniques on people that were not considered fully human (see, e.g., Elkins, 2022).

Social work emerged in the late nineteenth century as a quintessential modern profession navigating the relationship between the individual and society during the huge transitional period of industrialization, mass migration, and the formation of population sciences like demography and public health. Following the goals of the modern project, as social work theorist David Howe (1994, p. 517–518) has argued, the cornerstones of social work became care, control, and cure. From acting to ensure the best interests of children to supporting interpersonal relationships to challenging interlocking systems of oppression, social work theorizes and applies methods with the aim of enhancing human liberation and the fulfillment of fundamental human rights. However, as social work is also a profession grounded in the coloniality of the modern project embedded in the university, it often theorizes within anthropocentric and Eurocentric epistemologies.

Critiques of social work's theorizations of human rights point to the need to recognize and address the ongoing impact of colonialism and white supremacy in social work explanatory systems (Blackstock, 2019). This requires acknowledging the historical and ongoing harm done to Indigenous and racialized communities also in aspects beyond the human and working to actively decolonize and dismantle oppressive structures and systems. Recent scholarship has documented the complicity of social work in unjust practices like the forced incarceration of Japanese-Americans in World War II (Park, 2019), in British immigration centers (dos Ventos Lopes Heimer, 2023), and in international social work (Carranza, 2018). Some social work scholars have opened an important discussion on the role of social work in upholding coloniality in its theories and practices (Black Deer & Ocampo, 2022; Dettlaff et al., 2020; Qalinge & Van Breda, 2018). The push for historical accountability in the field of social work offers opportunities to confront and take responsibility for the profession's complicity with coloniality and white supremacy as well as to reimagine social work epistemologies and theorizations to move toward decolonial theorizations and practice. Ultimately, the limitations of dominant Eurocentric epistemologies must be recognized, and Indigenous and other marginalized knowledges must be included at the center of social work theorizations to address epistemic injustice, erasures, and power imbalances, especially regarding the impact of climate crisis.

The Epistemic Injustice of Coloniality and Envisioning Futures

Sea levels are rising, glaciers are melting, forests are burning, air quality is deteriorating, and oceans are acidifying. The cumulative impact of this huge environmental catastrophe will have devastating effects on human communities around the globe, though they will certainly be experienced very differently. Millions may soon be displaced from their homes, but not all will have the means or a place to migrate. Species extinction will have knock-on effects that may not be foreseen. Climate crisis demands new ways of theorizing the intrinsic rights of all living things and social work as a social justice profession has a critical role to play. Approaching climate crisis through the same colonial epistemological lens that produced slavery, land theft, and dispossession threatens the future existence of the planet. Climate crisis demands a radical reorientation in social work ways of knowing and acting.

Coloniality pervades our sense of self, social order, and relationship to the world beyond humans (Hoagland, 2020). Many calls for climate justice continue to replicate systems of oppression through their embeddedness in colonial epistemologies (Zografos, 2022). Philosopher Miranda Fricker (2007) has developed the concept of epistemic injustice, which she conceptualizes as how systemic silencing and exclusion rooted in the dominant power structures forms the basis of ways of knowing. Fricker discusses "epistemic injustice" as ways of knowing that systemically distort or exclude marginalized social groups from participating. A robust and critical approach to human rights must trouble the artificial epistemological boundaries between human and nonhuman, challenging the coloniality of many of its theorizations to embrace anti-colonial and Indigenous epistemologies (Ife & Tascon, 2016). New more-than-human approaches to social work challenge the limits of the coloniality of privileging of humans above other life forms and underline the importance of building relationships and acting with nonhuman entities, animals, and ecosystems (Bozalek & Pease, 2020). Challenging epistemic injustice in social work requires acknowledging and taking accountability for historical and ongoing injustices. It also requires active listening and the inclusion of marginalized voices to upend the hegemony of colonial epistemologies in social work.

There is a wealth of Indigenous knowledge systems that span the globe with deep historical roots. Many scholars have written about the breadth and depth of diverse Indigenous epistemologies and knowledge keepers (Bennett & Gates, 2022; Brave Heart et al., 2011; Little Bear, 2012; TallBear, 2014; Yellow Bird, 2016). This brief essay cannot possibly capture a heterogenous living tradition that stretches back across the millennia and is also in continual transformation. Indigenous knowledges can be characterized as complex epistemologies that are "holistic, affective, and spiritual" moving beyond "the cognitive to the kinetic" (Kovach, 2021, p. 268). Reciprocity, responsibility, and relationality to the planet are core Indigenous values (Redvers et al., 2020). However, it is crucial that the discipline of social work approaches Indigenous knowledge with respect and caution, ensuring that Indigenous voices are centered and the historical and ongoing impacts of colonization are acknowledged so that notions of decoloniality and Indigeneity are not simply appropriated and monetized following the same historical pattern as settler colonialism.

In recent years, decolonization has been the focus of many discussions on social change and equity. Social movements in Latin America have brought a new emancipatory decolonial perspective to social work (Motta, 2017). Leading theorists like de Sousa Santos (2016), Quijano (2007), Dussel (2012), Mignolo (2007), and Freire (1996) have brought an embodied, localized, and subaltern perspective to the analysis of coloniality in emancipatory epistemologies. These epistemologies challenge anthropocentrism and the value system of coloniality. The aim of decolonizing knowledge systems is to unsettle and fiercely interrogate the framework of modernist colonial thought that has dominated social work, which has privileged Eurocentric ways of knowing and acting. Aníbal Quijano (2002, p. 82) has argued that unless we challenge a horizon "totally and exclusively occupied by the predatory needs of financial capital," we will have no future. The first step toward challenging this horizon is recognizing how colonial epistemologies pervade our thinking in social work and how they are linked to ideologies of land theft, whiteness, and extractivism. Decolonial approaches demand the centering of Indigenous and marginalized voices by embarking on a process of acknowledging and making amends for historical and ongoing intersectional systems of oppression, including the key role that social work has played in repressive state interventions. Reimagining social work in the context of climate crisis requires new imaginaries grounded in decolonial principles and epistemologies to create more equitable theorizations and practices that can truly ensure the rights of all living things to thrive.

Discussion Questions

1. What ways of knowing did you learn during your social work education with and how does it shape how you understand the world as a professional?
2. How do you understand human rights from the perspective of social work?
3. How should social work address its historical complicity with systems of oppression?
4. What ways could social work address climate crisis in your context?

References

Bennett, B., & Gates, T. G. (2022). Decolonization and trauma-informed truth-telling about indigenous Australia in a social work diversity course: A cultural safety approach. *Journal of Ethnic & Cultural Diversity in Social Work*, 1–14.

Black Deer, A. A., & Ocampo, M. G. (2022). # SocialWorkSoWhite: A critical perspective on settler colonialism, white supremacy, and social justice in social work. *Advances in Social Work, 22*(2), 720–740.

Blackstock, C. (2019). The occasional evil of angels: Learning from the experiences of aboriginal peoples and social work. *First Peoples Child & Family Review, 14*(1), 137–152.

Bozalek, V., & Pease, B. (2020). *Post-anthropocentric social work: Critical posthuman and new materialist perspectives*. Taylor and Francis. https://doi.org/10.4324/9780429329982

Brave Heart, M. Y. H., Chase, J., Elkins, J., & Altschul, D. B. (2011). Historical trauma among indigenous peoples of the Americas: Concepts, research, and clinical considerations. *Journal of Psychoactive Drugs, 43*(4), 282–290.

Carranza, M. E. (2018). International social work: Silent testimonies of the coloniality of power. *International Social Work, 61*(3), 341–352.

Dettlaff, A. J., Weber, K., Pendleton, M., Boyd, R., Bettencourt, B., & Burton, L. (2020). It is not a broken system, it is a system that needs to be broken: The upEND movement to abolish the child welfare system. *Journal of Public Child Welfare, 14*(5), 500–517.

dos Ventos Lopes Heimer, R. (2023). Bodies as territories of exception: The coloniality and gendered necro-politics of state and intimate border violence against migrant women in England. *Ethnic and Racial Studies*, 1–29.

Dunbar-Ortiz, R. (2014). *An indigenous peoples' history of the United States* (Vol. 3). Beacon Press.

Dussel, E. D. (2012). Transmodernity and interculturality: An interpretation from the perspective of philosophy of liberation. *Transmodernity: Journal of Peripheral Cultural Production of the Luso-Hispanic World, 1*(3).

Elkins, C. (2022). *Legacy of violence: A history of the British empire*. Random House.

Fenelon, J. V., & Trafzer, C. E. (2014). From colonialism to denial of California genocide to misrepresentations: Special issue on indigenous struggles in the Americas. *American Behavioral Scientist, 58*(1), 3–29.

Freire, P. (1996). *Pedagogy of the oppressed (revised)* (Vol. 356, pp. 357–358). Continuum.

Fricker, M. (2007). Epistemic injustice : power and the ethics of knowing. Oxford University Press.

Healy, L. M. (2008). Exploring the history of social work as a human rights profession. *International Social Work, 51*(6), 735–748.

Hoagland, S. L. (2020). Aspects of the coloniality of knowledge. *Critical Philosophy of Race, 8*(1–2), 48–60.

Hoffman, P. T. (2015). *Why did Europe conquer the world?* Princeton University Press.

Howe, D. (1994). Modernity, postmodernity and social work. *The British Journal of Social Work, 24*(5), 513–532.

Ife, J., & Tascon, S. M. (2016). Human rights and critical social work: Competing epistemologies for practice. *Social Alternatives, 35*(4), 27–31. https://doi.org/10.3316/ielapa.872170562413761

International Federation of Social Work. (2014). *Global definition of social work*. https://www.ifsw.org/what-is-social-work/global-definition-of-social-work/.

Kovach, M. (2021). Indigenous methodologies : characteristics, conversations, and contexts (Second edition.).University of Toronto Press.

Lindqvist, S. (2021). *Exterminate all the brutes*. Granta books.

Little Bear, L. (2012). Traditional knowledge and humanities: A perspective by a Blackfoot. *Journal of Chinese Philosophy, 39*(4), 518–527.

Marks, S. (2020). *A false tree of liberty: Human rights in radical thought*. Oxford University Press, Incorporated. https://doi.org/10.1093/oso/9780199675456.001.0001

Middleton Manning, B. R., & Gayle, S. (2022). Enslaved in a free country: Legalized exploitation of Native Americans and African Americans in Early California and the Post-Emancipation South. *Journal of Law and Political Economy, 3*(2).
Mignolo, W. D. (2007). Delinking: The rhetoric of modernity, the logic of coloniality and the grammar of de-coloniality. *Cultural Studies, 21*(2–3), 449–514.
Moreton-Robinson, A. (2015). The white possessive: Property, power, and indigenous sovereignty. University of Minnesota Press.
Motta, S. C. (2017). Emancipation in Latin America: On the pedagogical turn. *Bulletin of Latin American Research, 36*(1), 5–20.
Musemwa, M. (2016). Sic utere tuo ut alienam non laedas. From wanton destruction of timber forests to environmentalism: The rise of colonial environmental and "sustainability" practices in colonial Zimbabwe, 1938-1961. *Environment and History, 22*(4), 521–559. https://doi.org/10.3197/096734016X14727286515772
Nixon, R. (2011). *Slow violence and the environmentalism of the poor*. Harvard University Press.
Park, Y. (2019). *Facilitating injustice: The complicity of social workers in the forced removal and incarceration of Japanese Americans, 1941–1946*. Oxford University Press.
Prakash, O. (2006). Wildlife destruction: A legacy of the colonial state in India. *Proceedings of the Indian History Congress, 67*, 692–702. http://www.jstor.org/stable/44147988
Pratt, M. L. (2022). Planetary longings. Duke University Press.
Preston, W. L. (1981). *Vanishing landscapes: Land and life in the Tulare Lake Basin*. Univ of California Press.
Qalinge, L., & Van Breda, A. D. (2018). Decolonising social work education in South Africa. *Southern African Journal of Social Work and Social Development, 30*(1), 4.
Quijano, A. (2002). The Return of the Future and Questions about Knowledge. *Current Sociology, 50*(1), 75–87. https://doi.org/10.1177/0011392102050001006
Quijano, A. (2007). Coloniality and modernity/rationality. *Cultural Studies, 21*(2), 168–178.
Redvers, N., Yellow Bird, M., Quinn, D., Yunkaporta, T., & Arabena, K. (2020). Molecular decolonization: An indigenous microcosm perspective of planetary health. *International Journal of Environmental Research and Public Health, 17*(12), 4586. https://doi.org/10.3390/ijerph17124586
Reisch, M., Ife, J., & Weil, M. (2013). Social justice, human rights, values, and community practice. In *The handbook of community practice* (pp. 73–103). SAGE Publications.
Roberts, C. N. (2017). Grasping at origins: Shifting the conversation in the historical study of human rights. *Chicago Journal of International Law, 17*(2), 573–608.
Rodney, W. (2018). *How Europe underdeveloped Africa*. Verso Books.
Santos, B. de S. (2014). Beyond Abyssal Thinking: From Global Lines to Ecologies of Knowledges. In Epistemologies of the South (pp. 130–147). Routledge. https://doi.org/10.4324/9781315634876-14
Santos, B. D. S. (2016). Epistemologies of the South and the future. *From the European South: a Transdisciplinary Journal of Postcolonial Humanities, 1*, 17–29.
TallBear, K. (2014). Standing with and speaking as faith: A feminist-indigenous approach to inquiry. *Journal of Research Practice, 10*(2), N17–N17.
Weatherford, J. (1988). *Indian givers: How the Indians of the Americas transformed the world*. Crown.
Witkin, S. L. (1998). Human rights and social work. *Social Work, 43*(3), 197–201.
Wolfe, P. (2006). Settler colonialism and the elimination of the native. *Journal of Genocide Research, 8*(4), 387–409. https://doi.org/10.1080/14623520601056240
Yellow Bird, M. (2016). Neuro-decolonization: Applying mindfulness research to decolonizing social work. In *Decolonizing social work* (pp. 293–310). Routledge.
Zografos, C. (2022). The contradictions of green new deals: Green sacrifice and colonialism: Large-scale solutions to the climate crisis drawn up in the global North too often remain embedded in colonial relations of injustice. *Soundings, 80*, 37. https://doi.org/10.3898/SOUN.80.03.2022

Kris Clarke is an Associate Professor of Social Work in the Faculty of Social Sciences at the University of Helsinki, Finland. Born in California, she immigrated to Finland over 25 years ago. Clarke worked in the area of multicultural social work and HIV. After returning to California for 12 years, she became interested in decolonizing social work through her work with Dr. Michael Yellow Bird. They published *Decolonizing Pathways Towards Integrative Healing in Social Work* in 2020 with Routledge. Clarke currently teaches courses on international and structural social work and works with themes surrounding decolonizing social work, LGBTQ+ issues, and HIV/AIDS.

Part V
Decolonized Approaches in Human Rights Advocacy

Chapter 10
Understanding the US-Mexico Border Through a Decolonial Lens

Nicholas D. Natividad

Introduction

In 2021, archaeologists and researchers presented evidence of the oldest fossilized human footprints in North America. The footprints were discovered in White Sands National Park located in southern New Mexico and based on radiocarbon dating, the footprints are estimated to have been made between 23,000 and 21,000 years ago. These footprints are one of the most significant archaeological findings in recent times (Bennett et al., 2021). The discovery has forced scientists to reconsider when humans first migrated to North America, which was originally thought to have occurred 13,000 years ago (Neuman, 2021). Interestingly, the ancient footprints mark the first known time period in which travelers migrated through the North American continent. Furthermore, what makes these oldest known markings of migration in North America so fascinating is that they are located just a little over 80 miles north of the US-Mexico border near El Paso, Texas. El Paso is a city so synonymous with migration that it was named "El Paso Del Norte" or the Passageway of the North. The juxtaposition and close proximity of the oldest known footprints due to migration on the continent to recent footprints being made today by those seeking asylum and safe refuge demonstrate the complexity and beauty of the borderland region. This chapter discusses this complexity and beauty and the nuances of the borderlands as a region caught in the crosshairs of multiple oppressions and at the same time the birthplace of new and innovative ways to rethink social organizing practices, community membership, and one's relationship to others.

N. D. Natividad (✉)
Department of Criminal Justice, Department of Borderlands and Ethnic Studies,
New Mexico State University, Las Cruces, NM, USA
e-mail: ndn@nmsu.edu

M. Madew et al. (eds.), *Decolonized Approaches to Human Rights and Social Work*,
https://doi.org/10.1007/978-3-031-33030-8_10

This chapter first explores background information on the border. It pays particular attention to the ways migration has helped to shape the most pressing issues in the borderlands. Second, it explores the lasting impact colonization has had in the region and uncovers new conceptual ways to view this impact. Third, this chapter examines different ways border theorists are reconceptualizing the border, community, and the self. This section provides a different model and method that can be utilized by those doing human rights and social work along the border. Lastly, this chapter discusses how we can begin to understand relations, community belonging, and membership in new and innovative ways.

Background

Several critical issues are impacting the US-Mexico border region today. Communities along the border have a long history of dealing with everything from rampant and deeply engrained inequalities (Heyman & Ribas-Mateos, 2019) to underdevelopment that has led to immense impoverishment (Betts et al., 2020; Davidson, 2000). In addition, recent extreme violence and gross human rights violations over the last several decades continue to plague the region (Androff & Tavassoli, 2012; Hansen et al., 2021; Staudt et al., 2009). Historically, the process and practice of border wall building and construction has caused drastic environmental transformation and degradation including disruption of migratory patterns of wildlife and depletion of natural resources (Alvarez, 2021). The region is currently facing environmental disasters as the toll of climate change is impacting local vegetation and quality of life for border residents (Wilder et al., 2013). Rapid militarization of the region has increased conflict within the borderland communities (Torres, 2014), while unprecedented expansion of policing has reshaped the region (Andreas, 2009). Implementation of the North American Free Trade Agreement (NAFTA) in the 1990s opened the doors for free passage of goods yet closed the doors to migration, opportunity, and advancement for others causing poverty and repression for many living on the border (Bacon, 2004). Transformation of the region is directly linked to the changes in economic laws and policies and national security agendas that reinforce and harden the border (Nevins, 2010). However, it is important to discuss in depth one of the most salient characteristics of the US-Mexico border, which is the constant ebb and flow of the migration and movement of people.

Political instability, extreme violence, poverty, climate change, and global crises have led to the forcible displacement of millions of people throughout the Western Hemisphere and throughout the world. In May 2022, the number of undocumented migrants arriving at the US-Mexico border hit the highest level in more than 21 years (Isacson, 2022). In a single month, US Customs and Border Protection Agency reported over 220,000 migrants arriving from countries like Venezuela, Colombia, Nicaragua, Haiti, Cuba, and as far as Russia and India (Kight, 2022). In 2021, US immigration authorities encountered almost 150,000 unaccompanied children arriving at the US-Mexico border, the largest number of unaccompanied minors arriving in a single year (Smith, 2022). In 2021, the US Border Patrol reported over 1.6 million encounters with migrants along the border making it the highest annual total on record of migrants coming to the border in a single fiscal year, according to government estimates (Gramlich & Scheller, 2021). The number of people arriving to the border has consistently risen over the years, and with an anticipated 1.2 billion people being displaced by the year 2050 due to climate change (Henley, 2020), those numbers will only continue to rise.

Under the United Nations 1951 Refugee Convention and 1967 Protocol, refugees have an international right to protection. According to the Convention, a refugee is "someone who is unable or unwilling to return to their country of origin owing to a well-founded fear of being persecuted for reasons of race, religion, nationality, membership of a particular social group, or political opinion" (U.N. General Assembly, 1951, 1967). In addition, those seeking asylum are also granted protection under international human rights law. An asylum seeker is often defined as a person seeking protection from persecution and/or serious human rights violations in another country but "who hasn't yet been legally recognized as a refugee and is waiting to receive a decision on their asylum claim" (Amnesty, 2022). Although there is no universally agreed upon definition of a migrant, human rights organizations often regard migrants as broadly people who reside outside their country of origin (Amnesty, 2022). Despite protections afforded in international human rights law, migrants traveling and arriving to the US-Mexico border face every step of the way a myriad of deadly and dangerous obstacles. Below outlines just few examples of the human rights abuses faced by migrants.

Organized Crime and Corruption

Migrants traveling through the Americas are constantly subjected to human rights violations perpetuated by organized criminal groups. These groups often prey upon the most vulnerable populations which results in hundreds of thousands of cases of kidnapping, rape, extortion, and murder of migrants traveling to seek refuge each year (Martínez & Goldman, 2014). Law enforcement and other agencies responsible for protecting migrants in other countries fail to protect migrants and at times, due to immense corruption, actively participate in their victimization (Bailey & Godson, 2000).

Repression at the Border

Historically, refugees and asylum seekers fleeing poverty, violence, and natural disasters have been met with restrictive immigration policies along the US-Mexico border (Nevins, 2010). Policies like "Operation Wetback" and "Operation Gatekeeper" have targeted particular migrant populations to either disallow entry at the border or increase deportations for those living undocumented in the United States (García, 1980; Nevins, 2010). These types of restrictive policies continue to this day with recent policies like the Migrant Protection Protocol (MPP) also known as "Remain in Mexico" policy and Title 42 policy which have resulted in denial of entry of asylum seekers and expulsion of hundreds of thousands of migrants (including unaccompanied children) entering the United States in the last several years (Morris & Saadi, 2022).

Mass Detention

The United States has the distinction of having the highest incarceration rate in the world. This model has been adopted by US state and federal governments to increasingly include mass detention of migrants (Dow, 2004). According to the Prison Policy Initiative, on average 6000 people are in federal prisons for criminal convictions of immigration offenses, and on average 16,000 are detained pretrial by US Marshals (Sawyer & Wagner, 2022). The majority of those incarcerated for criminal immigration offenses are not accused of serious offenses but rather unauthorized entry or crossing the border without permission. Detention of unaccompanied minors that have crossed the border has also steadily increased. Migrant children have spent days in jail-like detention centers at the border, while an estimated thousands every month are held in custody awaiting placement with parents, family, or friends (García Hernández, 2019). In addition, at any given time on average around 22,000 people are civilly detained not for committing any criminal offense but are awaiting deportation by the US Immigration and Customs Enforcement (ICE) (Sawyer & Wagner, 2022).

Conditions Inside Detention

Once in custody, investigations charting human rights violations taking place have been reported by numerous human rights agencies. Even the US government's own internal US Department of Homeland Security (DHS) reports have charted over 160 cases of misconduct and abuse of asylum applicants by CBP and Border Patrol agents over the last several years (Long, 2021). Reports of sexual abuse, denial of medical care, assault, unsanitary facilities, and dehumanizing treatment at the border have been experienced by migrants. There are also reports of harsh conditions experienced by migrants including being held in facilities with freezing cold temperatures and having to sleep on cement floors in overcrowded cinder block cells with other migrants. Unaccompanied minors are also exposed to these conditions. In 2022, one in three migrants held in Border Patrol facilities was minor. These children were also exposed to unsanitary conditions and overcrowded cells designed for adults (Flagg & Preston, 2022).

Most egregiously, US border enforcement agencies have separated thousands of migrant children from their families at US Border Patrol stations and holding centers along the border. Under the Trump administration, 3913 children were forcibly separated from families under the notorious Zero Tolerance Policy enacted in May 2018. Numerous professional associations, including the American Academy of Pediatrics, condemned the policy due to the severe trauma family separation inflicts on children (American Academy of Pediatrics, 2019). Although President Biden reversed the policy and signed an executive order to establish the Interagency Task Force on Reunification of Families in February 2021, the practice continues to be implemented at US Border Patrol stations and detention centers (Southern Poverty Law Center, 2022).

Private Contract Detention Centers in the United States

Some of the reasons why detention facilities have increasingly been committing human rights violations is because of the increase of privately run for-profit detention facilities in the United States. According to government estimates, over 70% of people are held in privately run immigrant detention facilities. Similar to the US criminal justice system, immigration detention facilities have become privatized over the years resulting in limited access and oversight of conditions in the detention centers (García Hernández, 2019).

Deaths

The most egregious human rights violations that have taken place along the US-Mexico border have come from the number of deaths that have occurred. In the mid-1990s, the US government implemented a "Prevention Through Deterrence" policy that was meant to steer unauthorized border crossings into the most environmentally dangerous terrain of land located along the border (Nevins, 2010). The strategy was meant to deter migrants from coming unauthorized by anticipating large stretches of dangerous desert would lessen the number of migrants attempting to cross. What has resulted since the implementation of this plan has been an estimated 5000–8000 migrants have died attempting to cross through the Sonoran Desert and other dangerous regions of the desert (Androff & Tavassoli, 2012). The 2022 fiscal year has been the deadliest year for migrant deaths along the border with more than 800 migrants dying while attempting to cross the border (Rose & Peñaloza, 2022).

What has been framed by so many politicians as a national security issue in the United States that requires laws, policies, and efforts to "secure the border" is contrasted with grassroots movements and human rights organizations attempting to reframe the migration situation at the US-Mexico border as a humanitarian crisis

(Fleuriet, 2021). Denying human rights obligations owed refugees is not only limited to the United States. Nations all over the world justify dehumanizing treatment of migrants as concomitant with and ancillary to maintaining and reinforcing nation-state sovereignty. Yet reframing the situation requires rehumanizing those that are most impacted by forced migration today. Resultantly, the global humanitarian crisis impacting the world today has deeper roots connected to practices and processes of dehumanization of certain populations worldwide. These practices and processes specifically in the United States have historically been linked to larger dynamics involving the remnants and history of colonization (Saldaña-Portillo, 2016) and the social construction and discourse of "illegality" in numerous institutional settings (De Genova, 2002, 2004; Ngai, 2014). Machinations of nation building and state construction have intentionally positioned and cast migrants as "others." Accordingly, migrants often find themselves used as pawns in political theater along national borders. In addition, national, ethnic, cultural, and racial differences often become embellished and exploited in political discourse in the United States and throughout the world for particular political gains in constant efforts to reinforce national borders and construct membership within borders (Chavez, 2013). As a result, much conversation on the numerous ways we can rethink human rights work, advocacy, and social work that can take place within border communities and with those that traverse these spaces becomes clouded by geopolitics, bureaucratization, and political rhetoric that leaves most with a desensitization toward human suffering. For these reasons, it is important to understand the US-Mexico border through a different lens.

Borders as Remnants of Colonization

In order to understand how the border between the United States and Mexico (and similar conditions at other borders throughout the world) has gotten to be this way, it is important to rethink origins and purposes of nation-state borders from a decolonial lens. To do advocacy work along the border requires more than just development of particular skills but also shifts in perceptions toward the ways communities organize which includes rethinking our relationships to land, power, and one another.

To begin this shift, we turn to Anibal Quijano's concept – the "coloniality of power" (Quijano, 2000). The "coloniality of power" maintains that the political and economic spheres of colonialism are linked with the idea that knowledge is part of the processes of colonialism. New ways to organize the world can only occur through new knowledge systems that inform how communities can exist and should coexist. The "coloniality of power" explains that classification of populations was used to control labor and develop a new global power around capitalist-wage labor relations. It argues that these different ways to classify populations included the "invention of race" and creation of other social identities that emerged alongside development of a world economy that relies on national boundaries and borders.

Quijano discusses how historically new identities were produced around the idea of race during the time the colonization of America (Quijano, 2000). These newly defined identities produced a milieu of social relations that became configured around domination, hierarchically arranged societies, and colonial expansion for the exploitation of labor. These social classifications became the identifying categories that separated the dominator from the dominated, i.e., colonizer from the colonized. Racial identity in particular became the instrument that would construct society's structure of power by placing individuals in social roles from birth. These invented social roles were determined by many factors including the color of one's skin.

The link of racial classification with capitalist-wage labor processes is described by Quijano as "new historical identities produced around the foundation of the idea of race in the new global structure of the control of labor were associated with social roles and geohistorical places. In this way, both race and the division of labor remained structurally linked and mutually reinforcing, in spite of the fact that neither of them were dependent on the other in order to exist or change" (Quijano, 2000, p. 536). In other words, systematic racial division of labor was utilized throughout the colonization period to subjugate both physically and epistemically the colonizer as well as the colonized.

Quijano's notion of coloniality of power contributes to understanding how colonization in the region paved the way for machinations of statecraft that control and limit social organizing practices and definitions of community. Coloniality of power also allows us to understand how reconfiguration of the self has been in relation to the new global structure meant for the control of labor. This new global structure was specifically linked to the creation of new social identities and geohistorical places (Quijano, 2000). For the border region, newly created "social roles" and "geohistorical places" during colonization resulted in the division of labor along racial lines to be structurally linked and mutually reinforcing. This new systematic racial division of labor as a new model of power during colonization then was able to be developed alongside the configuration of the nation-state. This new model of power, according to Quijano, is embedded and fortified in what he calls the "logic of coloniality" (Mignolo, 2007; Quijano, 2000, 2007). The logic maintains and supports exploitative and imperial-state practices by asserting modernity's rationality that justifies their existence. This is the aspect of Quijano's research that is most relevant to our understanding practices and processes of border building, namely, that the configuration of the nation-state, and specifically the construction of its borders, becomes justified in relation and in support with the logic of coloniality. This is important because, in becoming justified, the configuration of the state locates valorizing mechanisms and logics that further state projects such as the reinforcement of national borders. Many people assume colonization was a historical event that has no bearing on today's world. However, the logic of coloniality still exists by extending justification not just to the physical border but also into epistemological frameworks (ways we understand membership and belonging in reference to borders) that legitimate a legal-political functioning of the border.

Since Quijano's work on coloniality of power, the modernity/coloniality research project, which includes scholars as Walter Mignolo (2011), Walter Mignolo and Catherine Walsh (2018), Arturo Escobar (2011), Santiago Castro-Gomez (2015), Ramon Grosfoguel, and others (2006), has extended the concept of the coloniality of power (political and economic) to the "coloniality of knowledge" and of "being" (gender, sexuality, subjectivity, and knowledge). It has now been extended to understand the border region.

The history of colonization has produced new historical identities around the politics of territory in order to support a new global structure. What we find at the border is the crossroads of the coloniality of power. Understanding the coloniality of power helps to connect colonizing projects to modern-day knowledge systems that continually oppress populations along the border (Hernández, 2018). According to Hernández, "in effect, the coloniality framework points to the continuation of colonial situations without the presence of formal administrations and to the state/structural administration and self-administration of a colonial order, operating simultaneously—yet with distinct dynamics—at global, nation-state, and epistemological levels" (Hernández, 2018, p. 10). In other words, even though it is apparent through physical manifestations of the border like border walls, checkpoints, and security apparatuses, the detrimental toll of such projects is located at epistemological levels, i.e., the knowledge systems that have been built (and created) to separate an "us" from "them." Coloniality allows us to see how social construction, reproduction, and reinforcement of nation-state boundaries and identities are part of a longer historical trajectory geared toward desensitizing others to human suffering which undergirds the material and epistemic nature of violence on the border. This long trajectory has its roots in colonization in the Americas. Other scholarships by border theorists have been connecting the trajectory of a colonial past and helping to reformulate new theoretical tools and methods in order to view the social phenomena of borders differently.

Theorizing the Border: Toward a Decolonial Tool/Method/Lens

Borderland scholarship has been transforming its understanding of borders in recent years. Earlier understandings of the border as the relationship between sovereign nations shifted to understanding the border as geographic and political margins to later political geography understandings of the "territorial trap" and performance and practice of borders (Anderson, 2003; Brunet-Jailly, 2005, 2007; Diener & Hagen, 2012; Newman, 2006; Passi, 2011; Sassen, 1996; Wastl-Walter, 2011; Wilson & Donnan, 2015). Some of the more recent attempts to understand the border include bordering practices (Parker & Vaughan-Williams, 2012), borders as methods (Mezzadra & Neilson, 2013), multiple borders (Correa-Cabrera & Staudt, 2014), empirical boundaries (Jacobs & Van Assche, 2014), and walled borders

(Brown, 2014). However, scholarship on the concept of borderscapes provides a unique and nuanced approach to understand how we can begin to view the border through a decolonial lens.

Recent scholarship on the concept of borderscapes highlights the fluidity and movement of the border (Brambilla, 2015). Borderscapes were first used in the works by Guillermo Gómez-Peña and Roberto Sifuentes (Kun, 2000), Chavez (Chávez, 1999), (Harbers, 2003), and (Dolff-Bonekämper & Kuipers, 2004) and have developed over time to embrace ethical, normative, and justice discussions of inclusion and exclusion. Prem Kumar Rajaram and Carl Grundy-Warr explain the concept of borderscapes is an analytical tool for reconceptualizing categories of political belonging and is a point of departure to study the border as mobile, perspectival, and relational (Rajaram & Grundy-Warr, 2008). The authors emphasize the need to understand fluid border practices that fold "inward" and "outward." Suvendrini Perera (2008) asserts that the creation of the concept of borderscapes is linked to the immediate need to express the border as a space that is not static but fluid and shifting. What this points to is not just the fluidity and replication of borders but the fluidity and manifestation and re-manifestation of borders as a way of knowing that gets reconceptualized, reframed, and modified. Borderscapes point to the complexity of this process and as a result implicitly acknowledge how ways of knowing can be fluid. For human rights and social workers working with communities along the border, understanding borders not as static spaces but as constantly shifting and fluid helps them think through all the ways borders are always getting reinforced through media, academic scholarship, law, policy, and other social forces. Resultantly, it can help human rights and social workers recast their work not only toward assisting border residents but also focus to reshape social forces replicating oppression in the region.

In addition, it is not just about understanding the border as fluid but also the knowledge systems that work in-tandem to establish conceptions of nation-state borders that are also not static but fluid and ever-shifting. Chiara Brambilla notes that using borderscapes as a method can be helpful to open new spaces for political subjectivities by providing insight on "a space of negotiating actors, experiences, and representations articulated at the intersection of competing and even conflicting tensions revealing the border also as 'a site of struggle'" (Brambilla, 2015, p. 29). She argues that the shift in understanding the concept of border to bordering is not sufficient in fully capturing the complex link between the "persistence of old boundaries and the multiplication of new forms, functions and practices of borders" (Brambilla, 2015, p. 20). The author asserts that the multiplication of new forms results from changing globalized scenarios that are consistently affected by transnational flows and migration. Because human rights and social workers are at the forefront of the fight for justice, healing, and protection of vulnerable populations, they are contributing to articulating new configurations of community that become redefined when understanding how fluid and ever-changing borders are. These new configurations include not only borders as fluid but understandings of community as fluid and shifting and traversed by a complexity of experiences, emotions, and practices. Therefore, we often view people who do human rights and social work as existing outside communities yet not actively participating as community members helping to shape and reconfigure new ways of social organizing and being. This is because we view communities as static and stagnant. Using borderscapes as method helps us view communities as fluid and better captures facilitation of the services offered by human rights and social workers as contributing to reconfiguring how social organizing takes place across border and as a result how different and innovative conceptions of "community" can occur that can include communal organizing and relations beyond borders.

This is further verified by Rajaram and Grundy-Warr and Brambilla when they discuss how concepts of community may be reconfigured through borderscapes as a method. Discussing how borderscapes is a tool to rethink categories of belonging, they state that this is possible "through the articulation of new configurations based on a novel concept of 'community' that is (re)defined by giving attention to the fluidity of nation-state borders and the complexity of the experiences of those who live in them and/or across them" (Brambilla, 2015, p. 19). The articulation of new configurations is also seen in Perera's (2008) work when she describes new geographies and socio-spatial identities. However, it is important to extend those socio-spatial identities not just from the individualistic standpoint but also a new geographic possibility for socio-spatial identity of communities. If borders are in a constant state of becoming, as scholars have proposed (Parker & Vaughan-Williams, 2012), then this aligns with communities formed with those working in the margins. Human rights and social workers are in the same constant state of actualizing practices and negotiating and mediating organizing space as those that live and inhabit the borderlands.

Furthermore, Victor Konrad (2015) in his article "Toward a Theory of Borders in Motion" discusses the shift away from understanding borders as merely territorial lines but as spaces of movement and uncertainty. This paradigmatic shift positions borders as actively ordering and reordering space and as a result repositioning and displacing identities and social relations. Konrad discusses how space is differentiated and institutionalized from the creation of borders. Dichotomization and dialectical differentiation are part of the construction of borders that become internalized by those living along the border. Human rights and social workers are at the forefront of reminding that this internalization process is dehumanizing in nature. Having a deeper understanding of the complexity of relations and understandings of the self that manifest in the borderlands can help human rights and social workers understanding how, when, and why internalization of dichotomous thinking contributes to dehumanization along the border and how their role can be to unveil this complexity and nuance that often becomes overlooked. Konrad reminds us that "the border is not a single and coherent concept, and this overdetermined and multidimensional character of borders has increased rather than decreased in globalization, and as state delimitation has become more varied and complex" (Konrad, 2015, p. 5). For Konrad, borders in motion as a result derive energy manifested between polarities and where "border dialogue is formulated most effectively and definitively by stakeholders in the dialectical space" (Konrad, 2015, p. 6). What is important about Konrad's piece is how he links borders in motion to the dynamic and multilayered complexity of borders. This coincides with alternative methodologies and theoretical frameworks that acknowledge dynamic and multilayered relations that occur in and between communities. This active involvement and fluidity of participation demonstrates not only how manifestation of a dialectical space is constructed but also how certain knowledge is represented and acknowledged within this dialectical space and how, why, and for what reasons other knowledge is excluded. Just as Konrad identified that border dialog is created by stakeholders in a dialectical space – who determines who those stakeholders are and what knowledge contributes to the space has much to do with the long sociohistorical remnants of colonization in the region. Human rights and social workers need to draw on this understanding in order to provide the realized space and landscape of the borderlands from a decolonial perspective.

A Reality of Relation

Beginning to view the US-Mexico border through a decolonial lens will not necessarily result in decolonization of the region. Psychiatrist and philosopher Franz Fanon (Fanon, 1963) while writing during the decolonization and independence movements in Africa sheds light on the relationship between communities struggling to decolonize and fight against assimilation. He writes that the colonial world is a Manichean world. He asserts that it is not enough for the colonizer to limit the native physically through the force of the military and police but that the colonizer must also denigrate the native and paint them as a "sort of quintessence of evil" (Fanon, 1963, p. 41). But there is an underlying reason for this denigration. Fanon reminds us that the most important element to colonized people is also the most concrete and deeply embedded aspect of their lives. He writes "for a colonized people the most essential value, because the most concrete, is first and foremost the land: the land which will bring them bread and, above all, dignity" (p. 44). This doctrine can be considered concomitant to Enrique Dussel's (1995) Myth of Modernity where the "facile optimism of a rationalist, abstract universalism" that imposes Eurocentric standards is used in order to deny the trauma and misery caused from exclusion, oppression, and conquest of indigenous communities and land. Erasing a community's connection and identity deeply embedded to the land has always functioned to extract historical links and narratives that these communities have to and with the land. For those engaged in human rights and social work practice, acknowledging the connection of communities to land is something that cannot be measured or legislated. The alternative epistemological framework that is unearthed through this connection is beyond the dictates of law, policy, or a state. When working with border communities, there is a different understanding and connection to land that emerges that is born out of a history of real and symbolic territorial, corporeal, and cultural violence (Hernández, 2018). As a result, many border theorists assert it is important to change the ways we view not only community but also relationships to land and one another.

Caribbean philosopher Edouard Glissant is the best way to understand how we can create a different reality of relations in the world. He introduces the notion of *chaos-monde* – the immeasurable intermixing of cultures – and argues that memory within a community is capable of "transcending a state of non-history" (Glissant, 1997). It is important to expand that definition of *chaos-monde* to include the ability of individuals and communities to transcend the static, motionless, immutable notion of identity imposed by colonization and presented along borders, which limits our ability to develop different relationships within community and to land and one another. By framing human rights and social work as an activity taking place in the context of building relationships that can be potentially rich in communal and meaningful justice and healing, they have the ability to acknowledge, recognize, and valorize a collective epistemology that exists within oppressed communities despite their silencing by conditions of colonization (and while in doing so resists their condition of "non-history"). Working to elevate the specific collective consciousness of a community, where the prohibition and inclusion of actions and interactions among its members are mediated, structured, organized, and sustained by a number of factors that emanate from its geohistorical and epistemic location (Esteva & Prakash, 2014; Prakash & Esteva, 2008), is not recognized in a state-centric perception of community but is something that should help frame and undergird the human rights and social work being done at the border.

Conclusion

Research on border regions usually focuses on the harsh realities that occur when different economic, social, linguistic, and cultural worlds collide (Wilson & Donnan, 2015). We often think of borders as separating two different real and distinct populations and/or communities through a "line in the sand." We also tend to draw conclusions that borders have always historically separated culturally and linguistically distinct communities and/or nations. However, scholarship and advocacy argues that this is a completely mistaken perception of borders (Naples & Méndez, 2015; Parker & Vaughan-Williams, 2012). As Gloria Anzaldúa (1987) reminds us, "A border is a dividing line, a narrow strip along a steep edge. A borderland is a vague and undetermined place created by the emotional residue of an unnatural boundary" (Anzaldúa, 1987, p. 25). The socially constructed and reified "unnatural" border embodies archival attempts to separate communities and people. Therefore, rather than approach borders as mere "lines in the sand," we have to consider how borders are never fully present or established but rather in constant states of being reinforced (Parker & Vaughan-Williams, 2014). The US-Mexico border is no exception. So, to understand the history and current existence of the border between the United States and Mexico, it is important to examine how this border is being reinforced legally, socially, physically, and epistemically. Understanding this reinforcement and how it is continuously being created, sustained, and justified provides more insight into the current issues border communities and those that travel across the border face every day.

As was discussed at the beginning of this chapter, located in the sand dunes in White Sands National Park sit the ancient footprints of the first migrants traveling throughout the region. Since time immemorial, migration was a part of this land. Efforts to draw lines in the sand have deeper roots to a history of colonization that were meant to reconfigure the sense of self in order to desensitize one to human suffering. The remnants of this history can be found with those living in the borderland region that are having to work within systems and institutions designed for nation building and statecraft. As a result, reconfiguration of the sense of self has left many involved in the labor of statecraft "trained toward indifference to human suffering and destruction" (Torres, 2014, p.xxxiv). For those doing human rights and social work, their approach toward working in the borderlands must be to understand how colonization has impacted the region. Furthermore, their goal should be to undertake a new lens by which to view the borderlands, a lens that allows for different conceptions of community and social organizing to take place and be a part of. Lastly, by building a different reality toward relations, it can help to unearth alternative epistemologies that connect us to one another rather than separate us on prescribed social identities that remind us how limited social interaction, kindness, compassion, community, and change can be.

Discussion Questions

1. What distinguishes the US-Mexico border specifically in terms of human rights?
2. Can you give an example of a human rights violation that migrants experience along the border between the United States and Mexico?
3. What aspects of border can be considered colonial remnants?

References

Alvarez, C. J. (2021). *Border land, border water: A history of construction on the U.S.-Mexico divide*. University of Texas Press.

American Academy of Pediatrics. (2019, May 8). *AAP statement opposing separation of children and parents at the border.* https://www.aap.org/en/news-room/news-releases/aap/2018/aap-statement-opposing-separation-of-children-and-parents-at-the-border/

Amnesty International. (2022). *Refugees, asylum-seekers and migrants*. Amnesty.org. https://www.amnesty.org/en/what-we-do/refugees-asylum-seekers-and-migrants/

Anderson, J. B. (2003). The U.S.-Mexico border: A half century of change. *The Social Science Journal, 40*(4), 535–554. https://doi.org/10.1016/S0362-3319(03)00067-3

Andreas, P. (2009). *BorderGames: Policing the U.S.-Mexico divide* (2nd ed.). Cornell University Press.

Androff, D. K., & Tavassoli, K. Y. (2012). Deaths in the desert: The human rights crisis on the U.S.-Mexico Border. *Social Work, 57*(2), 165–173. https://doi.org/10.1093/sw/sws034

Anzaldúa, G. E. (1987). *Borderlands/La Frontera: The New Mestiza*. San Francisco: Aunt Lute Books.

Bacon, D. (2004). *The children of NAFTA: Labor wars on the U.S./Mexico border*. University of California Press.

Bailey, J. J., & Godson, R. (Eds.). (2000). *Organized crime & democratic governability: Mexico and the U.S.-Mexican borderlands*. University of Pittsburgh Press.

Bennett, M. R., Bustos, D., Pigati, J. S., Springer, K. B., Urban, T. M., Holliday, V. T., Reynolds, S. C., Budka, M., Honke, J. S., Hudson, A. M., Fenerty, B., Connelly, C., Martinez, P. J., Santucci, V. L., & Odess, D. (2021). Evidence of humans in North America during the Last Glacial Maximum. *Science, 373*(6562), 1528–1531. https://doi.org/10.1126/science.abg7586

Betts, D. C., Slottje, D. J., & Vargas-Garcia, J. (2020). *Crisis on the Rio Grande: Poverty, unemployment, and economic development on the Texas-Mexico border*. Routledge.

Brambilla, C. (2015). Exploring the critical potential of the borderscapes concept. *Geopolitics, 20*(1), 14–34. https://doi.org/10.1080/14650045.2014.884561

Brown, W. (2014). *Walled states, waning sovereignty*. Zone Books.

Brunet-Jailly, E. (2005). Theorizing borders: An interdisciplinary perspective. *Geopolitics, 10*(4), 633–649. https://doi.org/10.1080/14650040500318449

Brunet-Jailly, E. (2007). *Borderlands: Comparing border security in North America and Europe*. Univ. of Ottawa Press.

Chavez, L. R. (2013). *The Latino threat: Constructing immigrants, citizens, and the nation* (2nd ed.). Stanford University Press.

Chávez, R. C. (1999). W(R)i(t/d)ing on the Border: Reading our borderscape. *Theory & Research in Social Education, 27*(2), 248–272. https://doi.org/10.1080/00933104.1999.10505880

Correa-Cabrera, G., & Staudt, K. (2014). An introduction to the multiple U.S.-Mexico borders. *Journal of Borderlands Studies, 29*(4), 385–390. https://doi.org/10.1080/08865655.2014.98247 3

Davidson, M. (2000). *Lives on the line: Dispatches from the U.S.-Mexico border*. University of Arizona Press.

De Genova, N. (2004). The legal production of Mexican/Migrant "Iillegality". *Latino Studies, 2*(2), 160–185. https://doi.org/10.1057/palgrave.lst.8600085

De Genova, N. P. (2002). Migrant "illegality" and deportability in everyday life. *Annual Review of Anthropology, 31*(1), 419–447. https://doi.org/10.1146/annurev.anthro.31.040402.085432

Diener, A. C., & Hagen, J. (2012). *Borders: A very short introduction*. Oxford University Press.

Dolff-Bonekämper, G., & Kuipers, M. (2004). Boundaries in the landscape and in the city. In G. Dolff-Bonekämper (Ed.), *Dividing lines, connecting lines: Europe's cross-border heritage*. Council of Europe Publication.

Dow, M. (2004). *American gulag: Inside U.S. immigration prisons*. University of California Press.

Dussel, E. (1995). *The invention of the Americas: Eclipse of "the ther" and the myth of modernity* (trans. M. D. Barber). Continuum International Publication Group.

Escobar, A. (2011). *Encountering development: The making and unmaking of the Third World*. Princeton University Press.

Esteva, G., & Prakash, M. S. (2014). *Grassroots post-modernism: Remaking the soil of cultures*. Zed Books. http://public.eblib.com/choice/publicfullrecord.aspx?p=1758717

Fanon, F. (1963). *The wretched of the earth* (40th Printing edition). Grove Press.

Flagg, A., & Preston, J. (2022). No place for a child': 1 in 3 migrants held in border patrol facilities is a minor. *Politico Magazine*.

Fleuriet, K. J. (2021). *Rhetoric and reality on the U.S.-Mexico border: Place, politics, home*. Palgrave Macmillan.

García Hernández, C. C. (2019). *Migrating to prison: America's obsession with locking up immigrants*. The New Press.

García, J. R. (1980). *Operation Wetback: The mass deportation of Mexican undocumented workers in 1954*. Greenwood Press.

Glissant, É. (1997). *Poetics of relation*. University of Michigan Press.

Gómez, S. C. (2015). *Crítica de la razón latinoamericana*. Editorial Pontificia Universidad Javeriana.

Gramlich, J., & Scheller, A. (2021, November 9). What's happening at the U.S.-Mexico border in 7 charts. *Pew Research Center*.

Grosfoguel, R., Maldonado-Torres, N., & Saldivar, J. D. (2006). *Latino/as in the world-system: Decolonization struggles in the 21st Century U.S. empire*. Routledge.

Hansen, T., Robles Robles, M. E., Hill, D., & Honey, S. (Eds.). (2021). *Voices of the border: Testimonios of migration, deportation, and asylum*. Georgetown University Press.

Harbers, A. (2003). Borderscapes, the influence of national borders on European spatial planning. In R. Broesi (Ed.), *Euroscapes*. Must Publishers.

Henley, J. (2020). Climate crisis could displace 1.2bn people by 2050, report warns. *The Guardian*.

Hernández, R. D. (2018). *Coloniality of the US/Mexico border: Power, violence, and the decolonial imperative*. University of Arizona Press. https://doi.org/10.2307/j.ctv550cjh

Heyman, J., & Ribas-Mateos, N. (2019). Borders of wealth and poverty: Ideas stimulated by comparing the Mediterranean and U.S.-Mexico borders. *Archivio Antropologico Mediterraneo, 21*(2). https://doi.org/10.4000/aam.2019

Isacson, A. (2022). Weekly U.S.-Mexico border update: May migration data, caravan outcome, migrant deaths, Border Patrol troubles. *WOLA: Advocacy for Human Rights in the Americas*.

Jacobs, J., & Van Assche, K. (2014). Understanding empirical boundaries: A systems-theoretical avenue in border studies. *Geopolitics, 19*(1), 182–205. https://doi.org/10.1080/14650045.2013.830106

Kight, S. W. (2022). Border Agents set new record amid historic migrant trends. *Axios News*.

Konrad, V. (2015). Toward a Theory of Borders in Motion. *Journal of Borderlands Studies 30*(1) 1–17. https://doi.org/10.1080/08865655.2015.1008387

Kun, J. D. (2000). Audioscape 2000: The Pocha Nostra and the performance of sound. In R. Uno & L. M. S. P. Burns (Eds.), *The colour of theatre: A critical source book in race and performance*. Athlone.

Long, C. (2021, October 21). 'They treat you like you are worthless' Internal DHS Reports of abuses by U.S. Border Officials. *Human Rights Watch*.

Martínez, O., & Goldman, F. (2014). *The beast: Riding the rails and dodging narcos on the migrant trail* (Paperback edition). Verso.

Mezzadra, S., & Neilson, B. (2013). *Border as method, or, the multiplication of labor*. Duke University Press.

Mignolo, W. D. (2007). Delinking: The rhetoric of modernity, the logic of coloniality and the grammar of de-coloniality. *Cultural Studies, 21*(2–3), 449–514. https://doi.org/10.1080/09502380601162647

Mignolo, W. D. (2011). *The darker side of western modernity: Global futures, decolonial options* (1st ed.). Duke University Press Books.

Mignolo, W., & Walsh, C. E. (2018). *On decoloniality: Concepts, analytics, praxis*. Duke University Press.

Morris, J. E., & Saadi, A. (2022). The Biden administration's unfulfilled promise of humane border policies. *The Lancet, 399*(10340), 2013. https://doi.org/10.1016/S0140-6736(22)00741-3

Nail, T. (2016). *Theory of the border*. Oxford University Press.

Naples, N. A., & Méndez, J. B. (Eds.). (2015). *Border politics: Social movements, collective identities, and globalization*. NYU Press.

Nevins, J. (2010). *Operation Gatekeeper and beyond: The war on "illegals" and the remaking of the U.S. – Mexico boundary* (2nd ed.). Routledge.

Neuman, S. (2021). Ancient footprints suggest humans lived in the Americas earlier than once thought. *NPR News*. https://www.npr.org/2021/09/24/1040381802/ancient-footprints-new-mexico-white-sands-humans

Newman, D. (2006). The lines that continue to separate us: Borders in our `borderless' world. *Progress in Human Geography, 30*(2), 143–161. https://doi.org/10.1191/0309132506ph599xx

Ngai, M. M. (2014). *Impossible subjects: Illegal aliens and the making of modern America*. Princeton University Press.

Parker, N., & Vaughan-Williams, N. (2012). Critical border studies: Broadening and deepening the 'Lines in the Sand' agenda. *Geopolitics, 17*(4), 727–733. https://doi.org/10.1080/14650045.2012.706111

Parker, N., & Vaughan-Williams, N. (Eds.). (2014). *Critical border studies: Broadening and deepening the "Lines in the Dand" Agenda*. Routledge.

Passi, A. (2011). Border theory: An unattainable dream or a realistic aim for border scholars? In D. Wastl-Walter (Ed.), *The Ashgate research companion to border studies* (pp. 11–32). Ashgate.

Perera, S. (2008). A Pacific Zone? (In)security, sovereignty, and stories of the pacific borderscape. In P. K. Rajaram & C. Grundy-Warr (Eds.), *Borderscapes: Hidden geographies and politics at territory's edge* (pp. 201–227). Univ Of Minnesota Press.

Prakash, M. S., & Esteva, G. (2008). *Escaping education: Living as learning within grassroots cultures* (2nd ed.). P. Lang.

Quijano, A. (2000). Coloniality of power and eurocentrism in Latin America. *International Sociology, 15*(2), 215–232. https://doi.org/10.1177/0268580900015002005

Quijano, A. (2007). Questioning "race"∗. *Socialism and Democracy, 21*(1), 45–53. https://doi.org/10.1080/08854300601116704

Rajaram, P. K., & Grundy-Warr, C. (Eds.). (2008). *Borderscapes: Hidden geographies and politics at territory's edge*. University of Minnesota Press.

Rose, J., & Peñaloza, M. (2022). Migrant deaths at the U.S.-Mexico border hit a record high, in part due to drownings. *NPR News*.

Saldaña-Portillo, M. J. (2016). *Indian given: Racial geographies across Mexico and the United States*. Duke University Press.

Sassen, S. (1996). *Losing control?; Sovereignty in an age of globalization*. Columbia University Press.

Sawyer, W., & Wagner, P. (2022). Mass incarceration: The whole pie 2022. *Prison Policy Initiative Report*.

Southern Poverty Law Center. (2022, March 23). *Family separation: A timeline*. https://www.splcenter.org/news/2022/03/23/family-separation-timeline

Smith, K. (2022). Thousands of unaccompanied children cross the border each year, officials say. *Border Report*.

Staudt, K. A., Payan, T., & Kruszewski, Z. A. (Eds.). (2009). *Human rights along the U.S.-Mexico border: Gendered violence and insecurity*. University of Arizona Press.

Torres, N. I. (2014). *Walls of indifference: Immigration and the militarization of the US-Mexico border*. Paradigm Publishers.

UN General Assembly. (1951, July 28). *Convention relating to the status of refugees* (Treaty Series) (Vol. 189, p. 137). United Nations.

UN General Assembly. (1967, January 31). *Protocol Relating to the Status of Refugees* (Treaty Series) (Vol. 606, p. 267). United Nations.

Wastl-Walter, D. (2011). *The Ashgate research companion to border studies*. Ashgate.

Wilder, M., Garfin, G., Ganster, P., Eakin, H., Romero-Lankao, P., Lara-Valencia, F., Cortez-Lara, A. A., Mumme, S., Neri, C., Muñoz-Arriola, F., & Varady, R. G. (2013). Climate change and U.S.-Mexico border communities. In G. Garfin, A. Jardine, R. Merideth, M. Black, & S. LeRoy (Eds.), *Assessment of climate change in the Southwest United States* (pp. 340–384). Island Press/Center for Resource Economics. https://doi.org/10.5822/978-1-61091-484-0_16

Wilson, T. M., & Donnan, H. (Eds.). (2015). *A companion to border studies*. Wiley Blackwell.

Nicholas D. Natividad is an Associate Professor in the Department of Criminal Justice and Affiliated Faculty in the Department of Borderlands and Ethnic Studies at New Mexico State University. He obtained his Master's degree in International Human Rights Law from the University of Oxford and Doctorate in Justice Studies from Arizona State University. His research interests focus on transnational and local community practices of human rights that are informed by indigenous and decolonial methodologies. He is the cocreator of the museum exhibit Pasos Ajenos: Social Justice and Inequalities in the Borderlands, an art and cultural exhibit that focuses on regional issues of justice as they pertain to identity, environment, history, immigration, human rights, and law.

Chapter 11
Decoding a Colonial Impact: The Women's Movement in India

Nycil Romis Thomas

Introduction

For some, human rights are experienced as a birthright, while others need to struggle for its recognition within their own lives. The declaration and acceptance of the universal nature of human rights emphasize the rights of every single person despite differences in human characteristics. Women's rights have been overlooked for centuries. This chapter exclusively examines the "woman question" within the combined framework of postcolonialism and the universality of human rights. India has a long history of women's oppression because of a strong patriarchal culture that evolved through multiple colonial processes. Despite the country being the largest democracy in the world, women have not attained freedom from the direct and indirect bondage of inequality and subjugation. How women as subpopulation are affected by colonization and how they have responded to it collectively are essential factors in understanding the impact of colonial history. It is from here that a process of decolonization could happen in the subcontinent.

Historical Overview of Women's Status in India

The Vedic literature of the early medieval period in Indian history serves as authentic basis for understanding the status of women before the premodern colonization of the Mughals and the subsequent British colonization. In the Vedic period of ancient India (1500–600 BC), women's roles were respected in society even when these were differentiated from that of men (Upadhya, 1941; Goswami, 2021).

N. R. Thomas (✉)
Department of Social Work, Rajagiri College of Social Sciences, Kochi, Kerala, India
e-mail: nycil@rajagiri.edu

M. Madew et al. (eds.), *Decolonized Approaches to Human Rights and Social Work*,
https://doi.org/10.1007/978-3-031-33030-8_11

For instance, Rig Veda as the oldest of the Vedic texts describes mothers as mistresses of the households, while men took care of provisions and protection. Both roles were complementary and highly revered. But women's roles were not entirely restricted to homes. There were female teachers and Indo-Aryan women in military service, and women were generally active in all social realms. Young daughters represented the free spirit and life of the family enjoying freedom, including the freedom to choose husbands and entitlement to paternal wealth in the absence of brothers or when they remained unmarried. Widow remarriage was common. Marriage was a sacred alliance of equals as symbolized in the nuptial ceremony *Saptapadi*, a ritual of taking seven steps around the sacred fire where the bridegroom tells the bride, "We shall live together, sharing alike all goods and powers combined" (Upadhya, 1941, p. 209). But after marriage, women did not have the right to property ownership nor a right to her paternal possessions or husband's property, since the protection of wives or mothers was considered a husband's or a son's duty. The images of the goddesses in Rig Veda are reflections of women's roles in the households (Upadhya, 1941).

Toward the late Vedic period, the free-spirited roles performed by men and women became rigid and compartmentalized. The *Manusmriti*, the Hindu legal texts of the medieval period which formed the basis of Hindu law, instructs women to be obedient and seek protection from husbands after marriage. But at the same time, it also speaks about honoring women as embodiment of goddesses because "Gods rejoice wherever women are revered" (Olivelle, 2005, p.35). These were probably the most tampered verses in the Manusmriti because women's lives were now forced into the confines of households, with their existence and roles undervalued within the feminine space. This is evident in the stereotypes women uphold in present day culture. The resulting patriarchal culture crystallized over the centuries stripped women of choice and power but burdened them with duties. Religion bolstered how women were cast into subordinate roles. Extreme forms of oppression were seen in practices such as Sati, child marriage, and the banishment of young widows because the worth of women's lives depended on their husbands' longevity. If Sati was not practiced, then widows at a very young age were compelled to live in mourning their husbands until their death. The Mughal invasion exacerbated the condition of women with polygamy and strict gender roles, putting them behind purdahs and keeping them subjugated, poor, and invisible. The ensuing nine decades of British colonial rule concretized the existing oppressive practices by legalizing them. This exacerbated women's situation, double-locking them in cultural and legal oppression.

The nineteenth century saw the surge of several social reform movements like Brahma Samaj (1828), Arya Samaj (1875), Arya Mahila Samaj (1882), and Prarthana Samaj (1867), to name a few. These movements exhorted people to return to the essence of Vedas and denounced child marriage, Sati, and caste inequalities. They supported women's education and widow remarriage, leading to the abolition of child marriage and Sati. Educated men and women flocked to these movements, paving way for the nationalist movement in India (Heimsath, 1964, as cited in Nambiar, 1965). Several independent women's movements that took shape during this period were at the forefront of the freedom struggle. They signified critical historical milestones in Indian women's fight for equity. Supported by Mahatma Gandhi, the Father of the Nation and the first Prime Minister Jawaharlal Nehru, women were at the forefront of influential independent organizations such as the All-India Women's Conference (AIWC), Women's India Association (WIA), and National Council for Women in India (NCWI). These organizations made their way into global forums to represent Indian women worldwide. They worked and spoke for the equality of women. Independent India also witnessed women at the helm of welfare services across the country.

The 1950 constitution of India is another crucial historical instrument that declared the equality of rights for women. From the Preamble to the statement of Fundamental Rights, the constitution demonstrated a firm footing on the principles of gender equity. In addition, it also showed affirmative action toward women by empowering the State to adopt positive measures for the protection and empowerment of women to mitigate the impact of a patriarchal culture. India's constitution and adherence to UN declarations and conventions saw the country move progressively toward policies, laws, and programs that empowered women. As a constitutional mandate, the country enacted an array of legislations for the protection of women's rights which included maternity benefits, equal pay for equal work, freedom from child marriage, widow remarriage, dowry prohibition, protection against domestic violence, prevention and prohibition of sexual harassment, protection against indecent representation in media, property rights, and all other legislative measures affecting women's lives.

The focus on protection and prevention gradually shifted to empowerment when the country introduced the National Policy for the Empowerment of Women in 2001. The National Commission for Women was established in 1990 to safeguard women's rights and legal entitlements. The multipronged government programs for women closely followed the pro-women focus of the constitution, emphasizing women's reproductive and maternal health, education, skilling, employment, and care services. Nevertheless, these efforts have had a trickle-down effect on women's equality in India despite remarkable changes in women's education.

Current Status of Women

Women in India have been critically aware of their subordinated status with respect to men. In drafting the *Universal Declaration of Human Rights* (UDHR), it was the Indian delegates in the commission who asserted the use of the more inclusive phraseology "All human beings" to replace "All men" as the formal reference to all humankind. "All human beings are born free and equal" in Article 1 of UDHR was the contribution of Ms. Hansa Mehta, the female Indian delegate to the United Nations Commission on Human Rights in 1947–1948 (United Nations, 2018). Her *Indian Women's Charter* as introduced to the United Nations Sub-Commission on the Status of Women is widely considered a blueprint for global women's rights.

And the term "universality" of human rights, the sustained use of "nondiscrimination based on sex" throughout the UDHR, as well as the mention of "the equal rights of men and women" in the Preamble were the contribution of Ms. Lakshmi Menon, the Indian delegate to the General Assembly's Third Committee in 1948 (United Nations, 2018). This demonstrates the awareness of women from India, that words matter in shaping mindsets over a sustained period of time. The women delegates from India represented a society where the oppression of women set the direction for a global movement for women's parity.

Despite progress in recognizing women's rights, release from patriarchal clutches seem too difficult for women. The huge urban-rural divide backslides the rural women in the country because of their lack of access to public services. From the margin of society, they remain uninformed, illiterate, and impoverished. There is a vast majority of rural women who are traditionally trained to be confined to households and to accept this as a normal life course. Women who do not fit into traditional stereotypes face criticism and social disapproval. A situational analysis of women's participation in the social, economic, and political domains will be helpful in understanding the current status of women in India.

Women and Education

There are policies adopted in India, such as the Right to Education Act and the commitment to the Sustainable Development Goals, which should be responsive to the daunting rural female illiteracy at 64.7% (Census of India, 2011). This is 10% higher than the national average despite India achieving substantial progress in female education after independence. Even as female education lags, India tops the 2022 Global Gender Gap Index in gender parity for both primary and tertiary education enrolments (World Economic Forum, 2022).

Economic Participation

The economic involvement of women in India is the lowest in the world with less than 30% of women in the workforce as estimated by the World Bank (Kondylis & Loeser, 2020). Conversely, the International Labor Organization points to the underreporting of women's economic activity centered around households (Chowdhary & Verick, 2014). The percentage of women in professional, technical, and managerial jobs increased in 2021, with India gaining on several other parameters of women's parity in economic participation and opportunity. Ironically, India ranks 122 in global wage equality at all levels except in professional and technical jobs, where a considerable gap between men and women exists (World Economic Forum, 2022).

Along with gender bias toward men, women's workforce participation is hindered by several other factors, including stereotypes favoring women as caregivers and the difficulty of balancing multiple roles as employees and household workers (Chowdhary & Verick, 2014). This calls for systemic action by the government and workplaces to attract and sustain women in work.

Health

Health is another critical area where India demonstrates poor performance with a lower female birth ratio, higher mortality and morbidity rates, and malnutrition. However, 80% of healthcare providers are women (World Economic Forum, 2022). Generally, women in Indian households demonstrate poor health-seeking behavior for themselves (Modi et al., 2014; Das et al., 2018) since they are more focused on giving care to other family members. Mental health is another area of concern since the high vulnerability among women is considered almost a social taboo (Malhotra & Shah, 2015; Sharma & Pathak, 2015). The Global Gender Gap Report 2022 reports 4% higher stress levels among women than men in 2020–2021 (World Economic Forum, 2022). Little access to economic resources and quality healthcare impedes women's well-being, especially in rural areas. The female gap in literacy, geographical limitations, socioeconomic situation, class, and caste are factors influencing women's health (Cowling et al., 2014; Mishra et al., 2011).

Political Participation

The enactment of Panchayati Raj in 1992, with its decentralized system of governance, succeeded in designating a 33% reserved participation of women in governance. This is a historic achievement in ensuring the political participation of women. Community-based organizations (CBO) also contributed to a growing number of women in politics. The presence of women in local self-governments positively influenced local administration because women leaders focus on issues often neglected by male politicians (Qazi, 2021). However, women see themselves overpowered by men in decision-making either inside political parties or by husbands in the domestic sphere. Irrespective of ideologies, all political parties are entrenched in a patriarchal culture, making it difficult for women to prove themselves as political leaders.

Despite some setbacks, the contributions of women leaders in postindependence India can be regarded as models of how women could qualitatively influence political decisions (Nair, 2022).

Property Rights

Wealth and asset accumulation is another key area where women experience a huge gap. They own less than 30% of household wealth, according to the Global Wealth Report of Credit Suisse (Davies & Shorrocks, 2018). After marriage, women generally do not own property or assets in India. Unemployed women are made more vulnerable, leaving them powerless, voiceless, and in danger of falling into homelessness and poverty. Even when the country has laws for claiming inheritance, the proportion of women who are aware of these legal entitlements are not ready to take legal recourse because of familial pressure. This makes it easier to perpetuate patriarchal practices. Financial illiteracy and cultural norms put even earning women in poverty once they suffer poor health from hard work.

Women and Safety

Rising crimes against women, both in households and in public places, reveal yet another grave threat to the right of a woman to survive and live with dignity. The National Crime Records Bureau reports a 15% annual rise in crimes against women in 2021. Cruelty by husbands or relatives tops the list, accounting for nearly one-third of crimes (National Crime Records Bureau, 2021). The National Commission for Women (NCW) reports a 30% increase in crimes against women in 2021. Sexual harassment, domestic violence, harassment of married women, and dowry harassment have been increasingly reported. It should also be noted that 1537 complaints were registered, citing police apathy toward complainants (National Commission for Women, 2021).

Decoding the Colonial Impact on Women

The colonization of India ended with the declaration of independence in 1947, but the colonial mentality is still prevalent in the Indian population. The colonial impact on women cannot be discussed without first referring to the patriarchy (Patil, 2013). The solidification of the family law calcified the absolutist nature of power relationships (Patil, 2013) in the family by creating and maintaining a male-subjugated confined identity among women. This explains their deep sense of inferiority. Women's identity is attached to domestic chores, nourishing children, dutifully obeying husbands and in-laws, and leaving the external world to men. They learned to confine themselves within this world by focusing on being successful homeowners and effective mothers to daughters whose education must observe the traditional female mold. Behaving and dreaming out of this patriarchal mold is met with strong criticism and even punishment. Nonconformity to expectation results to internalized guilt and fear to break away from cultural dictates. This vicious cycle of becoming the ideal woman brought about many successful stereotypes which were upheld and replicated for generations. Breaking from this mold is a herculean task because generations of molding have so conditioned women to a point where they themselves do not feel the need for change. This is evidenced by the fact that more than half of women experiencing domestic violence acknowledged the right of their husbands to do as they did. This is normalized by cultural norms that expect a woman caught in an abusive relationship to preserve the marriage at all costs (Raj, 2019).

The British strategy of conveniently maintaining patriarchal and cultural divides served to instill a colonized mentality. The predominant male-oriented hierarchy in all social and political systems has institutionalized the subjugation of women, keeping them to the status of an "othered" person. To this day, a feudal value system effectively operates in the practice of questioning a woman's moral character if she herself files a case against a perpetrator of a crime.

Womanhood and Caste

The universality of human rights is of paramount importance in India owing to its steeply stratified population according to caste and class. The caste system in India is one of the oldest forms of social stratification. It divides Hindus into four hierarchical categories based on the livelihood they were allowed to do. On top of the hierarchy were Brahmins, who were regarded as priests and intellectuals. This was followed by the Kshatriyas, the warriors. The Vaishyas were traders and farmers, and the Shudras were laborers. There were people outside the caste system, who were regarded as untouchable outcasts called Dalits.

The country's constitution formally abolished the caste system and the notion of untouchability soon after independence. However, the caste system remains a cultural designation despite its divisive implications. A close examination of literature demonstrates the origins of the caste system in the Aryan invasion that pushed the conquered indigenous people into lower castes and outcastes. This stratification based on caste is complex, with its roots in multiple diversities, including categorizations in race, language, religion, physical appearance, and skin tone (Keppens, 2017).

British colonial rule unscrupulously reinforced the existing stratification system as a tool to drive deeper divisions among the people. To rule over a divided population is conveniently easy, and so was the unchecked oppression of women.

Women from lower castes face different challenges from those from higher castes. The hierarchies of caste, class, and gender condition the destinies of women. All depending on familial background, daughters of poor families end up uneducated and eventually married off to husbands from an appropriate caste. Women are known to oppress other women on the basis of caste differentiation. Sexual violence and other forms of violence have been used with effectiveness by upper-caste people, including the police, to sabotage Dalit movements that advocate for human rights (Human Rights Watch, 1999; Karat, 2017). These instances are only formally addressed when the media expose them. In most cases, abuses against the Dalit people do not proceed further in court because the accused is set free. Dalit women are subject to public stripping, gang rapes, and murder by upper-caste people (Chakraborthy, 2021; Shantha, 2017; Tomar, 2022). Honor killings in India could happen in intercaste marriages when upper-caste family members kill the spouse who happens to belong to a lower caste (Sharma & Chowdhary, 2022). Ironically, the issues of oppression experienced by Dalit women still have to find a strong place within women's movements in India (Human Rights Watch, 1999).

Dalit women are also known to migrate from state to state driven by economic necessity. Migrants are known to come from poorer households (Aggarwal et al., 2020). An interstate migrant woman is easily recognizable from the language she speaks or the behavior she exhibits, making her vulnerable to harassment, abuse, and discrimination in wages, healthcare, and other services. As migrants, they are regarded as outsiders who take advantage of services available within a state to which they do not belong.

The deep ethnic and regional divisions perpetuated by colonial rulers (Upadhya, 1941) damaged the collectivistic culture of India. These destructive divisions are so entrenched even today that violence committed against migrants, be they women or men, does not merit much attention from the majority public or law enforcers.

Ethnicity

Ethnicity is yet another social factor that defines the status of womanhood. Ethnic tribes constitute 8.6% of the Indian population, with 104 million tribal people (Census of India, 2011). People belonging to indigenous tribes face severe challenges from the majority non-tribal population and the police. Tribal women experience the harshest abuse from police or the military who weaponize rape and sexual violence against them. These result in outright murder or attempted murder (Karat, 2017), with perpetrators going unpunished (Minj, 2021).

The constitution of India formally enacted affirmative action policies to protect the rights of India's indigenous peoples, and like the Dalits, these enactments have still to impact the day to day lives of affected individuals and communities.

Hierarchy Set in Skin Color

Imperial rule has one critical legacy among Indians who are psychologically colonized by their special affinity to fair skin. It is a well-known fact that Indians, men and women alike, aspire to have a light skin tone similar to their once colonizers.

The aspiration for fair skin brought about a flourishing industry of fairness products (Mishra, 2015). Skin tone has become a factor in the increased harassment and shaming of women. It is also a legitimate reason for demanding compensatory dowry in a marriage negotiation. Within families, workplaces, schools, and other public spaces, skin tone has instigated ill treatment.

There was a time when the Indian yardstick for beauty was very different from western standards (Upadhya, 1941). Ancient literature gives evidence to this. Dark skin was considered beautiful because Gods were themselves dark-skinned as Lord Krishna and Goddess Kali. Colonization led to a significant shift in the perceptions of beauty, inducing a covert colonial mentality (David, 2010), with internalized negative views about appearance and identity. To be as fair skinned as the colonizing master remains an aspiration despite the ill treatment of Indians by the British, who equated them to dogs and banned them from entering clubs and restaurants frequented by white people (Mishra, 2015).

While maintaining the caste system in India, the British took advantage of perceptions of skin color as a marker of privilege and entitlement. The skin tone bias was well integrated into the caste system, with the higher castes having light skin at the top of the work hierarchy and the dark-skinned at the lowest. British discrimination based on skin color created and maintained a select group of fair-skinned people.

Today, lighter skinned people still wanted to look fairer, while those with dark skin wanted to be light-skinned. Eventually, skin tone has become another marker for differentiation and discrimination. The British rule of nearly a century left deep imprints on Indian minds about the superiority of fairness, which connotates power, privileges, status, and beauty (Mishra, 2015). In modern India, fair skin as a positive qualifier is not held above caste origin; however, fairness matters within the same caste.

The media encourage this affinity toward fairness. From pregnancy onward, women are lured to enhance the skin tone of their children through natural remedies. As children grow up, girl children are further forced by family members to appear fairer by using fairness products or natural remedies. Fairness is a qualifier for good marriage and career prospects. Matrimonial advertisements are relentless in seeking fair-skinned partners or introducing potential spouses as fair-skinned individuals (Mishra, 2015). With the custom of arranged marriages still prevalent in India, dark-skinned women are often shamed and mistreated. Young women face social rejection while dealing with their own internalized self-dejection.

Campaigns called "Dark is Beautiful" and "#unfairandlovely" have become stronger in recent years. There is a draft bill recommending a ban on fairness advertisements (Sharma, 2020). The Calcutta High Court in the State of West Bengal issued a verdict punishing cruelty toward wives on the ground of dark complexion (Sen, 2020). The verdict is considered a decolonizing landmark message, affirming once again that the struggle against colonial values is a continuing project (Shetty, 2018).

Affinity Toward the West

The psychological inferiority implanted in Indian minds does not end with the obsession with fairness. Middle and upper-class Indians show an affinity toward western standards, manner of living, individual freedom, and the English language, which they consider superior. Western education has helped Indians to fare well globally. But there are those who caution that "we are getting both sips of ambrosia as well as doses of poison" (Upadhya, 1941, p. 231). People leave behind their cultural moorings for the attraction of the West. This internal conflict between two cultures puts Indian women in an "in-between world" (Manning, 2021, p. 1204) of confusion and contradictions (Lugones, 2008 as cited in Manning, 2021), as they switch between the dichotomies of the ideal subdued woman and the modern woman; the valued female identity and the rejected identity (Shukla & Rathour, 2021). The modern woman is seen as a multitasker performing social and political roles without disturbing her traditional roles within the household. Colonization has thus led India into a paradoxical culture, where women are served as goddesses on the one hand and are brutally treated in families and public places on the other. Indian men and women admire women celebrities and political leaders, but they prefer traditional women in their homes (Evans et al., 2022). Therefore, the Indian woman is in constant flux, an entity who is in a constant state of being and becoming (Shukla & Rathour, 2021). In many situations, there is no certainty as to the identity she must present before the world and the one she keeps to herself (Beauvoir, 1989 as cited in Shukla & Rathour, 2021).

Women Advocating for Human Rights

The decolonization of human rights is fundamental for the dignity of life to take shape (Shetty, 2018). A landmark decolonization movement in India came about with the All India Women's Conference (AIWC) in 1927. It was led by Margaret Cousins and a group of Indian and British women. They considered education as the primary tool for realizing women's rights. The Indian women at the top of AIWC were at the forefront of the freedom struggle. The women in AIWC represented the Indian women's voices against the imperial culture before and after India gained independence. From local committees to organized conferences, the women leaders in AIWC deliberated on women's issues. These rights-based discussions were followed by representations and lobbying for legislative reforms. This included the Sarda Act to restrain child marriage and increase the legal age of female marriage. The Maternity Benefit Act provided support for mothers. They used various methods like literature, discourses, propaganda meetings, postcard campaign, posters, surveillance of child marriages, and sending warning circulars to parents to end child marriages (Nair, 2022).

Independent India had its priority focused on economic development, neglecting the equally important women's social issues. The report of the Committee on the Status of Women published by the AIWC brought to light the problems faced by Indian women. This was followed by joint lobbying and advocacy work of six women's organizations, including AIWC. Often referred to as "Six Sisters," they led India into ratifying the Convention on the Elimination of All Forms of Discrimination Against Women (Krishnaraj, 2012). The movement was a pathbreaker in many respects. The AIWC also made history by positively impacting global bodies and forums asserting women's rights. The AIWC delegates to the conferences of the League of Nations submitted a Memorandum on the Political, Legal, Social, and Educational Status of Women in India. Having a consultative UN status after World War II, the AIWC was a delegate to the different international forums under the United Nations. Hansa Mehta and Lakshmi Menon played crucial roles in the formulation of UDHR.

Independent India has also witnessed iconic women's movements that rose to address human rights issues, including the ecofeminist Chipko Movement and Narmada Bachao Aandolan. Relatively recent is Nirbhaya (Bakshi, 2017), a protest movement following a gang rape case in the capital city of Delhi. The contemporary women's movement represents an array of political causes that stretch from domestic patriarchy to resisting colonized identity. Below are a few examples of organizations that comprise a multifaceted women's movement in India.

1. *Sakshi or "Witness"* is an NGO founded in 1992 in New Delhi to closely follow and address sexual violence against women and children. The NGO took shape as a response to a gang rape case of a young girl by two police officers. This case exposed the insufficiency of legal provisions meant to protect rape survivors. Through campaigns, advocacy, lobbying, and landmark public interest litigations, Sakshi succeeded in bringing about systemic policy changes. Sakshi was credited for the enactment of two major legislations in India, the Prevention of Sexual Harassment at the workplace (POSH) and the Protection of Children against Sexual Offences (POCSO). Sexual violence perpetrators see women not as human beings but as objects of gratification, violating their human right to live with dignity. The organization used advocacy and stringent legislation to end these extreme expressions of patriarchy. They are now engaged in rights-based campaigns to educate and empower girl children and women regarding their right to be safe from violence.
2. *Kudumbashree Mission* works to promote family prosperity. It is the State Poverty Eradication Mission of the government of Kerala, the southern State of India. It functions at the grassroots level through a network of women collectives with the triple motto of social, economic, and women empowerment. Established in 1998, it has expanded to several states in India and Asian and African countries, winning several UN awards. Women leaders of Kudumbashree are active in local governance, winning seats as elected representatives (Roshni, 2022). Their collective victory signified the electoral power of the women's vote, so national parties now compete for their endorsement. This women's collective

has become indispensable to the functioning of local government. The organization is a model of staff efficiency, accessibility of services, and effective impact. Though not challenging patriarchy openly, Kudumbashree silently regains spaces in the public sphere by proving how committed work succeeds at constructing a feminine presence in spaces once dominated by men. This strategy gradually neutralizes patriarchal power. Their active presence at the grassroots level and the empowering nature of their collective work make them unignorable as they keep their voices amplified and acceptably nonthreatening.

3. *Gulabi Gang or Pink Gang* is a vigilante women's collective in the Uttar Pradesh State of North India. It began in 2006 when one village woman named Sampat Pal Devi realized that women must act on their own problems when nobody else does. She started the movement in response to widespread domestic violence against women and police indifference in arresting perpetrators. The gang of women adopted the pink sari as a symbol and armed themselves with wooden canes to give punishment against reported perpetrators. As village women, they established stations at strategic spots in their villages to gather reports on domestic violence, corruption, child marriage, and dowry issues. Villagers submit complaints to the local police station as the first step. If the police do not take action or are apathetic, the gang takes over the case by force. This movement resorts to outrightly confronting patriarchal practices by physically caning perpetrators. They engage in physical combat, at times clad in pink saris. They deliver a message that women are not assets acquired by men through marriage but human beings with equal rights in a marital relationship. In addition, the women of the Gulabi collective engage in education campaigns to raise awareness of women's rights. They engage in other community-oriented actions winning acceptance and respect with the effective work they do. Reports indicate that Gulabi members have begun helping men who suffer a loss of income when their crops fail (Prasad, 2008). These forms of community action have only increased the support the Gulabi Gang has received from various sectors of Indian society.
4. *Meira Paibis or Women with Bamboo Torches* is a strong movement of tribal women in the State of Manipur, which has a long history of resisting colonial oppression from both British and Indian rulers. Their history starts with a public demonstration in 1904 against the British. They successfully forced the British to withdraw the practice of forced labor on Manipuri men. In the 1930s, Manipuri women led a strong resistance against the food export policies of the colonial rulers, saving the people in Manipur from experiencing scarcity in the food supply. By the 1970s, the movement became a political force by successfully running an anti-liquor mass action. The movement gained international attention and support when they protested against brutal military abuses condoned under the Armed Forces Special Powers Act (AFSPA) in Northeast India. Purely resorting to nonviolent methods, the women prevented the abduction and death of their young men by holding night vigils in bamboo huts to alert villages against impending attacks. In July 2004, when a 31-year-old indigenous woman was raped and killed by the armed forces, 12 women protested in front of the paramilitary headquarters by disrobing themselves. They continued their fight

through sit-in protests and silent marches wearing funeral attire. In November 2000, 28-year-old Irom Chanu Sharmila began a hunger strike in protest of the Malom Massacre where paramilitary forces killed ten civilians, including an old lady and an 18-year-old. She is considered the longest hunger striker in the world and an icon of public resistance. She endured a 16-year-long strike, regular arrests, and bouts of forceful nasogastric intubation. The law was partially repealed in 2022, but the protest is still active. Meira Paibis continues to be a strong example of indigenous women's resistance.

Conclusion

Social work is a profession rooted in social justice and belief in the inherent dignity and worth of human beings. A decolonizing lens is crucial for social workers in the Global South to understand the complexities of their situation, which is very different from their western counterparts. Social workers have to professionally practice with a decolonizing lens upholding human rights. This comes with the awareness that violations committed against the principles of justice and equality have colonial underpinnings. The manner women in India have organized themselves against injustices gives evidence of the rootedness of their issues to a colonial past that perpetuated patriarchal structures.

Social work in India takes pride in the work of pioneering women before and after gaining independence. Women succeeded in influencing the adoption of the seminal Universal Declaration of Human Rights. Indigenous research and literature about women have to be revisited with the decolonized lens. Indigenous knowledge of gender issues could positively impact policies that are inclusive of all women.

There are many examples of how the power of small collectives brings about transformative change (Prillaman, 2020). These women collectives are models of good practices which social workers can draw lessons from. Gender education and advocacy should also become essential elements in a decolonization movement, to once again interrogate how colonial values have a damaging impact on women's sense of integrity in their identity.

Women in the Global South are not only representations of long-term oppression, but they also represent resistance and tenacity in taking action to address their problems when institutions fail them.

Discussion Questions

1. Critically analyze the status of women in the Global South in terms of access and power in their individual and social lives.
2. How does a decolonization approach empower women to reclaim their identity and space in society?

References

Aggarwal, V., Solano, G., Singh, P., & Singh, S. (2020). The integration of interstate migrants in India: A 7 state policy evaluation. *International Migration, 58*(5), 144–163. https://doi.org/10.1111/imig.12701

Bakshi, G. (2017). The 'Nirbhaya' movement: An Indian feminist revolution. *Gnovis, 17*(2), 43–56.

Census of India. (2011). *Primary census abstracts*. Office of the Registrar General and Census Commissioner, India. https://censusindia.gov.in/nada/index.php/catalog/42604/download/46256/Census%20of%20India%202011-PCA%20Release.pdf

Chakraborthy, P. (2021, December 29). Uttar Pradesh: Minor Dalit girl brutalized over suspicion of theft. *Times of India*. https://timesofindia.indiatimes.com/city/lucknow/two-arrested-for-thrashing-mentally-unstable-dalit-minor-girl-mistaking-her-as-a-thief/articleshow/88571843.cms

Chowdhary, R., & Verick, S. (2014). *Female labor force participation in India and beyond*. [ILO Asia- Pacific working paper series]. https://www.ilo.org/wcmsp5/groups/public/@asia/@ro-bangkok/@sro-new_delhi/documents/publication/wcms_324621.pdf

Cowling, K., Dandona, R., & Dandona, L. (2014). Social determinants of health in India: Progress and inequities across states. *International Journal for Equity in Health, 13*(1), Article 88. https://doi.org/10.1186/s12939-014-0088-0

Das, M., Angeli, F., Krumeich, A. J. S. M., & van Schayck, O. C. P. (2018). The gendered experience with respect to health-seeking behavior in an urban slum of Kolkata, India. *International Journal for Equity in Health, 17*(1), Article 24. https://doi.org/10.1186/s12939-018-0738-8

David, E. J. R. (2010). Testing the validity of the colonial mentality implicit association test and the interactive effects of covert and overt colonial mentality on Filipino American Mental Health. *Asian American Journal of Psychology, 1*(1), 31–45.

Davies, J., & Shorrocks, A. (2018). Women and wealth. Global Wealth Report 2018. *Credit Suisse*. https://www.credit-suisse.com/about-us/en/reports-research/global-wealth-report.html

Evans, J., Sahgal, N., Salazar, A. M., Starr, K. J., & Corichi, M. (2022). How Indians view gender roles in families and society. *PEW Research Center*. https://www.pewresearch.org/religion/2022/03/02/how-indians-view-gender-roles-in-families-and-society/

Goswami, M. (2021). Roles and rights of women during vedic and post-vedic age. *PalArch's Journal of Archaeology of Egypt/Egyptology, 18*(8), 589–594. https://archives.palarch.nl/index.php/jae/article/view/8682

Human Rights Watch. (1999). *Broken People Caste Violence Against India's "Untouchables"*. https://www.hrw.org/reports/1999/india/India994-11.htm

Karat, B. (2017, January 12). *When rape becomes a weapon against tribal women*. NDTV. https://www.ndtv.com/opinion/when-rape-becomes-a-weapon-against-tribal-women-1647667

Keppens, M. (2017). The Aryans and the ancient system of caste. In M. Farek, D. Jalki, S. Pathan, & P. Shah (Eds.), *Western foundations of the caste system* (pp. 221–251). Palgrave Macmillan.

Kondylis, F., & Loeser, J. (2020, January 15). 28%. *World Bank Blogs*. https://blogs.worldbank.org/impactevaluations/28#:~:text=28%20women%20for%20every%20100,world%20outside%20the%20middle%20east

Krishnaraj, M. (2012). The women's movement in India: A hundred year history. *Social Change, 42*(3), 325–333.

Malhotra, S., & Shah, R. (2015). Women and mental health in India: An overview. *Indian Journal of Psychiatry, 57*(Suppl. 2), 205–211. https://www.ncbi.nlm.nih.gov/pmc/articles/PMC4539863/

Manning, J. (2021). Decolonial feminist theory: Embracing the gendered colonial difference in management and organization studies. *Gender, Work and Organization, 28*(4), 1203–1219. https://doi.org/10.1111/gwao.12673

Minj, B. K. (2021, September 18). Crimes against India's Dalits, tribal people increased in pandemic. *UCA News*. https://www.ucanews.com/news/crimes-against-indias-dalits-tribal-people-increased-in-pandemic/94196

Mishra, N. (2015). India and colorism: The finer nuances. *Washington University Global Studies Law Review, 14*(4), 725–750. https://openscholarship.wustl.edu/law_globalstudies/vol14/iss4/14

Mishra, P. S., Veerapandian, K., & Choudhary, P. K. (2011). Impact of socio-economic inequity in access to maternal health benefits in India: Evidence from Janani Suraksha Yojana using NFHS data. *PLoS ONE, 16*(3), e0247935. https://doi.org/10.1371/journal.pone.0247935

Modi, A., Moitra, M., Patel, B. H., & Kantharia, S. (2014). Analysis of health seeking behavior among women healthcare providers. *Canadian Journal of Medical Research, 1*(1), 1–4. https://www.researchgate.net/publication/282731390

Nair, U. (2022). *AIWC at a Glance: The First Twenty-Five Years, 1927–1952*. http://www.aiwc.org.in/pdf/History.pdf

Nambiar, V. (1965). Nationalism and social reform in India [Review of the book *Indian nationalism and Hindu social reform*, by Charles H. Heimsath]. *Economic and Political Weekly. 17*(38), 1441. https://www.epw.in/system/files/pdf/1965_17/38/nationalism_and_social_reform_in_india.pdf

National Commission for Women. (2021). *Annual Report 2021–21*. http://ncwapps.nic.in/pdfReports/Annual_Report_2020_21_English_Full.pdf

National Crime Records Bureau. (2021). *Crime in India 2021, Vol 1*. https://ncrb.gov.in/sites/default/files/CII-2021/CII_2021Volume%201.pdf

Olivelle, P. (2005). *Manu's code of law – a critical edition and translation of the Manava-Dharmasastra*. Oxford University Press.

Patil, V. (2013). From patriarchy to intersectionality: A transnational feminist assessment of how far we've really come. *Signs, 38*(4), 847–867. https://doi.org/10.1086/669560

Prasad, R. (2008, February 15). Banda Sisters. *The Guardian*. https://www.theguardian.com/lifeandstyle/2008/feb/15/women.india

Prillaman, S. A. (2020). The power of women's collective action. *EDI COVID-19 Essay Series*. https://edi.opml.co.uk/wpcms/wp-content/uploads/2020/09/Prillaman_EDI_Brief_SecondDraft-29.9.20.pdf

Qazi, M. (2021, March 6). Women playing leading role in India's grassroot democracy; more participation needed for a better society. *National Herald*. https://www.nationalheraldindia.com/opinion/women-playing-leading-role-in-indias-grassroot-democracy-more-participation-needed-for-a-better-society

Raj, A. (2019). Public health impact of marital violence against women in India. *Indian Journal of Medical Research, 150*(6), 525–531. https://doi.org/10.4103/ijmr.IJMR_1427_19

Roshni, R. K. (2022, May 16). At 25, Kudumbashree gears up to face new challenges. *The Hindu*. https://www.thehindu.com/news/national/kerala/at-25-kudumbasree-gears-up-to-face-new-challenges/article65419912.ece

Sen, S. (2020, July 1). Cruelty to wife for dark skin punishable under 498A: Calcutta HC. *Times of India*. https://timesofindia.indiatimes.com/city/kolkata/cruelty-to-wife-for-dark-skin-punishable-under-498a-hc/articleshow/76720041.cms

Shantha, S. (2017, July 1). How a Maratha-Majority Village in Maharashtra witnessed mob violence against a Dalit woman but did not identify its participants. *Caravan*. https://caravanmagazine.in/vantage/maratha-majority-village-maharashtra-mob-violence-dalit-woman

Sharma, N. (2020, February 6). Govt proposes 5-year jail, Rs 50-lakh fine for ads promoting fair skin. *Economic Times*. https://economictimes.indiatimes.com/industry/services/advertising/govt-proposes-5-year-jail-rs-50-lakh-fine-for-ads-promoting-fair-skin/articleshow/73993170.cms?from=mdr

Sharma, K., & Chowdhary, M. (2022, May 25). How continuous caste-based 'honor' killings in India prove that mere love is not enough. *Feminism in India*. https://feminisminindia.com/2022/05/25/how-continuous-caste-based-honour-killings-in-india-prove-that-mere-love-is-not-enough/

Sharma, I., & Pathak, A. (2015). Women mental health in India. *Indian Journal of Psychiatry, 57*(Suppl. 2), S201–S204. https://doi.org/10.4103/0019-5545.161478

Shetty, S. (2018, May 22). *Decolonizing human rights*. [Speech transcript]. Amnesty International. https://www.amnesty.org/en/documents/doc10/8463/2018/en

Shukla, R., & Rathour, M. (2021, October 19). Deconstructing the idea of the 'Modern Indian Woman': Being versus becoming. *Feminism in India*. https://feminisminindia.com/2021/10/19/deconstructing-the-idea-of-the-modern-indian-woman-being-versus-becoming/

Tomar, S. (2022, March 14). Mob assaults tribal woman on camera in Madhya Pradesh, 3 arrested. *Hindustan Times*. https://www.hindustantimes.com/india-news/mob-assaults-tribal-woman-on-camera-in-madhya-pradesh-3-arrested-101647197782726.html

United Nations. (2018, December). *Women who shaped the universal declaration*. https://www.un.org/en/observances/human-rights-day/women-who-shaped-the-universal-declaration

Upadhya, B. S. (1941). *Women in Rig Veda*. Nand Kishore & Bros. https://indianculture.gov.in/reports-proceedings/women-rigveda

World Economic Forum. (2022). *Global Gender Gap Report 2022*. http://reports.weforum.org/globalgender-gap-report-2022

Nycil Romis Thomas is an Assistant Professor in the Department of Social Work and Coordinator of the BSW program at Rajagiri College of Social Sciences, India. Besides two decades of academic experience, she has practice experience with homeless people and Afghan refugees in India. Her doctoral thesis was in the area of Strength-Based Social Work Practice with Families of Adolescents. She has three funded research projects to her credit. She has presented papers at national and international conferences and has authored many articles. Her research interests include child and adolescent well-being, strength-based practices, and women's issues.

Chapter 12
From Anti-Colonial Revolutionaries to Subversive Feminists: Women in the Philippines

Melinda Madew

As in most countries in the Global South, the women's movement in the Philippines can be studied to distill lessons on how women assumed vital responsibilities in compelling their government to recognize human rights mandates. The passage of the universal declaration of human rights is marked as a historical turning point because the principles of human dignity and equality are so enshrined to compel governments who belong to the community of nations to agree to the mandate of protecting and upholding human rights in their constitution and judicial system. We will begin by tracing the status of women in precolonial times and the manner by which they took arms in solidarity with anti-colonial insurrectionists. We will examine how women rose against colonial slavery, led armed uprisings, and faced the consequences of capture, torture, and execution (FMA, 2017).

Today, women are winning political representation and amassing substantial legislative gains. The effectiveness of their actions is based on the ability to foresee the impact of oppressive structures around them, be these the results of continuing neocolonial occupation, corruption in government institutions, and the pervasiveness of patriarchal oppression as a cultural way of life. Women are assuming the critical task of addressing structures of domination while implementing multipronged strategies meant to address the need of putting food on the table while at the same time confronting entrenched social values that systematically silence them.

M. Madew (✉)
Department of Social Work, Protestant University of Applied Sciences Ludwigsburg, Ludwigsburg, Germany

Research Associate at the Department of Social Work, University of Johannesburg, Johannesburg, South Africa
e-mail: m.madew@eh-ludwigsburg.de

M. Madew et al. (eds.), *Decolonized Approaches to Human Rights and Social Work*,
https://doi.org/10.1007/978-3-031-33030-8_12

Colonial Incursions into Indigenous Identity

Spanish archival records describe the southern Philippine archipelago as having a system of leadership structured around a chieftain known as Datu. The mountain areas in the north were organized around councils of elders known as Nannakay (Scott, 2023). Women were the Babaylan or Mambunong – the shamans who were keepers of their people's historical narrative. As priestesses, they have immense knowledge extending to medicinal herbal healing; they were the givers of wise counsel, the interlocutors of natural phenomena, and most of all the mediators between the world of the seen and unseen. Their powers are not subsumed under male leadership because the reverence accorded to their roles guaranteed cohesion in tribal life. They presided over important rituals of birth, life, and death independent of male chieftainship (Mangahas & Llaguno, 2006).

The Spanish conquest of the Philippines did not come without a price paid by the Spanish crown in men and money. The tribal inhabitants of the archipelago had already evolved a class of warriors who waged territorial attacks against Spanish conquistadores. The first expedition to the archipelago financed by the Spanish crown in 1521 saw its most famous and important expedition commander Ferdinand Magellan killed by the chieftain Datu Lapu-Lapu in the battle of Mactan (Constantino, 2010).

Four hundred years of repeated military incursions in the islands eventually saw the slow subjection of the lowland majority[1] Filipinos to Spanish rule. The Spanish regime succeeded in a slow process of imposed cultural amnesia through the power of both sword and cross. The mystifying and domesticating influence of punitive Christianity did have lasting impact on women. The indigenous spirituality of the once revered Mambunong and Babaylan saw a slow corrosion in influence, with Catholic sacraments replacing their rituals. The colonial church prescribed how the human body is clothed and female sexuality became the domain of church edicts. Women comported themselves as wives, mothers, and servants of the church. The transformed ideal Filipina was one who assimilated into colonial values, the docile virginal woman, obedient to father, husband, and parish priest (Mangahas & Llaguno, 2006).

The process of colonial indoctrination did not influence those parts of the archipelago beyond the reach of Spanish colonial decrees. It was in the mountain highlands of Northern Luzon and the southern islands of Mindanao that indigenous cultures predominantly flourished beyond the reach of the sword and cross. To this day, indigenous tribes and clans thrive in these territories despite the systematic and historical discrimination they have endured from the assimilated lowland Filipinos and their colonial masters (Scott, 1992). Regarded as pagan savages, the indigenous peoples live predominantly in the Northern and Southern extremes of the archipelago. Spanish military campaign launched against indigenous tribes was

[1] Filipino majority or lowland Filipinos – terms used to refer to those assimilated by the colonial cultural system, while minority Filipinos are those who refused assimilation.

unsuccessful for two reasons. First, tribal people have a class of warriors who serve in the defense of territory. Second, indigenous warriors honed and tested in tribal warfare had a mastery of mountain terrain and jungle trails to waylay and successfully counterattack colonial military campaigners deployed to destroy their settlement (Scott, 1996). However, Spain's soldiers were no match to rugged mountain warfare waged by tribal people who had mastery over dangerous cliffs and gorges. Archival records (Scott, 1992, 1996) describe how Spanish conquistadores conscripted majority Filipinos living in lowland regions to engage in war against mountain savages in the North and heathens in the South. This colonial tactic of divide and rule created chasms in Filipino collective identity that is pervasive among assimilated Filipinos and their indigenous counterpart (Scott, 1996). Elements of animosity and suspicion continue to regionally exist among majority Filipinos and minority populations to this day.

Women Organizing and Mobilizing for Revolutionary Change

The tyranny of colonial rule and abuse of church power eventually compelled the majority Filipino population to organize pockets of insurrection throughout the islands, culminating in the revolution against Spain in 1896. Not only did women revolutionaries serve as couriers and spies to assist men, but they also led troops into the battle field. Gabriela Silang was one important woman, who, upon the capture and execution of her husband, assumed his role in leading a battalion of Filipino revolutionaries against Spanish forces. While women of the peasant and working classes engaged directly in armed insurrections, a group of elite women from the class of Illustrados[2] began the Asociacion Filantropica de la Cruz Roja to raise financial support for the revolution and provide medical care for the wounded. Revolutionary women persisted in their activities, despite what archival records reveal today that they were subjected to rape and harassment by their own revolutionary comrades (Goel, 2020; Hega et al., 2017; Kudaibergenova, 2016; Mabini, 1999).

While the archipelago was swept in insurrectionary campaigns, the now declining Spanish empire ceded the Philippines to the United States in 1998 for 20 million dollars. The revolutionaries persisted in the nationalist struggle, this time against a new colonial ruler in the United States. The US government under the administration of Pres. Theodore Roosevelt faced its first war in the Pacific losing 4200 US soldiers from 1899 to 1902. The Philippine-American War claimed the lives of 20,000 Filipino soldiers and 200,000 civilian casualties. The United States acquired their first ever colony in 1898 and ruled the country until 1946 (Constantino, 2010).

[2] Illustrados or Illustradas – elite class of educated Filipinos who were coopted into the Spanish colonial system.

Within this period was the ascendancy of the suffragist movement in the country, with the first ever organization of women who claimed a "feminist" character. In 1905, the *Asociacion Feminista Filipina* was organized by middle class women like Concepcion Felix Calderon at its helm. It was followed in 1937 by the anti-American and pro-independence *National League of Patriotic Women* which advocated and eventually won the right to vote for women in the country (Casambre & Rood, 2012).

The Question of Patriarchy Within the Wider Decolonizing Campaign

The ability to organize themselves and seek identity as a women's movement become more pronounced when the Philippines became the staging ground for military warfare during the Vietnam War in the 1970s. It is at this stage when anti-colonial sentiment progressed to anti-imperialist stance. Women critically studied the character of the country as a neocolonial state within the orbit of US military interest. The presence of US military bases in many parts of the country was interpreted as continuance of military aggression in the Pacific from the Korean to the Vietnam wars. Aside from this anti-imperialist stance, the women's movement was aware of other structural problems. Genuine land reform threatened the elite owners of vast tracts of farmland in the country, the so-called *haciendero* family dynasties who from generations back profited from the patronage of the Spanish colonial regime. Peasants working as indentured laborers within the hacienda system had no chance to break away from intergenerational slavery. It is in this situation of social disparities and unrest that saw the emergence of a younger nationalist stream of women in the movement calling itself MAKIBAKA or *Movement for Freedom by Progressive Women* (Hega et al., 2017).

MAKIBAKA members have been known to protest against the Vietnam War as a case of American hegemonic ambition in Asia. The movement succeeded in articulating a socialist Marxist line of women' participation in the struggle for equal rights within the framework of class struggle and anti-imperialism. Class struggle had to take place among the ranks of landless peasants against owners of haciendas and among workers in factories against foreign capitalist and their local representatives. As a neo-colony, the country was held at stranglehold by the World Band and the International Monetary Fund whose structural adjustment policies (SAP) compelled the country to open its natural resources to foreign exploitation, free trade, and the devaluations of its local currency (Bello et al., 2005, 2004). In retrospect, the politically progressive and nationalist women's movement had not clearly articulated a critical analysis against patriarchal domination as a cause for women's oppression. The Marxist line of thought argued that women's oppression is subsidiary to the more urgent task of national liberation. Women's liberation was not seen within the context of freedom from patriarchy, on the argument that the fundamental trajectory of the liberation struggle was against the imperialistic foreign domination of the economy and the still feudalistic landownership system in the country (Hega et al., 2017).

The articulation of patriarchal hegemony was sharpened by two prominent women's networks in the country, namely, Pilipina[3] founded in 1975 and Gabriela in 1984. These networks drew sharper definitions of the patriarchal character of Philippine society and raised the imperative of gender equality. The struggle against patriarchal oppression was integral to the overall systemic opposition against the feudal character of land ownership and the control of export oriented agricultural production by the landed rich who bankrolled the careers of corrupt politicians in government. This system of patronage politics in the country ensured how legislative policy decision-making protected the interest of rich landlords and owners of local industries. Women activists understood this and knew that a liberation movement had to address these century old problems that people in a neocolonial country are forced to endure (Schirmer & Shalom, 1987). Economic inequalities as evidenced by intergenerational poverty trace back to the time of colonial indentured labor. Given the neocolonial relationship of the government with other global trading partners, the country's resources are plundered by extractive industries such as mining, forestry, and fishing. Workers in manufacturing companies produce goods meant for the global market (Bello et al., 2005, 2004). And as rural poverty spreads, families are compelled to move to the cities setting up shanties as dwelling places wherever they find an open space. All these point to the reality that the women's movement cannot shield itself away from the historicity of political and economic structures that are the causes of intergenerational suffering among the poor.

The broad participation of women from various social sectors was strong and visible in Pilipina and Gabriela. Women activists, among them social work educators and their students, organized and mobilized among the urban poor in slum settlements. Social workers served as labor union organizers, reaching out to urban migrants trapped in factory sweatshops to earn slave wages. Social workers also served as peasant organizers who mobilized women together with their men in sugarcane and coconut plantations. Social workers in the women's movement in the Philippines played critical roles as community organizers and educators.

Unlike other women's movements in the West, Pilipina and Gabriela had to contend with the reality of oppression rooted in a colonial past.

[3] The two biggest networks of women – Katipunan ng Bagon Pilipina (Pilipina) and the General Assembly Binding Women for Reforms, Integrity, Equality, Leadership and Action (GABRIELA).

The Postcolonial Characteristics of Women's Advocacy Movements in the Global South

This chapter takes heavy reference to a history of colonization to trace the trajectory of the women's movement. The feminist analysis of historical poverty and social inequality can only be embedded in a society that is still grappling with its colonial past (Mohanty, 1984). We will now focus on some characteristics that set women's movements in Global South countries like the Philippines from other women's movements in the Global North. Within these differences lie the rich possibility of exploring decolonizing approaches in social work with women in the Global South who bear the responsibility of confronting patriarchal structures within the framework of a colonial past. Further methods in decolonization had compelled women to address the particularities of their history, their neoliberal present, and the vision they have for systemic change in their societies.

Identity Politics and Systemic Problems

Women's liberation movements in the West have legitimately created a body of work in identity politics to legitimize a sense of autonomy and integrity. It meant speaking in a different voice to redefine their strength and recreate their roles when participating more meaningfully in a society that is more respectful of their capabilities. It was a form of women's liberation from the correctly perceived male condescension and domination in western way of life. The character of this postwar women's liberation coalesced around the so-called problem without a name (Whitaker, 2017) because middle class white women saw themselves trapped in the drudgery of homemaking, childbearing, and keeping husbands happy – all these taking place within the comforts of liberal prosperous societies (Millett, 2016). The western woman's sense of oppression stems greatly from being shunted away from the perceived benefits and privileges that men had prerogative to claim as an entitlement of birth. The struggle against patriarchy was a struggle against male privilege which had institutionalized the marginalization of women (Mananzan, 1991; Millett, 2016).

While western women were addressing their need to attain a sense of selfhood and actualization in their personal capacities, women in the Global South faced pressing issues related to the many interrelated consequences of poverty, poor health, education of children, and unemployment, coupled with the absence of any viable perspectives their families could have to rise above a situation of hopelessness. The message articulated by women's networks like Pilipina and Gabriela resonated with other Filipino women in villages, factories, and farms because it was a message that answered questions they have always asked (Hega et al., 2017): that despite their willingness to labor from sunup to sundown, their families were still hungry, their children are unable to complete education, and their poverty will be an inevitable intergenerational cycle. If their individual efforts were not enough, then perhaps their organized capacities might make a difference to their collective lives.

The multi-sectoral organizing of women's groups grew into long term educational campaigns where women resorted to participatory processes in extracting insights from their lived experiences in fulfilling the multiple burden of productive and reproductive duties (Butler, 2015). It is the women in the Global South who substantiated the productive-reproductive dichotomy. Reproductive roles are fulfilled in the bearing and nurturance of children, in the care of extended family members including elderly parents, and keeping husbands contended. Productive roles refer to the extraordinary capacity of poor women to do all kinds of productive labor in marketplaces, in farms and gardens, in rich households, or in factories – always proving that for as long as a woman leaves her house each day, she will return with something that will ensure the family has something to eat the following day.

The seeming normality of multiple burdens borne by poor women cannot be set separate from external structures that politically consign them to these roles, duties, and expectations (Mananzan, 1991). Their culturally designated roles are intertwined with the political and the economic conditions of the larger society that is seemingly immune to the exploitation of women's labor and the unquestioned acceptance that it is primarily a woman's duty to put food on the table, while men can spend their income, when they happen to find employment, in other forms of distraction other than family need.

Poverty as a fundamental question affecting every aspect of women's lives has a different economic and political ramification in the Global South. Addressing disparities in gender roles cannot be set apart from a contextual analysis of cultural and political structures that perpetuate unjust situations. Therefore, women in the Global South understand that their personal struggles are intertwined with the overall societal condition from which they seem so helpless to confront. The gender roles within the private sphere of personal and family relations have to be undertaken within the context of the political and the economic structures of a country still very much at the grip of its colonial past and neocolonial present (Mohanty, 1984).

Nationalism and Its Anti-colonial Character

Nationalism can be equated to a supremacist ideology because of its adherence to the notion that people can be superior over other people. At times it can be an ethnocentric tendency to believe in the notion that one's nationality has to be held above all others. Nationalism can border to a belief that a set of people should have ascendancy over others. However, nationalism in the Philippine women's movement was equated to an assertion of a collective identity shaped by a history of struggle against colonialism (Schirmer & Shalom, 1987). Nationalism attains a different meaning in societies still struggling against the vestiges of colonialism and its continuing impact on the economic and politic structures of an independent nation. It is a disavowal of the legacies of colonialism on the country's institutions of religion and education (Mohanty, 1984). It is a denouncement of a government that allows foreign control over its national economic institutions and environmental resources. Nationalism comes with the assertion of the right to reclaim and revive a collective cultural identity that was once demeaned by dominating powers as primitive and pagan.

The women's movement in the Philippines took on a nationalist character because of the continuing military presence of the United States on sovereign territory. The country was a strategic launching base for military aggression in the Southeast Asia during the Korean and Vietnam wars. The United States built its biggest ever naval base outside American territory in the Philippines as a concrete show of nuclear capacity to intervene in conflicts in the strategically important Pacific Rim (Bello, 2005). Given this strategic value, a series of US administrations supported political regimes in the country which were submissive to the US interventionist interest in the region. The Marcos dictatorship lasted 20 years because of US economic support and military advice in the systematic and yet brutal suppression of civil rights until various mass movements in the country coalesced in the overthrow of the dictatorship in the popular uprising called the People Power Revolution of 1986. The women in the Philippines carried an anti-colonial character linking gender oppression to the broader nationalist movement that denounced the subservience of Philippine political leaders to US hegemonic interest.

The Politics of Empowerment

The politics of empowerment that emerged from the women's movement is all about a liberative approach in the Freirean tradition (Freire, 2017). Empowerment is an educative process of coming to terms with the fundamental causes of women's oppression. The process of awareness raising, popularized by Dom Halder Camara as conscientization, swept through the women's movement as an educational approach in community organizing (Cámara, 2009). Women from all walks of life engaged in small or big groups of conscientization processes in grassroots communities, in the academe, and in parishes, farms, and factories. Empowerment began as a process of claiming knowledge through years of protracted educational campaigns to disentangle the many reasons why women suffer most from a dysfunctional system. They began questioning underlying reasons for that daily struggle to put food on the table or the anxiety over not having any assurance that the children will have better life prospects in the future. And in the end, there was that active refusal to submit to a condition of helplessness.

It was a widely effective approach that allowed women to critically understand the dynamics of oppression in a systemic manner (Mananzan, 1991) on both personal and structural levels. It was restorative of that capacity to confidently participate in an analytic process of encouraging those affected by the impact of community problems to partake in action toward solutions. It is from a coherent and unified understanding of women's oppression that compelled the ranks of women to organize and mobilize.

The process of empowerment is not reduced to a system of doling out help and comfort to vulnerable women. It was a protracted process of critical awareness raising and strategic reflection on ways where systematic oppression is confronted in their daily lives. It is from this process that the women's movement moved forward in amassing gains in terms of membership participation in many mobilization efforts.

In a country where social welfare resources are inadequate if not absent, where social benefits are inaccessible to those who need it most, and where public institutions set up from taxpayers' money are mired in corruption and dysfunction, it is upon the strength of organized community-based women's groups that responded to immediate needs in self-help efforts to mitigate the impact of poverty and government neglect. Women perfected the concept of small income generating projects; they launched village campaigns against domestic violence; they formed vigilante groups to protect communal forests; they did literacy, theater, and cultural activities, all in line with the objective of building women's solidarity and self-sufficiency. The knowledge and skills women acquired while engaging in organized mutual self-help initiatives and building solidarity networks proved to be effective forms of political education. The processes of conscientization that led to critical reflection and organized action were the basic elements of community empowerment. These models in women and development (WAD) originating from women in the Global South have been written about and elevated into theoretical paradigms in scholarly publications without ever acknowledging the collective authorship of community women who lived the truest meaning of self-empowerment and participatory community organization.

The Women's Movement and Their Legislative Gains

The Philippines is said to be one of those countries in Southeast Asia with some of the most liberal laws recognizing the rights of women. The Philippine women's movement aside from its pronounced articulation of patriarchy as a cause of women's oppression also identifies the neocolonial characteristics of Philippines society as a fundamental reason why the liberation of women and all other suffering sectors is a continuing struggle. The two biggest networks of women – Katipunan ng Bago Pilipina (Pilipina) and the General Assembly Binding Women for Reforms, Integrity, Equality, Leadership and Action (GABRIELA) – coalesced around the anti-Marcos dictatorship in the 1980s and continued to support legislative initiatives together (Hega et al., 2017).

Their support saw the passage of various legislative measures such as the Women in Development and Nation Building (RA 7192), the integration of gender and development in the national budget, the passage of the Anti-Rape Law of 1997, and the recognition of women's rights as human rights, which all puts the country in the

17th place among 156 countries in the UN Global Gender Gap Report in the area of economic participation and opportunity (World Economic Forum, 2022). These legislative strides still do not address questions related to female sexuality, gender identity, and sexual orientation. As a predominantly Catholic country, church institutions hold sway over legislation deemed threatening to family cohesion and moral rectitude. Despite papal doctrine, the women's movement continues to push for legislation in areas such as LGBTQ rights, reproductive rights, and equality in marriage and divorce laws (Schirmer & Shalom, 1987).

The recognition of women's rights as human rights had given impetus for women in the Philippines to gain more legislative reforms as defined by the UN Convention on the Elimination of all Forms of Discrimination against Women (UN-CEDAW).

Conclusion: Social Work and the Decolonization of Women's Rights

The women's movement in the Philippines carries a nationalistic brand that is defined as anti-colonial and anti-neoliberal in character. Nationalism is not understood in the narrowed context of white supremacism or right-wing politics of the West. As in any other Global South country, the Philippine women's movement is compelled to glean lessons from various sources including their history of revolutionary struggle, from the people's sacrifices, to uphold community cohesion and national integrity.

Even as the war of independence has been won, the resistance against neoliberalism and neocolonialism is still raging in streets and communities led by various politically progressive people's movements in the country, including those led by women. The human rights mandate as specifically outlined in the UN-CEDAW provides the fundamental mandate from which women can continue to organize around their aspirations to achieve a life of integrity and safety.

Social workers in the country have been at the frontline of organizational work among community women. They have developed conscientization tools for grassroots education. They support human rights groups in opening legislative avenues to advance the collective interest of women. Even as there are ideological divisions in the identification of priorities and strategies, the two biggest women's networks (Pilipina and Gabriela) can unite in efforts in the pursuance of political agenda that are of national consequence. They can unite in decolonial human rights agenda that are embracive of a common vision in economic security, environmental justice, peace, and social justice.

The struggle against patriarchy is pursued in the context of structural problems impacting both the individual and societal spheres of women's lives. The women's movement is proud of their revolutionary history, and today, women continue with great effort to win incremental political concessions albeit in the legislative arena. The philosophical foundation of social work is not only congruent with human rights principles, but it is also a profession closely identified with women whose skills and dedication to work held societies together, so that in the course of history, human rights will be pursued, promoted, and protected.

Discussion Questions

1. Why are there differences in the manner women's movements developed in the Global South and Global North?
2. Why is it necessary for women to organize and mobilize their ranks before pursuing a common interest or political agenda?

References

Bello, W. (2005). *Dilemmas of domination: The unmaking of the American empire (1st ed.). The American empire project*. Metropolitan Books.

Bello, W. F., Docena, H., Guzman, M. de, & Malig, M. L. (2005, 2004). *The anti-development state: The political economy of permanent crisis in The Philippines* (2nd ed.). Dept. of sociology, College of Social Sciences and Philosophy, University of The Philippines Diliman and Focus on the Global South.

Butler, J. (2015). *Gender trouble: Feminism and the subversion of identity*. Routledge.

Cámara, H. (2009). *Dom Helder Camara: Essential writings. Modern spiritual masters series*. Orbis Books.

Casambre, L. A., & Rood, S. (2012). *Early Feminism in the Philippines*. Asia Foundation. https://asiafoundation.org/2012/03/07/early-feminism-in-the-philippines/#:~:text=The%20struggle%20for%20women's%20right,voters%20on%20April%2030%2C%201937

Constantino, R. (2010). *A history of The Philippines*. Monthly Review Press. https://ebookcentral.proquest.com/lib/kxp/detail.action?docID=6403046

Foundation for Media Alternatives. (2017, November 30). *This day in #Herstory: Courageous and strong women of the Katipunan*. https://fma.ph/2017/11/30/day-herstory-courageous-strong-women-katipunan/

Freire, P. (2017). *Pedagogy of the oppressed* (M. Bergman Ramos, Trans.) Penguin Books Ltd.

Goel, A. (2020). *The Philippine Revolution and the Role of Filipinas*. https://thekootneeti.in/2020/11/26/the-philippine-revolution-and-role-of-filipinas/

Harper, T. (2021). *Underground Asia. Global Revolutionaries and the Assault on Empire*. Belknap Press.

Hega, M., Alporha, V., & Evangelista, M. (Eds.). (2017). *Feminism and the Women's movement in the Philippiness: Struggles, advances, challenges*. Friedrich Ebert Stiftung.

Kudaibergenova, D. T. (2016). Between the state and the artist: Representations of femininity and masculinity in the formation of ideas of the nation in Central Asia. *Nationalities Papers, 44*(2), 225–246. https://doi.org/10.1080/00905992.2015.1057559

Mabini, A. (1999). *The letters of Apolinario Mabini*. Publications of the National Heroes Commission. National Historical Institute.

Mananzan, M. J. (1991). *The woman question in the Philippines*. Institute of Women's Studies.

Mangahas, F., & Llaguno, J. R. (2006). *Centennial crossings: Readings on Babaylan feminism in The Philippines*. C & E Pub.

Millett, K. (2016). *Sexual politics*. Columbia University Press.

Mohanty, C. T. (1984). Under Western Eyes: Feminist scholarship and colonial discourses. *Boundary 2, 12*(3), 333. https://doi.org/10.2307/302821
Schirmer, D. B., & Shalom, S. R. (Eds.). (1987). *The Philippines reader: A history of colonialism, neocolonialism, dictatorship, and resistance* (1st ed.). South End Press.
Scott, W. H. (1992). *Looking for the prehispanic Filipino and other essays in Philippine history (revised edition).* New Day Publishers.
Scott, W. H. (1996). *Cracks in the parchment curtain: And other essays in Philippine history*. New Day Publishers of the Christian Literature Society of the Philippines.
Scott, W. H. (2023, January 2). *The Igorot struggle for independence: William Henry Scott*. Malaya Books.
Whitaker, E. (2017). *The feminine mystique*. Taylor and Francis.
World Economic Forum (Ed.). (2022). *Global Gender Report [Special issue]*. WEF.

Melinda Madew is Professor in International Social Work at the Protestant University of Applied Sciences, Ludwigsburg, Germany, and a Research Associate of the University of Johannesburg, South Africa. She serves as Board Member of the European Social Work Research Association. Her teaching and research are in the areas of gender politics, postcolonial social work, and indigenous knowledge and practice in community organizing. She has served as education and research consultant for international development organizations. She conceptualized and implemented international projects under the auspices of European Union educational programs for North-South university collaboration.

Chapter 13
A Colonial History of Territorial Dislocation and Landlessness: Indigenous Peoples and Farmers' Food Sovereignty in the Philippines

Jason M. Leung

The hacienda system harks back to a feudal system of land ownership in the country where the colonial regime subdivided regions in the country for the cultivation of specific cash crops under the management of local elites whose loyalty to the Spanish crown was rewarded with ownership of vast tracts of land, thereby establishing the landlord class of *hacienderos* (Constatino & Constantino, 1975). To date, efforts to break this long-established monopoly of land ownership through the enactment of land reform laws proved ineffective and lacking in legislative clout given the strong collusion between the political and landlord classes in maintaining and protecting their intertwined interest. It is not unusual for members of landowning dynasties to occupy important political positions given that electoral contests are run on the basis of money and patronage (Abelinde & de la Rosa, 2018; de Dios & Hutchcroft, 2003; Ramos, 2021).

Indigenous land ownership applies to those regions in the country relatively unaffected by efforts to assimilate people in the colonial arrangement (Scott, 1992). To this day, indigenous tribes continue to assert ancestral land ownership based on customary law. Extractive industries such as mining and logging have been allowed to set up decade-long operations and only shut down when forests have been devastated of its ecological diversity and mountains once rich in mineral deposits are flattened and reduced to gaping excavations in once pristine environments. It is a tenuous existence for indigenous peoples since the nonrecognition of the Philippine government of customary law subjects them to the constant threat of state confiscation of their ancestral land, this being justified by the Doctrine of Eminent Domain

J. M. Leung (✉)
Department of Environmental Science, Benguet State Univeristy, La Trinidad, Benguet, Philippines

Philippine Department of Science and Technology Research – Extractive Mining and Indigenous Communities, Baguio City, Philippines
e-mail: j.leung@bsu.edu.ph

M. Madew et al. (eds.), *Decolonized Approaches to Human Rights and Social Work*, https://doi.org/10.1007/978-3-031-33030-8_13

that dictates how land under the collective custody of a people can be appropriated for public purposes (Aguilar et al., 2016; Soriano, 2012).

This chapter cites aspects of advocacy work done by peasants and the indigenous peoples in the Philippines. The economic and political circumstances from which the peasant and indigenous people's movements grew in strength are reflections of a postcolonial reality in the country where millions of peasant families continue to suffer from the impact of landlessness and indigenous peoples north of the country, to this day, still struggle to have their right to live in their ancestral territories legally recognized (Delina, 2020). The parallel realities of peasants and indigenous peoples in the Philippines are the remaining vestiges of around four centuries of colonial subjugation that succeeded in forcibly appropriating land ownership for the colonial crown and enslaving the people who once lived from the land (Constatino & Constantino, 1975). Dislocation from land had meant hunger on one hand and forcible submission to a new colonial master on the other.

The postcolonial struggle to redeem the past for landless peasants in the Philippines has found expression in a farmers' movement (Bello et al., 2006). The indigenous people have likewise formed a coalition of tribal organizations that has since developed into a movement advocating for ancestral land ownership recognized in consonance with international standards of customary law (Borras, 2007).

In this chapter, we refer to farmers as those who work on other people's land or are owners of subsistence farms themselves. The farmer is interchangeably a peasant who engages in small scale agricultural production for subsistence and market purposes. The farmer or the peasant has a special dependency and attachment to the land as a means of economic survival and community belonging (United Nations Declaration on the Rights of Peasants and Other People Working in Rural Areas, 2018).

The United Nations does not define who is an indigenous person or community and instead describes them as inheritors and practitioners of cultural lifeways that are attuned to the characteristics of their distinct ecosystem. Despite the impact of colonization on other people in their country, they have protected and retained their social, cultural, and political practices in contrast to the dominant population which could have assimilated into the colonial or neocolonial setup. As self-identified indigenous peoples, they are holders of unique languages, knowledge systems, beliefs, and practices that maintain their caring relationship with natural resources in their territories (United Nations Permanent Forum on Indigenous Peoples' Issues, 2019).

The Farmers' Movement: From the Hacienda System to Multinational Corporate Farming

The biggest organization of farmers in the Philippines – the *Kilusang Magbubukid ng Pilipinas or KMP* (Peasant Movement of the Philippines) – stays by the estimate that seven out of ten farmers in the Philippines do not own the land they farm. KMP describes how 75% of what they harvest go to landowners. This reality is a propagation of the hacienda system of indentured farm labor where peasants are constantly under threat of eviction for nonpayment of debts. Within 35 years of existence as a mass organization, the KMP has articulated an advocacy for genuine land reform on the principles of social justice which is a far cry from what politicians agree to promulgate in congress (One Earth, n.d.). As a militant movement, the KMP has seen its member harassed, abducted, and murdered. Seared in the movement's memory were the 13 farmers who lost their lives and scores of other injured in the infamous Mendiola massacre of 1987 when the police and paramilitary forces fired at a demonstration calling for genuine land reform (Serafica, 2017).

With its membership of around two million spread over various regions in the Philippines, they have actively exposed how local and foreign landlords are responsible for the displacement of farmer families. They have challenged policies that allow agricultural corporations to establish cash crop plantations reducing farmers who once tended to the land as agricultural workers over vast tracts of land planted to exportable crops such as bananas, coffee, and pineapples. Corporate farming while claiming to provide income for farmers has nonetheless devastated vast tracts of land because monoculture farming is highly dependent on harmful chemical inputs. The hacienda system transitioned to corporate farming with land ownership allowed to foreigners with the added incentive that multinational corporations can take exemption from the land reform law that stipulates land redistribution to farmers (Peasant Movement of the Philippines, n.d.).

Farmer landlessness in the Philippines has multipronged consequences. Not only is it impossible for farmers to attain food security and food sovereignty, but they can also not invest in long-term effort at nurturing healthy soil systems and implement diversified agroecological efforts to alleviate their dependence on store-bought food. Corporate farming has systematically taken people away from their roles as producers of their own food (McMichael, 2014). The ability of farmers to assert agency in decisions over the cultivation of crops that maintain good health and to choose crops attuned to the environmental conditions of their regions while adhering to culturally appropriate practices is the prescription to the right to food sovereignty which has long been denied to farmers.

Indigenous People's Movement: The Right to Ancestral Land

One other important advocacy movement with respect to land ownership is one carried out by the indigenous peoples in the Cordillera region of Northern Philippines. It is a region abundant in natural resources but suffers from discriminatory government neglect despite the region's huge contribution to the national coffers given the presence of industries such as mining, hydraulic energy, tourism, and forestry. The Philippine legal system does not recognize customary law applicable to the right of individuals and communities to claim ownership of ancestral territories. As such, people who farmed on land for ages face the imminent threat of displacement from their territories and dispossession of their materials and immaterial cultural lifeways (Cordillera Peoples Alliance, 2014; Franco, 2008). Land to indigenous peoples is the very source of life, importantly as a source of physical nurturance in the cultivation of crops but also in the manner a physical territory becomes the integrated locus of collective memory and life-bonding sense of identity (Buendia, 1987).

In 1984, various tribes in the region formed an alliance to address a shared task of working toward the establishment of a Cordillera autonomous region where the rights of indigenous peoples to self-determination would be respected. The Cordillera People's Alliance (CPA) as an indigenous peoples' movement has been at the forefront of guarding the rights and freedoms of the people specifically against the abuse of environmental resources and usurpation of their land. It is environmental defense that advances the interest of peasants to the fundamental right to food sovereignty. This is in adherence to the United Nations Declaration on the Rights of Indigenous Peoples to live in their ancestral territories and pursue community life in consonance with their distinct values and traditions. The right to self-determination carries with it the right to food sovereignty where people can exercise decision-making process over the use of land and the raising of crops that are appropriate to their food systems. Recognizing the right to food sovereignty is an important tool for indigenous peoples to negotiate with power structures, which is the core of social advocacy (Cariño, 2016). The CPA has fearlessly worked on these causes undaunted by the harassment of its members. As a peoples' movement, the CPA has weathered various forms of politically driven persecution. Through the years, it has seen the murder of tribal leaders, the abduction and disappearance of its workers, and the constant harassment of members (Cabreza, 2022; de Vera, 2022; Delina, 2020; Soriano, 2012).

Social Movements and Social Advocacy

From the short description of two social movements, this chapter illustrates some prominent characteristics of the KMP and the CPA to expound on their long-term goal of advocating for the land rights and food sovereignty of farmers and self-determination in the use of natural resources in the ancestral domain of indigenous peoples. The farmers' movement and the indigenous people's movement have extensive demands that when achieved will result in massive changes in the country's political and economic institutions. These social movements are not spontaneous arrangements where people converge in order to achieve a short-term objective. The Filipino peasants and indigenous peoples could trace a history of intergenerational oppression from a colonial system that institutionalized the exploitation of the peasantry and marginalized those who refused submission to the colonial setup. These are social movements that came about as a resistance to oppression and a resolute determination to find ways in working toward changing their conditions (Bello et al., 2004). Social movements such as the CPA and KMP have members who understand that it is only in taking the responsibility of working for change themselves that their lives could achieve some sense of hope and meaning. They are segments of the Philippine population who have endured betrayals from their political leaders and abuse by landlords. It is in extreme condition of deprivation that people come together over a common desire to join others who share the same motivation of bringing about change and ensuring that their legitimate interest is protected and advanced (de Cadiz, 2014).

The CPA and the KMP have an established following, not only of individual members but organizations which are federated around their program of action. It is important to note that social movements are not spontaneous uprisings, but instead KMP and CPA developed in a carefully planned recruitment of membership through educational campaigns that articulated the systemic and historical reasons that explain why famers and indigenous peoples are threatened by hunger, dispossession, and displacement in a country rich in resources and how a process of cumulative change can come about in their organized and mobilized numbers.

Both people's movements cited here count years of protracted advocacy work with CPA at 39 and KMP at 35 years. Records would indicate how decades of dedicated work necessitated a constant review of strategy and programmatic action when national and global conditions shifted according to political and economic undercurrents. As social movements advocating for systemic change, the KMP and CPA have not declined in membership nor flagged in their political relevance through the years. They have adopted a democratic structure of leadership and management style that is typical of a mass-based peoples' organization.

The urgency of their programs of action expanded their coalitions, so that today the KMP and CPA are integrated in the global justice movements. They have formed international coalitions and are represented in various high profile UN gatherings on justice and ecological issues. The KMP is in coalition with *La Via Campesina* (Way of the Peasants) which is the biggest global network of peasants advocating for the right to uphold food sovereignty pursue this within an agricultural system respects the integrity of peoples' cultural lifeways (La Via Campesina, 2017). The CPA as a highly respected proponent of indigenous people's right to ancestral domain is represented in UN supported bodies which oppose extractive industries in indigenous lands not only in the Philippines but in other continents as well (Center for World Indigenous Studies, 1999).

While social movements are expected to break apart when measures of success have been achieved or when they have been co-opted into the government system (Blumer, 1969; Mauss, 1975; Tilly, 1978), the existence of the KMP and CPA will continue to have significant relevance in so far as the historical oppression of landless farmers and indigenous peoples is not addressed by the Philippine state. The KMP will persist in its advocacy for genuine land reform and food sovereignty within the auspices of the UN Declaration on the Rights of Peasants and Rural Workers, and the CPA will likewise persists in holding the Philippine governments accountable to its responsibility in upholding the principles embodied in the UN Declaration on the Rights of Indigenous Peoples.

Food Sovereignty and the Protection of Peasant and Indigenous Peoples Rights

Food sovereignty, peasant landlessness, and indigenous peoples' loss of territorial domain are interlocking issues that can only be addressed by social advocacy movements in a unified manner. We will proceed to draw the connection of food sovereignty to the aspiration of peasants and indigenous peoples to partake, contribute, and benefit from social, political, and cultural development as a universally recognized human right (United Nations Declaration on the Rights of Peasants and Other People Working in Rural Areas, 2018).

Food sovereignty is defined as the right of food producers to raise their own crops and to decide on what to grow according to their culturally appropriate needs and lifestyle. After decades of advocacy by broad coalitions of democratic farmers' unions including the KMP, the veritable meaning of food sovereignty was enshrined in the UN Declaration on the Rights of Peasants and Other People Working in Rural Areas in 2018. The advocacy to the right to food sovereignty began in 1996 when *La Via Campesina* disavowed the notion of food security as neoliberal protection of the right of consumers to access food at all times in all places without conscious regard for the human conditions by which food is raised as well as the impact of this on the environment (Nicholson & Delforge, 2008). The UN Food and Agricultural Organization had defined food security as the physical, social, and economic access to food that is sufficient, safe, and nutritious to meet the needs and preferences of people for a healthy and active life (FAO, 2002). For two decades, the limitedness of this definition was challenged by peasant and indigenous peoples' movements, beginning in 1996 when *La Via Campesina* articulated the meaning of food sovereignty in an international peasant congress held in Tlaxcala, Mexico.

The global promotion of food security was integrated into the neoliberal program of trade liberalization in the complex chain of food production and distribution. The monopolies in agricultural industry regard food as nothing more than a commodity (Magdoff, 2012), whereas peasants and indigenous peoples regard food as a living system of connectivity among food growers and food users (Argumedo et al., 2020). Under the doctrine of free trade and liberalization of market resources, huge agricultural businesses had untrammeled prerogative to purchase indigenous land from colluding governments who were dismissive of the damage caused on human well-being and the environment with profits accumulating exponentially from the global glorification of corporate food and the mass production of chemically enhanced agricultural products for human and animal consumption (Bello, 2009).

To the peasant and indigenous people's movements, food sovereignty has come to mean the right to produce food in a manner that is freed of control from governments or business interest. It carries the right to perpetuate dietary preferences that are culturally valued because these are sourced from heritage crops grown under conditions that support their communities' ecosystem as it adapts and regenerates in natural cycles (McMichael, 2009). Peasant organizations under the broad auspices of the *La Via Campesina* had persistently lobbied governments and the United

Nations for the inclusion of food sovereignty principles in the recently adopted UN Declaration on the Rights of Peasants and other People Working in Rural Areas. This declaration has now unequivocally recognized principles of food sovereignty as the right of peasants and indigenous peoples to define their food and agricultural systems and the right to healthy and culturally appropriate food produced through ecologically sound and sustainable methods that respect human rights (United Nations Declaration on the Rights of Peasants and Other People Working in Rural Areas, 2018). The declaration is also significant in its reaffirmation of the rights of indigenous peoples including their right to ancestral domain. The UN Declaration on the Rights of Peasants is a strong complementation of another UN Declaration on the Rights of Indigenous Peoples to pursue a cultural way of life in consonance with customary laws that dictate the protection of natural resources and the conservation of indigenous knowledge systems in food production.

Thus, food sovereignty formally entered the UN lexicon in 2018 with the recognition that the goal of zero hunger, positioned as second among the 17 Sustainable Development Goals, would never be achieved until the world's landless peasants and indigenous peoples are finally accorded their longstanding aspiration to live on land they can call their own, freed from the threat of displacement, eviction, and military harassment. It a groundbreaking document that factored the hazardous and exploitative nature of corporate farming when landless peasants or indigenous peoples are reduced to rural farm workers forced to accept exploitative daily wages without the assurance of long-term social security.

When people exercise that human right to participate in decision-making on processes related to food sovereignty, it would mean putting into question the dominating control of global agribusiness in the production, distribution, and consumption of food. The neoliberal order that has long protected the global food chain stands in serious critic by social movements which are equipped with skills and knowledge in protracted political and social advocacy (Alkon, 2013). This would have potential structural impact on the lifestyle of people in the Global North. At the same time, it will bring more opportunities for peasants and indigenous peoples to claim their right to humane living conditions when they benefit from the resources drawn from the land they had worked and protected from generation to generation (Claeys & Delgado Pugley, 2017).

Social Work: Accumulating Lessons from the Past While Working for a Decolonized Present

Recounting aspects of work done by the peasant and indigenous people's movements could provide social workers with important insights on the kind of social advocacy we are called to do in the face of global challenges. In this section, we will identify some characteristics of advocacy movements whereby social workers could make significant contributions in critically understanding the history of oppression experienced by landless farmers and indigenous peoples. More than three decades of advocacy work in farmers and indigenous peoples' movement have the inherent potential to bring about change in an incremental manner. We can proceed to identify some characteristics of this advocacy work.

1. *The Historical Underpinnings of Social Problems.* We have briefly characterized the parallel social movements launched by the landless farmers and indigenous peoples in the Philippines illustrating how social change is a cumulative undertaking. Their situation is not unique to the country. Throughout the world, farmers and indigenous peoples experience the same situation wherever the history of colonialism left its mark on the lives of people. The social movements launched by millions of affected people who have historically borne the burden of colonization will have continuing relevance in Global South countries where governments have submitted to the neocolonial order of open trade policies of the World Trade Organization (Mann, 2014). The liberalization of global markets has disadvantaged countries whose economies are still dependent on agricultural production and, therefore, sectors such as farmers and indigenous peoples who as losers in the globalization experiment are shunted at the sidelines of the global market economy (McMichael, 2014). They do not have the aspiration of competing in a global neoliberal economy. Instead, their call for a paradigm shift in conceiving a just and equitable world includes the institutionalization of the food sovereignty as a most basic element to survival with food being a collective human right.
2. *Social Movements in a Neocolonial Global Order.* Analyzing the colonial historicity of hunger, landlessness, abuse of peasant labor, and dislocation and dispossession of peoples compel social workers to raise questions when and how a neocolonial global order can be transformed. When colonization as the outright occupation of a territory and enslavement of a people cannot be internationally condoned today, a system that perpetuates the (Desmarais, 2002) unequal political and economic relationship between the once imperial powers in the Global North and their former colonies continues to operate today in a global neoliberal order. The deceptions of free market and liberal trade order built into neoliberal international relations are the prolongation of colonial regimes known in modern parlance as neocolonialism. On its own, social work may not have the capacity to overturn a neocolonial order or even transform neoliberal policies. Social workers are trained on advocacy skills in promoting the interest of individuals in casework or, at times, to advocate for their own professional interest. It is in the Global South that a significant number of social workers are in significant positions of leadership in social movements that address structural problems with long-term political and economic implications. For them, the impact of success or failure would have repercussions not only on individual lives but on entire communities. Social work in the Global South has a strong tradition in social action and radical community organizing. It is to the credit of social movements in the Global South which amassed facts and stood to give evidence over the historical wrongs committed against landless farmers and indigenous peoples

(Mann, 2014). This brought the UN to its defining moments in compelling countries to ratify declarations that definitively outlined the way forward in restorative justice. It took the United States, Australia, New Zealand, and Canada years before they signed into the 1997 Declaration on the Rights of Indigenous Peoples.

3. *The Decolonizing Project in Social Work.* The neocolonial characteristics of countries in the Global South have inspired social workers to assimilate into the politicized work of social movements. Decolonized social work addresses structural problems that continue to impact the lives of people because of entrenched inequalities in global relations. While this chapter focused on the parallel plight of landless peasants and indigenous peoples in a Global South country such as the Philippines, decolonized social work theory and practice is essentially the observance of human rights principles when advocating for social change in the Global North as well. In Europe or North America, postcolonial theory can explain why people experiencing poverty take the decision to leave family and land for the uncertain, if not tragic fate, in an affluent country.

Conclusion: Advocacy from Grassroots Community Organizing to the Corridors of Power

Social work with grassroots organizations requires the formulation of long-term programmatic strategies in organizing and mobilization skills. It calls for analytical competence to propose alternative conceptual frameworks from which action can be taken to address entrenched forms of injustices. Advocacy work in social movements is an incremental process because of the stepwise approach in accumulating gains. A vision toward structural change is pursued at different levels at different phases so that members of a movement derive a sense of success at every stage of the work despite experiencing setbacks. Grassroots organizations start achieving a sense of long-term purpose knowing that they face massive opposition from those who benefit from their oppression (Bello et al., 2004). As a case in point, farmers and indigenous peoples' organizations know that neoliberal governments protect big landowning business and that exposing unjust arrangements requires strong voices and massive resources (McKeon, 2011). Therefore, coalitions on national and global levels have to be forged in order to reach those corridors power grassroots organizations cannot access. The UN Declarations on the Rights of Farmers and Indigenous Peoples would not have been adopted had not the global movement of farmers and indigenous peoples coalesced to have their political voices heard. The task at hand is still long and hard for social workers if they are to work in solidarity with farmers and indigenous peoples' organizations. It is necessary for social workers to have community organizing skills where methods in social action also mean conducting research and documentation on the issues and concerns relevant to the movement as well as the skills in mobilizing individuals and groups to act in informed and strategic ways to achieve a movement's strategic goals.

Discussion Questions

1. In the context of colonial history, what can the social work profession learn from peasant and indigenous people's movements?
2. What areas of advocacy work can you identify based on lessons learned from the Philippine peasant and indigenous people's movements?

References

Abelinde, J.-A. M., & de la Rosa, L. (2018, February 2018). *Is agrarian reform a dying issue?* Rappler. https://www.rappler.com/voices/imho/196826-agrarian-reform-dying-issue/

Aguilar, D. T., Abonado, A. I. M., Pavo, R. R., Beltrán Ulate, E. J., & Kahlmeyer-Mertens, R. S. (2016). Land ownership among indigenous people through the lens of John Locke's State of Nature. *ARETÉ: International Journal for Liberal Arts, Education, Social Sciences and Philosophical Studies, 4*(1), 67–84.

Alkon, A. H. (2013). Food sovereignty and the challenge of neoliberalism. *Food Sovereignty: A Critical Dialogue*. www.tni.org

Argumedo, A., Song, Y., Khoury, C. K., Hunter, D., & Dempewolf, H. (2020). Support indigenous food system biocultural diversity. *The Lancet Planetary Health, 4*(12), e554. https://doi.org/10.1016/S2542-5196(20)30243-6

Bello, W. (2009). *The food wars*. Verso.

Bello, W., Bové, J., Cassen, B., & Graeber, D. (2004). In T. Mertes (Ed.), *A movement of movements: Is another world really possible?* Verso.

Bello, W., Docena, H., de Guzman, M., & Malig, M. L. (2006). *The anti-development state: The political economy of permanent crisis in The Philippines*. Zed.

Blumer, H. G. (1969). Collective behavior. In A. M. Lee (Ed.), *Principles of sociology* (3rd ed., pp. 65–121). Barnes & Noble, Inc.

Borras, S., Jr. (2007). *Pro-poor land reform*. University of Ottawa Press. https://doi.org/10.1353/book.4451

Buendia, R. (1987). The case of the cordillera: An unresolved national question. *Philippine Journal of Public Administration, 31*(2), 157–187. https://www.researchgate.net/publication/321097118_The_Case_of_the_Cordillera

Cabreza, V. (2022, November 3). Cordillera activists fail to get writ of amparo vs red-taggers. *Philippine Daily Inquirer*. https://newsinfo.inquirer.net/1688573/cordillera-activists-fail-to-get-writ-of-amparo-vs-red-taggers

Cariño, J. K. (2016, August 31). *Genuine regional autonomy as self-determination in the Cordillera*. Cordillera Peoples Alliance. https://www.cpaphils.org/gra.html

Center for World Indigenous Studies. (1999). *Cordillera Peoples' Alliance*. https://hartford-hwp.com/archives/54a/081.html

Claeys, P., & Delgado Pugley, D. (2017). Peasant and indigenous transnational social movements engaging with climate justice. *Canadian Journal of Development Studies, 38*(3), 325–340. https://doi.org/10.1080/02255189.2016.1235018

Constatino, R., & Constantino, L. R. (1975). *The Philippines: A past revisited* (Vol. 1). Tala.

Cordillera Peoples Alliance. (2014, October 14). *IPRA and NCIP: 17 years of IP rights violations*. https://cpaphils.org/ipra-and-ncip-17-years-of-ip-violations.html

de Cadiz, G. B. (2014). A critical analysis of social movements in The Philippines. *"LIFE": Paving the way for a more resilient and sustainable Haiyan communities in Central Philippines*. https://doi.org/10.2139/SSRN.2483104

de Dios, E. S., & Hutchcroft, P. D. (2003). The Philippine economy. In *The Philippine economy: Development, policies, and challenges* (pp. 45–74). Oxford University Press. https://doi.org/10.1093/0195158989.003.0002

de Vera, S. (2022, August 22). *Abducted Cordillera activist found*. Rappler. https://www.rappler.com/nation/luzon/cordillera-activist-stephen-tauli-abduction-updates-kalinga-august-2022/.

Delina, L. L. (2020). Indigenous environmental defenders and the legacy of Macli-ing Dulag: Anti-dam dissent, assassinations, and protests in the making of Philippine energyscape. *Energy Research & Social Science, 65*, 101463. https://doi.org/10.1016/J.ERSS.2020.101463

Desmarais, A.-A. (2002). PEASANTS SPEAK – the Vía Campesina: Consolidating an international peasant and farm movement. *The Journal of Peasant Studies, 29*(2), 91–124. https://doi.org/10.1080/714003943

FAO. (2002). *The State of Food Insecurity in the World 2001*.

Franco, J. C. (2008). Peripheral justice? Rethinking justice sector reform in The Philippines. *World Development, 36*(10), 1858–1873. https://doi.org/10.1016/J.WORLDDEV.2007.10.011

La Via Campesina. (2017, July 1). *Kilusang Magbubukid ng Pilipinas (KMP)*. https://viacampesina.org/en/kilusang-magbubukid-ng-pilipinas-kmp/

Magdoff, F. (2012, January 1). Food as a commodity. *Monthly Review*. https://monthlyreview.org/2012/01/01/food-as-a-commodity/

Mann, A. (2014). *Global activism in food politics*. Palgrave Macmillan UK. https://doi.org/10.1057/9781137341402

Mauss, A. L. (1975). *Social problems as social movements*. Lippincott.

McKeon, N. (2011). Now's the time to make it happen: The UN's committee on food security. In E. Holt-Giménez (Ed.), *Food movements unite! Strategies to transform our food systems*. Food First.

McMichael, P. (2009). A food regime analysis of the 'world food crisis'. *Agriculture and Human Values, 26*(4), 281–295. https://doi.org/10.1007/s10460-009-9218-5

McMichael, P. (2014). Historicizing food sovereignty. *The Journal of Peasant Studies, 41*(6), 933–957. https://doi.org/10.1080/03066150.2013.876999

Nicholson, P., & Delforge, I. (2008). Via Campesina: Responding to global systemic crisis. *Development, 51*(4), 456–459. https://doi.org/10.1057/dev.2008.51

One Earth. (n.d.). *Empowering the peasant movement of the Philippines to secure land tenure rights and create a climate-resilient food system*. https://www.oneearth.org/projects/empowering-the-peasant-movement-of-the-philippines-to-secure-land-tenure-rights-and-create-a-climate-resilient-food-system/

Peasant Movement of the Philippines. (n.d.). *About – updates from the peasant movement of the Philippines*. https://peasantmovementph.com/about/

Ramos, C. G. (2021). The return of strongman rule in The Philippines: Neoliberal roots and developmental implications. *Geoforum, 124*, 310–319. https://doi.org/10.1016/J.GEOFORUM.2021.04.001

Scott, W. H. (1992). *Looking for the pre-Hispanic Filipino and other essays in Philippine history* (3rd ed.).

Scott, W. H. (1996). *Cracks in the parchment curtain and other essays in Philippine history*. New Day.

Serafica, R. (2017, January 21). *4 things to know about the Mendiola Massacre*. Rappler. https://www.rappler.com/moveph/159028-mendiola-massacre-anniversary/

Soriano, C. R. (2012). The arts of indigenous online dissent: Negotiating technology, indigeneity, and activism in the Cordillera. *Telematics and Informatics, 29*(1), 33–44. https://doi.org/10.1016/J.TELE.2011.04.004

Tilly, C. (1978). *From mobilization to revolution*. Addison-Wesley.

United Nations Declaration on the Rights of Peasants and Other People Working in Rural Areas. (2018). http://digitallibrary.un.org/record/1650694

United Nations Permanent Forum on Indigenous Peoples' Issues. (2019).

Jason M. Leung is Department Head of the environmental studies program at the Benguet State University, Philippines. His areas of teaching and research are in human ecology, food regimes and sovereignty, and community rural development. He has published in Germany where he completed his masters' studies in environmental science. He spent years of teaching in Korea and did research work on food sovereignty in Germany. He is currently undertaking a nationwide research with the Philippine Department of Science and Technology on the impact of extractive mining industries on indigenous communities.

Chapter 14
Lessons from Social Movements: Farmers and Food Sovereignty in India

Kiran Thampi

Introduction

Food is a basic human right. Food sovereignty provides control over the production, distribution, and consumption of food. It is the right of people to healthy and to have access to culturally appropriate food produced through ecologically sound and sustainable methods (Desmarais, 2007). Considering food as more than just a commodity, we place people's need for food at the center of policies which also consider value for food providers, localizing food systems and control at the local level by promoting knowledge and skills in harmony with nature (Nyeleni Steering Committee, 2007). It is important to note that "ecological integrity" is a striving term, which considers maintaining biodiversity while achieving food sovereignty.

Biodiversity and ecological integrity are at risk due to human interventions. Biodiversity is the "variety of living animal and plant life from all sources and includes diversity within and between species and ecosystems" (Biodiversity Conservation Act, 2016). Ecological integrity entails maintaining the diversity and quality of ecosystems and enhancing their capacity to adapt to change and provide for the needs of future generations. We need an eco-centric view which is nature-centered in adopting an integrated approach in food systems that encompasses ecological justice and that upholds the principle of "interrelation" between all the elements in the environment. A shift from an anthropocentric worldview will ensure the sustenance in food system and will respect the rights and functions of all the elements in the food chain needed. In short, food sovereignty is a concept that integrates the promotion of ecological integrity so that a just society is ensured.

K. Thampi (✉)
Department of Social Work, Rajagiri College of Social Sciences (Autonomous), Kochi, Kerala, India
e-mail: kiran@rajagiri.edu

M. Madew et al. (eds.), *Decolonized Approaches to Human Rights and Social Work*,
https://doi.org/10.1007/978-3-031-33030-8_14

Economic liberalization in the 1990s in India expanded the industrialist capital system in food throughout the country which went through the phases of "White Revolution" and "Green Revolution" (which provided growth and sustainability of milk products and green products, respectively). The neocolonial surge in agriculture is reflected in taking the control in the whole process ranging from food production to distribution. Corporate engagement has resulted in forcing farmers to adopt crop-intensive strategies in farming including pesticides, fertilizers, and genetically modified seeds, which in a direct way is adversely affecting the ecological balance. The market chain control models adopted by the multinational companies also restrict farmers from using traditional and local distribution channels. This has deepened the inequalities existing in rural society based on the economic, cultural, and social realms.

This chapter deals with the colonial and postcolonial struggles in India toward food sovereignty. It also unravels governmental and voluntary efforts in India to promote food security and food sovereignty. This chapter also reflects on lessons learned in community mobilization from the farmers' movements and the professional implications of social work.

India: A Situational Analysis

India has experienced a large number of famines – especially during British colonial India (Siegel, 2018; Simonow, 2022). The Great Bengal Famine of 1770, Chalisa Famine of 1783–1784, Doji Bara Famine of 1791–1792, Agra Famine of 1837–1838, Upper Doab Famine of 1860–1861, Great Famine of 1876–1878, Indian Famine of 1896–1897, and the Indian Famine of 1899–1900 generated high mortality rates that were aggravated by British policies (Earle, 2020). However, the Bengal Famine of 1943 was one of the largest famines in South Asia in terms of mortality rates (Simonow, 2022). This was partly due to the negligence of authorities to take note of the famine codes which was a reason for accelerating the unrest which propelled the decolonization of British India (Human Rights Watch, 1992). Learning from these experiences, food security has since been a key goal in the planning processes in postindependence India. Wood (2016) notes that despite the food shortages and famines in the postcolonial era, there were no such famines like those of the colonial period. Agriculture was 15.4% of the national economy of India in 2017 (WFB, 2022). Around 41.49% of total labor was associated with agriculture in 2020 (World Bank, 2021). Farmer suicides account for 11.2% of all suicides in India (NCRB, 2014). India has made progress in the agriculture production especially after the Green Revolution due to the adoption of new techniques in farming, diversification of seed variety, improvement of irrigation facilities, and the extension of electricity (Prajapathi & Dutta, 2014). It has been empirically demonstrated that agricultural growth is significantly beneficial for reducing poverty and increasing per capita income (Virmani, 2008). There is large gap between the income of agricultural workers and nonagricultural workers, and farmers earn one-third of income of nonfarm workers (Chand, 2019). The reasons could be attributed to climate change, non-sustainable farming, and a shift in the distribution channels.

Pre-independence and postindependence famines and disasters have instilled a fear of loss among the farmers, and it is evident in the current era where climate predictability is at risk. A study conducted in 2014 found that there are three specific characteristics associated with high-risk farmers – "those that grow cash crops such as coffee and cotton, those with 'marginal' farms of less than 1 hectare, and those with debts of 300 rupees or more" – and the same is applied to those Indian states with highest famer suicides (Kennedy & King, 2014). Economic factor is stressed as the major challenge for the farmers and they require expert guidance to make decisions on strategies for farming and management along with psychosocial support to confront with multiple challenges.

Government Intervention Efforts

The National Food Security Act of 2013 (NFSA) caused a paradigm shift from welfare approach to a rights-based approach. Food security ensures that all people get physical, social, and economic access to secure, sufficient, and nutritious food for a healthy life. Food sovereignty stresses the idea of democratic food system where existing food systems are protected and distributed. Both these concepts advocate for sustainable productivity (Gordillo & Jeronimo, 2013).

The act established the following key initiatives. The Food Corporation of India (FCI) is entrusted with effective price support operations for Indian farmers. Maintaining the buffer stocks for distribution is also one of the key functions of FCI, and thus it plays a major role in supporting farmers (FCI, 2022). The connected schemes for ensuring the food security are as follows:

(a) Antyodaya Anna Yojana (scheme for poorest of the poor with the purpose of providing food security) and also considering priority households (PHH) for entitlements. The scheme ensures supply of food and essential commodities for a subsidized rate for the poor people on a monthly basis (DFPD, 2022a).
(b) Scheme of ICDS (Integrated Child Development Services) for supplementary nutritional care to bridge the gap between recommended dietary allowance (RDA) and the average daily intake (ADI) for children under 6 years as well as pregnant women and lactating mothers. It represents one of the world's largest and unique programs for early childhood care and development (MOWCD, 2022).The ICDS scheme is operated through Anganwadi centers (community based centers), and the team is comprised of Anganwadi workers, Anganwadi helpers, supervisors, child development project officers (CDPOs), and district program officers (DPOs).The Anganwadi worker is the female representative selected from the community itself who is the community based frontline honorary worker in ICDS.

(c) Public Distribution System (PDS) was established under the Ministry of Consumer Affairs, Food, and Public Distribution. The central and state governments are responsible for the effectiveness of PDS and ensure minimum support prices (MSP) for farmers as center procures food grains from them and sells it to states at central issue prices. The beneficiaries receive the food grains through fair price shops at central issue prices, and this is further subsidized by several states which make it affordable to beneficiaries (NFSP, 2023).
(d) *Midday Meal Program* under the Ministry of Education is a centrally sponsored scheme that was launched in 1995. It is the world's largest school meal program with a goal of universalization of primary education. In 2021, it was renamed the "Pradhan Mantri Poshan Shakti Nirman" scheme (PM Poshan scheme). It is designed to address the issue of malnutrition among school children and to prevent the dropouts due to hunger. This is a key initiative to address the challenges in food security (P M Poshan, 2022).

According to the Situation Assessment Survey (SAS) of Agricultural Households and Land and Livestock Holdings of Households in Rural India, the households getting primary income from agriculture have gone from 54% in 2013 to 58% in 2019 which reflects the importance of agriculture in rural society (NSO, 2019). The survey also has highlighted the nominal increase of income from agriculture as 59% between 2013 and 2019. The government has been actively promoting farmer producer organizations (FPOs) for better organization and collective support. In the year 2013–2014, the budget allocation for the Department of Agriculture was only ₹21,933.50 crores. This has been increased to ₹1,23,017.57 crores in 2021–2022.

Voluntary Intervention Efforts

Apart from government efforts to ensure food security and food sovereignty, many voluntary organizations as well as activists are working for environment protection and conservation and for empowering communities through negotiation with government systems, providing platforms to sell the products, provision of manure and irrigation options, and sharing of technological inputs and other resources. Ms. Vandana Shiva with her ecofeminist philosophy and environment activism has contributed to sustainable fair trade and organic farming practices. Navdanya is an Earth-centric, woman-centric, and farmer-led movement for the protection of biological and cultural diversity initiated for the fight for food sovereignty. The Navdanya Movement has promoted agricultural biodiversity through organizing communities and organizations (0.2 million farmers), conserving rice and wheat varieties, initiating community seed banks, and organizing local food festivals for farmers (Navdanya, 2022).

The voluntary sector takes a lead role in seed preservation management techniques, organic farming initiatives, organizing farmer/producer forums, etc., which contributes to the empowerment of the rural community.

Colonial and Postcolonial Struggles for Food Security

In India, there have been struggles by farmers through different organized movements and challenges for ensuring social justice and human rights. The pre-independence era marked several struggles against oppression, exploitations, new land rules, and imposition of taxes by the colonial system. The Indigo Revolt flared up in Bengal (1859–1960), which was initiated by indigo growers against the planters. It instilled national sentiment against the British rule in India. The Kol rebellion (1832) was another movement in Chotta Nagpur by the Kol tribesmen against the exploitation of East India Company agents. Other struggles include the Mappila rebellion in Kerala (1841–1920), the Santhal rebellion in Jharkhand (1855), the Deccan Uprising in Mumbai (1875), the Munda Ulgulan in Ranchi (1899–1900), the Thebhaga Movement in Bengal (1946–1947), and the Telengana Movement (1946–1952). These struggles led by the peasants eventually contributed to an uprising spirit of nationalism. The postindependence era was marked by farmers who struggled against the oppression of human rights. The movements called the New Farmers' Movements were against the globalization, imperialism, and capitalism. The movements were not completely effective in addressing some of the radical issues faced by the farmer's community. Internal conflicts and the sporadic nature of the movements contributed to this situation. The issues of marginal classes and small farmers were sidelined in most of the movements as the prominent beneficiaries who led the struggles were representing the rich class in the farming community. But these movements gave a new face to the struggle as it was considered to be the struggle for basic rights of farmers.

Current farmers' movements are linked to the perceived threat associated with the implementation of new policies in India. The Farmers' Produce Trade and Commerce (Promotion and Facilitation) Act 2020 will create instability in agricultural markets affecting small and marginal farmers the most and also may affect the Public Distribution System (PDS). Two other bills, the Essential Commodities (Amendment) Act 2020 and the Farmers (Empowerment and Protection) Agreement on Price Assurance and Farm Services Act 2020 or the Contract Farming Act 2020, will contribute to food price instability and also give unrestricted entry to corporations.

There is much to learn from the farmers' struggles against neoliberal policies as perceived by them as anti-farmer and inhumane. Some of the agricultural reforms took place as a result of the continuous struggles such as land settlement policy for farmers. The struggle saw the emergence of leaders in the farmers' movement and also established their leadership to the larger cause to achieve freedom from colonial rule. Farmers' movements have had a lasting effect during pre-independence and postindependence eras that market-based policies and capitalism need to position the famer as the key stakeholder. Farmers' movements have primarily addressed local issues, but the new farmers' movements could mobilize farmers from many other regions also in the common struggle against the harmful policies. Farmers' struggles utilized different strategies including demonstrations, civil disobedience, legal and political pressure, negotiations, and noncooperation movements. Recent struggles have demanded minimum support prices for commodities and procurement at one and a half times the comprehensive cost of production as recommended by the National Commission of Farmers. Another was to revoke the move to increase electricity tariff which in many means burdens the cost of production.

Community Organization and People's Mobilization Lessons

A key feature across the recent struggles was community representation, including women, children, and the elderly. It motivated the beneficiaries to oppose certain policies and legal measures irrespective of gender, religion, caste, and political denominations. The intersectionality framework analyzes the vulnerability of farming community and the privileges of caste and economic power in food system. The farmer, being the representative of certain caste in the society, is not privileged to own land, and this forms the basic challenge to food production. Stratification in Indian communities between the landowners and landless laborer has historically resulted in revolts and struggles. After the Green Revolution in India, the evolution of rich capitalist farmers has contributed to categorization of farmers on socioeconomic dimensions. Though it was not prominent in later movements as such, the landlessness has posed severe challenges for the farmers economically in making them powerless in decision-making regarding the cultivation pattern, quantity and quality of the products, and marketing cycle. The role of the voluntary sector was much evident in mobilizing rural communities and was shaped by cardinal principles such as collective decision-making, structured mobilization strategies across the borders from many states (especially from the states of Punjab, Haryana, Rajasthan, Uttar Pradesh, and Madhya Pradesh), networking among organizations and peoples cooperatives, consensus building among the various stakeholders through Kisan Mahapanchayats, and empowering local leadership. Another notable feature of the struggle was the involvement of youth in mobilizing the community and giving proper public messages using the potential of information technology. The community kitchens organized and controlled by the protesters offered a reflection of determination to democratize the food chain system.

Sustainable farming efforts need to be supported through some of the initiatives such as opening the space for biotechnology, natural resource management including water and solar energy, planned crop yield across the regions to ensure sustainability, and special agriculture zones with special support. In the current era of information technology, farmers should be empowered to continue the use of high-tech farming practices which will support them in managing the farming cycle to produce a maximum yield. The Electronic National Agriculture Market (eNAM) is an initiative taken by the government of India which is a pan-India electronic program that aims to create a unified national market for agricultural commodities (SFAC, 2022). The accessibility to digital facility is a question, but still the technology assisted farming methods need to be accepted considering the possible inclusion of farmers. There needs to have accessible dashboards (dashboards where the organizations and local self-government offices will be able to track and communicate progress toward Sustainable Development Goals). The Sustainable Development Goal 2 (SDG 2) aims at zero hunger, and it could be percolated to local farming groups which are monitored by local self-governments. Technology assisted storage spaces are much needed in the context of climate change to ensure food security and minimum production cost for farmers. The food grains and perishables wasted due to improper storage could be sufficient to feed a portion of the poor population in the world.

Social Work and Food Sovereignty

Social work as a profession is not alien from social issues including ensuring food sovereignty. The absolute number of people in hunger and malnutrition is increasing, and even before COVID-19, the trend is the same (FAO, 2020). "Increasing the democratic control over the food systems" is one of the key principles in food sovereignty (Claeys, 2013) and is a way to address these macro issues. This could be done by integrating stakeholder participation in decision-making and further implementation, considering locality specific formation of cooperatives. Giving impetus to farmers' movements rooted on cooperative governing systems can be supported by social work institutions and voluntary associations. There are many models of cooperative societies who lead the local farmers and collectively bargain for their entitlements including minimum price support and other relevant government policy decisions.

Community empowerment through informing the farmers and citizens with appropriate knowledge has led to achievement of rights (Chappell, 2018). This could be supported by the social work profession by adopting proper Information, Education, and Communication (IEC) strategies. These strategies could focus on the intergenerational transfer of indigenous knowledge in farming practices and its documentation. The popular strategies to celebrate local food fests, promoting responsible tourism through locally specific farming techniques, organizing campaigns for protecting the rights of farmers, and action research on possibilities and prospects of food chain could help establish food sovereignty. Advocacy support is also required for the producers and cooperatives as they are competing with corporations and bigger organizations that have the resources to invest. Involving the young generation in the process of production to distribution is another key aspect. They need to be supported with aggrotech start-ups through educational institutions as well as through communities by empowering them to explore the potential of information technology. Farmer-oriented research is another area which could involve need assessment, situational analysis, policy analysis, high yield farming methodologies, and market research.

Another key aspect to be ensured is the gender equity in food chain system. In a country like India, the traditional norm approves male members as household heads who have more power in decision-making. Though women are in workforce, including the agricultural sector, it needs to be ensured that they are treated appropriately in terms of social, economic, and political entitlements. Women-led agri supply chain models (UNDP, 2022) experimented in Uttar Pradesh state (with the support of the Uttar Pradesh State Rural Livelihoods Mission in partnership with the United Nations Development Program) could be tried which has impacted in enhancing income as well as helped to break stereotypes in the society.

Conclusion

The farmers' struggles and collective movements were expressly against the forces that disrupt fair trade practices and ecological justice. It is imperative that the common people and the bureaucrats are made aware of the eco-centric approach to managing the food chain and food system. Colonial and postcolonial policies have triggered the farming community to be united and to advocate for their rights. Even though there are many initiatives in the public, private, and voluntary sector to support the farmers, there needs to be more sustainable measures that address the concerns the farmers are having in the context of neoliberal policies. Cooperative initiatives and farmer producer organizations are to be strengthened, and they could be empowered to use new age farming tools and techniques utilizing the possibilities of digital interventions. The social work profession, being based on the pillars of social justice and human rights, has recognized the relevance of farm producers' rights and freedoms and has supported their needs and demands in organized way. The potential of social workers and farmers to associate and cooperate could be harnessed in such a way that they are included through participatory decision-making in the implementation of welfare measures. The "market-ecology-land" issues need relevant attention and urgent action from all the stakeholders in food system so that balance is brought to sustainable development policy.

Discussion Questions

1. Can you describe the relationship between food sovereignty, human rights, and environmental justice?
2. How do community organization and people's mobilization can contribute to food sovereignty?
3. What role do social workers play in ensuring food sovereignty?

References

Biodiversity Conservation Act. (2016). *Western Australia Act*. https://www.legislation.wa.gov.au/legislation/prod/filestore.nsf/FileURL/mrdoc_41658.pdf/$FILE/Biodiversity%20Conservation%20Act%202016%20-%20%5B00-d0-01%5D.pdf?OpenElement

Claeys, P. (2013). From food sovereignty to peasants' rights: an overview of La Via Campesina's rights-based claims over the last 20 years. In *Food sovereignty: A critical dialogue* (pp. 1–11). Yale University Press.

Chappell, M. J. (2018). *Beginning to end hunger: Food and the environment in Belo Horizonte, Brazil, and beyond*. University of California Press.

Chand, R. (2019). Innovative policy interventions for transformation of agriculture sector. *Agricultural Economics Research Review, 32*(1), 1–10.

Desmarais, A. (2007). *La Vía Campesina: Globalization and the power of peasants*. Fernwood Publishing and Pluto Press.

Department of Food & Public Distribution. (2022a). *Anthyodaya Anna Yojana*. Ministry of Consumer Affairs, Government of India. https://dfpd.gov.in/pds-aay.htm

Department of Food & Public Distribution. (2022b). *Public distribution system*. Ministry of Consumer Affairs, Government of India. https://nfsa.gov.in/portal/PDS_page

Earle, R. (2020). *Feeding the people: The politics of the potato* (p. 114). Cambridge University Press.

Food Corporation of India. (2022). *Overview of Food Corporation of India*. https://fci.gov.in/

FAO. (2020). *Impacts of COVID-19 on food security and nutrition: Developing effective policy responses to address the hunger and malnutrition pandemic*. Food and Agriculture Organization of the United Nations.

Gordillo, G. & Jeronimo, O. M. (2013). *Food security and sovereignty*. Food and Agriculture Organization of the United Nations. https://www.fao.org/3/ax736e/ax736e.pdf

Watch, H. R. (1992). *Individual human rights: The relationship of political and civil rights to survival, subsistence and poverty* (Vol. 3). Human Rights Watch.

Kennedy, J., & King, L. (2014). The political economy of farmers' suicides in India: indebted cash-crop farmers with marginal landholdings explain state-level variation in suicide rates. *Globalization and Health, 10*(1), 16. https://doi.org/10.1186/1744-8603-10-16

Ministry of Women and Child Development. (2022). *Integrated Child Development Scheme*. http://icds-wcd.nic.in/icds.aspx

National Statistics Office (NSO) of Ministry of Statistics and Programme Implementation (MoSPYI). (2019). Situation assessment of agricultural households and land and livestock Holdings of Households in rural India, Report No. 587.

Navdanya Organisation. (2022). *Colonialism and Globalisation*. https://www.navdanya.org/eco-feminism/women-feed-the-world?id=616

National Crime Reports Bureau. (2014). *Distribution of suicides by profession, Accidental Deaths and Suicides in India Report, Government of India*. https://ncrb.gov.in/sites/default/files/adsi-2014%20full%20report.pdf

National Food Security Portal. (2023). Public Distribution System. Department of Food and Public Distribution, Government of India. https://nfsa.gov.in/portal/PDS_page

Nyeleni Steering Committee. (2007). *Six pillars of food sovereignty*. Report of Forum for food sovereignty, Mali. https://nyeleni.org/DOWNLOADS/Nyelni_EN.pdf

Prajapathi, H. R., & Dutta, I. (2014). Future of Indian agriculture: Prospects and challenges, agricultural situation in India, Ministry of Agriculture, Government of India, New Delhi, *21*(6), 5–18.

Poshan, P. M. (2022). *Mid-day meal in schools*. Ministry of Education, Government of India. https://pmposhan.education.gov.in/

Simonow, J. (2022). Famine relief in colonial South Asia, 1858–1947: Regional and global perspectives. In H. Fischer-Tiné & M. Framke (Eds.), *Routledge handbook of the history of colonialism in South Asia* (pp. 497–509). Routledge.

Siegel, B. R. (2018). *Hungary nation: Food, famine, and the making of modern India* (p. 6). Cambridge University Press.
Small Farmers Agri Business Consortium. (2022). *e NAM Platform*, Department of Agriculture & Family Welfare, Ministry of Agriculture & Family Welfare, Government of India. https://enam.gov.in/web/
The World Bank. (2021). *International Labour Organization, ILOSTAT database*. Accessed from https://data.worldbank.org/indicator/SL.AGR.EMPL.ZS?locations=IN
UNDP. (2022). *Women lead the way: from farm to market*. https://www.undp.org/india/stories/women-lead-way-farm-market
Virmani. (2008, January 12). Growth and poverty: Policy implications for lagging states. *Economic and Political Weekly, 43*(2), 54–62.
World Factbook. (2022). *U.S Government*. https://www.cia.gov/the-world-factbook/countries/india/
Wood, A. T. (2016). Asian democracy in world history. In *Themes in world history* (p. 39). Routledge.

Kiran Thampi is Assistant Professor in the Department of Social Work, Rajagiri College of Social Sciences. He has 17 years of experience in teaching and practice. His research interests include voluntary sector organizations, social audit, participatory project planning and management, participatory rural appraisal techniques, and the mental health of professionals and youth. He was appointed as an Adjunct Faculty in the School of Health and Human Services, Nazareth College, USA, for the summer semester in 2015. He is currently leading an IASSW project with Israel and Australia.

Chapter 15
Decolonizing Social Work Education

Mark Lusk and Marcin Boryczko

Introduction

Social work education has never exactly been at the ramparts of social change or far-reaching social movements in pursuit of social justice. At best, social work educators write and talk about the need for social justice, equity, and inclusion, and some organize, advocate, and protest when their professional obligations and work permit. Unfortunately, one of the last places to learn about progressive changes in the status quo is at a convention of social workers. Similarly, decolonization at many universities and schools of social work is an afterthought and too often is little more than making minor adjustments in curricula or paying verbal homage to the need for recalibrating the narrative of social work on its role in maintaining the status quo.

The failure of social work education to confront its conservative roots is aided and abetted by student demand for a curriculum that prepares them for careers in clinical social work and psychotherapy – a labor of microcosmic social change that, while it addresses important work in helping individuals cope with trauma and dysfunction, does little or nothing to address the causes of trauma, dysfunction, and the social and economic structures of violence that lead to the psychological injury of people in the first place. One does not see many clinicians at the ramparts or barricades defending human rights, advocating for indigenous rights, or striking to end global ecocide. Ideally, social work should be in the business of putting itself out of business by ferreting out and resolving the causes of trauma, structural violence,

M. Lusk (✉)
School of Social Work, New Mexico State University, Las Cruces, NM, USA
e-mail: marklusk@nmsu.edu

M. Boryczko
Department of Social Work, Faculty of Social Sciences, University of Gdańsk, Gdańsk, Poland
e-mail: marcin.boryczko@ug.edu.pl

M. Madew et al. (eds.), *Decolonized Approaches to Human Rights and Social Work*,
https://doi.org/10.1007/978-3-031-33030-8_15

and poverty, yet few go there. Lawrence Shulman has suggested that if macro-practice is not part of social workers' practice, then they are not engaged in social work (Shulman, 2020).

Part of the problem lies in the conservative roots of Western social work, and another part is rooted in the regressive nature of higher education in neoliberal economies. The stunning collapse of social work's emancipatory potential in the face of cognitive-instrumental rationality's domination is a sign that it has been reduced to market principles and has merely evolved into a productive force in society (Gottschalk & Witkin, 1991). de Sousa Santos (2014a) characterizes this process as the gradual colonization of other rationalities; nonetheless, he believes that Western modernity is still in the process of development and separates the two types of knowledge that he labels the "pillars of modernity," which are also found in social work. In contrast to market and state regulation, he contends that community regulation is one that has been neglected. Modern science is characterized by the absence of the community principle, and social work, regrettably, is still to a large extent dominated by an individualistic perspective. Therefore, we need new explorations of waking emancipatory energies neglected by Eurocentric models of knowledge.

Contemporary universities, on balance, can serve a key role in promoting the public good through the education of people who would otherwise not have an opportunity to participate fully in the culture and economies of their nations and communities and also in the production of community engaged research that improves the well-being of citizens by generating knowledge based on evidence that results in positive outcomes in the general population. Universities, on the other hand, must be decolonized on the basis of knowledge-as-emancipation rooted in solidarity, rather than knowledge-as-regulation. de Sousa Santos (2014a, b) proposes constructing universities-as-public-good on the foundation of counter-hegemonic globalization. However, seeing this type of project in action and identifying details are difficult. These will be addressed in the sections that follow in this chapter.

While early universities were strictly exclusive institutions for male elites that replicated the social order and trained the ruling classes, contemporary universities, particularly publicly funded colleges, have served a broader function. Yet, as higher education has become increasingly seen as a private commodity rather than a public good, net inflation adjusted state funding has declined, and students are too often left to fend for themselves to fund their schooling with debt and labor (Pew, 2019). In the United States, in particular, higher education is primarily seen as job training rather than an education in the arts, sciences and humanities for citizenship and service. In many countries, access to universities is minimally subsidized by the state, admission is highly controlled, student rights and self-governance are negligible, and students are increasingly taught by untenured contract workers rather than professors. Increasingly, the ranks of social work educators are filled with part-time adjuncts who hustle for classes to teach like gig workers – a cheaper and more compliant workforce that produces student credit hours at lower cost – workers so disempowered and poorly paid that they would hardly dare to rock the boat.

Outside of Western Europe, universities are commonly fee-based with some public support, like a market commodity one purchases in the economy, for career development. College majors that are perceived as less utilitarian, such as the humanities and arts, are cut, while resources are redirected toward "practical" fields, such as engineering and business. As Natividad and Lauderdale note, university administrations are based on authoritarian corporate models, good research is defined by how much money it brings to the school, and neoliberal absolutism has shifted universities to corporate structures based on profitability (Natividad & Lauderdale, 2010).

Indeed, tuition at public universities is regressive. It essentially makes it more expensive for lower income students to attend college when tuition is not subsidized, income-based, or free. Viewing colleges as an asset to be purchased in a free-market economy is to see the *value* of the degree in relation to *price* rather than *worth*. Degrees are likened to a fungible asset when they are commoditized, and while degrees cannot be transferred or exchanged once they are earned, universities in neoliberal economies are very much in the business of selling them, usually for a very heavy set of fees. The default rate in college loans in the United States is but one example of market failure when one takes a public good, the education of a productive citizen, and monetizes it. Coupled with the endless pursuit of external contracts and grants on the slippery slope to national and international recognition, too many colleges have lost the spirit of acting in the public good as legislatures and government ministries strangle them by cutting state support.

Social work education often is carried out in precisely this type of regressive environment, where prospective social workers, often from humble economic origins, are conscripted into debt servitude to eke out a degree that will place them in the lower rungs of the professional classes. And the promise at the end of the social work education journey is not that they will transform the system in which they are trapped but will offer individualized services and programs to fellow casualties, essentially reproducing the status quo and providing a labor force to pacify the marginalized and excluded.

Social work educators infrequently examine their own role in perpetuating the prevailing state of affairs or in reproducing the social order. Indeed, social work, as commonly practiced, is steadfastly entrenched in the status quo, promoting minimal, even punitive interventions allegedly to "benefit" marginalized groups and individuals.

There are other paths to the profession. Like the founders, those associated with Charity Organization Societies or started settlement houses, many from places of unearned privilege, have found their way to the profession to practice a form of *noblesse oblige* by helping the "disadvantaged" break the presumed bad habits that keep them in destitution. Such social bureaucrats try to disrupt the self-perpetuating culture of poverty, thereby reinforcing the idea that the poor have no one to blame but themselves. Many "fixers" join the profession to solve problems, correct behaviors, and work out past injuries through individual treatment and casework. Focusing on the technical aspects of their jobs, such social workers fail to ask inconvenient questions about inequality, poverty, and oppression (Ioakimidis, 2016). Having secured professional status, such as it is, through licensure and accreditation, social work in its bureaucratic form, fails altogether to grasp the historical, economic, social, and colonial origins of the problems its clientele confronts.

Moreover, social work is regulated in several ways that stifle its ability to flexibly and assertively address social justice issues. These include accreditation agencies that to a large degree mandate curriculum and monitor budgets, administration, and faculty credentials. In addition, professional associations in social work at the national, state, and local levels regulate the practice of social work, investigate and adjudicate professional conduct, and seek to secure exclusivity over domains of practice and licensure, particularly clinical practice. These private organizations can function as self-perpetuating trade associations that operate with minimal or no public or governmental oversight or scrutiny.

Notwithstanding these obstacles, "doing good" is important work. Doing so as a full-time professional is a calling. Working with people who are hurt takes no small amount of patience, skill, and courage. But to be clear, ministering in individual and small group settings to those who have been damaged or traumatized *in the absence of working toward fundamental social and economic change* is to be complicit in the ongoing and seemingly endless cycle of a system of oppression that will, like a perpetual motion machine, continue to harm, hurt, and traumatize as long as it is not disrupted from its course.

As was eloquently elaborated by Specht and Courtney, social work, born in the progressive era in solidarity with the poor, immigrants, and endangered children, was waylaid by the desire for professional recognition and became instead preoccupied with the pathologies of the poor, and social workers acted as "priests in the church of individual repair" by offering a cheaper version of psychotherapy (Specht & Courtney, 1994; Reid & Lowe, 1999; Stoesz et al., 2010). This is encapsulated in the technology of focusing on client problems through the lens of their failures to succeed in a system that is rigged against them. The forces and factors in society that generate social problems remain concealed, and as Steyaert (2019) observes, "…social work became a partner in crime in the culture of silence around social justice."

Since its founding, social work has continually been challenged by ideological conservatism. Traditional conservatism and its more contemporary variants, neoconservatism and neoliberalism, are based on the idea that government's function is to be small with respect to regulation of the elites and powerful with respect to the regulation of the poor and different – capitalism for the poor and socialism for the rich. Investments in law enforcement and other forms of social control are seen as necessary and prudent, while any regulation of the market is seen as government excess. In such a view, social work that seeks to disrupt the status quo and empower workers and families is heresy. Far better that social agencies and bureaucrats manage delinquent kids, pacify families with the dole, and regulate and pacify families affected by violence, abuse, or substance use. And the origins of such social problems must be ever left unexamined. Ideally, conservative media and politicians will enlist, or shall we say indoctrinate, the poor into blaming liberals for their problems. We see this anomaly in contemporary versions of authoritarian nationalism and

Trumpism throughout the Global North and South (e.g., Hungary, Poland, Brazil, the United States).

Poor people's social movements and protests that demand changes in the social order are driven by the desperation and defiance as members of disempowered and oppressed groups (Piven & Cloward, 1979). Social work cannot stand idly by and fail to engage when conditions call for sweeping and fundamental change. While some may wish to remain neutral on issues of social justice, poverty, and human rights, as noted journalist Christiane Amanpour has observed: "There are some situations one simply cannot be neutral about, because when you are neutral you are an accomplice" (Schmitt, 1996).

Progressive and Radical Social Work

From time to time, progressive social workers have chafed at the passivity and compliance of mainstream social work (Galper, 1980; de Maria, 1992). Fatigued with the idea that social workers are destined to be handmaidens to physicians (Katz, 1984) or "therapists" who work for paying customers or, worse, agency social workers who dole out substandard minimal benefits to the poor while forcing them to enroll in workfare programs, some social workers have taken a different path.

One excellent example derives from the progressive mobilization of the *Movimiento Estudiantil* (student movement) in Latin America during the late 1960s, particularly in Argentina, that inspired student activism throughout Latin American in the context of authoritarian national governments and the repressive role of higher education throughout the region. Spawned between the Argentinian coups of 1966 and 1976, students rebelled and engaged in strikes, marches, boycotts, sit-ins, and the occupation of campus buildings to bring attention to student rights and the lack of representation in university governance. This broad-based student movement was a catalyst for social action throughout Latin American universities and earned many students' fuller representation in governance through the *tercio estudiantil* (one-third student vote) that included students in the selection of rectors, administrators, and the curriculum. Corollary movements emerged in Paris, Berkeley, New York, and Mexico City as students became more involved in global protests against wars, particularly in Southeast Asia, and the international civil rights movement.

The *Movimiento Estudiantil* kindled a sea change in Latin American social work and social work education toward populism, poor people's movements, and *concientización* as an organizing principle in social work practice, a movement that was partly inspired by liberation theology (Dos Santos et al., 2021; Lusk & Corbett, 2021). Social workers in Latin America became involved in community organization at the grassroots in *barrios* and *favelas* – poor communities that lack basic services. They worked with unions, helping to organized workers, and also built *comunidades de base* (base communities) dedicated to self-sufficiency, local autonomy, and microfinance. Social work educators throughout the region taught social activism skills, community organizing, outreach, and action research. This was a significant shift for social work in the Global South, which had traditionally been organized along lines that emulated theory and methods from the developed nations of the North (Midgley, 1981).

Throughout Europe and North America, social workers were asking the same questions as their counterparts in Latin America. The student movements in the South paralleled a similar surge of activism in the North. The civil rights movement that had begun in earnest in the 1950s was joined in the 1960s by a global anti-war movement, the rise of feminism, gay rights activism, Black Power, indigenous peoples' movements, environmentalism, and a global rise of concern over the rights of people with disabilities. Social workers in Britain, for example, inspired by Saul Alinsky, Paulo Freire, Ivan Illich, and Franz Fanon, among others, pressed for change in the paradigm of mainstream social work. They challenged the narrow concentration of the profession on work with the individual and introduced a broader set of issues which put politics at the center of the agenda (Langan & Lee, 1989). Yet, austerity policies in the United Kingdom and the United States established by Thatcher and Reagan and continued by Blair and Clinton convinced most middle-class social workers to address the immediate needs of individuals and families who faced the effects of "welfare reform" and agency downsizing rather than the structural factors exacerbating poverty. The consequences of austerity and welfare reform reduced benefits programs and exacerbated homelessness and food insecurity. The austerity programs, which continue to this day in the United Kingdom and United States, confront clients with the challenges of navigating a repressive system of dwindling benefits and declining relative earnings, which is coupled with political and media stereotyping of the poor as lazy misfits. In the face of neoconservatism, social workers became scapegoats for failures of the child welfare system, and the profession has continued to be driven back into enforcing the coercive regulation of poor families.

During the 1960s and 1970s, grassroots social workers had begun to push back against the social work establishment. Practitioners began to publish manifestos, newsletters, and magazines, such as *Case Con*, in which they called for the profession to address structural causes and critiqued the seeming compliance of social work by being apolitical in intensely political times. Two books emerged which formulated an alternative approach: *Radical Social Work* and *Radical Social Work and Practice*, both by Bailey and Brake. In 1990, the *Journal of Progressive Human Services* was founded in the United States to cover "...political, social, personal, and professional problems in human services from a progressive perspective" (Journal of Progressive Human Services, 2022). A newer journal emerged in 2013, *Critical & Radical Social Work*, which continues to be published today in the United Kingdom by Bristol University Press (Steyaert, 2019).

The move toward a structural view was also motivated by a recognition that social work needed to move away from focusing on client pathology – using diagnostic criteria to label clients for their deficiencies, defects, and mental disorders. Radical social workers, by focusing on causes of client problems, set the stage for seeing clients based on their strengths and their capacities to survive and sometimes thrive, despite oppression and deprivation – a *strength's* perspective that empowers clients not just to survive but to *resist* (Guo & Tsui, 2010).

It is hard to overstate the importance of a strength's perspective in the history of social work. For a change, social workers gave a chance to people to stop ruminating over their supposed limitations in order to start realizing what they really can do. Clients possess remarkable capabilities of navigating weak labor markets, marginal social safety nets, oppressive social service agencies, and the managerialism that has transformed social work into a field that focuses on meeting targets, rationing resources, managing risks, and pressuring clients to conform to work requirements and other bureaucratic impediments, to emancipate themselves from the perils of neoliberal austerity (Rogowski, 2020).

Decolonial Social Work

As progressive models of social work have evolved and critiques of status quo maintaining social work practice techniques have sharpened, attention has turned to the global sequelae of colonialism and its relation to neoliberal paradigms. The huge and lasting legacy of colonialism has been widely studied and assessed in historical and political narratives and has increasingly become more relevant to social work education, theory, and practice. Bearing in mind that most of the planet's nations have at one time or another been colonies of empires, kingdoms, or international commonwealths, few parts of the community of nations have been unaffected by the pernicious legacy of colonial exploitation, either as a subjugated or dominant state.

Decolonization occurs in stages. Initially, it entails efforts by colonized states and territories to secure independence through revolutionary wars, succession, independence movements, and the decoupling of dependent economies from imperial or externally dominant states. In modern history, this is exemplified by the wars of independence that freed colonies throughout the Americas from Great Britain, Spain, Portugal, and France to be replaced by emergent democracies, as in North America, or by neocolonial government of and for *criollo* elites, as in Latin America. A subsequent phase was the collapse of European empires in the postwar era of the twentieth century, such as when the British Empire ceased to be the "empire on which the sun never sets." Nation states in South Asia and Africa established independent rule or installed puppet governments under the influence of former powers. Other nations were caught up in the crossfire of the Cold War as proxy states for the conflict between the Soviet Union and the West such as was seen in Southeast Asia, West Africa, and Central and South America.

The stages of decolonization which are of concern to social workers, activists, and social justice warriors are of a more contemporary variety – the process of disassembling colonial and postcolonial power in all of its cultural and institutional after achieving political independence. After a colony achieves independence, through whatever means, there is typically a replication of colonial structures, policies, and unfavorable trade economies of cheap exports and expensive imports (mercantilism). Moreover, colonial cultural and educational institutions, staffed by colonists, are replaced by local elites and middleman minorities in organizations that mimic their predecessors. Thus, the essence of colonialism is perpetuated through local control. The economy continues to be dependent on the export of agricultural products, natural resources, and unprocessed good coupled with the import of high value manufactured goods, technology, and intellectual capital. Cheap labor and natural resources bolster unfavorable terms of trade for the emerging economy. This mercantile exploitation is accompanied by a continued cultural imperialism in the form of a class system that maintains hierarchies based on access to elite institutions at home and abroad. Even well after nations have shed their economic dependency and established domestic industry and restored cultural institutions based on local traditions, colonialism persists through the legacy of class, social status, and positionality in identity such as race, color, ethnicity, class, education, indigeneity, rurality, gender, migration status, and other forms of intersectionality. Local elites become entrenched and imbued with colonial cultural and social values through their preferential access to the perks and privileges of the *comprador* class.

A consequence of neocolonialism is that traditional modes of understanding are ignored, lost, or eradicated, local languages fall into disuse or extinction, oral traditions become muted, local arts and humanities are denigrated as "folk culture," and indigenous cultures are either caricatured or disappeared (Hambrol, 2017).

Of critical importance in decolonization is the historic and contemporary treatment of indigenous populations. In virtually all cases of conquest and settlement of colonized spaces, the original First Peoples have been displaced, overrun, imprisoned, enslaved, or exterminated. Peaceful coexistence has not been the norm on any continent. From settlement colony slave states like the early United States or settlement colonies with no slaves, like Canada, to *Conquistador* colonies based on precious resource extraction and plantation agriculture, like the colonies of Spain and Portugal, all have carried out at least some degree of physical and cultural genocide. European colonies in Africa and South Asia were also organized as slave-based economies coupled with trade monopolies, as the East India Company, and the displacement and commodification of humans as property were common. The ancient peoples of each region were routinely dispossessed of their lands. First Nations were pushed from rich lands to reservations and geographic and economic peripheries. Indigenous children were treated as chattel, and many were sent to remote state boarding schools for cultural indoctrination.

The ongoing discovery of graveyards of native children at former Indian schools in Canada and the United States exemplifies the degree to which native peoples were dehumanized and exterminated even after conquest and settlement. Postcolonial genocide continues as evidenced by the exposure of the American Navajo Nation to radiation during a period of uranium mining, the ongoing extermination of indigenous peoples during the dirty wars in Guatemala, and the displacement and murder of native populations in the Amazon under Brazilian President Bolsonaro, among others.

Much of this began with the "Doctrine of Discovery" in which European nations invaded and dominated lands as if they were uninhabited – lands in the case of the Americas that had been settled by preexisting civilizations for over 17,000 years. The logic was that indigenous extermination, removal, and allotment to "new" lands were a natural consequence of their inferiority as rationalized by paternalism, racism, territoriality (belief in the property rights of the settlers to "claimed lands"), and divine right (Godly authority) (Black, 2015). The losses of knowledge, culture, languages, and traditions under the colonization and destruction of indigenous peoples would be incalculable. The death of each indigenous healer, chief, leader, curandera, and native woman is comparable to burning a library.

Decolonizing Social Work Education

The work of decolonizing social work education is dependent upon context. In the vast swathes of territory comprised of former colony nation states, the task is a complex effort to roll back the effects of *ethnocide* (cultural destruction), *ecocide* (destruction of original landscape and natural resources), *genocide* (elimination of peoples, tribes, and nations) and *linguicide* (destruction of languages) (Yellow Bird, 2016). In the former colonizing countries, such as in Western Europe, the task is to take ownership of the irreversible harms inflicted upon the colonies of the Global South and correct the course of politics and justice to reach reconciliation, restoration, and inclusion.

Maton's (2014) conceptual framework enables viewing nuances and possibilities of knowledge creation and development, as well as processes of knowledge reproduction, in the context of society as a whole and in social work education. He coined the term "epistemic-pedagogical device" (henceforth: EPD) to describe what he sees as the "focus of domination and resistance, struggle and negotiation, both within education and across wider society" (Maton, 2014, p. 53). Assuming that current knowledge is shaped by globalization processes that, crucially in the context of decolonizing social work, create either "localized globalisms" or "globalized localisms," this approach can shed light on how certain epistemic traditions remain absent in the field of knowledge production in social work and encourage us to consider potential developments (Santos, 2006).

Like the humanities, social work is based on hierarchies of knowledge, where theories frequently clash or complement one another rather than build up as they do in science (Maton, 2014). In higher education, several institutions and actors struggle for control of the three-field epistemic-pedagogic device: (a) knowledge production field where new knowledge is being produced (based on epistemic logic), (b) recontextualization field where knowledge that was previously developed is recontextualized and integrated into curricula (based on recontextualization logic), and (c) reproduction field – sites of teaching and learning – where knowledge turns into pedagogic discourse (based on evaluative logic). The whole process has two dynamics: "curriculization" which extends from production to recontextualization and "pedagogization" which ranges from recontextualization to reproduction.

At this point, we might ask about conditions for epistemic decolonization in social work where this process would entail re-centring social work knowledge on Global South traditions and changing the field of knowledge production. This condition would entail the shift from knowledge production as a Western academic domain (theories as scientific descriptions) to communities that hold traditional knowledge and develop new forms of knowledge as acts of resistance and adaptation. Contrary to Cartesian dualism, non-Western epistemologies are characterized by the intersectionality of the relationship between self and the word (Purcell, 1998; Tamale, 2020); more importantly, this differentiation also makes up a significant portion of social work history and theory.

As a part of the processes of "curriculization," it would demand the shift in recontextualization logic that, in the context of social work, is based on abyssal thinking that excludes non-Western forms of knowledge. Through this process, new knowledge is converted into a pedagogic discourse. Today, this field is the primary setting for the reproduction of colonialism where academics ensure that the abyssal line is maintained through linguistic imperialism and ubiquitous exclusion, selection, and denials. The critical question remains as to what are and will be the future principles ("rules of the game") of content inclusion in social work curriculum and who will have power over it. The role of researchers, reviewers, research institutions and funds, research associations, and networks that promote knowledge developed in the Global South is critical for decolonizing social work curricula. Given that this is seen as the foundation of academic freedom – the ability to select the content of the curriculum, as well as how academics carry out teaching and learning practices without undue colonial imposition – the question should be asked to what extent neoliberal absolutism reproduces colonial matrix of power. Decolonization of social work should also be examined in the context of the reproduction field that includes sites of teaching and learning based on evaluative logic that regulates learning and teaching of pedagogic discourse and practice. This field is crucial as a setting for learning processes because it requires an understanding of how different hegemonic systems – including colonial systems of power – work and the ability to develop transformative forms of practice in social work through critical thinking and action.

We contend that all three fields are tightly packed with colonial thinking based on the "abyssal line" and that they are battlegrounds for control of each field and the relationship between fields. The problem identified by Maton (2014) is that the "rules of the game" are frequently ambiguous, perceived as universal, and mostly uncontested; thus, we must be aware of how relationships influence the positions and practices of social work activists, researchers, intellectuals, "recontextualizers," teachers, and students. Recontextualization is the process by which meanings from the production field are transformed into pedagogic discourse. This pedagogized knowledge is then transformed into reproduction fields, such as classrooms or lecture halls, where lecturers and professors can recontextualize discourse once more (Bernstein, 1990).

Social work curricula look surprisingly similar throughout the schools of social work in member states of the International Federation of Social Workers (IFSW). Although change is underway to educationally address structural violence, racism, intersectionality, oppression, environmental collapse, and colonialism, the course structures look more alike than not (IFSW, 2020). There is the standard array of classes in social work practice skills, social policy, ethics, field practicum, and electives with a sprinkling of courses on diversity. Decisively important topics such as critical race theory, radical feminism, and queer theory get occasional treatment but face backlash from paranoid state politicians and faint-hearted college administrators. Fortunately, there is increasing attention to human rights and social and economic and environmental justice, but evidence of attention to decolonization is scarce despite long-standing calls for its inclusion (IFSW, 2020; Almeida et al., 2019; Tamburro, 2013; Gray et al., 2016).

But to decolonize social work education, it has to be preceded or accompanied by decolonizing academic social work departments. Can we truthfully say that such units are presently at the cutting edge of university reform, student emancipation, faculty self-governance, and progressive thought? Far better to look at faculty in rhetoric or literature for that. Our experience is one of staid if not stale Eurocentric curricula, paternalistic management, and retrograde authoritarian university managers who are hell-bent on generating tuition fees, student credit hours, and money from grants and contracts. The metrics by which universities are governed resemble those of a for-profit corporation more than a learning institution, and small armies of highly paid university administrators are tasked with setting and monitoring measurable outputs congruent with costly strategic plans that as the word *bureaucrat* suggests govern from the desk.

A reconceptualization of the work itself could change the structure and focus of academic social work. To be capable of working to emancipate those who are being crushed by poverty, brutality, hunger, housing insecurity, family violence, drug use, police harassment, gender discrimination, state paternalism, voter disenfranchisement, and the apartheid of cumulative intersectional multiple oppressions requires knowledge and skills that are now only at the margins of many mainstream academic departments.

Themes of a New Approach to Social Work Education

Democratization

The discipline of social work is the best illustration of how to establish the connection between social sciences and the knowledge that serves humans in relation to their environment and create a theoretical and practical background for a decent life and well-being. The global definition of social work, which states that it is a "practice-based profession and an academic discipline that promotes social change and development, social cohesion, and the empowerment and liberation of people," expresses the idea that social work as a practice and discipline can and should enhance human well-being (IFSW, 2014). The question of how social work as a practice and discipline can improve human well-being is critical not only for the discipline but also for practice in the context of decolonial struggles. Decolonized social work advocates for the need for a new social criticism that values grassroots voices and actions instead of grand narratives of emancipation based on Eurocentric globalized rationality. It is crucial to distinguish *knowledge-as-emancipation* from *knowledge-as-regulation* insofar as Eurocentric knowledge based on applied neutrality is still a significant component of the social work discipline (de Sousa Santos, 2014a). Given that it is believed to be based on the supposition that cognition is equated with building solidarity and the need for appreciation of other forms of knowledge, this approach may be helpful in addressing decolonized human rights and social work. A different type of social critique that is capable of including excluded worldviews is necessary in the context of colonial reality. There are a number of obstacles to certain aporias of modern critical thought, such as an emphasis on limiting to the scientific language of description and referring solely to Eurocentric ideas. Western social work is in crisis partially because we continue to frame social issues in Western-Eurocentric ways for which we are unable to find solutions. A change in attitudes regarding southern epistemologies and the elimination of "abyssal thinking" in the framework of social work theory, curriculum, and research would be essential components of true democratization.

If we expect to teach democratic governance, participatory supervision, professional peer review, group consensus, and occupational autonomy, our own academic units need to be organized along those lines. How do we achieve that? To begin, we flatten the hierarchy. Social work is not built to model corporate or military models that stress compliance, structural hierarchy, and order. To be successful, professionals work with high degrees of autonomy, seek out supervision when needed, and self-regulate. It is not incongruent to set expectations high while delegating leadership to the unit rather than monopolizing it at the top. While many social work educators find themselves working in comparative freedom and are fairly included in the representative governance of their units, many readers will resonate with a call for greater inclusion in decision-making. It follows that academic units must function with high levels of transparency versus administrative opacity or secrecy. Much as in society at large, democratic academic organizations and departments cannot work in the absence of freely flowing and open information, especially about programs, curriculum, as well as recruitment, hiring, and promotion decisions. Indeed, even the budget should not be a state secret. Opaque and hierarchical management reflects the values of neocolonialism in which the staff are treated like house servants or field sharecroppers. Democratization flourishes when recruitment emphasizes a diversity of opinion and ideology as well as a wide range of background, social class, ethnicity, gender expression, and other identities. It also requires the affirmative recruitment of indigenous voices and ongoing efforts and incentives for the retention and promotion of individuals who have been part of marginalized groups.

Leadership need not be restricted to senior faculty and administrators. There are valid reasons to include shared governance with alumni, emeritus faculty, and community leaders. They might serve not only on the advisory board but also on internal committees that oversee curriculum, recruitment, and field placements. Community members also have a role on research committees to help make the linkage to community engaged research and to facilitate faculty engagement in agencies and the community. Also relevant is the inclusion of students themselves, not as token members of committees but as peer voting members who represent the key clientele of higher education. It makes sense to bring student organizations to the table with meaningful roles and voting privileges on student issues and collective bargaining for graduate assistants and the advisory board.

Perhaps the most important step in reforming a department is the inclusion of people and communities-at-risk. Including social work clients and members of at-risk groups in the social work academy could be transformative by bringing the periphery to the core and incorporating client voices as part of the academic space. Rather than being "othered" as recipients of services, client partners might become catalysts for fundamentally different approaches to the field. The voices of indigenous groups, migrants, and trauma survivors would transform the social work education narrative through sharing alternative perspectives on the nature of the work we do. Departments that function with these factors in mind create a model for how students could function upon graduation and transform their agencies and the profession.

Conclusion: Curriculum and Postcolonial Lobotomy

Exclusion undergirds the social work curriculum. According to de Sousa Santos (2014a), there is an abyssal line between what is allowed to be copresent or thought and what is not present and non-imaginable in contemporary Western thought. In terms of colonial realities, it is clear that dominant Western versions of social work theory and practice are based on the division of metropolitan and peripheral societies, where practices, knowledge, and imagination that were on the other side of the abyssal line could not be a part of practices and theories on the Eurocentric side as this would make them questionable and nonuniversal. It is unnecessary to point out that the abyssal line also exists in the area of social work curriculum, which is dominated by the Eurocentric perspective (Hall, 2005), "whiteness" expressed in negligence of contributors of color (Specht & Courtney, 1994), and colonial epistemic frameworks (Clarke, 2022).

The basic core of social work curriculum with its exclusivist emphasis on working with individuals and groups has remained relatively unchanged at the most fundamental level for generations. Although models of practice have evolved to be more grounded in evidence, such as the emphasis on cognitive behavioral theory, the basic paradigm centers on fixing disruptions at the interface between clients and their environment (person-in-environment model) at the microlevel. True, social work schools employ faculty who work in macro-practice and social policy as part of the curriculum, but as we have noted, a critical approach that seeks to restructure a society that systematically marginalizes and impoverishes peoples, classes, tribes, and communities is wanting. Theory in schools of social work, such as it is, revolves around individuals and their functional abilities to navigate personal troubles.

We propose that theory be broadened in social work education to embrace *structural approaches* to social work as articulated by Mullaly and Dupre (2018). The elements of this approach include content on the progressive era, the neoconservative and neoliberal paradigms, critical and conflict theory, radical humanism, and the structural approach to oppression (Mullaly & Dupre, 2018). In addition, current theoretical approaches to be included would be feminist theory, critical race theory, human rights theory, queer theory, environmentalism, postmodernism, decolonization theory, Ubuntu, eco-social work, theory of radical needs, and diatopic hermeneutics (Mayaka & Truell, 2021; de Sousa Santos, 2014a; Heller, 1976). Central topics in this theoretical sphere include intersectionality, oppression, human needs and rights, environmental rights, postcolonialism, unearned privilege, social class, health disparities, globalization, indigenous peoples and First Nations, center/periphery models, human influence on climate and environmental collapse, decolonizing the social work lineage (Clarke, 2022), and subaltern cosmopolitanism (de Sousa Santos, 2014a). Students are asked in this context to envision a *meta-social work* that is postindustrial, post-profit, post-growth, post-consumerist, and postcolonial. This theoretical shakeup would be augmented by enriching the array of macro praxis field experiences to include human rights groups, unions, indigenous spaces, community gardens, migrant advocacy and legal services, social justice agencies, environmental organizations, advocacy groups, integrative arts, and placements with progressive political parties and their elected officials.

The assumption is that, going forward at this perilous moment in our history, professors do not have the answers but side by side with students are forging new futures for social work.

Discussion Questions

1. Is social work historically a profession that defends the status quo or an occupation that assertively works to end structural violence and oppression? Please provide examples.
2. Is clinical social work fundamentally incompatible with macro social work and social justice work or can a middle ground be found?
3. To what degree should professional social workers be involved in social reform, social justice work, and efforts to decolonize the profession? Is this a political activity that is outside of the bounds of professional propriety?

References

Almeida, R. V., Werkmeister Rozas, L. M., Cross-Denny, B., Kyeunghae Lee, K., & Yamada, A. M. (2019). Coloniality and intersectionality in social work education and practice. *Journal of Progressive Human Services, 30*(2). https://doi.org/10.1080/10428232.2019.1574195

Bernstein, B. (1990). *Class, codes and control* (The structuring of pedagogic discourse) (Vol. 4). Routledge.

Black, J. M. (2015). *American Indians and the rhetoric of removal and allotment*. University of Mississippi Press. https://doi.org/10.14325/mississippi/9781628461961.001.0001

Clarke, K. (2022). Reimagining social work ancestry: Toward epistemic decolonization. *Affilia, 37*(2), 266–278. https://doi.org/10.1177/08861099211051326

De Maria, W. (1992). On the trail of a radical pedagogy for social work education. *The British Journal of Social Work, 22*(3). https://doi.org/10.1093/oxfordjournals.bjsw.a055862

de Sousa Santos, B. (2014a). Globalizations. *Theory Culture Society, 23*, 393. https://doi.org/10.1177/026327640602300268

de Sousa Santos, B. (2014b). *Epistemologies of the South: Justice against epistemicide*. Paradigm Publishers.

Dos Santos, C. M., Eiras, A. A. L. T. S., Defilippo, A. D., & Yazbek, M. C. (2021). The Latin American movement for reconceptualization and radical social work (1960–80): Possible similarities. *Critical and Radical Social Work, 9*(1) https://bristoluniversitypressdigital.com/view/journals/crsw/9/1/article-p129.xml

Galper, J. (1980). *Social work practice: A radical perspective*. Prentice Hall.

Gottschalk, S., & Witkin, S. (1991). Rationality in social work: A critical examination. *The Journal of Sociology & Social Welfare, 18*(4) https://scholarworks.wmich.edu/jssw/vol18/iss4/9

Gray, M., Coats, J., Yellow Bird, M., & Hetherington, T. (2016). *Decolonizing social work*. Routledge.

Guo, W., & Tsui, M. (2010). From resilience to resistance: A reconstruction of the strength's perspective in social work practice. *International Social Work, 53*(2), 233–245. https://doi.org/10.1177/0020872809355391

Hall, R. E. (2005). Eurocentrism in social work education. *Journal of Social Work*, 5. https://doi.org/10.1177/1468017305051238

Hambrol, N. (2017, October 4). Decolonization. *Literary Theory and Criticism*. https://literariness.org/2017/10/04/decolonization/

Heller, A. (1976). *The theory of need in Marx*. Verso.

Journal of Progressive Human Services. (2022). *Aims and scope*. https://www.tandfonline.com/action/journalInformation?show=aimsScope&journalCode=wphs20

Katz, A. H. (1984). Reflections on an elusive vision: Social work in health. *Journal of Public Health Policy, 5*(3), 410–422. https://doi.org/10.2307/3342165

Mayaka, B., & Truell, R. (2021). Ubuntu and its potential impact on the international social work profession. *International Social Work, 64*(5), 649–662. https://doi.org/10.1177/00208728211022787

Natividad, N., & Lauderdale, P. (2010). Global indigenous rights and resistance. *Oxford Encyclopedia of International Studies*, 29. https://doi.org/10.1093/acrefore/9780190846626.013.445

International Federation of Social Workers (IFSW). (2020). *Global standards for social work education and training*. https://www.ifsw.org/global-standards-for-social-work-education-and-training/

International Federation of Social Workers (IFSW). (2014). *Global definition of social work*. https://www.ifsw.org/what-is-social-work/global-definition-of-social-work/

Ioakimidis, V. (2016, May 24). A guide to radical social work. *The Guardian*. https://www.theguardian.com/social-care-network/2016/may/24/radical-social-work-quick-guide-change-poverty-inequality

Langan, M., & Lee, P. (1989). Whatever happened to radical social work? In M. Langan & P. Lee (Eds.), *Radical social work today* (pp. 1–18). Unwin Hyman.

Lusk, M., & Corbett, D. (2021). Liberation theology and international social work. *Journal of Religion & Spirituality in Social Work: Social Thought, 40*(1). https://doi.org/10.1080/15426432.2020.1848750

Maton, K. (2014). *Knowledge and knowers: Towards a realist sociology of education*. Routledge.

Midgley, J. (1981). *Professional imperialism: Social work in the Third World*. Heinemann.

Mullaly, B., & Dupre, M. (2018). *The new structural social work: Ideology, theory and practice*. Oxford University Press.

Pew. (2019, October 15). *Two decades of change in federal and state higher education funding*. Pew Charitable Trusts. https://www.pewtrusts.org/en/research-and-analysis/issue-briefs/2019/10/two-decades-of-change-in-federal-and-state-higher-education-funding

Piven, F. F., & Cloward, R. A. (1979). *Poor people's movements: Why they succeed, how they fail*. Vintage.

Purcell, T. W. (1998). Indigenous knowledge and applied anthropology: Questions of definition and direction. *Human Organization, 57*(3) http://www.jstor.org/stable/44127271

Reid, P. N., & Lowe, G. R. (1999). The professionalization of poverty: Common themes and contributions. In G. R. Lowe & P. N. Reid (Eds.), *The professionalization of poverty: Social work and the poor in the Twentieth Century* (pp. 1–8). Aldine de Gruyter.

Rogowski, S. (2020). *Social work: The rise and fall of a profession?* Policy Press.

Schmitt, E. (1996, May 12). Five years later, the Gulf War story is still being told. *The New York Times*. https://writing.upenn.edu/~afilreis/Coursetexts/gulf-war-arnett.html

Shulman, L. (2020). *The skills of helping individuals, families, groups and communities*. Cengage.

Specht, H., & Courtney, M. (1994). *Unfaithful angels: How social work has abandoned its mission*. Free Press.

Steyaert, J. (2019). Radical social work: Refocusing social work, seeing more than the individual. *History of Social Work*. https://www.historyofsocialwork.org/eng/details.php?cps=26

Stoesz, D., Karger, H., & Carrilio, T. (2010). *A dream deferred: How social work education lost its way and what can be done*. Aldine.

Tamale, S. (2020). *Decolonization and Afro-feminism*. Daraja Press.

Tamburro, A. (2013). Including decolonization in social work education and practice. *Journal of Indigenous Social Development., 2*(1) https://journalhosting.ucalgary.ca/index.php/jisd/article/view/63048/46993

Mark Lusk is a Faculty Member in the School of Social Work at New Mexico State University. Professor Lusk was Senior Fulbright Scholar at the Catholic University of Peru in Lima and also a Fulbright Research Scholar at the Catholic University of Rio de Janeiro in Brazil. He currently works with forced migrants and refugees from Central America and Mexico and related human rights issues. Dr. Lusk was founding director of the School of Social Work at Boise State University (Idaho) and has served as Associate Provost at the University of Georgia.

Marcin Boryczko is an Associate Professor at the University of Gdańsk, Poland, where he teaches social work on bachelors and masters levels. He serves in the board of several international and national associations such as the Polish Federation of Social Workers and Social Service Employees Unions (Polska Federacja Związków Zawodowych Pracowników Socjalnych i Pomocy Społecznej), the European Social Work Research Association, and the International Advisory Board of the *European Social Work Research Journal* and as a Polish representative in the International Federation of Social Workers (IFSW). His main research interests include social work education, critical social work theory, human rights, decolonization, neoliberal governmentality, and populism in Central Europe.

Chapter 16
A Path Forward for Social Work, Human Rights, and Decolonization

Marcin Boryczko, Melinda Madew, and Mark Lusk

The Balkanization of Human Rights: Relativism as the "Invariable Alibi of Tyranny"

Balkanization is a drive toward relativization and instrumentalization of human rights and humanitarian law that creates a threat to its universal applicability. This process is based on political fragmentation and revisionism centered on relativist ideas of cultural appreciation and strongly emphasizes discordant local versions of human rights. There is a visible trend toward developing a new political economy of human rights that is distinct from the liberal tradition (Koceba & Stambuslki, 2020). Balkanization can be described as a set of processes leading to the defragmentation and unmaking of certain symbolic spaces such as literature (Hasanović, 2021), architecture (Bobic, 2020), or human rights. Even if the term "Balkanization" may sound odd in the context of human rights, we want to highlight the new manner that human rights are being treated and instrumentalized in the context of the interdependence of global and local politics. Some interpretations of human rights fall under the skepticism ingrained in three types of relativism as was mentioned in the

M. Boryczko (✉)
Department of Social Work, Faculty of Social Sciences, University of Gdańsk, Gdańsk, Poland
e-mail: marcin.boryczko@ug.edu.pl

M. Madew
Department of Social Work, Protestant University of Applied Sciences Ludwigsburg, Ludwigsburg, Germany

Department of Social Work, University of Johannesburg, Johannesburg, South Africa
e-mail: m.madew@eh-ludwigsburg.de

M. Lusk
School of Social Work, New Mexico State University, Las Cruces, NM, USA
e-mail: marklusk@nmsu.edu

M. Madew et al. (eds.), *Decolonized Approaches to Human Rights and Social Work*,
https://doi.org/10.1007/978-3-031-33030-8_16

second chapter of this book: (1) descriptive relativism, which acknowledges that values and norms associated with human rights are tightly connected to specific culture or civilization, (2) normative relativism which holds that we should not accept any norm as legitimate universally, and (3) epistemological relativism which argues that there are no grounds for justifying norms that merely depend on the settings of their occurrence (Namli, 2018). This viewpoint contends that human rights and the norms that justify them depend upon the cultural contexts. In this view, norms themselves cannot be universally recognized.

We focus on two aspects of the Balkanization of human rights: national (related to state populism) and international (related to global politics). First, there is a political threat of instrumentalization of human rights that stems from populism, authoritarianism, and nationalism which use them for their own localized interests all over the world. Political regimes not only violate human rights but hijack them, (Neuman 2022). The global reemergence of populism has become a serious threat to democracy and human rights. Human rights violations take on a new form as they become part of a discourse that legitimizes authoritarian regimes and nationalist government actions. On the one hand, populist governments frequently act as defenders of the human rights of a particular population of voters (the majority), but on the other, they pose a threat to the rights of that same majority and come into conflict with international human rights protection institutions. Populists claim to be in the position of majority voice, a majority that in this way is capable of expressing discontent and resentment to improvements of human rights of minorities such as LGBTQ+ or racial groups, such as in Central European or American right-wing populism. We observe populists maintaining a balance between international organizations and local threats to the rights of those they govern, exposing populist regimes to criticism from international human rights organizations, which they largely ignore or dispute. Populist discourse assumes that human rights go against the will of the majority that is supposedly protected by populists. In this balancing act, the tension between the supposed majority's will and human rights requirements becomes tangible.

Taking populist governments in Central and Eastern Europe as an example, they typically criticize international human rights agreements as conflicting with national sovereignty. Preelection and postelection tactics that criticize and question human rights are the two primary sorts of this interference in the international system that we observe. In their populist programs during election campaigns, Eurosceptics frequently criticize international organizations that support human rights, claiming that they are erasing national identity and that the European Court of Human Rights is imposing human rights on the majority defined in opposition to corrupted EU elites. Different tactics include rejecting or contesting in the postelection period the international treaties obligations. Yet they are nevertheless legally binding due to earlier agreements. A good example is the European Convention on Human Rights, which the Polish Constitutional Tribunal, under the control of the populist government of Morawiecki, has questioned and declared to be unconstitutional (Biuletyn Informacji Publicznej RPO, 2022). All of these strategies are being used to protect the majority that once was "betrayed" for fighting against corrupted "EU elites."

How do populist policies affect human rights and how do they relate to social work? The ambiguous relationship between populism and human rights may be demonstrated by the paradox of restrictions placed on minority rights (refugees, women, LGBTQ+, etc.) through marginalization practices in public spaces or bureaucracy rather than through explicit laws. More significantly, populism aligns social rights advancements in national social policy with relatively universal access to everyone. We are dealing with a new dialectic of human rights, one in which the deterioration of some aspects coexists with improvements in others. It's a tricky situation because populism seeks to establish a new political economy of human rights that is distinct from the liberal tradition based on individual rights while simultaneously not negating them as under authoritarian or fascist regimes that violate human rights. In the liberal tradition, everyone is given equal access to rights and liberties. The moral and metaphysical community, which is often defined as a nation, race, or religious group, is where populism breaks down in the way rights are distributed.

According to authoritarian populist perspectives, rights and liberties are distributed by an imagined community; in less abstract terms, it is a state represented by the ruling party. This distribution frequently affects communities and groups rather than individuals. Populism not only distributes rights but also creates and strengthens certain types of communities, starting from a traditional family and ending with the nation, race, etc. This type of distribution may also be described in terms of paternalism which means "populists' arrogation of the right to identify the interests of 'the people' for whom they claim to speak, rather than listen to the views of real citizens about their preferences" (O'Connell, 2020, p. 101). The new notion of community is frequently promoted by social policy and social transfers to certain groups such as families and religious groups, while minorities continue to be excluded from the public sphere. Populist strategies can be classified as new a politics of rights, creating communities that serve the aims of politics (Hans-George & Immerfall, 1998).

The rise of right-wing populism is profoundly transforming social policies and programs globally where they become selective and conditional, socially exclusive, and instrumentalized (Noble & Ottmann, 2020). Their role is more complicated since they often are expressed as the right of majority, and, in fact, social rights are being realized more broadly, such as Central and Eastern European populism, where social programs are more universally distributed yet do not include minorities (Baranowski, 2022). The obvious question in the context of social work concerns populist inclusion-exclusion policies designed to marginalize "second class citizens and minorities. In the framework of authoritarian populism, at least two future trends of social work can be distinguished: resistance and education. Globally, social workers are fighting back against right-wing populism from demonstrations and imprisonment in Hungary, where populists made dumpster diving and living on the street a misdemeanor punishable by fines or imprisonment (Social Work Network Action, 2011), opposing anti-immigrant measures across Europe (Noble & Ottmann, 2020) to Peruvian indigenous protests against poverty and racism ignited by populists (Villegas & Machicao, 2023). All of these experiences and practices of public fights against racism, inequality, injustice, and political corruption are persuasive in terms of the urgent need for human rights-based social work as a role model.

There is a need for critically informed, anti-racist and decolonized social work. In addition, nationalist authoritarianism and populism are a new challenge that will shape future developments in social work. As noted by Zaidi and Aaslund, "...social work education needs to employ critical reflections about political context, identity, organizational expectations and collective action framing, and the interactions between these entities to help social workers meet the complex plethora of movements and protests in late modern welfare states" (Zaidi & Aaslund, 2021, p. 10). This need will be more obvious in the context of populism since social workers are not generally "immune" to right-wing authoritarianism and populism (Fazzi & Nothdurfter, 2020). Here we return to the idea of social workers' critical consciousness and the necessity for education in order to expose nationalist, racist, and conservative policies that contribute to the oppression of minorities and strengthen repressive identities such as whiteness, masculinity, religion, etc.

We believe that one of the upcoming changes in social work will be the social work practice with radicalized youth and adults in the setting of various forms of radicalism ranging from fundamentalist to political. Nonetheless, authoritarian populism appears to play an important part in future political developments, as it becomes a clear direction for at least some young people experiencing democratic disenchantment as a result of relative deprivation, dropping wages, debts, and shrinking ownership among its population (Foa & Mounk, 2019). Studies have revealed that right-wing populism is becoming popular among young people (Mrozowicki et al., 2019). We believe that decolonization processes, defined as the presence of pluriverse perspectives in a global world, have the potential to reverse authoritarian populism support trends. Anti-discriminatory, anti-racist, critically informed social work must be coupled with antidemocratic resilience education (Pausch et al., 2021). This populist resilience education should focus on the following topics:

- Knowledge and critical understanding of the media and competence in identifying "false media"
- Building resilience toward antidemocratic tendencies among youths
- Civic education for resilient democracies
- Decolonial approaches to global education devoid of colonial matrix of power
- Ethical global issues pedagogy

The second facet of human rights Balkanization concerns international relations. Human rights in the modern period are seen as being just conventional operatives since they are primarily supported by legal order or the result of a series of political agreements. Some individuals believe that human rights must have a metaphysical foundation because, without it, the potential of cultural relativism opens the door to skepticism (Bob, 2019). Human rights are fundamentally dependent on moral communities, which frequently clash with one another because they adhere to diverse values and perhaps conflicting interests. What if the issue of instrumentalization should be one of the primary concerns with respect for human rights across the world today? We should be aware of how human rights are applied to accomplish political or religious objectives. Two examples given here show how human rights are being used for political (China's case) and religious (Islam case) purposes.

Important points in the discussion on universal human rights should be raised as a political tendency to relativize the idea of human rights trying to conceive to the public that they are always limited by local context and determined by the historical point of view. It occurs not only on the national level (such as limitations of human rights by authoritarian or populist regimes) but also by new emerging authoritarian powers such as China or more deliberately Russia destroying civil society in its own territory and committing mass atrocities in Ukraine. In today's situation, the universality of human rights is not necessarily hampered by theoretical or legal discussions but mostly by political situations that create a genuine threat to the universal applicability of human rights that are supported by multilateral organizations that oppose the universality of human rights and the rights and freedoms of individuals (Benakis, 2022). We observe disturbing reports of multilateral agreements relativizing human rights as in a joint Russia and China declaration that officially stated that "every nation has its own unique national features, history, culture, social system and level of social and economic development, universal nature of human rights should be seen through the prism of the real situation in every particular country, and human rights should be protected in accordance with the specific situation in each country and the needs of its population" (Joint Statement, 2022). This revisionist drive attempts to redefine democracy and human rights that are not shaped by the Global North and retain resistance to possible Western influence. We think that the underlying issue is that the "swing nations," or the Global South, are the actual targets of authoritarian revisionism (Benakis, 2022) that is aimed at dismantling international law and human rights protection as a consequence of instrumentalization of human rights.

It is seen in the strategies of non-Western imperialist powers like China, which continues to interpret international law and standards in light of its national conditions. Given China's colonial history and foreign intrusions, the suspicion about Western origins and universal values of human rights should come as no surprise. Furthermore, this attitude of seeking to reconcile universalism with national and local realities has been maintained since the 1990s, when Tian Jin, a member of the Chinese government's delegation, officially accepted the universality of human rights for the first time (Zhao, 2015). Today we see many examples of this attitude expressed among others during the European Union and China Human Rights Dialogues when the Chinese delegation stressed that international laws and standards should be interpreted in the light of its national conditions (The Diplomatic Service of the European Union, 2019). Another example is President Xi Jinping's major speech specifically about how the Chinese attitude toward human rights must be respected (China's approach to human rights of minorities, 2019). Given that these declarations are being made during times of international crisis, such as today's war in Ukraine, where joint statements such as those cited above, of two imperial powers violating human rights on a large scale, demonstrate that this instrumentalization is more than just an attitude, but a political strategy that may be labeled as Balkanization.

In this worldwide scenario of fragmentation, relativization, and instrumentalization, we see, on the one hand, a movement from individual to social and economic rights, which populists all over the world regularly invoke (no mention of a minority or religious rights). On the other hand, a subordination of human rights to the will of the majority or imagined community, as in China, will result in the suffering of millions of minority representatives, expressing the dialectics of human rights instrumentalization frequently used by populists who politically secure the rights of the majority while excluding minorities. As it was highlighted by Xi Jinping, "Human rights are not unique advantages given on select people or a small minority, but universal rights to be enjoyed by all people" (China's approach to human rights of minorities, 2019).

The case of Islam illustrates a more general question of whether political actors or institutions should at all (or to what extent) influence democratic political discourse. The religious impact cannot be overlooked because it is prevalent in the most people's worldviews. In this case, the question of the compatibility of human rights and Islam is far too difficult for the purposes of this chapter, while the answer may be simple – it depends on what kind of Islam we are considering. Efforts to reconcile the global initiatives of human rights with the Muslim world are expressed in the Islamist perspectives on human rights – *Cairo Declaration on Human Rights in Islam* – where it was stated that "Believing that fundamental rights and freedoms (…) are an integral part of the Islamic religion and that no one shall have the right as a matter of principle to abolish them either in whole or in part or to violate or ignore them" (Cairo Declaration on Human Rights in Islam, 1990). Yet, from today's perspective, some evident components are absent, such as individual equality and nondiscrimination based on gender, as well as non-Muslim rights. Further, the Declaration on Human Rights by the Organization of Islamic Cooperation marked a potentially major improvement in approaching the Universal Declaration of Human Rights and distancing from using SO law to limit universal freedoms (Kayaoglu, 2020).

Today, human rights differences in the Muslim world are based on the linkage between Sharia law, positive law, and international human rights. As a result of the dominance of Sharia-derived customary law over secular law in Islamic states in the twentieth century, puritanic interpretations of Sharia imposed tremendous restrictions on liberties in those countries. The question for the future is how Sharia will interact with state law and, more importantly, how fundamentalist regimes will use and interpret it. It should be highlighted that many fundamentalist groups imposing extreme interpretations of Islamic law seek to harken back to historical Muslim empires as a way to strengthen resistance to alleged Western dominance in the region (Robinson, 2021). We believe that this may appear to be a false promise of decolonization where Islamic rights have taken the place of universal human rights and with the return of fundamentalist regimes rather than a world capable of accepting many alternative perspectives, ideologies, and world views.

Religious interpretations, particularly regarding Islamic human rights, are usually applied as an antidote to the so-called dominant liberal and individualistic human rights paradigm (An-Na'im, 2021; Bonnet, 2015; Saghaye-Biria, 2018). Islamic academics argue for a paradigm shift beyond Western human rights and are optimistic that they will "...find solidarity with progressive activists around the world in their struggles to keep great powers accountable for the plight of their people and other people around the world" (Saghaye-Biria, 2018). First and foremost, we must address an underlying assumption about the Western, liberal, and individualistic nature of human rights. As we indicated in Chap. 2, we should question ourselves honestly: why are human rights seen as exclusively Western conceptions? In the case of the Islamic critique of human rights, this assumption serves as a tool for criticism toward its supposed Western origins. As previously said, human rights are pluriversal in nature, and it is exceedingly naive to believe that human rights came from a single source. This type of argumentation can be seen as a paradoxical result of the postcolonial condition, as reflected in Chakrabarty's (2008) notion of the impossibility of thinking outside of Western thought. It is also important to note that the so-called dominant Western human rights perspective is not dominant at all, given that a small minority of the global population lives in countries that are democratic and free.

Interestingly, a critical review of Arabic peer-reviewed articles on human rights from an Islamic perspective reveals that in scholarly discourse the Universal Declaration of Human Rights is perceived as part of Western hegemony and an ineffective mechanism of protection. Moreover, this study confirms that there is a polarization within human rights discourse in the context of compatibility and incompatibility of human rights and Islam (Almahfali & Avery, 2023). Almahfali and Avery (2023) assure that, after studying academic articles in Arabic, the reader is regarded to be a "believer" already convinced by the theological reasons offered by these scholars, as references rarely employ legal contexts or have an academic grounding. On the other side, well-known Muslim intellectuals such as An-Na′im deploy lowbrow arguments against the universality of human rights, stating that: "...human rights are actually accepted by the vast majority of people around the world, cannot be true if it is rejected by Muslims, an estimated quarter of humanity today" (An-Na'im, 2012, p.). This empirical justification is just another example of the relativist claim that the universality of human rights presupposes its acceptance by all the people, much as if the justification of morality would demand that everyone, including Muslims, adhere to it. An-Na'im (2012) also states that Sharia law should not affect the implementation of human rights treaties by Muslim-majority states as principles cannot by definition be secured by the state law. Even religious criticism of human rights cannot impair the state's legal enforcement of such rules. This legal interpretation of relations between Sharia and state law is unfortunately incompatible with the experience of populations in Muslim-majority countries where universal human rights are replaced by Islamic rights. Afghanistan may serve as the best illustration of this replacement that forges its "Emirate of Afghanistan" where human rights are defined accordingly to the Sharia interpretation of "God's law," such as banning secondary education for girls (George, 2023).

In the context of current developments, we can interpret fragmentation, relativization, instrumentalization of human rights and the growth of authoritarian populism as catastrophic omens of a post-liberal future (Ibrahim, 2022). What must be emphasized is the distinction between relativist claims that use cynical pluralism of human rights to undermine them or sneak its contradictions veiled in the local version of human rights and relativism based on local differences and pluralism of human rights that are meant to protect them from total criticism of their universality. We believe that decolonization is a process leading to a pluriversal world with a capacity to embrace many philosophies, ideologies, faiths, and world views including non-Western values, perspectives, and methodologies that address climate change, inequality, and the decline of democracy.

The Wisdom of Resistance

If social work promotes quality of life for all people, it has failed to define what constitutes life quality in different cultures in different historical periods. Nor has social work been always capable of determining its own definitive political position in the face of various power struggles that have created global crises and endangered human well-being (Besthorn, 2014). Our professional history is replete with examples where social work has had its darkest moments, as in the case of the Holocaust, the forced institutionalization of indigenous children, and the condoning of state sanctioned expulsion of endangered migrants, to name but a few (Littlechild et al., 2014).

The human rights regime as it emerged after World War II gave us a plethora of human rights instruments issued by international organizations such as the United Nations and the European Union. Human rights declarations, covenants, and international resolutions have articulated a universal agreement on the inviolability of human life and the importance of human dignity; however, such agreement does not necessarily integrate pluriversal cosmologies that are present in many societies that viably succeed at leading lives at the periphery of Western modernity (Escobar, 2020). There are contrasting and at times conflicting positions taken by groups living in various parts of the world regarding human rights as well as actions taken to protect quality of life. There are cultural beliefs and principles that determine how this inviolability is pursued and secured. Cultural values, spiritualities, and history shape what is perceived as closest to truth. This section describes some complexities previously discussed by some authors in chapters of this book. Authors have complementary viewpoints as to how the inviolability of life calls for an accountability to nurture and promote those social and environmental conditions that ensure this. Such accountability cannot be an exclusive act, but one that embraces contending positions and divergences over how the future can be determined by decisions taken today.

Early pioneers in the social work profession were not particularly engaged with the question of how cultural perspectives must factor into what constitutes a good human life, nor have they been clear about the conditionalities by which this is achieved (Cox & Pawar, 2018). Social work was and is still is motivated by the fundamental good intention of alleviating human needs with emphasis on the social functionality of individuals to adapt to social conditions within a given world order. The embedding of social work theory and practice in the Eurocentric and Western tradition has deemphasized the honing of competences in interventional skills and creation of transformative knowledge needed to confront unjust social structures that produce inequalities beyond individual causal responsibility (Lorenz, 2006). Aligning social work with a pluriversal human rights orientation compels us to interrogate our own exclusionary stance in disregarding and delegitimizing other perspectives which do not conform to the rules of Western rationality (Mignolo & Walsh, 2018).

In recent decades, voices in the social work community have articulated lessons and positionalities derived from global social movements in environmental justice, indigenous land rights, and decolonizing strategies (Littlechild et al., 2014). These are critical areas in social work not only because of their global repercussions but also because past failures to comprehend the implications of these problems have taken us backward in our capacities to engage in serious inquiry and commit to more structurally transformative action.

This book describes the sectoral situation of indigenous peoples, landless farmers, refugees and asylum seekers, and women, who, while still grappling with the vestiges of a colonial past, are also defining for themselves an aspiration to be fully human within the current human rights regime. We can glean valuable lessons about collective resilience from these often silenced and repressed sectors. The study of decolonized social work and human rights today inherits the legacy of undefeated resistance by those who refused dehumanization. That act of refusal is evidenced by the truth that the pluriversal pursuit of quality of life, even when wrought in centuries of struggle, is incomplete (Escobar, 2020). Decolonized social work recognizes that it is in the resolute ability of communities to rise and rise again despite the many betrayals of the past, that we can extract wisdom and truth from those who paid the price of resistance and won their right to collective life.

The acts of resistance in its many forms are counter-structures enacted by marginalized groups to guard against the annihilation of communities, the erasure of entire cultures, the dispossession of language and knowledge systems, the displacement from ancestral land, and subjection and enslavement by tyrannical governments (Escobar, 2020). The profession now bears witness to the protracted resistance waged by women, indigenous peoples, migrants, asylum seekers, and survivors of genocidal wars – all whose very existence compel our interrogative discourse in the decolonization of human rights and social work. There are deep lessons that can be gleaned, even as our attempt to distill them in these pages will not give justice to the depth of experience. Ours is but an attempt to honor those whose stories found their way into our study so that we and many others may know – to know that the uprooted, dislocated, and dispossessed are, in truth, the most invested in finding new locations where effective configurations in decoloniality could apply (Gray et al., 2016).

Social Work as Witness to Wisdom

A serious unearthing of discourses in decolonized social work must include pluriversal human rights, ecological justice, and indigenous knowledge systems. To do so is to participate in a momentous long-term challenge to reconceptualize social work (Ramsay & Boddy, 2016). Those who have stood at the forefront of social movements in ancestral land rights, ecological justice, advocacy in migration and asylum rights, and other areas of justice and peace work are the bearers of wisdom in social work practice.

Physical Places and Social Spaces

There could still be deeper wisdom derived from acknowledging that individual and collective interest are never divorced from social and physical ecosystems. To have a rightful claim to a territorial place and the experience of belonging to a social space are prerequisites to quality of life. Denying this to anyone is as much as denying the right to life. Tribal systems have long recognized this by installing knowledge systems that protect ancestral identity and encourage mutual recognition of responsibility in ensuring cohesion and solidarity. From here we learn about the person-in-environment perspective which reminds us of the truth that each is embedded in humanity. A humanity with a shared territorial place and an interactive space where a respectful relationship with the natural world is prerequisite to viable survival. The protection of a person's space and place redounds to the protection of a system of relationship with an entire ecosystem (Besthorn, 2014).

A recounting of relationships from a plurality of perspectives constitutes the histories of peoples who interpret events lived then and now according to standpoints and choices they had the agency to make or unmake. Social work can still be invited into these spaces and places to seek validation over its own sites of knowledge and engage in contestations that will transform our colonized paradigms.

Creation-Centered Social Work

The emerging environmental justice discourse in social work has made us realize that, indeed, quality of life is only possible when there is a wise and respectful relationship with the Earth's natural resources (Berry, 2013). It is a fundamental cross-cutting concern that affects the Global North and South at varying levels of urgency and gravity. Social work has joined the ranks of other disciplines calling for transformative strategies that will slow or reverse the damage committed by centuries of treating creation as something to be subdued and exploited to meet humanity's insatiable demand for wealth (Gray et al., 2013). There is a call to stewardship over the

Earth's resources which is a reversal of the dominating and colonizing position taken by those who regard creation as something to subdue and exploit. Social work can still draw wisdom from those existing uncolonized physical places and social spaces where indigenous knowledge thrives. It is here where there is an unquestioned acceptance that all forms of life are intertwined in mutual dependence (Berry, 2013).

Celebrated today in Western discourse is the "discovery" of creation-centered spirituality – a way of life endemic to indigenous groups who were once persecuted for practicing animistic rituals honoring all that is seen and unseen, the animate or inanimate, the material and immaterial. To them, every river, mountain, forest, air, and rain breathe with their own life – sustaining all who depend on them. Such is the elemental interconnectedness of life which finds source in the Great Transcendent. What was derided as paganistic nature worship is now elevated to the intellectual and spiritual sophistry of academics and theologians alike who cultivate this in their written tracts.

Atrocities were committed by colonizing missionaries when indigenous peoples refused Christian conversion. Despite persecution, tribal keepers of knowledge systems and presiders of spiritual rituals have zealously guarded the secrets of their Transcendent, succeeding to transmit this to chosen keepers from generation to generation. There is wisdom and truth in appropriating honor and respect for creation because everything is purposed for the sustenance of life in its diverse yet equal forms. Indigenous wisdom, once derided and banned as primitive animistic paganism, has attained relevance and legitimacy in today's search for transformative paradigms.

Creation-centered spirituality has entered the social work lexicon through discourses in environmental justice (Dominelli, 2014; Pellow, 2018). The care and stewardship over our common ecosystem is now an accepted social work mandate. The profession of social work and the politics of human rights could expand its global discourse on how the Anthropocene era is not marked by destruction alone but one evidenced by human strivings to rediscover greater wisdom in convivial living with all of creation (Berry, 2013).

Beyond the Anthropocene

Virtually every square meter of the Earth's surface has been affected, usually adversely, by human activity. From microplastics discovered in the snow on the top of Mt. Everest (Chomolungma) to a plastic bag at the deepest point of the Mariana Trench, human waste and destruction is omnipresent. The extent of the changes wrought by humanity's explosive growth and dominance of the planet's physical and natural resources that long term and possibly irreversible shifts in ecosystems, climate, the oceans and the Earth's surface that scientists have named the current era the Anthropocene. A geological epoch in which the magnitude, variety, and longevity of human impacts on the atmosphere and land masses, the Anthropocene era is said to succeed Holocene Epoch (Lewis & Maslin, 2015). While no definitive date has been agreed upon regarding its beginning, one could claim that the discovery of human-made fire is the inflection point at which the fuels were used to create energy from early simple forms up to the nuclear age, and coupled with the evolution, human ingenuity, rapaciousness, and in-group preferences led to what is called the "social conquest of the Earth" (Wilson, 2012).

Indigenous and traditional societies have given primary standing to the rights to "nature" and to the ecosystems from which they draw sustenance and with which they interact respectfully. As noted throughout this book, Western conceptions of rights have been radically individual, with some conceptions of inherent rights being present in cultures, groups, and nationalities, but few or no rights granted to the living systems on which Western civilization parasitically draws. This utter failure of philosophical imagination has left the West with few tools to navigate the current and ongoing crises of climate change, desertification, despeciation, and ecosystem collapse that imperil the longevity of species. Moreover, the impacts of global climate change and other devolutionary human effects such as air and water pollution, rising seas, shrinking lakes, deforestation, and pandemics are disproportionately borne by vulnerable populations including poor nations, children, women, and indigenous peoples (Mapp, 2021).

As a result of human activity, the planet's average temperature is rising faster than it has for over 800,000 years (Council on Foreign Relations, 2022). The consequences of climate change include increased average global temperature with adverse effects on agricultural production, soil erosion, drought, increasing flood events, and increased risks in infectious diseases and epidemics. These changes in environmental and health risks pose a threat to human, cultural, and economic rights and pose a particular risk to the rights of the poor; the environmental calamity requires effort to mitigate the unevenly distributed sequelae of climate change on human society (Levy & Patz, 2015).

Climate change is a risk multiplier that results in numerous interacting effects and disasters that displace people and create a pressing need for humanitarian assistance. Displaced, marginalized, and stateless people are a particular risk and are driving mass global migration resulting from environmental hazards; some 25 million environmental refugees are displaced by weather and climate disasters in a given year (Gaynor, 2020).

Unrestrained by global policy initiatives and international cooperation to check unlimited growth and to reverse the use of fossil fuels, a catastrophe is rapidly accelerating as the vast majority of the world's population remain blissfully unaware or, worse, defiant and in denial. Efforts such as the Paris Accords, signed in 2015 to address an ambitious climate action program to slow global warming and to limit temperature increases to 1.5 °C, have been largely at the discretion of nation states, and progress falls far short of stated goals. Even with the Kyoto Protocol and the Paris Accords, the average temperature is already up by 1.2° and, with no significant changes in policy, will reach an estimated +2.7° by 2100 (Council on Foreign Relations, 2022).

Global ecological disaster is in large part a by-product of a colonial mindset in relation to natural and environmental resources – much like the colonies provided raw materials for the industrialized colonial powers which with vast use of carbon-based energy converted the goods into products exchanged at unfavorable terms of trade with the colonized south. Western economic models are based on a colonization of the Earth, which is seen intrinsically as an unlimited resource to be exploited for economic growth that favors industrialists at the expense of workers and resource providers. The tenets of the colonial capitalism are so ingrained in Western economics and culture as to be beyond challenge. Notions of the "rational economic actor" and the "invisible hand" of the marketplace are so instilled into contemporary ideology as to be a form of unquestioned dogma. To see the natural resource base as a fragile and dynamic, fluctuating, living ecosystem requires a radical decolonization of the mind. The colonial project was based on seized lands, genocide, cultural eradication, linguicide, the rupture of community relationships to their resources, and the conversion of traditional lands and ecosystems to the mass production of industrial and consumer products with no regard for the responsibilities to protect the self-determination, sovereignty, and cultures of the colonized. And so it is with nature that colonial mindset sees it as a territory to occupy, control, exploit, and erase. With such an unfathomably arrogant outlook, the only recourse is to embark on a project of the decolonization of the mind (Ngũgĩ wa Thiong'o, 1981).

The Social Work Response

While social work is not a major player in international politics, the profession is advancing efforts to introduce new paradigms in thinking about environmental rights and responsibilities. Accreditation agencies such as the Council on Social Work Education have introduced innovative curricular requirements and guidelines to address environmental justice in university social work education programs (CSWE, 2020). Professional social work associations, such as the National Association of Social Workers in the United States, have placed environmental justice and climate change at the center of their policy agenda at the state and national levels (NASW, 2023), and the American Academy of Social Work and Social Welfare (AASWSW) has identified the creation of social responses to a changing environment as one of the grand challenges facing the global profession (AASWSW, 2018). At the global level, the International Federation of Social Workers (IFSW), which represents over 50 million social workers in 143 countries, is assertively addressing climate change and environmental justice through a number of initiatives. The IFSW statement on *The Role of Social Workers in Advancing a New Eco-Social World* (2022) calls for a newly reconceptualized human rights framework that diverges from the individualism of traditional human rights concepts to assert a holistic rights framework that extends "…the existing UN Human Rights Declaration to a Holistic Rights Framework to encompass social human rights, cultural rights, ecosystem rights, and the broader rights of nature to ensure that the global crises of climate change, pandemics, and conflict are addressed and that a new eco-social world can flourish" (IFSW, 2022, p. 1).

The International Federation of Social Workers is at the vanguard of reformulating established human rights frameworks to fit a contemporary reality that is much more inclusive of indigenous traditions, community rights, cultures, as well as the inherent rights of humans in the natural and physical environments which sustain them. A broader holistic rights framework encompasses civil and political rights as they have been defined in the modern era but expands those individualized entitlements to account for the global crises of environmental destruction, international conflict and war, and global inequality. A holistic framework takes an activist position that social workers have responsibilities to advance social protection systems to protect vulnerable populations and to reverse environmental description by engaging and partnering with civil society, national governments, NGOs, and international organizations such as the United Nations with the goal of building a more sustainable and just world (IFSW, 2022). The IFSW action plan is to seek sustainability using the UN's framework, which includes the rights and dignity of *People*, the need to protect the *Planet* with an eco-social approach that accounts for the embeddedness of people in the ecosystem, the critical importance of shared *Prosperity* in which economic structures support human well-being, the importance of *Peace* that results from sharing resources and mutual respect across cultures and nations, and the importance of *Partnership* or the spirit of global solidarity based on cooperation in building sustainable futures (IFSW, 2022).

The International Federation of Social Workers has launched a Global Agenda for Social Work and Social Development for the decade 2010 to 2020 as a plan of action for the international social work community. During that decade, emphasis was given to promoting social and economic equality, to the dignity and worth of peoples and cultures, and to advancing community and environmental sustainability. The Agenda has sought to expand the profession beyond its narrower traditions of helping individuals and groups through micro and mezzo practice to global level macro practice that shapes a broader set of goals and which engages more directly with global institutions.

For the decade 2020–2030, IFSW launched the second cycle of social work and social development around the concept of Ubuntu – an African philosophical tradition that emphasizes the values of justice, responsibility, equality, collectiveness, community, social change, and related values (Mayaka & Truell, 2021). Of critical importance to Ubuntu is the concept of environmental justice as traditionally defined in collaborative land use, sharing of natural resources, communal land, and reciprocal relationships. An underlying principle is to approach resource and the environment by improving upon its long-term sustainability – to leave the world and its resources a better place than that in which it was found. Thus, the tradition is unlike Western social work notions of alleviating poverty and engaging in humanitarian and charitable work but rather seeks to engage people to remove barriers to inclusion that impede social development (Mayaka & Truell, 2021). The tradition is distinctly communitarian rather than individualistic in its approach to social problems as diverse as child welfare, crime, poverty, and social isolation. Ubuntu invokes reconciliation, restoration, and responsibilities toward others. The approach specifically rejects the importation of colonial Western models of social work that tend to individualize social problems as personal pathology. Importantly for environmental justice, Ubuntu sees natural resources and ecosystems as shared "property" to which all should have equitable access and which should be managed collectively in the interests of the community rather than a few elite landowners as was the case during the colonial period. The IFSW and social workers from the Global South are calling for a paradigm shift that emphasizes communities as a form of social and environmental protection – "natural organic systems that support people" (Mayaka & Truell, 2021, p. 660).

Whether it is through Ubuntu or other traditional, indigenous, or postcolonial models and philosophies, clearly social work has reached an inflection point where a new perspective is needed to revolutionize the profession by decolonizing and recentering the social work mind. The alternative is to continue on the path of rugged individualism, nationalism, conflict, and environmental destruction.

We identified guiding principles for decolonizing practice and knowledge in social work while mapping approaches to decolonization in the first chapter. It's time to rethink the range of potential outcomes and possible futures. We assumed there would be at least two possible ways of decolonizing human rights and social work – integrative, universalistic approaches or separating localized essentialisms. Future struggle to establish ways and approaches of decolonization will probably stretch between essentialism and universalism. The essentialist approaches consider content of knowledge and related practices of the "local," traditional, and culturally dependent knowledge, such as indigenous or non-Western traditions. Universalistic approaches could be based on new decolonized universalisms that go beyond Eurocentric universalism. We labeled it as pluriversalism and described it in this chapter as well as in second chapter.

Theories and practices that address the decolonization of social work will incorporate the integrative principle, moving toward a knowledge code and elite code in legitimation code theory, where epistemic and social relations are more relevant. It is reasonable to predict that we will experience the consolidation of multiple traditions resulting in integrative interplay of potentially localized ways of decolonizing social work, as in case of Afrocentric Ubuntu or South American *Sumak Kawsay*. These may be strong candidates for the role of "game changers" in future decolonization processes as they progressively become accepted globally.

Yet, alternative, gloomier, development scenarios are also possible. We can describe them by using legitimation code theory and the specialization codes detailed in Chap. 1. We could expect the following development patterns: growth of relativist, knower, and knowledge codes. The growth of *relativist codes* whereby anything can be legitimately accepted, neither expert knowledge nor knower characteristics are relevant. In the future, this could result in the instrumentalization of human rights, when everything would be acceptable and neither expert knowledge nor knower traits would matter. This "anything goes" stance is already used by political and religious leaders under claims over the need of decolonization and de-Westernization of human rights. This trend will likely become more pronounced as populist leaders instrumentalize and Balkanize human rights as counternarratives to universal orders. They will do this while disguising their actions as respecting cultural or religious integrity or protecting local versions of human rights in order to gain political advantage and mask social class related exploitation.

The *knower code*, where emphasis is on specialized knowledge, principles, or procedures, is minimized, and the qualities of actors are highlighted as indicators of achievement will become more important in the context of right-wing populism rise. Populists and authoritarians frequently deploy a false rhetoric of decolonization and human rights discourses, as well as instrumentalization, to protect particular interests of certain community or political goals. Balkanization is how we to describe this phenomenon. A good example of meta-narrative backing populist claims is religion. International human rights policies and institutions will almost certainly be shaped by authoritarian populist and global religious movements. Sadly, a religion is frequently "depoliticized" in different parts of the world as a result. The knower codes in this context could take the shape of ethnic elitism, ethnocentric, or environmental destruction.

The last prospect is related to *knowledge codes* where emphasis is given to specialized knowledge, principles, or procedures and the qualities of actors are unimportant. In this context, we can expect that the developments in decolonization may be based on postcolonial or radical philosophy but most probably on coalitions of social movements globally.

By consolidating traditional ways of knowing with an eco-social work perspective, we can engage in a reformulation of social work that thorough wisdom and social resistance position the profession to advance human rights, decolonize socio-economic systems, and advance environmental justice.

Discussion Questions

1. How can you characterize Balkanization of human rights?
2. Aside from being a human right profession, why is there a growing call for social work to be a creation-centered profession?
3. What is the meaning of environmental justice and how does it relate to social work?
4. What actions are being undertaken by the International Federation of Social Workers in environmental protection?
5. What are possible future developments in decolonization of human rights and social work?

References

Almahfali, M., & Avery, H. (2023). Human rights from an Islamic perspective: A critical review of Arabic peer-reviewed articles. *Social Sciences, 12*(2), 106. https://doi.org/10.3390/socsci12020106

American Academy of Social Work & Social Welfare. (2018). *Create social responses to a changing environment.* https://grandchallengesforsocialwork.org/wp-content/uploads/2015/12/180604-GC-Environment.pdf

An-Na'im, A. A. (2012). Islam and human tights. In J. Witte & M. C. Green (Eds.), *Religion and human rights: An introduction*. Oxford University Press.

An-Na'im, A. A. (2021). *Decolonizing human rights*. Cambridge University Press.

Baranowski, M. (2022). The illiberal turn in politics and ideology through commodified social policy of the 'Family 500+' Programme. *Forum for Social Economics*, 1. https://doi.org/10.1080/07360932.2022.2138936

Benakis, T. (2022, February 23). *Why we must resist when authoritarian regimes try to re-define international rules*. European Interest. https://www.europeaninterest.eu/article/why-we-must-resist-when-authoritarian-regimes-try-to-re-define-international-rules/

Berry, T. (2013). *The great work: Our way into the future*. Crown.

Besthorn, F. H. (2014). Environment. In C. Franklin (Ed.), *Encyclopaedia of social work*. National Association of Social Workers Press and Oxford University Press. https://doi.org/10.1093/acrefore/9780199975839.013.131

Biuletyn Informacji Publicznej RPO. (2022). Trybunał Konstytucyjny ponownie orzekł oniekonstytucyjności Europejskiej Konwencji Praw Człowieka. RPO wnosił o umorzenie sprawy [The Constitutional Tribunal again ruled on the unconstitutionality of the European Convention on Human Rights]. https://bip.brpo.gov.pl/pl/content/rpo-tk-wyrok-etpcz-prawo-do-sadu

Bob, C. (2019). *Rights as weapons instruments of conflict, tools of power*. Princeton University Press.

Bobic, N. (2020). *Balkanization and global politics*. Routledge.

Bonnet, S. (2015). Overcoming Eurocentrism in human rights: Postcolonial critiques – Islamic answers? *Muslim World Journal of Human Rights, 12*(1), 1–24. https://doi.org/10.1515/mwjhr-2014-0010

Cairo Declaration on Human Rights in Islam. (1990). http://hrlibrary.umn.edu/instree/cairodeclaration.html

China's approach to human rights of minorities. (2019, October 5). *Business standard*. https://www.business-standard.com/article/international/president-xi-jinping-defends-china-s-approach-to-human-rights-of-minorities-122100500189_1.html

Chakrabarty, D. (2008). *Provincializing Europe: Postcolonial thought and historical difference*. Princeton University Press.

Council on Foreign Relations. (2022, November 4). *Global climate agreements: Successes and failures*. https://www.cfr.org/backgrounder/paris-global-climate-change-agreements

Council on Social Work Education. (2020). *Curricular guide for environmental justice*. https://www.cswe.org/getattachment/Education-Resources/2015-Curricular-Guides/2015-Environmental-Justice-Guide-Web-Version.pdf

Cox, D. R., & Pawar, M. S. (2018). In 2nd (Ed.), *International social work: Issues, strategies, and programs*. SAGE Publications.

Escobar, A. (2020). Pluriversal politics: The real and the possible. *Revista Crítica De Ciências Sociais, 26*, 153–156. https://doi.org/10.4000/rccs.12507

Dominelli, L. (2014). *Green social work: From environmental crises to environmental justice*. Polity Press. https://ebookcentral.proquest.com/lib/kxp/detail.action?docID=1524246

Escobar, A. (2020). *Pluriversal politics: The real and the possible. Latin America in translation*. Duke University Press. https://doi.org/10.2307/j.ctv11315v0

Fazzi, L., & Nothdurfter, U. (2020). Why are you backing such positions? Types and trajectories of social workers' right-wing populist support. *The British Journal of Social Work, 51*(2), 636–654. https://doi.org/10.1093/bjsw/bcaa199

Foa, R. S., & Mounk, Y. (2019). Youth and the populist wave. *Philosophy & Social Criticism, 45*(9–10), 1013–1024. https://doi.org/10.1177/0191453719872314
Gaynor, T. (2020, November 30). *Climate change is the defining crisis of our time and it particularly impacts the displaced*. United Nations High Commission on Refugees. https://www.unhcr.org/news/latest/2020/11/5fbf73384/climate-change-defining-crisis-time-particularly-impacts-displaced.html
George, S. (2023, February 18). Inside the Taliban campaign to forge a religious emirate. *The Washington Post*. https://www.washingtonpost.com/
Gray, M., Coates, J., & Hetherington, T. (Eds.). (2013). *Environmental social work* (1st ed.). Routledge. https://www.taylorfrancis.com/books/9781136212826. https://doi.org/10.4324/9780203095300
Gray, M., Coates, J., & Yellow Bird, M. (Eds.). (2016). *Contemporary social work studies. Indigenous social work around the world: Towards culturally relevant education and practice*. Routledge, Taylor & Francis Group.
Hans-George, B., & Immerfall, S. (Eds.). (1998). *The new politics of the right*. Macmillan.
Hasanović, J. (2021). Mirroring Europeanization: Balkanization and auto-colonial narrative in Bosnia and Herzegovina. In B. Radeljić (Ed.), *The Unwanted Europeanness? Understanding division and inclusion in contemporary Europe*. De Gruyter.
Ibrahim, A. (2022). *Authoritarian century: Omens of a post-liberal future*. Hurst Publishers.
International Federation of Social Workers. (2022, May 22). *The role of social workers in advancing a new eco-social world.* https://www.ifsw.org/the-role-of-social-workers-in-advancing-a-new-eco-social-world/
Kayaoglu, T. (2020). *The Organization of Islamic cooperation's declaration on human rights: Promises and pitfalls*. https://www.brookings.edu/research/the-organization-of-islamic-cooperations-declaration-on-human-rights-promises-and-pitfalls/
Koceba, K., & Stambuslki, M. (2020). Populizm a polityka praw człowieka. *Studenckie Prace Prawnicze, Administratywistyczne i Ekonomiczne, 31*, 135–156.
Levy, B. S., & Patz, J. A. (2015). Climate change, human rights and social justice. *Annals of Global Health, 81*(3), 310–322. https://doi.org/10.1016/j.aogh.2015.08.008
Lewis, S., & Maslin, M. (2015). Defining the anthropocene. *Nature, 519*, 171–180. https://doi.org/10.1038/nature14258
Littlechild, B., Noble, C., & Strauss, H. (2014). *Global social work: Crossing borders, blurring boundaries*. Sydney University Press. https://doi.org/10.2307/j.ctv1fxm2q
Lorenz, W. (2006). *Perspectives on European social work: From the birth of the nation state to the impact of globalization*. Barbara Budrich Verlag.
Mapp, S. C. (2021). *Human rights and social justice in global perspective: An introduction to international social work*. Oxford University Press.
Mayaka, B., & Truell, R. (2021). Ubuntu and its potential impact on the international social work profession. *International Social Work, 64*(5), 649–662. https://doi.org/10.1177/00208728211022787
Mignolo, W., & Walsh, C. E. (2018). *On decoloniality: Concepts, analytics, praxis. On decoloniality*. Duke University Press.
Mrozowicki, A., Trappmann, V., Seehaus, A., & Kajta, J. (2019). Who is a right-wing supporter? on the biographical experiences of young right-wing voters in Poland and Germany. *Qualitative Sociology Review, 15*(4), 212–235. https://doi.org/10.18778/1733-8077.15.4.10
Namli, E. (2018). *Critique of Human Rights Universalism*. In: Stenmark, M., Fuller, S., Zackariasson, U. (Eds) Relativism and Post-Truth in Contemporary Society. Palgrave Macmillan.
National Association of Social Workers. (2023). *Environmental justice and climate change*. https://www.socialworkers.org/Advocacy/Social-Justice/Environmental-Justice
Neuman, G. L. (2022). *Human rights in a time of populism challenges and responses*. Cambridge University Press.

Ngũgĩ wa Thiong'o. (1981). *Decolonising the mind: The politics of language in African literature*. East African Educational Publishers.
Noble, C., Ottmann, G. F. (2020). *The challenge of nationalist populism for social work a human rights approach*. Routledge.
O'Connell, J. (2020). Representation, paternalism, and exclusion: The divergent impacts of the AKP's populism on human rights in Turkey. In L. Gerald & K. Neuman (Eds.), *Human Rights in a time of populism: Challenges and responses* (pp. 100–129). Cambridge University Press.
Pausch, M., Hladschik, P., Pazderski, P., & Nagem, R. (2021). *Resilience against anti-democratic tendencies through education handbook for youth and social workers. Competences for democratic culture in European social and youth work*. Council of Europe and Institute of Public Affairs.
Pellow, D. N. (2018). *What is critical environmental justice?* Polity.
President Xi Jinping defends China's (2022, October 5). *Buisness Standard*. https://www.business-standard.com/article/international/president-xi-jinping-defends-china-s-approach-to-human-rights-of-minorities-122100500189_1.html
Joint statement of the Russian Federation and the people's republic of China on the International Relations entering a new era and the Global Sustainable Development. President of Russia. (2022, February 4). http://en.kremlin.ru/supplement/5770
Ramsay, S., & Boddy, J. (2016). Environmental social work: A concept analysis. *British Journal of Social Work, bcw078*, bcw078. https://doi.org/10.1093/bjsw/bcw078
Robinson, K. (2021). *Understanding Sharia: The intersection of Islam and the law*. https://www.cfr.org/backgrounder/understanding-sharia-intersection-islam-and-law
Saghaye-Biria, H. (2018). Decolonizing the "Universal" human rights regime: Questioning American exceptionalism and Orientalism. *ReOrient, 4*(1), 59–77. https://doi.org/10.13169/reorient.4.1.0059
Social Work Network Action. (2011). *Norbert Ferencz is NOT the sinner! Statement from our Hungarian colleagues*, https://socialworkfuture.org/norbert-ferencz-is-not-the-sinner-statement-from-our-hungarian-colleagues/
The Diplomatic Service of the European Union. (2019). *The European Union and China held their 37th human rights dialogue*. https://www.eeas.europa.eu/node/60561_enfrom:
Villegas, A., & Machicao, M. (2023 February). *'I am Inca blood:' Peru protests fire up a divided nation*. https://www.reuters.com/world/americas/i-am-inca-blood-peru-protests-fire-up-divided-nation-2023-01-30/
Wilson, E. O. (2012). *The social conquest of Earth*. WW Norton & Company.
Zaidi, M., & Aaslund, H. (2021). Pedagogy of the protest: Teaching social workers about collective action and the social policy context. *Social Work & Society, 19*(2), 1–16.
Zhao, J. (2015). China and the uneasy case for universal human rights. *Human Rights Quarterly, 37*(1), 29–52. https://doi.org/10.1353/hrq.2015.0020

Marcin Boryczko is an Associate Professor at the University of Gdańsk, Poland, where he teaches social work on bachelors and masters levels. He serves in the board of several international and national associations such as the Polish Federation of Social Workers and Social Service Employees Unions (Polska Federacja Związków Zawodowych Pracowników Socjalnych i Pomocy Społecznej), the European Social Work Research Association, and the International Advisory Board of the *European Social Work Research Journal* and as a Polish representative in the International Federation of Social Workers (IFSW). His main research interests include social work education, critical social work theory, human rights, decolonization, neoliberal governmentality, and populism in Central Europe.

Melinda Madew is Professor in International Social Work at the Protestant University of Applied Sciences, Ludwigsburg, Germany, and a Research Associate of the University of Johannesburg, South Africa. She serves as Board Member of the European Social Work Research Association.

Her teaching and research are in the areas of gender politics, postcolonial social work and indigenous knowledge, and practice in community organizing. She has served as Education and Research Consultant for international development organizations. She conceptualized and implemented international projects under the auspices of the European Union educational programs for north-south university collaboration.

Mark Lusk is a Faculty Member in the School of Social Work at New Mexico State University. Professor Lusk was Senior Fulbright Scholar at the Catholic University of Peru in Lima and also a Fulbright Research Scholar at the Catholic University of Rio de Janeiro in Brazil. He currently works with forced migrants and refugees from Central America and Mexico and related human rights issues. Dr. Lusk was Founding Director of the School of Social Work at Boise State University (Idaho) and has served as Associate Provost at the University of Georgia.

Index

M. Madew et al. (eds.), *Decolonized Approaches to Human Rights and Social Work*, https://doi.org/10.1007/978-3-031-33030-8

The manufacturer's authorised representative in the EU is Springer Nature Customer Service Centre GmbH, Europaplatz 3, 69115 Heidelberg, Germany. If you have any concerns regarding our products, please contact ProductSafety@springernature.com

Printed and bound by CPI Group (UK) Ltd, Croydon, CR0 4YY
28/09/2026
02224070-0008